EXPANDED INTEREST TABLES

For Economic Analysis Problems

Fourth Edition

Michael R. Lindeburg, P.E.

PROFESSIONAL PUBLICATIONS, INC.
Belmont, CA 94002

In the ENGINEERING REVIEW MANUAL SERIES

Engineer-In-Training Review Manual
Engineering Fundamentals Quick Reference Cards
Mini-Exams for the E-I-T Exam
1001 Solved Engineering Fundamentals Problems
E-I-T Review: A Study Guide
Civil Engineering Reference Manual
   Civil Engineering Quick Reference Cards
   Civil Engineering Sample Examination
   Civil Engineering Review Course on Cassettes
   Seismic Design for the Civil P.E. Exam
   Timber Design for the Civil P.E. Exam
Structural Engineering Practice Problem Manual
Mechanical Engineering Review Manual
   Mechanical Engineering Quick Reference Cards
   Mechanical Engineering Sample Examination
   Mechanical Engineering Review Course on Cassettes
Electrical Engineering Review Manual
Chemical Engineering Reference Manual
   Chemical Engineering Practice Exam Set
Land Surveyor Reference Manual
Metallurgical Engineering Practice Problem Manual
Petroleum Engineering Practice Problem Manual
Expanded Interest Tables
Engineering Law, Design Liability, and Professional Ethics
Engineering Unit Conversions

In the ENGINEERING CAREER ADVANCEMENT SERIES

How to Become a Professional Engineer
The Expert Witness Handbook—A Guide for Engineers
Getting Started as a Consulting Engineer
Intellectual Property Protection—A Guide for Engineers
E-I-T/P.E. Course Coordinator's Handbook

Distributed by: Professional Publications, Inc.
               1250 Fifth Avenue
               Department 77
               Belmont, CA 94002
               (415) 593-9119

**EXPANDED INTEREST TABLES for Economic Analysis Problems
Fourth Edition**

Printed in the United States of America

ISBN: 0-932276-70-9

Current printing of this edition (last number): 6 5 4 3 2 1

PREFACE

EXPANDED INTEREST TABLES is an important resource for solving economic analysis problems (also known as "present worth," "engineering economy," and "time value of money" problems). This book will be particularly valuable for professionals in various fields who are preparing for their licensing exams.

Most economic analysis problems are not computationally difficult. Almost all problems can be solved with a four-function calculator. However, most real-world problems tend to be long, both in the problem statement and in the solution procedure. Some problem types, particularly those involving the determination of rate of return, tend to be iterative. The extensive interest tables contained in *EXPANDED INTEREST TABLES* will simplify solutions by reducing, if not eliminating, the need for interpolation and use of factor formulas.

No other book contains as many different interest tables as *EXPANDED INTEREST TABLES*. Unlike most textbooks, which include only even interest rates in a limited range, this book includes tables for both odd and even interest rates over a wide range of values. Furthermore, factors are calculated for up to 100 compounding periods for the higher interest rates that are becoming common.

The factors in this book were calculated by a FORTRAN progam using double-precision variables throughout. All numbers have been rounded at the last decimal place.

This book should be considered an important complement to your primary economic analysis textbook.

Michael R. Lindeburg
Belmont, CA
July 1988

ACKNOWLEDGMENTS

Thank you, Joanne Bergeson, for resurrecting and perfecting my ten-year-old FORTRAN program that generated the factors in this book. I know that the problems seemed, at least initially, insurmountable. You had to first learn a new programming language, and then struggle with elusive accuracy in order to finish the project.

Thank you, Cindy Arnold of Professional Publications' art department, for the cover design. I also have to thank you for doing all of the paste-up and other composition work on this book.

I am indebted to Henry Hollwedel who took our data on diskette and produced the final film output when Professional Publications' facilities were busy. How fortuitous of you to mention at a Rotary meeting that your company did such work.

Finally, a big thank you to Lisa Rominger, supervisor of Professional Publications' production department, who managed to find time to coordinate yet another of my book ideas. The project was in good hands.

Michael R. Lindeburg
Belmont, CA
July 1988

STANDARD CASH FLOW FACTORS

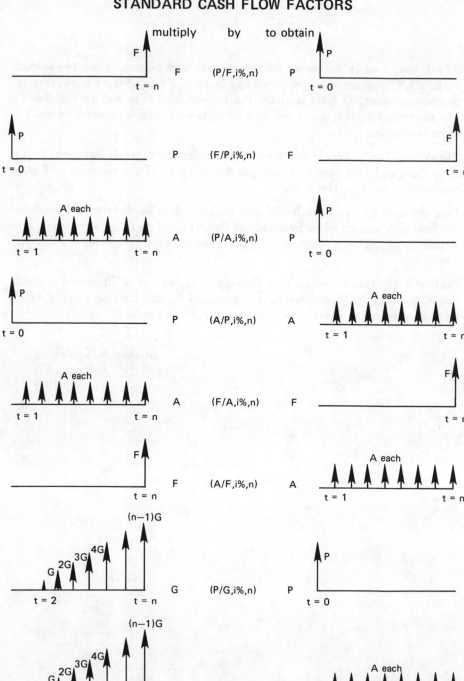

$I = 0.25\%$

n	(P/F)	(P/A)	(P/G)	(F/P)	(F/A)	(A/P)	(A/F)	(A/G)	n
1	0.9975	0.9975	0.0000	1.0025	1.0000	1.0025	1.0000	0.000	1
2	0.9950	1.9925	0.9950	1.0050	2.0025	0.5019	0.4994	0.499	2
3	0.9925	2.9851	2.9801	1.0075	3.0075	0.3350	0.3325	0.998	3
4	0.9901	3.9751	5.9503	1.0100	4.0150	0.2516	0.2491	1.496	4
5	0.9876	4.9627	9.9007	1.0126	5.0251	0.2015	0.1990	1.995	5
6	0.9851	5.9478	14.8263	1.0151	6.0376	0.1681	0.1656	2.492	6
7	0.9827	6.9305	20.7223	1.0176	7.0527	0.1443	0.1418	2.990	7
8	0.9802	7.9107	27.5839	1.0202	8.0704	0.1264	0.1239	3.486	8
9	0.9778	8.8885	35.4061	1.0227	9.0905	0.1125	0.1100	3.983	9
10	0.9753	9.8639	44.1842	1.0253	10.1133	0.1014	0.0989	4.479	10
11	0.9729	10.8368	53.9133	1.0278	11.1385	0.0923	0.0898	4.975	11
12	0.9705	11.8073	64.5886	1.0304	12.1664	0.0847	0.0822	5.470	12
13	0.9681	12.7753	76.2053	1.0330	13.1968	0.0783	0.0758	5.965	13
14	0.9656	13.7410	88.7587	1.0356	14.2298	0.0728	0.0703	6.459	14
15	0.9632	14.7042	102.2441	1.0382	15.2654	0.0680	0.0655	6.953	15
16	0.9608	15.6650	116.6567	1.0408	16.3035	0.0638	0.0613	7.446	16
17	0.9584	16.6235	131.9917	1.0434	17.3443	0.0602	0.0577	7.940	17
18	0.9561	17.5795	148.2446	1.0460	18.3876	0.0569	0.0544	8.432	18
19	0.9537	18.5332	165.4106	1.0486	19.4336	0.0540	0.0515	8.925	19
20	0.9513	19.4845	183.4851	1.0512	20.4822	0.0513	0.0488	9.417	20
21	0.9489	20.4334	202.4634	1.0538	21.5334	0.0489	0.0464	9.908	21
22	0.9466	21.3800	222.3410	1.0565	22.5872	0.0468	0.0443	10.399	22
23	0.9442	22.3241	243.1131	1.0591	23.6437	0.0448	0.0423	10.890	23
24	0.9418	23.2660	264.7753	1.0618	24.7028	0.0430	0.0405	11.380	24
25	0.9395	24.2055	287.3230	1.0644	25.7646	0.0413	0.0388	11.870	25
26	0.9371	25.1426	310.7516	1.0671	26.8290	0.0398	0.0373	12.359	26
27	0.9348	26.0774	335.0566	1.0697	27.8961	0.0383	0.0358	12.848	27
28	0.9325	27.0099	360.2334	1.0724	28.9658	0.0370	0.0345	13.337	28
29	0.9301	27.9400	386.2776	1.0751	30.0382	0.0358	0.0333	13.825	29
30	0.9278	28.8679	413.1847	1.0778	31.1133	0.0346	0.0321	14.313	30
31	0.9255	29.7934	440.9502	1.0805	32.1911	0.0336	0.0311	14.800	31
32	0.9232	30.7166	469.5696	1.0832	33.2716	0.0326	0.0301	15.287	32
33	0.9209	31.6375	499.0386	1.0859	34.3547	0.0316	0.0291	15.773	33
34	0.9186	32.5561	529.3528	1.0886	35.4406	0.0307	0.0282	16.259	34
35	0.9163	33.4724	560.5076	1.0913	36.5292	0.0299	0.0274	16.745	35
36	0.9140	34.3865	592.4988	1.0941	37.6206	0.0291	0.0266	17.230	36
37	0.9118	35.2982	625.3219	1.0968	38.7146	0.0283	0.0258	17.715	37
38	0.9095	36.2077	658.9727	1.0995	39.8114	0.0276	0.0251	18.199	38
39	0.9072	37.1149	693.4468	1.1023	40.9109	0.0269	0.0244	18.683	39
40	0.9050	38.0199	728.7399	1.1050	42.0132	0.0263	0.0238	19.167	40
41	0.9027	38.9226	764.8476	1.1078	43.1182	0.0257	0.0232	19.650	41
42	0.9004	39.8230	801.7658	1.1106	44.2260	0.0251	0.0226	20.133	42
43	0.8982	40.7212	839.4900	1.1133	45.3366	0.0246	0.0221	20.615	43
44	0.8960	41.6172	878.0162	1.1161	46.4499	0.0240	0.0215	21.097	44
45	0.8937	42.5109	917.3400	1.1189	47.5661	0.0235	0.0210	21.578	45
46	0.8915	43.4024	957.4572	1.1217	48.6850	0.0230	0.0205	22.060	46
47	0.8893	44.2916	998.3637	1.1245	49.8067	0.0226	0.0201	22.540	47
48	0.8871	45.1787	1040.0552	1.1273	50.9312	0.0221	0.0196	23.020	48
49	0.8848	46.0635	1082.5276	1.1301	52.0585	0.0217	0.0192	23.500	49
50	0.8826	46.9462	1125.7767	1.1330	53.1887	0.0213	0.0188	23.980	50
51	0.8804	47.8266	1169.7983	1.1358	54.3217	0.0209	0.0184	24.459	51
52	0.8782	48.7048	1214.5885	1.1386	55.4575	0.0205	0.0180	24.937	52
53	0.8760	49.5809	1260.1430	1.1415	56.5961	0.0202	0.0177	25.415	53
54	0.8739	50.4548	1306.4577	1.1443	57.7376	0.0198	0.0173	25.893	54
55	0.8717	51.3264	1353.5286	1.1472	58.8819	0.0195	0.0170	26.371	55
60	0.8609	55.6524	1600.0845	1.1616	64.6467	0.0180	0.0155	28.751	60
65	0.8502	59.9246	1864.9427	1.1762	70.4839	0.0167	0.0142	31.121	65
70	0.8396	64.1439	2147.6111	1.1910	76.3944	0.0156	0.0131	33.481	70
75	0.8292	68.3108	2447.6069	1.2059	82.3792	0.0146	0.0121	35.830	75
80	0.8189	72.4260	2764.4568	1.2211	88.4392	0.0138	0.0113	38.169	80
85	0.8088	76.4901	3097.6963	1.2364	94.5753	0.0131	0.0106	40.498	85
90	0.7987	80.5038	3446.8700	1.2520	100.7885	0.0124	0.0099	42.816	90
95	0.7888	84.4677	3811.5311	1.2677	107.0797	0.0118	0.0093	45.124	95
100	0.7790	88.3825	4191.2417	1.2836	113.4500	0.0113	0.0088	47.421	100

EXPANDED INTEREST TABLES

$I = 0.50\%$

n	(P/F)	(P/A)	(P/G)	(F/P)	(F/A)	(A/P)	(A/F)	(A/G)	n
1	0.9950	0.9950	0.0000	1.0050	1.0000	1.0050	1.0000	0.000	1
2	0.9901	1.9851	0.9901	1.0100	2.0050	0.5038	0.4988	0.498	2
3	0.9851	2.9702	2.9604	1.0151	3.0150	0.3367	0.3317	0.996	3
4	0.9802	3.9505	5.9011	1.0202	4.0301	0.2531	0.2481	1.493	4
5	0.9754	4.9259	9.8026	1.0253	5.0503	0.2030	0.1980	1.990	5
6	0.9705	5.8964	14.6552	1.0304	6.0755	0.1696	0.1646	2.485	6
7	0.9657	6.8621	20.4493	1.0355	7.1059	0.1457	0.1407	2.980	7
8	0.9609	7.8230	27.1755	1.0407	8.1414	0.1278	0.1228	3.473	8
9	0.9561	8.7791	34.8244	1.0459	9.1821	0.1139	0.1089	3.966	9
10	0.9513	9.7304	43.3865	1.0511	10.2280	0.1028	0.0978	4.458	10
11	0.9466	10.6770	52.8526	1.0564	11.2792	0.0937	0.0887	4.950	11
12	0.9419	11.6189	63.2136	1.0617	12.3356	0.0861	0.0811	5.440	12
13	0.9372	12.5562	74.4602	1.0670	13.3972	0.0796	0.0746	5.930	13
14	0.9326	13.4887	86.5835	1.0723	14.4642	0.0741	0.0691	6.419	14
15	0.9279	14.4166	99.5743	1.0777	15.5365	0.0694	0.0644	6.906	15
16	0.9233	15.3399	113.4238	1.0831	16.6142	0.0652	0.0602	7.394	16
17	0.9187	16.2586	128.1231	1.0885	17.6973	0.0615	0.0565	7.880	17
18	0.9141	17.1728	143.6634	1.0939	18.7858	0.0582	0.0532	8.365	18
19	0.9096	18.0824	160.0360	1.0994	19.8797	0.0553	0.0503	8.850	19
20	0.9051	18.9874	177.2322	1.1049	20.9791	0.0527	0.0477	9.334	20
21	0.9006	19.8880	195.2434	1.1104	22.0840	0.0503	0.0453	9.817	21
22	0.8961	20.7841	214.0611	1.1160	23.1944	0.0481	0.0431	10.299	22
23	0.8916	21.6757	233.6768	1.1216	24.3104	0.0461	0.0411	10.780	23
24	0.8872	22.5629	254.0820	1.1272	25.4320	0.0443	0.0393	11.261	24
25	0.8828	23.4456	275.2686	1.1328	26.5591	0.0427	0.0377	11.740	25
26	0.8784	24.3240	297.2281	1.1385	27.6919	0.0411	0.0361	12.219	26
27	0.8740	25.1980	319.9523	1.1442	28.8304	0.0397	0.0347	12.697	27
28	0.8697	26.0677	343.4332	1.1499	29.9745	0.0384	0.0334	13.174	28
29	0.8653	26.9330	367.6625	1.1556	31.1244	0.0371	0.0321	13.651	29
30	0.8610	27.7941	392.6324	1.1614	32.2800	0.0360	0.0310	14.126	30
31	0.8567	28.6508	418.3348	1.1672	33.4414	0.0349	0.0299	14.601	31
32	0.8525	29.5033	444.7618	1.1730	34.6086	0.0339	0.0289	15.075	32
33	0.8482	30.3515	471.9055	1.1789	35.7817	0.0329	0.0279	15.548	33
34	0.8440	31.1955	499.7583	1.1848	36.9606	0.0321	0.0271	16.020	34
35	0.8398	32.0354	528.3123	1.1907	38.1454	0.0312	0.0262	16.491	35
36	0.8356	32.8710	557.5598	1.1967	39.3361	0.0304	0.0254	16.962	36
37	0.8315	33.7025	587.4934	1.2027	40.5328	0.0297	0.0247	17.431	37
38	0.8274	34.5299	618.1054	1.2087	41.7354	0.0290	0.0240	17.900	38
39	0.8232	35.3531	649.3883	1.2147	42.9441	0.0283	0.0233	18.368	39
40	0.8191	36.1722	681.3347	1.2208	44.1588	0.0276	0.0226	18.835	40
41	0.8151	36.9873	713.9372	1.2269	45.3796	0.0270	0.0220	19.302	41
42	0.8110	37.7983	747.1886	1.2330	46.6065	0.0265	0.0215	19.767	42
43	0.8070	38.6053	781.0815	1.2392	47.8396	0.0259	0.0209	20.232	43
44	0.8030	39.4082	815.6087	1.2454	49.0788	0.0254	0.0204	20.696	44
45	0.7990	40.2072	850.7631	1.2516	50.3242	0.0249	0.0199	21.159	45
46	0.7950	41.0022	886.5376	1.2579	51.5758	0.0244	0.0194	21.621	46
47	0.7910	41.7932	922.9252	1.2642	52.8337	0.0239	0.0189	22.083	47
48	0.7871	42.5803	959.9188	1.2705	54.0978	0.0235	0.0185	22.543	48
49	0.7832	43.3635	997.5116	1.2768	55.3683	0.0231	0.0181	23.003	49
50	0.7793	44.1428	1035.6966	1.2832	56.6452	0.0227	0.0177	23.462	50
51	0.7754	44.9182	1074.4670	1.2896	57.9284	0.0223	0.0173	23.920	51
52	0.7716	45.6897	1113.8162	1.2961	59.2180	0.0219	0.0169	24.377	52
53	0.7677	46.4575	1153.7372	1.3026	60.5141	0.0215	0.0165	24.834	53
54	0.7639	47.2214	1194.2236	1.3091	61.8167	0.0212	0.0162	25.289	54
55	0.7601	47.9814	1235.2686	1.3156	63.1258	0.0208	0.0158	25.744	55
60	0.7414	51.7256	1448.6458	1.3489	69.7700	0.0193	0.0143	28.006	60
65	0.7231	55.3775	1675.0272	1.3829	76.5821	0.0181	0.0131	30.247	65
70	0.7053	58.9394	1913.6427	1.4178	83.5661	0.0170	0.0120	32.468	70
75	0.6879	62.4136	2163.7525	1.4536	90.7265	0.0160	0.0110	34.667	75
80	0.6710	65.8023	2424.6455	1.4903	98.0677	0.0152	0.0102	36.847	80
85	0.6545	69.1075	2695.6389	1.5280	105.5943	0.0145	0.0095	39.006	85
90	0.6383	72.3313	2976.0769	1.5666	113.3109	0.0138	0.0088	41.145	90
95	0.6226	75.4757	3265.3298	1.6061	121.2224	0.0132	0.0082	43.263	95
100	0.6073	78.5426	3562.7934	1.6467	129.3337	0.0127	0.0077	45.361	100

$I = 0.75\%$

n	(P/F)	(P/A)	(P/G)	(F/P)	(F/A)	(A/P)	(A/F)	(A/G)	n
1	0.9926	0.9926	0.0000	1.0075	1.0000	1.0075	1.0000	0.000	1
2	0.9852	1.9777	0.9852	1.0151	2.0075	0.5056	0.4981	0.498	2
3	0.9778	2.9556	2.9408	1.0227	3.0226	0.3383	0.3308	0.995	3
4	0.9706	3.9261	5.8525	1.0303	4.0452	0.2547	0.2472	1.490	4
5	0.9633	4.8894	9.7058	1.0381	5.0756	0.2045	0.1970	1.985	5
6	0.9562	5.8456	14.4866	1.0459	6.1136	0.1711	0.1636	2.478	6
7	0.9490	6.7946	20.1808	1.0537	7.1595	0.1472	0.1397	2.970	7
8	0.9420	7.7366	26.7747	1.0616	8.2132	0.1293	0.1218	3.460	8
9	0.9350	8.6716	34.2544	1.0696	9.2748	0.1153	0.1078	3.950	9
10	0.9280	9.5996	42.6064	1.0776	10.3443	0.1042	0.0967	4.438	10
11	0.9211	10.5207	51.8174	1.0857	11.4219	0.0951	0.0876	4.925	11
12	0.9142	11.4349	61.8740	1.0938	12.5076	0.0875	0.0800	5.411	12
13	0.9074	12.3423	72.7632	1.1020	13.6014	0.0810	0.0735	5.895	13
14	0.9007	13.2430	84.4720	1.1103	14.7034	0.0755	0.0680	6.378	14
15	0.8940	14.1370	96.9876	1.1186	15.8137	0.0707	0.0632	6.860	15
16	0.8873	15.0243	110.2973	1.1270	16.9323	0.0666	0.0591	7.341	16
17	0.8807	15.9050	124.3887	1.1354	18.0593	0.0629	0.0554	7.820	17
18	0.8742	16.7792	139.2494	1.1440	19.1947	0.0596	0.0521	8.298	18
19	0.8676	17.6468	154.8671	1.1525	20.3387	0.0567	0.0492	8.775	19
20	0.8612	18.5080	171.2297	1.1612	21.4912	0.0540	0.0465	9.251	20
21	0.8548	19.3628	188.3253	1.1699	22.6524	0.0516	0.0441	9.726	21
22	0.8484	20.2112	206.1420	1.1787	23.8223	0.0495	0.0420	10.199	22
23	0.8421	21.0533	224.6682	1.1875	25.0010	0.0475	0.0400	10.671	23
24	0.8358	21.8891	243.8923	1.1964	26.1885	0.0457	0.0382	11.142	24
25	0.8296	22.7188	263.8029	1.2054	27.3849	0.0440	0.0365	11.611	25
26	0.8234	23.5422	284.3888	1.2144	28.5903	0.0425	0.0350	12.080	26
27	0.8173	24.3595	305.6387	1.2235	29.8047	0.0411	0.0336	12.547	27
28	0.8112	25.1707	327.5416	1.2327	31.0282	0.0397	0.0322	13.012	28
29	0.8052	25.9759	350.0867	1.2420	32.2609	0.0385	0.0310	13.477	29
30	0.7992	26.7751	373.2631	1.2513	33.5029	0.0373	0.0298	13.940	30
31	0.7932	27.5683	397.0602	1.2607	34.7542	0.0363	0.0288	14.402	31
32	0.7873	28.3557	421.4675	1.2701	36.0148	0.0353	0.0278	14.863	32
33	0.7815	29.1371	446.4746	1.2796	37.2849	0.0343	0.0268	15.323	33
34	0.7757	29.9128	472.0712	1.2892	38.5646	0.0334	0.0259	15.781	34
35	0.7699	30.6827	498.2471	1.2989	39.8538	0.0326	0.0251	16.238	35
36	0.7641	31.4468	524.9922	1.3086	41.1527	0.0318	0.0243	16.694	36
37	0.7585	32.2053	552.2969	1.3185	42.4614	0.0311	0.0236	17.149	37
38	0.7528	32.9581	580.1511	1.3283	43.7798	0.0303	0.0228	17.602	38
39	0.7472	33.7053	608.5451	1.3383	45.1082	0.0297	0.0222	18.054	39
40	0.7416	34.4469	637.4693	1.3483	46.4465	0.0290	0.0215	18.505	40
41	0.7361	35.1831	666.9144	1.3585	47.7948	0.0284	0.0209	18.955	41
42	0.7306	35.9137	696.8709	1.3686	49.1533	0.0278	0.0203	19.404	42
43	0.7252	36.6389	727.3297	1.3789	50.5219	0.0273	0.0198	19.851	43
44	0.7198	37.3587	758.2815	1.3893	51.9009	0.0268	0.0193	20.297	44
45	0.7145	38.0732	789.7173	1.3997	53.2901	0.0263	0.0188	20.742	45
46	0.7091	38.7823	821.6283	1.4102	54.6898	0.0258	0.0183	21.185	46
47	0.7039	39.4862	854.0056	1.4207	56.1000	0.0253	0.0178	21.628	47
48	0.6986	40.1848	886.8404	1.4314	57.5207	0.0249	0.0174	22.069	48
49	0.6934	40.8782	920.1243	1.4421	58.9521	0.0245	0.0170	22.508	49
50	0.6883	41.5664	953.8486	1.4530	60.3943	0.0241	0.0166	22.947	50
51	0.6831	42.2496	988.0050	1.4639	61.8472	0.0237	0.0162	23.385	51
52	0.6780	42.9276	1022.5852	1.4748	63.3111	0.0233	0.0158	23.821	52
53	0.6730	43.6006	1057.5810	1.4859	64.7859	0.0229	0.0154	24.256	53
54	0.6680	44.2686	1092.9842	1.4970	66.2718	0.0226	0.0151	24.689	54
55	0.6630	44.9316	1128.7869	1.5083	67.7688	0.0223	0.0148	25.122	55
60	0.6387	48.1734	1313.5189	1.5657	75.4241	0.0208	0.0133	27.266	60
65	0.6153	51.2963	1507.0910	1.6253	83.3709	0.0195	0.0120	29.380	65
70	0.5927	54.3046	1708.6065	1.6872	91.6201	0.0184	0.0109	31.463	70
75	0.5710	57.2027	1917.2225	1.7514	100.1833	0.0175	0.0100	33.516	75
80	0.5500	59.9944	2132.1472	1.8180	109.0725	0.0167	0.0092	35.539	80
85	0.5299	62.6838	2352.6375	1.8873	118.3001	0.0160	0.0085	37.531	85
90	0.5104	65.2746	2577.9961	1.9591	127.8790	0.0153	0.0078	39.494	90
95	0.4917	67.7704	2807.5694	2.0337	137.8225	0.0148	0.0073	41.427	95
100	0.4737	70.1746	3040.7453	2.1111	148.1445	0.0143	0.0068	43.331	100

EXPANDED INTEREST TABLES

$I = 1.00$ %

n	(P/F)	(P/A)	(P/G)	(F/P)	(F/A)	(A/P)	(A/F)	(A/G)	n
1	0.9901	0.9901	0.0000	1.0100	1.0000	1.0100	1.0000	0.000	1
2	0.9803	1.9704	0.9803	1.0201	2.0100	0.5075	0.4975	0.497	2
3	0.9706	2.9410	2.9215	1.0303	3.0301	0.3400	0.3300	0.993	3
4	0.9610	3.9020	5.8044	1.0406	4.0604	0.2563	0.2463	1.487	4
5	0.9515	4.8534	9.6103	1.0510	5.1010	0.2060	0.1960	1.980	5
6	0.9420	5.7955	14.3205	1.0615	6.1520	0.1725	0.1625	2.471	6
7	0.9327	6.7282	19.9168	1.0721	7.2135	0.1486	0.1386	2.960	7
8	0.9235	7.6517	26.3812	1.0829	8.2857	0.1307	0.1207	3.447	8
9	0.9143	8.5660	33.6959	1.0937	9.3685	0.1167	0.1067	3.933	9
10	0.9053	9.4713	41.8435	1.1046	10.4622	0.1056	0.0956	4.417	10
11	0.8963	10.3676	50.8067	1.1157	11.5668	0.0965	0.0865	4.900	11
12	0.8874	11.2551	60.5687	1.1268	12.6825	0.0888	0.0788	5.381	12
13	0.8787	12.1337	71.1126	1.1381	13.8093	0.0824	0.0724	5.860	13
14	0.8700	13.0037	82.4221	1.1495	14.9474	0.0769	0.0669	6.338	14
15	0.8613	13.8651	94.4810	1.1610	16.0969	0.0721	0.0621	6.814	15
16	0.8528	14.7179	107.2734	1.1726	17.2579	0.0679	0.0579	7.288	16
17	0.8444	15.5623	120.7834	1.1843	18.4304	0.0643	0.0543	7.761	17
18	0.8360	16.3983	134.9957	1.1961	19.6147	0.0610	0.0510	8.232	18
19	0.8277	17.2260	149.8950	1.2081	20.8109	0.0581	0.0481	8.701	19
20	0.8195	18.0456	165.4664	1.2202	22.0190	0.0554	0.0454	9.169	20
21	0.8114	18.8570	181.6950	1.2324	23.2392	0.0530	0.0430	9.635	21
22	0.8034	19.6604	198.5663	1.2447	24.4716	0.0509	0.0409	10.099	22
23	0.7954	20.4558	216.0660	1.2572	25.7163	0.0489	0.0389	10.562	23
24	0.7876	21.2434	234.1800	1.2697	26.9735	0.0471	0.0371	11.023	24
25	0.7798	22.0232	252.8945	1.2824	28.2432	0.0454	0.0354	11.483	25
26	0.7720	22.7952	272.1957	1.2953	29.5256	0.0439	0.0339	11.940	26
27	0.7644	23.5596	292.0702	1.3082	30.8209	0.0424	0.0324	12.397	27
28	0.7568	24.3164	312.5047	1.3213	32.1291	0.0411	0.0311	12.851	28
29	0.7493	25.0658	333.4863	1.3345	33.4504	0.0399	0.0299	13.304	29
30	0.7419	25.8077	355.0021	1.3478	34.7849	0.0387	0.0287	13.755	30
31	0.7346	26.5423	377.0394	1.3613	36.1327	0.0377	0.0277	14.205	31
32	0.7273	27.2696	399.5858	1.3749	37.4941	0.0367	0.0267	14.653	32
33	0.7201	27.9897	422.6291	1.3887	38.8690	0.0357	0.0257	15.099	33
34	0.7130	28.7027	446.1572	1.4026	40.2577	0.0348	0.0248	15.544	34
35	0.7059	29.4086	470.1583	1.4166	41.6603	0.0340	0.0240	15.987	35
36	0.6989	30.1075	494.6207	1.4308	43.0769	0.0332	0.0232	16.428	36
37	0.6920	30.7995	519.5329	1.4451	44.5076	0.0325	0.0225	16.868	37
38	0.6852	31.4847	544.8835	1.4595	45.9527	0.0318	0.0218	17.306	38
39	0.6784	32.1630	570.6616	1.4741	47.4123	0.0311	0.0211	17.742	39
40	0.6717	32.8347	596.8561	1.4889	48.8864	0.0305	0.0205	18.177	40
41	0.6650	33.4997	623.4562	1.5038	50.3752	0.0299	0.0199	18.610	41
42	0.6584	34.1581	650.4514	1.5188	51.8790	0.0293	0.0193	19.042	42
43	0.6519	34.8100	677.8312	1.5340	53.3978	0.0287	0.0187	19.472	43
44	0.6454	35.4555	705.5853	1.5493	54.9318	0.0282	0.0182	19.900	44
45	0.6391	36.0945	733.7037	1.5648	56.4811	0.0277	0.0177	20.327	45
46	0.6327	36.7272	762.1765	1.5805	58.0459	0.0272	0.0172	20.752	46
47	0.6265	37.3537	790.9938	1.5963	59.6263	0.0268	0.0168	21.175	47
48	0.6203	37.9740	820.1460	1.6122	61.2226	0.0263	0.0163	21.597	48
49	0.6141	38.5881	849.6237	1.6283	62.8348	0.0259	0.0159	22.017	49
50	0.6080	39.1961	879.4176	1.6446	64.4632	0.0255	0.0155	22.436	50
51	0.6020	39.7981	909.5186	1.6611	66.1078	0.0251	0.0151	22.853	51
52	0.5961	40.3942	939.9175	1.6777	67.7689	0.0248	0.0148	23.268	52
53	0.5902	40.9844	970.6057	1.6945	69.4466	0.0244	0.0144	23.682	53
54	0.5843	41.5687	1001.5743	1.7114	71.1410	0.0241	0.0141	24.094	54
55	0.5785	42.1472	1032.8148	1.7285	72.8525	0.0237	0.0137	24.504	55
60	0.5504	44.9550	1192.8061	1.8167	81.6697	0.0222	0.0122	26.533	60
65	0.5237	47.6266	1358.3903	1.9094	90.9366	0.0210	0.0110	28.521	65
70	0.4983	50.1685	1528.6474	2.0068	100.6763	0.0199	0.0099	30.470	70
75	0.4741	52.5871	1702.7340	2.1091	110.9128	0.0190	0.0090	32.379	75
80	0.4511	54.8882	1879.8771	2.2167	121.6715	0.0182	0.0082	34.249	80
85	0.4292	57.0777	2059.3701	2.3298	132.9790	0.0175	0.0075	36.080	85
90	0.4084	59.1609	2240.5675	2.4486	144.8633	0.0169	0.0069	37.872	90
95	0.3886	61.1430	2422.8811	2.5735	157.3538	0.0164	0.0064	39.626	95
100	0.3697	63.0289	2605.7758	2.7048	170.4814	0.0159	0.0059	41.342	100

$I = 1.25\%$

n	(P/F)	(P/A)	(P/G)	(F/P)	(F/A)	(A/P)	(A/F)	(A/G)	n
1	0.9877	0.9877	0.0000	1.0125	1.0000	1.0125	1.0000	0.000	1
2	0.9755	1.9631	0.9755	1.0252	2.0125	0.5094	0.4969	0.496	2
3	0.9634	2.9265	2.9023	1.0380	3.0377	0.3417	0.3292	0.991	3
4	0.9515	3.8781	5.7569	1.0509	4.0756	0.2579	0.2454	1.484	4
5	0.9398	4.8178	9.5160	1.0641	5.1266	0.2076	0.1951	1.975	5
6	0.9282	5.7460	14.1569	1.0774	6.1907	0.1740	0.1615	2.463	6
7	0.9167	6.6627	19.6571	1.0909	7.2680	0.1501	0.1376	2.950	7
8	0.9054	7.5681	25.9949	1.1045	8.3589	0.1321	0.1196	3.434	8
9	0.8942	8.4623	33.1487	1.1183	9.4634	0.1182	0.1057	3.917	9
10	0.8832	9.3455	41.0973	1.1323	10.5817	0.1070	0.0945	4.397	10
11	0.8723	10.2178	49.8201	1.1464	11.7139	0.0979	0.0854	4.875	11
12	0.8615	11.0793	59.2967	1.1608	12.8604	0.0903	0.0778	5.352	12
13	0.8509	11.9302	69.5072	1.1753	14.0211	0.0838	0.0713	5.826	13
14	0.8404	12.7706	80.4320	1.1900	15.1964	0.0783	0.0658	6.298	14
15	0.8300	13.6005	92.0519	1.2048	16.3863	0.0735	0.0610	6.768	15
16	0.8197	14.4203	104.3481	1.2199	17.5912	0.0693	0.0568	7.236	16
17	0.8096	15.2299	117.3021	1.2351	18.8111	0.0657	0.0532	7.702	17
18	0.7996	16.0295	130.8958	1.2506	20.0462	0.0624	0.0499	8.165	18
19	0.7898	16.8193	145.1115	1.2662	21.2968	0.0595	0.0470	8.627	19
20	0.7800	17.5993	159.9316	1.2820	22.5630	0.0568	0.0443	9.087	20
21	0.7704	18.3697	175.3392	1.2981	23.8450	0.0544	0.0419	9.545	21
22	0.7609	19.1306	191.3174	1.3143	25.1431	0.0523	0.0398	10.000	22
23	0.7515	19.8820	207.8499	1.3307	26.4574	0.0503	0.0378	10.454	23
24	0.7422	20.6242	224.9204	1.3474	27.7881	0.0485	0.0360	10.905	24
25	0.7330	21.3573	242.5132	1.3642	29.1354	0.0468	0.0343	11.355	25
26	0.7240	22.0813	260.6128	1.3812	30.4996	0.0453	0.0328	11.802	26
27	0.7150	22.7963	279.2040	1.3985	31.8809	0.0439	0.0314	12.247	27
28	0.7062	23.5025	298.2719	1.4160	33.2794	0.0425	0.0300	12.691	28
29	0.6975	24.2000	317.8019	1.4337	34.6954	0.0413	0.0288	13.132	29
30	0.6889	24.8889	337.7797	1.4516	36.1291	0.0402	0.0277	13.571	30
31	0.6804	25.5693	358.1912	1.4698	37.5807	0.0391	0.0266	14.008	31
32	0.6720	26.2413	379.0227	1.4881	39.0504	0.0381	0.0256	14.443	32
33	0.6637	26.9050	400.2607	1.5067	40.5386	0.0372	0.0247	14.876	33
34	0.6555	27.5605	421.8920	1.5256	42.0453	0.0363	0.0238	15.307	34
35	0.6474	28.2079	443.9037	1.5446	43.5709	0.0355	0.0230	15.736	35
36	0.6394	28.8473	466.2830	1.5639	45.1155	0.0347	0.0222	16.163	36
37	0.6315	29.4788	489.0176	1.5835	46.6794	0.0339	0.0214	16.588	37
38	0.6237	30.1025	512.0952	1.6033	48.2629	0.0332	0.0207	17.011	38
39	0.6160	30.7185	535.5039	1.6233	49.8662	0.0326	0.0201	17.432	39
40	0.6084	31.3269	559.2320	1.6436	51.4896	0.0319	0.0194	17.851	40
41	0.6009	31.9278	583.2681	1.6642	53.1332	0.0313	0.0188	18.268	41
42	0.5935	32.5213	607.6009	1.6850	54.7973	0.0307	0.0182	18.683	42
43	0.5862	33.1075	632.2195	1.7060	56.4823	0.0302	0.0177	19.096	43
44	0.5789	33.6864	657.1130	1.7274	58.1883	0.0297	0.0172	19.506	44
45	0.5718	34.2582	682.2710	1.7489	59.9157	0.0292	0.0167	19.915	45
46	0.5647	34.8229	707.6832	1.7708	61.6646	0.0287	0.0162	20.322	46
47	0.5577	35.3806	733.3393	1.7929	63.4354	0.0283	0.0158	20.727	47
48	0.5509	35.9315	759.2296	1.8154	65.2284	0.0278	0.0153	21.129	48
49	0.5441	36.4755	785.3442	1.8380	67.0437	0.0274	0.0149	21.530	49
50	0.5373	37.0129	811.6738	1.8610	68.8818	0.0270	0.0145	21.929	50
51	0.5307	37.5436	838.2091	1.8843	70.7428	0.0266	0.0141	22.326	51
52	0.5242	38.0677	864.9409	1.9078	72.6271	0.0263	0.0138	22.721	52
53	0.5177	38.5854	891.8604	1.9317	74.5349	0.0259	0.0134	23.113	53
54	0.5113	39.0967	918.9588	1.9558	76.4666	0.0256	0.0131	23.504	54
55	0.5050	39.6017	946.2277	1.9803	78.4225	0.0253	0.0128	23.893	55
60	0.4746	42.0346	1084.8429	2.1072	88.5745	0.0238	0.0113	25.808	60
65	0.4460	44.3210	1226.5421	2.2422	99.3771	0.0226	0.0101	27.674	65
70	0.4191	46.4697	1370.4513	2.3859	110.8720	0.0215	0.0090	29.491	70
75	0.3939	48.4890	1515.7904	2.5388	123.1035	0.0206	0.0081	31.260	75
80	0.3702	50.3867	1661.8651	2.7015	136.1188	0.0198	0.0073	32.982	80
85	0.3479	52.1701	1808.0598	2.8746	149.9682	0.0192	0.0067	34.657	85
90	0.3269	53.8461	1953.8303	3.0588	164.7050	0.0186	0.0061	36.285	90
95	0.3072	55.4211	2098.6973	3.2548	180.3862	0.0180	0.0055	37.868	95
100	0.2887	56.9013	2242.2411	3.4634	197.0723	0.0176	0.0051	39.405	100

EXPANDED INTEREST TABLES

$I = 1.50 \%$

n	(P/F)	(P/A)	(P/G)	(F/P)	(F/A)	(A/P)	(A/F)	(A/G)	n
1	0.9852	0.9852	0.0000	1.0150	1.0000	1.0150	1.0000	0.000	1
2	0.9707	1.9559	0.9707	1.0302	2.0150	0.5113	0.4963	0.496	2
3	0.9563	2.9122	2.8833	1.0457	3.0452	0.3434	0.3284	0.990	3
4	0.9422	3.8544	5.7098	1.0614	4.0909	0.2594	0.2444	1.481	4
5	0.9283	4.7826	9.4229	1.0773	5.1523	0.2091	0.1941	1.970	5
6	0.9145	5.6972	13.9956	1.0934	6.2296	0.1755	0.1605	2.456	6
7	0.9010	6.5982	19.4018	1.1098	7.3230	0.1516	0.1366	2.940	7
8	0.8877	7.4859	25.6157	1.1265	8.4328	0.1336	0.1186	3.421	8
9	0.8746	8.3605	32.6125	1.1434	9.5593	0.1196	0.1046	3.900	9
10	0.8617	9.2222	40.3675	1.1605	10.7027	0.1084	0.0934	4.377	10
11	0.8489	10.0711	48.8568	1.1779	11.8633	0.0993	0.0843	4.851	11
12	0.8364	10.9075	58.0571	1.1956	13.0412	0.0917	0.0767	5.322	12
13	0.8240	11.7315	67.9454	1.2136	14.2368	0.0852	0.0702	5.791	13
14	0.8118	12.5434	78.4994	1.2318	15.4504	0.0797	0.0647	6.258	14
15	0.7999	13.3432	89.6974	1.2502	16.6821	0.0749	0.0599	6.722	15
16	0.7880	14.1313	101.5178	1.2690	17.9324	0.0708	0.0558	7.183	16
17	0.7764	14.9076	113.9400	1.2880	19.2014	0.0671	0.0521	7.643	17
18	0.7649	15.6726	126.9435	1.3073	20.4894	0.0638	0.0488	8.099	18
19	0.7536	16.4262	140.5084	1.3270	21.7967	0.0609	0.0459	8.553	19
20	0.7425	17.1686	154.6154	1.3469	23.1237	0.0582	0.0432	9.005	20
21	0.7315	17.9001	169.2453	1.3671	24.4705	0.0559	0.0409	9.455	21
22	0.7207	18.6208	184.3798	1.3876	25.8376	0.0537	0.0387	9.901	22
23	0.7100	19.3309	200.0006	1.4084	27.2251	0.0517	0.0367	10.346	23
24	0.6995	20.0304	216.0901	1.4295	28.6335	0.0499	0.0349	10.788	24
25	0.6892	20.7196	232.6310	1.4509	30.0630	0.0483	0.0333	11.227	25
26	0.6790	21.3986	249.6065	1.4727	31.5140	0.0467	0.0317	11.664	26
27	0.6690	22.0676	267.0002	1.4948	32.9867	0.0453	0.0303	12.099	27
28	0.6591	22.7267	284.7958	1.5172	34.4815	0.0440	0.0290	12.531	28
29	0.6494	23.3761	302.9779	1.5400	35.9987	0.0428	0.0278	12.961	29
30	0.6398	24.0158	321.5310	1.5631	37.5387	0.0416	0.0266	13.388	30
31	0.6303	24.6461	340.4402	1.5865	39.1018	0.0406	0.0256	13.813	31
32	0.6210	25.2671	359.6910	1.6103	40.6883	0.0396	0.0246	14.235	32
33	0.6118	25.8790	379.2691	1.6345	42.2986	0.0386	0.0236	14.655	33
34	0.6028	26.4817	399.1607	1.6590	43.9331	0.0378	0.0228	15.073	34
35	0.5939	27.0756	419.3521	1.6839	45.5921	0.0369	0.0219	15.488	35
36	0.5851	27.6607	439.8303	1.7091	47.2760	0.0362	0.0212	15.900	36
37	0.5764	28.2371	460.5822	1.7348	48.9851	0.0354	0.0204	16.311	37
38	0.5679	28.8051	481.5954	1.7608	50.7199	0.0347	0.0197	16.719	38
39	0.5595	29.3646	502.8576	1.7872	52.4807	0.0341	0.0191	17.124	39
40	0.5513	29.9158	524.3568	1.8140	54.2679	0.0334	0.0184	17.527	40
41	0.5431	30.4590	546.0814	1.8412	56.0819	0.0328	0.0178	17.928	41
42	0.5351	30.9941	568.0201	1.8688	57.9231	0.0323	0.0173	18.326	42
43	0.5272	31.5212	590.1617	1.8969	59.7920	0.0317	0.0167	18.722	43
44	0.5194	32.0406	612.4955	1.9253	61.6889	0.0312	0.0162	19.116	44
45	0.5117	32.5523	635.0110	1.9542	63.6142	0.0307	0.0157	19.507	45
46	0.5042	33.0565	657.6979	1.9835	65.5684	0.0303	0.0153	19.896	46
47	0.4967	33.5532	680.5462	2.0133	67.5519	0.0298	0.0148	20.282	47
48	0.4894	34.0426	703.5462	2.0435	69.5652	0.0294	0.0144	20.666	48
49	0.4821	34.5247	726.6884	2.0741	71.6087	0.0290	0.0140	21.048	49
50	0.4750	34.9997	749.9636	2.1052	73.6828	0.0286	0.0136	21.427	50
51	0.4680	35.4677	773.3629	2.1368	75.7881	0.0282	0.0132	21.804	51
52	0.4611	35.9287	796.8774	2.1689	77.9249	0.0278	0.0128	22.179	52
53	0.4543	36.3830	820.4986	2.2014	80.0938	0.0275	0.0125	22.551	53
54	0.4475	36.8305	844.2184	2.2344	82.2952	0.0272	0.0122	22.921	54
55	0.4409	37.2715	868.0285	2.2679	84.5296	0.0268	0.0118	23.289	55
60	0.4093	39.3803	988.1674	2.4432	96.2147	0.0254	0.0104	25.093	60
65	0.3799	41.3378	1109.4752	2.6320	108.8028	0.0242	0.0092	26.839	65
70	0.3527	43.1549	1231.1658	2.8355	122.3638	0.0232	0.0082	28.529	70
75	0.3274	44.8416	1352.5600	3.0546	136.9728	0.0223	0.0073	30.163	75
80	0.3039	46.4073	1473.0741	3.2907	152.7109	0.0215	0.0065	31.742	80
85	0.2821	47.8607	1592.2095	3.5450	169.6652	0.0209	0.0059	33.267	85
90	0.2619	49.2099	1709.5439	3.8189	187.9299	0.0203	0.0053	34.739	90
95	0.2431	50.4622	1824.7224	4.1141	207.6061	0.0198	0.0048	36.160	95
100	0.2256	51.6247	1937.4506	4.4320	228.8030	0.0194	0.0044	37.529	100

$I = 1.75\%$

n	(P/F)	(P/A)	(P/G)	(F/P)	(F/A)	(A/P)	(A/F)	(A/G)	n
1	0.9828	0.9828	0.0000	1.0175	1.0000	1.0175	1.0000	0.000	1
2	0.9659	1.9487	0.9659	1.0353	2.0175	0.5132	0.4957	0.495	2
3	0.9493	2.8980	2.8645	1.0534	3.0528	0.3451	0.3276	0.988	3
4	0.9330	3.8309	5.6633	1.0719	4.1062	0.2610	0.2435	1.478	4
5	0.9169	4.7479	9.3310	1.0906	5.1781	0.2106	0.1931	1.965	5
6	0.9011	5.6490	13.8367	1.1097	6.2687	0.1770	0.1595	2.449	6
7	0.8856	6.5346	19.1506	1.1291	7.3784	0.1530	0.1355	2.930	7
8	0.8704	7.4051	25.2435	1.1489	8.5075	0.1350	0.1175	3.408	8
9	0.8554	8.2605	32.0870	1.1690	9.6564	0.1211	0.1036	3.884	9
10	0.8407	9.1012	39.6535	1.1894	10.8254	0.1099	0.0924	4.356	10
11	0.8263	9.9275	47.9162	1.2103	12.0148	0.1007	0.0832	4.826	11
12	0.8121	10.7395	56.8489	1.2314	13.2251	0.0931	0.0756	5.293	12
13	0.7981	11.5376	66.4260	1.2530	14.4565	0.0867	0.0692	5.757	13
14	0.7844	12.3220	76.6227	1.2749	15.7095	0.0812	0.0637	6.218	14
15	0.7709	13.0929	87.4149	1.2972	16.9844	0.0764	0.0589	6.676	15
16	0.7576	13.8505	98.7792	1.3199	18.2817	0.0722	0.0547	7.131	16
17	0.7446	14.5951	110.6926	1.3430	19.6016	0.0685	0.0510	7.584	17
18	0.7318	15.3269	123.1328	1.3665	20.9446	0.0652	0.0477	8.033	18
19	0.7192	16.0461	136.0783	1.3904	22.3112	0.0623	0.0448	8.480	19
20	0.7068	16.7529	149.5080	1.4148	23.7016	0.0597	0.0422	8.924	20
21	0.6947	17.4475	163.4013	1.4395	25.1164	0.0573	0.0398	9.365	21
22	0.6827	18.1303	177.7385	1.4647	26.5559	0.0552	0.0377	9.803	22
23	0.6710	18.8012	192.5000	1.4904	28.0207	0.0532	0.0357	10.238	23
24	0.6594	19.4607	207.6671	1.5164	29.5110	0.0514	0.0339	10.671	24
25	0.6481	20.1088	223.2214	1.5430	31.0275	0.0497	0.0322	11.100	25
26	0.6369	20.7457	239.1451	1.5700	32.5704	0.0482	0.0307	11.527	26
27	0.6260	21.3717	255.4210	1.5975	34.1404	0.0468	0.0293	11.951	27
28	0.6152	21.9870	272.0321	1.6254	35.7379	0.0455	0.0280	12.372	28
29	0.6046	22.5916	288.9623	1.6539	37.3633	0.0443	0.0268	12.790	29
30	0.5942	23.1858	306.1954	1.6828	39.0172	0.0431	0.0256	13.206	30
31	0.5840	23.7699	323.7163	1.7122	40.7000	0.0421	0.0246	13.618	31
32	0.5740	24.3439	341.5097	1.7422	42.4122	0.0411	0.0236	14.028	32
33	0.5641	24.9080	359.5613	1.7727	44.1544	0.0401	0.0226	14.435	33
34	0.5544	25.4624	377.8567	1.8037	45.9271	0.0393	0.0218	14.839	34
35	0.5449	26.0073	396.3824	1.8353	47.7308	0.0385	0.0210	15.241	35
36	0.5355	26.5428	415.1250	1.8674	49.5661	0.0377	0.0202	15.639	36
37	0.5263	27.0690	434.0715	1.9001	51.4335	0.0369	0.0194	16.035	37
38	0.5172	27.5863	453.2094	1.9333	53.3336	0.0362	0.0187	16.428	38
39	0.5083	28.0946	472.5264	1.9672	55.2670	0.0356	0.0181	16.819	39
40	0.4996	28.5942	492.0109	2.0016	57.2341	0.0350	0.0175	17.206	40
41	0.4910	29.0852	511.6512	2.0366	59.2357	0.0344	0.0169	17.591	41
42	0.4826	29.5678	531.4363	2.0723	61.2724	0.0338	0.0163	17.973	42
43	0.4743	30.0421	551.3554	2.1085	63.3446	0.0333	0.0158	18.352	43
44	0.4661	30.5082	571.3980	2.1454	65.4532	0.0328	0.0153	18.729	44
45	0.4581	30.9663	591.5540	2.1830	67.5986	0.0323	0.0148	19.103	45
46	0.4502	31.4165	611.8135	2.2212	69.7816	0.0318	0.0143	19.474	46
47	0.4425	31.8589	632.1670	2.2600	72.0027	0.0314	0.0139	19.842	47
48	0.4349	32.2938	652.6054	2.2996	74.2628	0.0310	0.0135	20.208	48
49	0.4274	32.7212	673.1196	2.3398	76.5624	0.0306	0.0131	20.571	49
50	0.4200	33.1412	693.7010	2.3808	78.9022	0.0302	0.0127	20.931	50
51	0.4128	33.5540	714.3413	2.4225	81.2830	0.0298	0.0123	21.289	51
52	0.4057	33.9597	735.0322	2.4648	83.7055	0.0294	0.0119	21.644	52
53	0.3987	34.3584	755.7660	2.5080	86.1703	0.0291	0.0116	21.996	53
54	0.3919	34.7503	776.5351	2.5519	88.6783	0.0288	0.0113	22.346	54
55	0.3851	35.1354	797.3321	2.5965	91.2302	0.0285	0.0110	22.693	55
60	0.3531	36.9640	901.4954	2.8318	104.6752	0.0271	0.0096	24.388	60
65	0.3238	38.6406	1005.3872	3.0884	119.3386	0.0259	0.0084	26.018	65
70	0.2969	40.1779	1108.3333	3.3683	135.3308	0.0249	0.0074	27.585	70
75	0.2722	41.5875	1209.7738	3.6735	152.7721	0.0240	0.0065	29.089	75
80	0.2496	42.8799	1309.2482	4.0064	171.7938	0.0233	0.0058	30.532	80
85	0.2289	44.0650	1406.3828	4.3694	192.5393	0.0227	0.0052	31.916	85
90	0.2098	45.1516	1500.8798	4.7654	215.1646	0.0221	0.0046	33.240	90
95	0.1924	46.1479	1592.5069	5.1972	239.8402	0.0217	0.0042	34.508	95
100	0.1764	47.0615	1681.0886	5.6682	266.7518	0.0212	0.0037	35.721	100

PROFESSIONAL PUBLICATIONS, INC. ● Belmont, CA

EXPANDED INTEREST TABLES

$I = 2.00\ \%$

n	(P/F)	(P/A)	(P/G)	(F/P)	(F/A)	(A/P)	(A/F)	(A/G)	n
1	0.9804	0.9804	0.0000	1.0200	1.0000	1.0200	1.0000	0.000	1
2	0.9612	1.9416	0.9612	1.0404	2.0200	0.5150	0.4950	0.495	2
3	0.9423	2.8839	2.8458	1.0612	3.0604	0.3468	0.3268	0.986	3
4	0.9238	3.8077	5.6173	1.0824	4.1216	0.2626	0.2426	1.475	4
5	0.9057	4.7135	9.2403	1.1041	5.2040	0.2122	0.1922	1.960	5
6	0.8880	5.6014	13.6801	1.1262	6.3081	0.1785	0.1585	2.442	6
7	0.8706	6.4720	18.9035	1.1487	7.4343	0.1545	0.1345	2.920	7
8	0.8535	7.3255	24.8779	1.1717	8.5830	0.1365	0.1165	3.396	8
9	0.8368	8.1622	31.5720	1.1951	9.7546	0.1225	0.1025	3.868	9
10	0.8203	8.9826	38.9551	1.2190	10.9497	0.1113	0.0913	4.336	10
11	0.8043	9.7868	46.9977	1.2434	12.1687	0.1022	0.0822	4.802	11
12	0.7885	10.5753	55.6712	1.2682	13.4121	0.0946	0.0746	5.264	12
13	0.7730	11.3484	64.9475	1.2936	14.6803	0.0881	0.0681	5.723	13
14	0.7579	12.1062	74.7999	1.3195	15.9739	0.0826	0.0626	6.178	14
15	0.7430	12.8493	85.2021	1.3459	17.2934	0.0778	0.0578	6.630	15
16	0.7284	13.5777	96.1288	1.3728	18.6393	0.0737	0.0537	7.079	16
17	0.7142	14.2919	107.5554	1.4002	20.0121	0.0700	0.0500	7.525	17
18	0.7002	14.9920	119.4581	1.4282	21.4123	0.0667	0.0467	7.968	18
19	0.6864	15.6785	131.8139	1.4568	22.8406	0.0638	0.0438	8.407	19
20	0.6730	16.3514	144.6003	1.4859	24.2974	0.0612	0.0412	8.843	20
21	0.6598	17.0112	157.7959	1.5157	25.7833	0.0588	0.0388	9.276	21
22	0.6468	17.6580	171.3795	1.5460	27.2990	0.0566	0.0366	9.705	22
23	0.6342	18.2922	185.3309	1.5769	28.8450	0.0547	0.0347	10.131	23
24	0.6217	18.9139	199.6305	1.6084	30.4219	0.0529	0.0329	10.554	24
25	0.6095	19.5235	214.2592	1.6406	32.0303	0.0512	0.0312	10.974	25
26	0.5976	20.1210	229.1987	1.6734	33.6709	0.0497	0.0297	11.391	26
27	0.5859	20.7069	244.4311	1.7069	35.3443	0.0483	0.0283	11.804	27
28	0.5744	21.2813	259.9392	1.7410	37.0512	0.0470	0.0270	12.214	28
29	0.5631	21.8444	275.7064	1.7758	38.7922	0.0458	0.0258	12.621	29
30	0.5521	22.3965	291.7164	1.8114	40.5681	0.0446	0.0246	13.025	30
31	0.5412	22.9377	307.9538	1.8476	42.3794	0.0436	0.0236	13.425	31
32	0.5306	23.4683	324.4035	1.8845	44.2270	0.0426	0.0226	13.823	32
33	0.5202	23.9886	341.0508	1.9222	46.1116	0.0417	0.0217	14.217	33
34	0.5100	24.4986	357.8817	1.9607	48.0338	0.0408	0.0208	14.608	34
35	0.5000	24.9986	374.8826	1.9999	49.9945	0.0400	0.0200	14.996	35
36	0.4902	25.4888	392.0405	2.0399	51.9944	0.0392	0.0192	15.380	36
37	0.4806	25.9695	409.3424	2.0807	54.0343	0.0385	0.0185	15.762	37
38	0.4712	26.4406	426.7764	2.1223	56.1149	0.0378	0.0178	16.140	38
39	0.4619	26.9026	444.3304	2.1647	58.2372	0.0372	0.0172	16.516	39
40	0.4529	27.3555	461.9931	2.2080	60.4020	0.0366	0.0166	16.888	40
41	0.4440	27.7995	479.7535	2.2522	62.6100	0.0360	0.0160	17.257	41
42	0.4353	28.2348	497.6010	2.2972	64.8622	0.0354	0.0154	17.623	42
43	0.4268	28.6616	515.5253	2.3432	67.1595	0.0349	0.0149	17.986	43
44	0.4184	29.0800	533.5165	2.3901	69.5027	0.0344	0.0144	18.346	44
45	0.4102	29.4902	551.5652	2.4379	71.8927	0.0339	0.0139	18.703	45
46	0.4022	29.8923	569.6621	2.4866	74.3306	0.0335	0.0135	19.057	46
47	0.3943	30.2866	587.7985	2.5363	76.8172	0.0330	0.0130	19.407	47
48	0.3865	30.6731	605.9657	2.5871	79.3535	0.0326	0.0126	19.755	48
49	0.3790	31.0521	624.1557	2.6388	81.9406	0.0322	0.0122	20.100	49
50	0.3715	31.4236	642.3606	2.6916	84.5794	0.0318	0.0118	20.442	50
51	0.3642	31.7878	660.5727	2.7454	87.2710	0.0315	0.0115	20.780	51
52	0.3571	32.1449	678.7849	2.8003	90.0164	0.0311	0.0111	21.116	52
53	0.3501	32.4950	696.9900	2.8563	92.8167	0.0308	0.0108	21.449	53
54	0.3432	32.8383	715.1815	2.9135	95.6731	0.0305	0.0105	21.778	54
55	0.3365	33.1748	733.3527	2.9717	98.5865	0.0301	0.0101	22.105	55
60	0.3048	34.7609	823.6975	3.2810	114.0515	0.0288	0.0088	23.696	60
65	0.2761	36.1975	912.7085	3.6225	131.1262	0.0276	0.0076	25.214	65
70	0.2500	37.4986	999.8343	3.9996	149.9779	0.0267	0.0067	26.663	70
75	0.2265	38.6771	1084.6393	4.4158	170.7918	0.0259	0.0059	28.043	75
80	0.2051	39.7445	1166.7868	4.8754	193.7720	0.0252	0.0052	29.357	80
85	0.1858	40.7113	1246.0241	5.3829	219.1439	0.0246	0.0046	30.606	85
90	0.1683	41.5869	1322.1701	5.9431	247.1567	0.0240	0.0040	31.792	90
95	0.1524	42.3800	1395.1033	6.5617	278.0850	0.0236	0.0036	32.918	95
100	0.1380	43.0984	1464.7527	7.2446	312.2323	0.0232	0.0032	33.986	100

PROFESSIONAL PUBLICATIONS, INC. ● Belmont, CA

I = 2.25 %

n	(P/F)	(P/A)	(P/G)	(F/P)	(F/A)	(A/P)	(A/F)	(A/G)	n
1	0.9780	0.9780	0.0000	1.0225	1.0000	1.0225	1.0000	0.000	1
2	0.9565	1.9345	0.9565	1.0455	2.0225	0.5169	0.4944	0.494	2
3	0.9354	2.8699	2.8273	1.0690	3.0680	0.3484	0.3259	0.985	3
4	0.9148	3.7847	5.5719	1.0931	4.1370	0.2642	0.2417	1.472	4
5	0.8947	4.6795	9.1507	1.1177	5.2301	0.2137	0.1912	1.955	5
6	0.8750	5.5545	13.5258	1.1428	6.3478	0.1800	0.1575	2.435	6
7	0.8558	6.4102	18.6604	1.1685	7.4906	0.1560	0.1335	2.911	7
8	0.8369	7.2472	24.5190	1.1948	8.6592	0.1380	0.1155	3.383	8
9	0.8185	8.0657	31.0672	1.2217	9.8540	0.1240	0.1015	3.851	9
10	0.8005	8.8662	38.2718	1.2492	11.0757	0.1128	0.0903	4.316	10
11	0.7829	9.6491	46.1007	1.2773	12.3249	0.1036	0.0811	4.777	11
12	0.7657	10.4148	54.5231	1.3060	13.6022	0.0960	0.0735	5.235	12
13	0.7488	11.1636	63.5089	1.3354	14.9083	0.0896	0.0671	5.688	13
14	0.7323	11.8959	73.0293	1.3655	16.2437	0.0841	0.0616	6.139	14
15	0.7162	12.6122	83.0565	1.3962	17.6092	0.0793	0.0568	6.585	15
16	0.7005	13.3126	93.5635	1.4276	19.0054	0.0751	0.0526	7.028	16
17	0.6851	13.9977	104.5243	1.4597	20.4330	0.0714	0.0489	7.467	17
18	0.6700	14.6677	115.9139	1.4926	21.8928	0.0682	0.0457	7.902	18
19	0.6552	15.3229	127.7082	1.5262	23.3853	0.0653	0.0428	8.334	19
20	0.6408	15.9637	139.8837	1.5605	24.9115	0.0626	0.0401	8.762	20
21	0.6267	16.5904	152.4180	1.5956	26.4720	0.0603	0.0378	9.187	21
22	0.6129	17.2034	165.2894	1.6315	28.0676	0.0581	0.0356	9.608	22
23	0.5994	17.8028	178.4770	1.6682	29.6992	0.0562	0.0337	10.025	23
24	0.5862	18.3890	191.9607	1.7058	31.3674	0.0544	0.0319	10.438	24
25	0.5733	18.9624	205.7210	1.7441	33.0732	0.0527	0.0302	10.848	25
26	0.5607	19.5231	219.7393	1.7834	34.8173	0.0512	0.0287	11.255	26
27	0.5484	20.0715	233.9974	1.8235	36.6007	0.0498	0.0273	11.658	27
28	0.5363	20.6078	248.4782	1.8645	38.4242	0.0485	0.0260	12.057	28
29	0.5245	21.1323	263.1648	1.9065	40.2888	0.0473	0.0248	12.453	29
30	0.5130	21.6453	278.0412	1.9494	42.1953	0.0462	0.0237	12.845	30
31	0.5017	22.1470	293.0920	1.9933	44.1447	0.0452	0.0227	13.233	31
32	0.4907	22.6377	308.3022	2.0381	46.1379	0.0442	0.0217	13.619	32
33	0.4799	23.1175	323.6576	2.0840	48.1760	0.0433	0.0208	14.000	33
34	0.4693	23.5868	339.1444	2.1308	50.2600	0.0424	0.0199	14.378	34
35	0.4590	24.0458	354.7493	2.1788	52.3908	0.0416	0.0191	14.753	35
36	0.4489	24.4947	370.4598	2.2278	54.5696	0.0408	0.0183	15.124	36
37	0.4390	24.9337	386.2635	2.2779	56.7974	0.0401	0.0176	15.491	37
38	0.4293	25.3630	402.1488	2.3292	59.0754	0.0394	0.0169	15.855	38
39	0.4199	25.7829	418.1045	2.3816	61.4046	0.0388	0.0163	16.216	39
40	0.4106	26.1935	434.1197	2.4352	63.7862	0.0382	0.0157	16.573	40
41	0.4016	26.5951	450.1840	2.4900	66.2214	0.0376	0.0151	16.927	41
42	0.3928	26.9879	466.2877	2.5460	68.7113	0.0371	0.0146	17.277	42
43	0.3841	27.3720	482.4211	2.6033	71.2574	0.0365	0.0140	17.624	43
44	0.3757	27.7477	498.5752	2.6619	73.8606	0.0360	0.0135	17.968	44
45	0.3674	28.1151	514.7412	2.7218	76.5225	0.0356	0.0131	18.308	45
46	0.3593	28.4744	530.9109	2.7830	79.2443	0.0351	0.0126	18.645	46
47	0.3514	28.8259	547.0761	2.8456	82.0273	0.0347	0.0122	18.978	47
48	0.3437	29.1695	563.2293	2.9096	84.8729	0.0343	0.0118	19.308	48
49	0.3361	29.5057	579.3632	2.9751	87.7825	0.0339	0.0114	19.635	49
50	0.3287	29.8344	595.4708	3.0420	90.7576	0.0335	0.0110	19.959	50
51	0.3215	30.1559	611.5454	3.1105	93.7997	0.0332	0.0107	20.279	51
52	0.3144	30.4703	627.5807	3.1805	96.9102	0.0328	0.0103	20.596	52
53	0.3075	30.7778	643.5707	3.2520	100.0906	0.0325	0.0100	20.910	53
54	0.3007	31.0785	659.5095	3.3252	103.3427	0.0322	0.0097	21.220	54
55	0.2941	31.3727	675.3917	3.4000	106.6679	0.0319	0.0094	21.528	55
60	0.2631	32.7490	753.7795	3.8001	124.4504	0.0305	0.0080	23.016	60
65	0.2354	33.9803	830.0710	4.2473	144.3256	0.0294	0.0069	24.428	65
70	0.2107	35.0821	903.8386	4.7471	166.5396	0.0285	0.0060	25.763	70
75	0.1885	36.0678	974.7681	5.3058	191.3677	0.0277	0.0052	27.026	75
80	0.1686	36.9498	1042.6394	5.9301	219.1176	0.0271	0.0046	28.217	80
85	0.1509	37.7389	1107.3101	6.6280	250.1329	0.0265	0.0040	29.341	85
90	0.1350	38.4449	1168.7019	7.4080	284.7981	0.0260	0.0035	30.399	90
95	0.1208	39.0766	1226.7883	8.2797	323.5426	0.0256	0.0031	31.394	95
100	0.1081	39.6417	1281.5847	9.2540	366.8465	0.0252	0.0027	32.329	100

EXPANDED INTEREST TABLES

$I = 2.50\%$

n	(P/F)	(P/A)	(P/G)	(F/P)	(F/A)	(A/P)	(A/F)	(A/G)	n
1	0.9756	0.9756	0.0000	1.0250	1.0000	1.0250	1.0000	0.000	1
2	0.9518	1.9274	0.9518	1.0506	2.0250	0.5188	0.4938	0.493	2
3	0.9286	2.8560	2.8090	1.0769	3.0756	0.3501	0.3251	0.983	3
4	0.9060	3.7620	5.5269	1.1038	4.1525	0.2658	0.2408	1.469	4
5	0.8839	4.6458	9.0623	1.1314	5.2563	0.2152	0.1902	1.950	5
6	0.8623	5.5081	13.3738	1.1597	6.3877	0.1815	0.1565	2.428	6
7	0.8413	6.3494	18.4214	1.1887	7.5474	0.1575	0.1325	2.901	7
8	0.8207	7.1701	24.1666	1.2184	8.7361	0.1395	0.1145	3.370	8
9	0.8007	7.9709	30.5724	1.2489	9.9545	0.1255	0.1005	3.835	9
10	0.7812	8.7521	37.6032	1.2801	11.2034	0.1143	0.0893	4.296	10
11	0.7621	9.5142	45.2246	1.3121	12.4835	0.1051	0.0801	4.753	11
12	0.7436	10.2578	53.4038	1.3449	13.7956	0.0975	0.0725	5.206	12
13	0.7254	10.9832	62.1088	1.3785	15.1404	0.0910	0.0660	5.654	13
14	0.7077	11.6909	71.3093	1.4130	16.5190	0.0855	0.0605	6.099	14
15	0.6905	12.3814	80.9758	1.4483	17.9319	0.0808	0.0558	6.540	15
16	0.6736	13.0550	91.0801	1.4845	19.3802	0.0766	0.0516	6.976	16
17	0.6572	13.7122	101.5953	1.5216	20.8647	0.0729	0.0479	7.409	17
18	0.6412	14.3534	112.4951	1.5597	22.3863	0.0697	0.0447	7.837	18
19	0.6255	14.9789	123.7546	1.5987	23.9460	0.0668	0.0418	8.261	19
20	0.6103	15.5892	135.3497	1.6386	25.5447	0.0641	0.0391	8.682	20
21	0.5954	16.1845	147.2575	1.6796	27.1833	0.0618	0.0368	9.098	21
22	0.5809	16.7654	159.4556	1.7216	28.8629	0.0596	0.0346	9.511	22
23	0.5667	17.3321	171.9230	1.7646	30.5844	0.0577	0.0327	9.919	23
24	0.5529	17.8850	184.6391	1.8087	32.3490	0.0559	0.0309	10.323	24
25	0.5394	18.4244	197.5845	1.8539	34.1578	0.0543	0.0293	10.724	25
26	0.5262	18.9506	210.7403	1.9003	36.0117	0.0528	0.0278	11.120	26
27	0.5134	19.4640	224.0887	1.9478	37.9120	0.0514	0.0264	11.513	27
28	0.5009	19.9649	237.6124	1.9965	39.8598	0.0501	0.0251	11.901	28
29	0.4887	20.4535	251.2949	2.0464	41.8563	0.0489	0.0239	12.286	29
30	0.4767	20.9303	265.1205	2.0976	43.9027	0.0478	0.0228	12.666	30
31	0.4651	21.3954	279.0739	2.1500	46.0003	0.0467	0.0217	13.043	31
32	0.4538	21.8492	293.1408	2.2038	48.1503	0.0458	0.0208	13.416	32
33	0.4427	22.2919	307.3073	2.2589	50.3540	0.0449	0.0199	13.785	33
34	0.4319	22.7238	321.5602	2.3153	52.6129	0.0440	0.0190	14.150	34
35	0.4214	23.1452	335.8868	2.3732	54.9282	0.0432	0.0182	14.512	35
36	0.4111	23.5563	350.2751	2.4325	57.3014	0.0425	0.0175	14.869	36
37	0.4011	23.9573	364.7135	2.4933	59.7339	0.0417	0.0167	15.223	37
38	0.3913	24.3486	379.1910	2.5557	62.2273	0.0411	0.0161	15.573	38
39	0.3817	24.7303	393.6972	2.6196	64.7830	0.0404	0.0154	15.919	39
40	0.3724	25.1028	408.2220	2.6851	67.4026	0.0398	0.0148	16.262	40
41	0.3633	25.4661	422.7559	2.7522	70.0876	0.0393	0.0143	16.600	41
42	0.3545	25.8206	437.2898	2.8210	72.8398	0.0387	0.0137	16.935	42
43	0.3458	26.1664	451.8150	2.8915	75.6608	0.0382	0.0132	17.267	43
44	0.3374	26.5038	466.3234	2.9638	78.5523	0.0377	0.0127	17.594	44
45	0.3292	26.8330	480.8070	3.0379	81.5161	0.0373	0.0123	17.918	45
46	0.3211	27.1542	495.2586	3.1139	84.5540	0.0368	0.0118	18.238	46
47	0.3133	27.4675	509.6710	3.1917	87.6679	0.0364	0.0114	18.555	47
48	0.3057	27.7732	524.0375	3.2715	90.8596	0.0360	0.0110	18.868	48
49	0.2982	28.0714	538.3519	3.3533	94.1311	0.0356	0.0106	19.178	49
50	0.2909	28.3623	552.6081	3.4371	97.4843	0.0353	0.0103	19.483	50
51	0.2838	28.6462	566.8004	3.5230	100.9215	0.0349	0.0099	19.786	51
52	0.2769	28.9231	580.9234	3.6111	104.4445	0.0346	0.0096	20.085	52
53	0.2702	29.1932	594.9722	3.7014	108.0556	0.0343	0.0093	20.380	53
54	0.2636	29.4568	608.9419	3.7939	111.7570	0.0339	0.0089	20.672	54
55	0.2572	29.7140	622.8280	3.8888	115.5509	0.0337	0.0087	20.960	55
60	0.2273	30.9087	690.8656	4.3998	135.9916	0.0324	0.0074	22.351	60
65	0.2009	31.9646	756.2806	4.9780	159.1183	0.0313	0.0063	23.660	65
70	0.1776	32.8979	818.7643	5.6321	185.2841	0.0304	0.0054	24.888	70
75	0.1569	33.7227	878.1152	6.3722	214.8883	0.0297	0.0047	26.039	75
80	0.1387	34.4518	934.2181	7.2096	248.3827	0.0290	0.0040	27.116	80
85	0.1226	35.0962	987.0269	8.1570	286.2786	0.0285	0.0035	28.123	85
90	0.1084	35.6658	1036.5499	9.2289	329.1543	0.0280	0.0030	29.062	90
95	0.0958	36.1692	1082.8381	10.4416	377.6642	0.0276	0.0026	29.938	95
100	0.0846	36.6141	1125.9747	11.8137	432.5487	0.0273	0.0023	30.752	100

$I = 2.75 \%$

n	(P/F)	(P/A)	(P/G)	(F/P)	(F/A)	(A/P)	(A/F)	(A/G)	n
1	0.9732	0.9732	0.0000	1.0275	1.0000	1.0275	1.0000	0.000	1
2	0.9472	1.9204	0.9472	1.0558	2.0275	0.5207	0.4932	0.493	2
3	0.9218	2.8423	2.7909	1.0848	3.0833	0.3518	0.3243	0.981	3
4	0.8972	3.7394	5.4824	1.1146	4.1680	0.2674	0.2399	1.466	4
5	0.8732	4.6126	8.9750	1.1453	5.2827	0.2168	0.1893	1.945	5
6	0.8498	5.4624	13.2239	1.1768	6.4279	0.1831	0.1556	2.420	6
7	0.8270	6.2894	18.1861	1.2091	7.6047	0.1590	0.1315	2.891	7
8	0.8049	7.0943	23.8205	1.2424	8.8138	0.1410	0.1135	3.357	8
9	0.7834	7.8777	30.0874	1.2765	10.0562	0.1269	0.0994	3.819	9
10	0.7624	8.6401	36.9490	1.3117	11.3328	0.1157	0.0882	4.276	10
11	0.7420	9.3821	44.3689	1.3477	12.6444	0.1066	0.0791	4.729	11
12	0.7221	10.1042	52.3124	1.3848	13.9921	0.0990	0.0715	5.177	12
13	0.7028	10.8070	60.7461	1.4229	15.3769	0.0925	0.0650	5.621	13
14	0.6840	11.4910	69.6380	1.4620	16.7998	0.0870	0.0595	6.060	14
15	0.6657	12.1567	78.9577	1.5022	18.2618	0.0823	0.0548	6.495	15
16	0.6479	12.8046	88.6758	1.5435	19.7640	0.0781	0.0506	6.925	16
17	0.6305	13.4351	98.7644	1.5860	21.3075	0.0744	0.0469	7.351	17
18	0.6137	14.0488	109.1966	1.6296	22.8934	0.0712	0.0437	7.772	18
19	0.5972	14.6460	119.9468	1.6744	24.5230	0.0683	0.0408	8.189	19
20	0.5813	15.2273	130.9906	1.7204	26.1974	0.0657	0.0382	8.602	20
21	0.5657	15.7929	142.3045	1.7677	27.9178	0.0633	0.0358	9.010	21
22	0.5506	16.3435	153.8661	1.8164	29.6856	0.0612	0.0337	9.414	22
23	0.5358	16.8793	165.6541	1.8663	31.5019	0.0592	0.0317	9.814	23
24	0.5215	17.4008	177.6481	1.9176	33.3682	0.0575	0.0300	10.209	24
25	0.5075	17.9083	189.8286	1.9704	35.2858	0.0558	0.0283	10.600	25
26	0.4939	18.4023	202.1771	2.0245	37.2562	0.0543	0.0268	10.986	26
27	0.4807	18.8830	214.6757	2.0802	39.2808	0.0530	0.0255	11.368	27
28	0.4679	19.3508	227.3077	2.1374	41.3610	0.0517	0.0242	11.746	28
29	0.4553	19.8062	240.0570	2.1962	43.4984	0.0505	0.0230	12.120	29
30	0.4431	20.2493	252.9082	2.2566	45.6946	0.0494	0.0219	12.489	30
31	0.4313	20.6806	265.8467	2.3187	47.9512	0.0484	0.0209	12.854	31
32	0.4197	21.1003	278.8587	2.3824	50.2699	0.0474	0.0199	13.215	32
33	0.4085	21.5088	291.9309	2.4479	52.6523	0.0465	0.0190	13.572	33
34	0.3976	21.9064	305.0508	2.5153	55.1002	0.0456	0.0181	13.925	34
35	0.3869	22.2933	318.2066	2.5844	57.6155	0.0449	0.0174	14.273	35
36	0.3766	22.6699	331.3868	2.6555	60.1999	0.0441	0.0166	14.617	36
37	0.3665	23.0364	344.5807	2.7285	62.8554	0.0434	0.0159	14.958	37
38	0.3567	23.3931	357.7782	2.8036	65.5839	0.0427	0.0152	15.294	38
39	0.3471	23.7402	370.9697	2.8807	68.3875	0.0421	0.0146	15.626	39
40	0.3379	24.0781	384.1459	2.9599	71.2681	0.0415	0.0140	15.954	40
41	0.3288	24.4069	397.2983	3.0413	74.2280	0.0410	0.0135	16.278	41
42	0.3200	24.7269	410.4187	3.1249	77.2693	0.0404	0.0129	16.598	42
43	0.3114	25.0384	423.4994	3.2108	80.3942	0.0399	0.0124	16.914	43
44	0.3031	25.3415	436.5331	3.2991	83.6050	0.0395	0.0120	17.226	44
45	0.2950	25.6365	449.5130	3.3899	86.9042	0.0390	0.0115	17.534	45
46	0.2871	25.9236	462.4325	3.4831	90.2940	0.0386	0.0111	17.838	46
47	0.2794	26.2030	475.2857	3.5789	93.7771	0.0382	0.0107	18.138	47
48	0.2719	26.4749	488.0669	3.6773	97.3560	0.0378	0.0103	18.435	48
49	0.2647	26.7396	500.7706	3.7784	101.0333	0.0374	0.0099	18.727	49
50	0.2576	26.9972	513.3920	3.8823	104.8117	0.0370	0.0095	19.016	50
51	0.2507	27.2479	525.9262	3.9891	108.6940	0.0367	0.0092	19.301	51
52	0.2440	27.4918	538.3689	4.0988	112.6831	0.0364	0.0089	19.582	52
53	0.2374	27.7293	550.7160	4.2115	116.7819	0.0361	0.0086	19.860	53
54	0.2311	27.9604	562.9638	4.3273	120.9934	0.0358	0.0083	20.134	54
55	0.2249	28.1853	575.1086	4.4463	125.3207	0.0355	0.0080	20.404	55
60	0.1964	29.2227	634.1838	5.0923	148.8091	0.0342	0.0067	21.701	60
65	0.1715	30.1285	690.2945	5.8320	175.7098	0.0332	0.0057	22.911	65
70	0.1497	30.9194	743.2423	6.6793	206.5184	0.0323	0.0048	24.038	70
75	0.1307	31.6100	792.9269	7.6496	241.8027	0.0316	0.0041	25.084	75
80	0.1141	32.2129	839.3240	8.7609	282.2129	0.0310	0.0035	26.055	80
85	0.0997	32.7394	882.4684	10.0336	328.4935	0.0305	0.0030	26.954	85
90	0.0870	33.1992	922.4387	11.4912	381.4976	0.0301	0.0026	27.785	90
95	0.0760	33.6006	959.3459	13.1605	442.2017	0.0298	0.0023	28.551	95
100	0.0663	33.9510	993.3240	15.0724	511.7244	0.0295	0.0020	29.257	100

EXPANDED INTEREST TABLES

$I = 3.00\%$

n	(P/F)	(P/A)	(P/G)	(F/P)	(F/A)	(A/P)	(A/F)	(A/G)	n
1	0.9709	0.9709	0.0000	1.0300	1.0000	1.0300	1.0000	0.000	1
2	0.9426	1.9135	0.9426	1.0609	2.0300	0.5226	0.4926	0.492	2
3	0.9151	2.8286	2.7729	1.0927	3.0909	0.3535	0.3235	0.980	3
4	0.8885	3.7171	5.4383	1.1255	4.1836	0.2690	0.2390	1.463	4
5	0.8626	4.5797	8.8888	1.1593	5.3091	0.2184	0.1884	1.940	5
6	0.8375	5.4172	13.0762	1.1941	6.4684	0.1846	0.1546	2.413	6
7	0.8131	6.2303	17.9547	1.2299	7.6625	0.1605	0.1305	2.881	7
8	0.7894	7.0197	23.4806	1.2668	8.8923	0.1425	0.1125	3.345	8
9	0.7664	7.7861	29.6119	1.3048	10.1591	0.1284	0.0984	3.803	9
10	0.7441	8.5302	36.3088	1.3439	11.4639	0.1172	0.0872	4.256	10
11	0.7224	9.2526	43.5330	1.3842	12.8078	0.1081	0.0781	4.704	11
12	0.7014	9.9540	51.2482	1.4258	14.1920	0.1005	0.0705	5.148	12
13	0.6810	10.6350	59.4196	1.4685	15.6178	0.0940	0.0640	5.587	13
14	0.6611	11.2961	68.0141	1.5126	17.0863	0.0885	0.0585	6.021	14
15	0.6419	11.9379	77.0002	1.5580	18.5989	0.0838	0.0538	6.450	15
16	0.6232	12.5611	86.3477	1.6047	20.1569	0.0796	0.0496	6.874	16
17	0.6050	13.1661	96.0280	1.6528	21.7616	0.0760	0.0460	7.293	17
18	0.5874	13.7535	106.0137	1.7024	23.4144	0.0727	0.0427	7.708	18
19	0.5703	14.3238	116.2788	1.7535	25.1169	0.0698	0.0398	8.117	19
20	0.5537	14.8775	126.7987	1.8061	26.8704	0.0672	0.0372	8.522	20
21	0.5375	15.4150	137.5496	1.8603	28.6765	0.0649	0.0349	8.923	21
22	0.5219	15.9369	148.5094	1.9161	30.5368	0.0627	0.0327	9.318	22
23	0.5067	16.4436	159.6566	1.9736	32.4529	0.0608	0.0308	9.709	23
24	0.4919	16.9355	170.9711	2.0328	34.4265	0.0590	0.0290	10.095	24
25	0.4776	17.4131	182.4336	2.0938	36.4593	0.0574	0.0274	10.476	25
26	0.4637	17.8768	194.0260	2.1566	38.5530	0.0559	0.0259	10.853	26
27	0.4502	18.3270	205.7309	2.2213	40.7096	0.0546	0.0246	11.225	27
28	0.4371	18.7641	217.5320	2.2879	42.9309	0.0533	0.0233	11.593	28
29	0.4243	19.1885	229.4137	2.3566	45.2189	0.0521	0.0221	11.955	29
30	0.4120	19.6004	241.3613	2.4273	47.5754	0.0510	0.0210	12.314	30
31	0.4000	20.0004	253.3609	2.5001	50.0027	0.0500	0.0200	12.667	31
32	0.3883	20.3888	265.3993	2.5751	52.5028	0.0490	0.0190	13.016	32
33	0.3770	20.7658	277.4642	2.6523	55.0778	0.0482	0.0182	13.361	33
34	0.3660	21.1318	289.5437	2.7319	57.7302	0.0473	0.0173	13.701	34
35	0.3554	21.4872	301.6267	2.8139	60.4621	0.0465	0.0165	14.037	35
36	0.3450	21.8323	313.7028	2.8983	63.2759	0.0458	0.0158	14.368	36
37	0.3350	22.1672	325.7622	2.9852	66.1742	0.0451	0.0151	14.695	37
38	0.3252	22.4925	337.7956	3.0748	69.1594	0.0445	0.0145	15.018	38
39	0.3158	22.8082	349.7942	3.1670	72.2342	0.0438	0.0138	15.336	39
40	0.3066	23.1148	361.7499	3.2620	75.4013	0.0433	0.0133	15.650	40
41	0.2976	23.4124	373.6551	3.3599	78.6633	0.0427	0.0127	15.959	41
42	0.2890	23.7014	385.5024	3.4607	82.0232	0.0422	0.0122	16.265	42
43	0.2805	23.9819	397.2852	3.5645	85.4839	0.0417	0.0117	16.566	43
44	0.2724	24.2543	408.9972	3.6715	89.0484	0.0412	0.0112	16.862	44
45	0.2644	24.5187	420.6325	3.7816	92.7199	0.0408	0.0108	17.155	45
46	0.2567	24.7754	432.1856	3.8950	96.5015	0.0404	0.0104	17.444	46
47	0.2493	25.0247	443.6515	4.0119	100.3965	0.0400	0.0100	17.728	47
48	0.2420	25.2667	455.0255	4.1323	104.4084	0.0396	0.0096	18.008	48
49	0.2350	25.5017	466.3031	4.2562	108.5406	0.0392	0.0092	18.285	49
50	0.2281	25.7298	477.4803	4.3839	112.7969	0.0389	0.0089	18.557	50
51	0.2215	25.9512	488.5535	4.5154	117.1808	0.0385	0.0085	18.825	51
52	0.2150	26.1662	499.5191	4.6509	121.6962	0.0382	0.0082	19.090	52
53	0.2088	26.3750	510.3742	4.7904	126.3471	0.0379	0.0079	19.350	53
54	0.2027	26.5777	521.1157	4.9341	131.1375	0.0376	0.0076	19.607	54
55	0.1968	26.7744	531.7411	5.0821	136.0716	0.0373	0.0073	19.860	55
60	0.1697	27.6756	583.0526	5.8916	163.0534	0.0361	0.0061	21.067	60
65	0.1464	28.4529	631.2010	6.8300	194.3328	0.0351	0.0051	22.184	65
70	0.1263	29.1234	676.0869	7.9178	230.5941	0.0343	0.0043	23.214	70
75	0.1089	29.7018	717.6978	9.1789	272.6309	0.0337	0.0037	24.163	75
80	0.0940	30.2008	756.0865	10.6409	321.3630	0.0331	0.0031	25.035	80
85	0.0811	30.6312	791.3529	12.3357	377.8570	0.0326	0.0026	25.834	85
90	0.0699	31.0024	823.6302	14.3005	443.3489	0.0323	0.0023	26.566	90
95	0.0603	31.3227	853.0742	16.5782	519.2720	0.0319	0.0019	27.235	95
100	0.0520	31.5989	879.8540	19.2186	607.2877	0.0316	0.0016	27.844	100

$I = 3.25\%$

n	(P/F)	(P/A)	(P/G)	(F/P)	(F/A)	(A/P)	(A/F)	(A/G)	n
1	0.9685	0.9685	0.0000	1.0325	1.0000	1.0325	1.0000	0.000	1
2	0.9380	1.9066	0.9380	1.0661	2.0325	0.5245	0.4920	0.492	2
3	0.9085	2.8151	2.7551	1.1007	3.0986	0.3552	0.3227	0.978	3
4	0.8799	3.6950	5.3948	1.1365	4.1993	0.2706	0.2381	1.460	4
5	0.8522	4.5472	8.8037	1.1734	5.3357	0.2199	0.1874	1.936	5
6	0.8254	5.3726	12.9306	1.2115	6.5091	0.1861	0.1536	2.406	6
7	0.7994	6.1720	17.7271	1.2509	7.7207	0.1620	0.1295	2.872	7
8	0.7742	6.9462	23.1468	1.2916	8.9716	0.1440	0.1115	3.332	8
9	0.7499	7.6961	29.1458	1.3336	10.2632	0.1299	0.0974	3.787	9
10	0.7263	8.4224	35.6823	1.3769	11.5967	0.1187	0.0862	4.236	10
11	0.7034	9.1258	42.7164	1.4216	12.9736	0.1096	0.0771	4.680	11
12	0.6813	9.8071	50.2103	1.4678	14.3953	0.1020	0.0695	5.119	12
13	0.6598	10.4669	58.1283	1.5156	15.8631	0.0955	0.0630	5.553	13
14	0.6391	11.1060	66.4360	1.5648	17.3787	0.0900	0.0575	5.982	14
15	0.6189	11.7249	75.1012	1.6157	18.9435	0.0853	0.0528	6.405	15
16	0.5995	12.3244	84.0930	1.6682	20.5592	0.0811	0.0486	6.823	16
17	0.5806	12.9049	93.3825	1.7224	22.2273	0.0775	0.0450	7.236	17
18	0.5623	13.4673	102.9418	1.7784	23.9497	0.0743	0.0418	7.643	18
19	0.5446	14.0119	112.7449	1.8362	25.7281	0.0714	0.0389	8.046	19
20	0.5275	14.5393	122.7668	1.8958	27.5642	0.0688	0.0363	8.443	20
21	0.5109	15.0502	132.9842	1.9575	29.4601	0.0664	0.0339	8.836	21
22	0.4948	15.5450	143.3747	2.0211	31.4175	0.0643	0.0318	9.223	22
23	0.4792	16.0242	153.9174	2.0868	33.4386	0.0624	0.0299	9.605	23
24	0.4641	16.4883	164.5924	2.1546	35.5254	0.0606	0.0281	9.982	24
25	0.4495	16.9379	175.3808	2.2246	37.6799	0.0590	0.0265	10.354	25
26	0.4354	17.3732	186.2651	2.2969	39.9045	0.0576	0.0251	10.721	26
27	0.4217	17.7949	197.2284	2.3715	42.2014	0.0562	0.0237	11.083	27
28	0.4084	18.2033	208.2550	2.4486	44.5730	0.0549	0.0224	11.440	28
29	0.3955	18.5988	219.3301	2.5282	47.0216	0.0538	0.0213	11.792	29
30	0.3831	18.9819	230.4396	2.6104	49.5498	0.0527	0.0202	12.140	30
31	0.3710	19.3529	241.5705	2.6952	52.1602	0.0517	0.0192	12.482	31
32	0.3594	19.7123	252.7103	2.7828	54.8554	0.0507	0.0182	12.819	32
33	0.3480	20.0603	263.8476	2.8732	57.6382	0.0498	0.0173	13.152	33
34	0.3371	20.3974	274.9714	2.9666	60.5114	0.0490	0.0165	13.480	34
35	0.3265	20.7239	286.0714	3.0630	63.4780	0.0483	0.0158	13.803	35
36	0.3162	21.0401	297.1383	3.1626	66.5411	0.0475	0.0150	14.122	36
37	0.3062	21.3463	308.1631	3.2654	69.7037	0.0468	0.0143	14.436	37
38	0.2966	21.6429	319.1375	3.3715	72.9690	0.0462	0.0137	14.745	38
39	0.2873	21.9302	330.0537	3.4811	76.3405	0.0456	0.0131	15.050	39
40	0.2782	22.2084	340.9045	3.5942	79.8216	0.0450	0.0125	15.350	40
41	0.2695	22.4779	351.6832	3.7110	83.4158	0.0445	0.0120	15.645	41
42	0.2610	22.7389	362.3837	3.8316	87.1268	0.0440	0.0115	15.936	42
43	0.2528	22.9917	373.0001	3.9561	90.9584	0.0435	0.0110	16.223	43
44	0.2448	23.2365	383.5271	4.0847	94.9146	0.0430	0.0105	16.505	44
45	0.2371	23.4736	393.9599	4.2175	98.9993	0.0426	0.0101	16.783	45
46	0.2296	23.7032	404.2939	4.3545	103.2168	0.0422	0.0097	17.056	46
47	0.2224	23.9256	414.5251	4.4961	107.5713	0.0418	0.0093	17.325	47
48	0.2154	24.1411	424.6496	4.6422	112.0674	0.0414	0.0089	17.590	48
49	0.2086	24.3497	434.6641	4.7931	116.7096	0.0411	0.0086	17.850	49
50	0.2021	24.5518	444.5654	4.9488	121.5026	0.0407	0.0082	18.107	50
51	0.1957	24.7475	454.3507	5.1097	126.4515	0.0404	0.0079	18.359	51
52	0.1895	24.9370	464.0176	5.2757	131.5611	0.0401	0.0076	18.607	52
53	0.1836	25.1206	473.5638	5.4472	136.8369	0.0398	0.0073	18.851	53
54	0.1778	25.2984	482.9873	5.6242	142.2841	0.0395	0.0070	19.091	54
55	0.1722	25.4706	492.2864	5.8070	147.9083	0.0393	0.0068	19.327	55
60	0.1468	26.2537	536.8703	6.8140	178.8930	0.0381	0.0056	20.449	60
65	0.1251	26.9210	578.2021	7.9957	215.2509	0.0371	0.0046	21.477	65
70	0.1066	27.4897	616.2692	9.3822	257.9135	0.0364	0.0039	22.418	70
75	0.0908	27.9744	651.1340	11.0092	307.9744	0.0357	0.0032	23.276	75
80	0.0774	28.3874	682.9114	12.9183	366.7164	0.0352	0.0027	24.056	80
85	0.0660	28.7394	711.7527	15.1585	435.6450	0.0348	0.0023	24.765	85
90	0.0562	29.0394	737.8316	17.7871	516.5265	0.0344	0.0019	25.408	90
95	0.0479	29.2950	761.3346	20.8716	611.4338	0.0341	0.0016	25.988	95
100	0.0408	29.5129	782.4537	24.4910	722.7992	0.0339	0.0014	26.512	100

EXPANDED INTEREST TABLES

$I = 3.50\%$

n	(P/F)	(P/A)	(P/G)	(F/P)	(F/A)	(A/P)	(A/F)	(A/G)	n
1	0.9662	0.9662	0.0000	1.0350	1.0000	1.0350	1.0000	0.000	1
2	0.9335	1.8997	0.9335	1.0712	2.0350	0.5264	0.4914	0.491	2
3	0.9019	2.8016	2.7374	1.1087	3.1062	0.3569	0.3219	0.977	3
4	0.8714	3.6731	5.3517	1.1475	4.2149	0.2723	0.2373	1.457	4
5	0.8420	4.5151	8.7196	1.1877	5.3625	0.2215	0.1865	1.931	5
6	0.8135	5.3286	12.7871	1.2293	6.5502	0.1877	0.1527	2.399	6
7	0.7860	6.1145	17.5031	1.2723	7.7794	0.1635	0.1285	2.862	7
8	0.7594	6.8740	22.8189	1.3168	9.0517	0.1455	0.1105	3.319	8
9	0.7337	7.6077	28.6888	1.3629	10.3685	0.1314	0.0964	3.771	9
10	0.7089	8.3166	35.0691	1.4106	11.7314	0.1202	0.0852	4.216	10
11	0.6849	9.0016	41.9185	1.4600	13.1420	0.1111	0.0761	4.656	11
12	0.6618	9.6633	49.1981	1.5111	14.6020	0.1035	0.0685	5.091	12
13	0.6394	10.3027	56.8710	1.5640	16.1130	0.0971	0.0621	5.520	13
14	0.6178	10.9205	64.9021	1.6187	17.6770	0.0916	0.0566	5.943	14
15	0.5969	11.5174	73.2586	1.6753	19.2957	0.0868	0.0518	6.360	15
16	0.5767	12.0941	81.9092	1.7340	20.9710	0.0827	0.0477	6.772	16
17	0.5572	12.6513	90.8245	1.7947	22.7050	0.0790	0.0440	7.179	17
18	0.5384	13.1897	99.9766	1.8575	24.4997	0.0758	0.0408	7.579	18
19	0.5202	13.7098	109.3394	1.9225	26.3572	0.0729	0.0379	7.975	19
20	0.5026	14.2124	118.8882	1.9898	28.2797	0.0704	0.0354	8.365	20
21	0.4856	14.6980	128.5996	2.0594	30.2695	0.0680	0.0330	8.749	21
22	0.4692	15.1671	138.4517	2.1315	32.3289	0.0659	0.0309	9.128	22
23	0.4533	15.6204	148.4240	2.2061	34.4604	0.0640	0.0290	9.501	23
24	0.4380	16.0584	158.4970	2.2833	36.6665	0.0623	0.0273	9.870	24
25	0.4231	16.4815	168.6526	2.3632	38.9499	0.0607	0.0257	10.232	25
26	0.4088	16.8904	178.8735	2.4460	41.3131	0.0592	0.0242	10.590	26
27	0.3950	17.2854	189.1438	2.5316	43.7591	0.0579	0.0229	10.942	27
28	0.3817	17.6670	199.4485	2.6202	46.2906	0.0566	0.0216	11.289	28
29	0.3687	18.0358	209.7734	2.7119	48.9108	0.0554	0.0204	11.631	29
30	0.3563	18.3920	220.1055	2.8068	51.6227	0.0544	0.0194	11.967	30
31	0.3442	18.7363	230.4324	2.9050	54.4295	0.0534	0.0184	12.298	31
32	0.3326	19.0689	240.7427	3.0067	57.3345	0.0524	0.0174	12.624	32
33	0.3213	19.3902	251.0257	3.1119	60.3412	0.0516	0.0166	12.946	33
34	0.3105	19.7007	261.2714	3.2209	63.4532	0.0508	0.0158	13.262	34
35	0.3000	20.0007	271.4706	3.3336	66.6740	0.0500	0.0150	13.573	35
36	0.2898	20.2905	281.6147	3.4503	70.0076	0.0493	0.0143	13.879	36
37	0.2800	20.5705	291.6959	3.5710	73.4579	0.0486	0.0136	14.180	37
38	0.2706	20.8411	301.7067	3.6960	77.0289	0.0480	0.0130	14.476	38
39	0.2614	21.1025	311.6403	3.8254	80.7249	0.0474	0.0124	14.767	39
40	0.2526	21.3551	321.4907	3.9593	84.5503	0.0468	0.0118	15.054	40
41	0.2440	21.5991	331.2519	4.0978	88.5095	0.0463	0.0113	15.336	41
42	0.2358	21.8349	340.9189	4.2413	92.6074	0.0458	0.0108	15.613	42
43	0.2278	22.0627	350.4867	4.3897	96.8486	0.0453	0.0103	15.885	43
44	0.2201	22.2828	359.9511	4.5433	101.2383	0.0449	0.0099	16.153	44
45	0.2127	22.4955	369.3081	4.7024	105.7817	0.0445	0.0095	16.417	45
46	0.2055	22.7009	378.5542	4.8669	110.4840	0.0441	0.0091	16.675	46
47	0.1985	22.8994	387.6861	5.0373	115.3510	0.0437	0.0087	16.929	47
48	0.1918	23.0912	396.7010	5.2136	120.3883	0.0433	0.0083	17.179	48
49	0.1853	23.2766	405.5964	5.3961	125.6018	0.0430	0.0080	17.425	49
50	0.1791	23.4556	414.3700	5.5849	130.9979	0.0426	0.0076	17.666	50
51	0.1730	23.6286	423.0199	5.7804	136.5828	0.0423	0.0073	17.902	51
52	0.1671	23.7958	431.5445	5.9827	142.3632	0.0420	0.0070	18.135	52
53	0.1615	23.9573	439.9422	6.1921	148.3459	0.0417	0.0067	18.363	53
54	0.1560	24.1133	448.2121	6.4088	154.5381	0.0415	0.0065	18.587	54
55	0.1508	24.2641	456.3530	6.6331	160.9469	0.0412	0.0062	18.807	55
60	0.1269	24.9447	495.1050	7.8781	196.5169	0.0401	0.0051	19.848	60
65	0.1069	25.5178	530.5987	9.3567	238.7629	0.0392	0.0042	20.793	65
70	0.0900	26.0004	562.8962	11.1128	288.9379	0.0385	0.0035	21.649	70
75	0.0758	26.4067	592.1213	13.1986	348.5300	0.0379	0.0029	22.423	75
80	0.0638	26.7488	618.4385	15.6757	419.3068	0.0374	0.0024	23.120	80
85	0.0537	27.0368	642.0370	18.6179	503.3674	0.0370	0.0020	23.746	85
90	0.0452	27.2793	663.1189	22.1122	603.2050	0.0367	0.0017	24.308	90
95	0.0381	27.4835	681.8902	26.2623	721.7808	0.0364	0.0014	24.810	95
100	0.0321	27.6554	698.5547	31.1914	862.6117	0.0362	0.0012	25.259	100

$$I = 3.75\ \%$$

n	(P/F)	(P/A)	(P/G)	(F/P)	(F/A)	(A/P)	(A/F)	(A/G)	n
1	0.9639	0.9639	0.0000	1.0375	1.0000	1.0375	1.0000	0.000	1
2	0.9290	1.8929	0.9290	1.0764	2.0375	0.5283	0.4908	0.490	2
3	0.8954	2.7883	2.7199	1.1168	3.1139	0.3586	0.3211	0.975	3
4	0.8631	3.6514	5.3091	1.1587	4.2307	0.2739	0.2364	1.454	4
5	0.8319	4.4833	8.6366	1.2021	5.3893	0.2231	0.1856	1.926	5
6	0.8018	5.2851	12.6457	1.2472	6.5914	0.1892	0.1517	2.392	6
7	0.7728	6.0579	17.2826	1.2939	7.8386	0.1651	0.1276	2.852	7
8	0.7449	6.8028	22.4969	1.3425	9.1326	0.1470	0.1095	3.307	8
9	0.7180	7.5208	28.2407	1.3928	10.4750	0.1330	0.0955	3.755	9
10	0.6920	8.2128	34.4689	1.4450	11.8678	0.1218	0.0843	4.197	10
11	0.6670	8.8798	41.1389	1.4992	13.3129	0.1126	0.0751	4.632	11
12	0.6429	9.5227	48.2108	1.5555	14.8121	0.1050	0.0675	5.062	12
13	0.6197	10.1424	55.6468	1.6138	16.3676	0.0986	0.0611	5.486	13
14	0.5973	10.7396	63.4112	1.6743	17.9814	0.0931	0.0556	5.904	14
15	0.5757	11.3153	71.4707	1.7371	19.6557	0.0884	0.0509	6.316	15
16	0.5549	11.8702	79.7937	1.8022	21.3927	0.0842	0.0467	6.722	16
17	0.5348	12.4050	88.3507	1.8698	23.1950	0.0806	0.0431	7.122	17
18	0.5155	12.9205	97.1139	1.9399	25.0648	0.0774	0.0399	7.516	18
19	0.4969	13.4173	106.0572	2.0127	27.0047	0.0745	0.0370	7.904	19
20	0.4789	13.8962	115.1562	2.0882	29.0174	0.0720	0.0345	8.286	20
21	0.4616	14.3578	124.3879	2.1665	31.1055	0.0696	0.0321	8.663	21
22	0.4449	14.8027	133.7307	2.2477	33.2720	0.0676	0.0301	9.034	22
23	0.4288	15.2315	143.1647	2.3320	35.5197	0.0657	0.0282	9.399	23
24	0.4133	15.6448	152.6711	2.4194	37.8517	0.0639	0.0264	9.758	24
25	0.3984	16.0432	162.2322	2.5102	40.2711	0.0623	0.0248	10.112	25
26	0.3840	16.4272	171.8317	2.6043	42.7813	0.0609	0.0234	10.460	26
27	0.3701	16.7973	181.4544	2.7020	45.3856	0.0595	0.0220	10.802	27
28	0.3567	17.1540	191.0859	2.8033	48.0875	0.0583	0.0208	11.139	28
29	0.3438	17.4978	200.7132	2.9084	50.8908	0.0571	0.0196	11.470	29
30	0.3314	17.8292	210.3239	3.0175	53.7992	0.0561	0.0186	11.796	30
31	0.3194	18.1487	219.9066	3.1306	56.8167	0.0551	0.0176	12.117	31
32	0.3079	18.4565	229.4509	3.2480	59.9473	0.0542	0.0167	12.431	32
33	0.2968	18.7533	238.9469	3.3698	63.1954	0.0533	0.0158	12.741	33
34	0.2860	19.0393	248.3858	3.4962	66.5652	0.0525	0.0150	13.045	34
35	0.2757	19.3150	257.7591	3.6273	70.0614	0.0518	0.0143	13.345	35
36	0.2657	19.5807	267.0594	3.7633	73.6887	0.0511	0.0136	13.638	36
37	0.2561	19.8369	276.2797	3.9045	77.4520	0.0504	0.0129	13.927	37
38	0.2469	20.0837	285.4135	4.0509	81.3565	0.0498	0.0123	14.211	38
39	0.2379	20.3217	294.4552	4.2028	85.4073	0.0492	0.0117	14.489	39
40	0.2293	20.5510	303.3993	4.3604	89.6101	0.0487	0.0112	14.763	40
41	0.2210	20.7720	312.2413	4.5239	93.9705	0.0481	0.0106	15.031	41
42	0.2131	20.9851	320.9767	4.6935	98.4944	0.0477	0.0102	15.295	42
43	0.2054	21.1905	329.6017	4.8695	103.1879	0.0472	0.0097	15.554	43
44	0.1979	21.3884	338.1129	5.0522	108.0575	0.0468	0.0093	15.808	44
45	0.1908	21.5792	346.5073	5.2416	113.1096	0.0463	0.0088	16.057	45
46	0.1839	21.7631	354.7821	5.4382	118.3512	0.0459	0.0084	16.302	46
47	0.1772	21.9403	362.9351	5.6421	123.7894	0.0456	0.0081	16.541	47
48	0.1708	22.1111	370.9643	5.8537	129.4315	0.0452	0.0077	16.777	48
49	0.1647	22.2758	378.8679	6.0732	135.2852	0.0449	0.0074	17.008	49
50	0.1587	22.4345	386.6445	6.3009	141.3584	0.0446	0.0071	17.234	50
51	0.1530	22.5875	394.2930	6.5372	147.6593	0.0443	0.0068	17.456	51
52	0.1474	22.7349	401.8125	6.7824	154.1965	0.0440	0.0065	17.673	52
53	0.1421	22.8770	409.2023	7.0367	160.9789	0.0437	0.0062	17.887	53
54	0.1370	23.0140	416.4620	7.3006	168.0156	0.0435	0.0060	18.096	54
55	0.1320	23.1460	423.5913	7.5744	175.3162	0.0432	0.0057	18.300	55
60	0.1098	23.7379	457.2860	9.1051	216.1369	0.0421	0.0046	19.264	60
65	0.0914	24.2303	487.7779	10.9453	265.2074	0.0413	0.0038	20.130	65
70	0.0760	24.6399	515.1914	13.1573	324.1952	0.0406	0.0031	20.908	70
75	0.0632	24.9807	539.6998	15.8164	395.1043	0.0400	0.0025	21.604	75
80	0.0526	25.2641	561.5051	19.0129	480.3441	0.0396	0.0021	22.225	80
85	0.0438	25.4999	580.8234	22.8554	582.8109	0.0392	0.0017	22.777	85
90	0.0364	25.6961	597.8747	27.4745	705.9861	0.0389	0.0014	23.267	90
95	0.0303	25.8592	612.8752	33.0271	854.0551	0.0387	0.0012	23.700	95
100	0.0252	25.9950	626.0325	39.7018	1032.0488	0.0385	0.0010	24.082	100

$I = 4.00\%$

n	(P/F)	(P/A)	(P/G)	(F/P)	(F/A)	(A/P)	(A/F)	(A/G)	n
1	0.9615	0.9615	0.0000	1.0400	1.0000	1.0400	1.0000	0.000	1
2	0.9246	1.8861	0.9246	1.0816	2.0400	0.5302	0.4902	0.490	2
3	0.8890	2.7751	2.7025	1.1249	3.1216	0.3603	0.3203	0.973	3
4	0.8548	3.6299	5.2670	1.1699	4.2465	0.2755	0.2355	1.451	4
5	0.8219	4.4518	8.5547	1.2167	5.4163	0.2246	0.1846	1.921	5
6	0.7903	5.2421	12.5062	1.2653	6.6330	0.1908	0.1508	2.385	6
7	0.7599	6.0021	17.0657	1.3159	7.8983	0.1666	0.1266	2.843	7
8	0.7307	6.7327	22.1806	1.3686	9.2142	0.1485	0.1085	3.294	8
9	0.7026	7.4353	27.8013	1.4233	10.5828	0.1345	0.0945	3.739	9
10	0.6756	8.1109	33.8814	1.4802	12.0061	0.1233	0.0833	4.177	10
11	0.6496	8.7605	40.3772	1.5395	13.4864	0.1141	0.0741	4.609	11
12	0.6246	9.3851	47.2477	1.6010	15.0258	0.1066	0.0666	5.034	12
13	0.6006	9.9856	54.4546	1.6651	16.6268	0.1001	0.0601	5.453	13
14	0.5775	10.5631	61.9618	1.7317	18.2919	0.0947	0.0547	5.865	14
15	0.5553	11.1184	69.7355	1.8009	20.0236	0.0899	0.0499	6.272	15
16	0.5339	11.6523	77.7441	1.8730	21.8245	0.0858	0.0458	6.672	16
17	0.5134	12.1657	85.9581	1.9479	23.6975	0.0822	0.0422	7.065	17
18	0.4936	12.6593	94.3498	2.0258	25.6454	0.0790	0.0390	7.453	18
19	0.4746	13.1339	102.8933	2.1068	27.6712	0.0761	0.0361	7.834	19
20	0.4564	13.5903	111.5647	2.1911	29.7781	0.0736	0.0336	8.209	20
21	0.4388	14.0292	120.3414	2.2788	31.9692	0.0713	0.0313	8.577	21
22	0.4220	14.4511	129.2024	2.3699	34.2480	0.0692	0.0292	8.940	22
23	0.4057	14.8568	138.1284	2.4647	36.6179	0.0673	0.0273	9.297	23
24	0.3901	15.2470	147.1012	2.5633	39.0826	0.0656	0.0256	9.647	24
25	0.3751	15.6221	156.1040	2.6658	41.6459	0.0640	0.0240	9.992	25
26	0.3607	15.9828	165.1212	2.7725	44.3117	0.0626	0.0226	10.331	26
27	0.3468	16.3296	174.1385	2.8834	47.0842	0.0612	0.0212	10.664	27
28	0.3335	16.6631	183.1424	2.9987	49.9676	0.0600	0.0200	10.990	28
29	0.3207	16.9837	192.1206	3.1187	52.9663	0.0589	0.0189	11.312	29
30	0.3083	17.2920	201.0618	3.2434	56.0849	0.0578	0.0178	11.627	30
31	0.2965	17.5885	209.9556	3.3731	59.3283	0.0569	0.0169	11.937	31
32	0.2851	17.8736	218.7924	3.5081	62.7015	0.0559	0.0159	12.241	32
33	0.2741	18.1476	227.5634	3.6484	66.2095	0.0551	0.0151	12.539	33
34	0.2636	18.4112	236.2607	3.7943	69.8579	0.0543	0.0143	12.832	34
35	0.2534	18.6646	244.8768	3.9461	73.6522	0.0536	0.0136	13.119	35
36	0.2437	18.9083	253.4052	4.1039	77.5983	0.0529	0.0129	13.401	36
37	0.2343	19.1426	261.8399	4.2681	81.7022	0.0522	0.0122	13.678	37
38	0.2253	19.3679	270.1754	4.4388	85.9703	0.0516	0.0116	13.949	38
39	0.2166	19.5845	278.4070	4.6164	90.4091	0.0511	0.0111	14.215	39
40	0.2083	19.7928	286.5303	4.8010	95.0255	0.0505	0.0105	14.476	40
41	0.2003	19.9931	294.5414	4.9931	99.8265	0.0500	0.0100	14.732	41
42	0.1926	20.1856	302.4370	5.1928	104.8196	0.0495	0.0095	14.982	42
43	0.1852	20.3708	310.2141	5.4005	110.0124	0.0491	0.0091	15.228	43
44	0.1780	20.5488	317.8700	5.6165	115.4129	0.0487	0.0087	15.469	44
45	0.1712	20.7200	325.4028	5.8412	121.0294	0.0483	0.0083	15.704	45
46	0.1646	20.8847	332.8104	6.0748	126.8706	0.0479	0.0079	15.935	46
47	0.1583	21.0429	340.0914	6.3178	132.9454	0.0475	0.0075	16.161	47
48	0.1522	21.1951	347.2446	6.5705	139.2632	0.0472	0.0072	16.383	48
49	0.1463	21.3415	354.2689	6.8333	145.8337	0.0469	0.0069	16.600	49
50	0.1407	21.4822	361.1638	7.1067	152.6671	0.0466	0.0066	16.812	50
51	0.1353	21.6175	367.9289	7.3910	159.7738	0.0463	0.0063	17.020	51
52	0.1301	21.7476	374.5638	7.6866	167.1647	0.0460	0.0060	17.223	52
53	0.1251	21.8727	381.0686	7.9941	174.8513	0.0457	0.0057	17.422	53
54	0.1203	21.9930	387.4436	8.3138	182.8454	0.0455	0.0055	17.616	54
55	0.1157	22.1086	393.6890	8.6464	191.1592	0.0452	0.0052	17.807	55
60	0.0951	22.6235	422.9966	10.5196	237.9907	0.0442	0.0042	18.697	60
65	0.0781	23.0467	449.2014	12.7987	294.9684	0.0434	0.0034	19.490	65
70	0.0642	23.3945	472.4789	15.5716	364.2905	0.0427	0.0027	20.196	70
75	0.0528	23.6804	493.0408	18.9453	448.6314	0.0422	0.0022	20.820	75
80	0.0434	23.9154	511.1161	23.0498	551.2450	0.0418	0.0018	21.371	80
85	0.0357	24.1085	526.9384	28.0436	676.0901	0.0415	0.0015	21.856	85
90	0.0293	24.2673	540.7369	34.1193	827.9833	0.0412	0.0012	22.282	90
95	0.0241	24.3978	552.7307	41.5114	1012.7846	0.0410	0.0010	22.655	95
100	0.0198	24.5050	563.1249	50.5049	1237.6237	0.0408	0.0008	22.980	100

$I = 4.25\%$

n	(P/F)	(P/A)	(P/G)	(F/P)	(F/A)	(A/P)	(A/F)	(A/G)	n
1	0.9592	0.9592	0.0000	1.0425	1.0000	1.0425	1.0000	0.000	1
2	0.9201	1.8794	0.9201	1.0868	2.0425	0.5321	0.4896	0.489	2
3	0.8826	2.7620	2.6854	1.1330	3.1293	0.3621	0.3196	0.972	3
4	0.8466	3.6086	5.2253	1.1811	4.2623	0.2771	0.2346	1.448	4
5	0.8121	4.4207	8.4737	1.2313	5.4434	0.2262	0.1837	1.916	5
6	0.7790	5.1997	12.3688	1.2837	6.6748	0.1923	0.1498	2.378	6
7	0.7473	5.9470	16.8523	1.3382	7.9585	0.1682	0.1257	2.833	7
8	0.7168	6.6638	21.8698	1.3951	9.2967	0.1501	0.1076	3.281	8
9	0.6876	7.3513	27.3704	1.4544	10.6918	0.1360	0.0935	3.723	9
10	0.6595	8.0109	33.3062	1.5162	12.1462	0.1248	0.0823	4.157	10
11	0.6326	8.6435	39.6327	1.5807	13.6624	0.1157	0.0732	4.585	11
12	0.6069	9.2504	46.3081	1.6478	15.2431	0.1081	0.0656	5.006	12
13	0.5821	9.8325	53.2936	1.7179	16.8909	0.1017	0.0592	5.420	13
14	0.5584	10.3909	60.5526	1.7909	18.6088	0.0962	0.0537	5.827	14
15	0.5356	10.9265	68.0513	1.8670	20.3997	0.0915	0.0490	6.228	15
16	0.5138	11.4403	75.7581	1.9463	22.2666	0.0874	0.0449	6.622	16
17	0.4928	11.9332	83.6436	2.0291	24.2130	0.0838	0.0413	7.009	17
18	0.4727	12.4059	91.6803	2.1153	26.2420	0.0806	0.0381	7.390	18
19	0.4535	12.8594	99.8429	2.2052	28.3573	0.0778	0.0353	7.764	19
20	0.4350	13.2944	108.1077	2.2989	30.5625	0.0752	0.0327	8.131	20
21	0.4173	13.7116	116.4528	2.3966	32.8614	0.0729	0.0304	8.493	21
22	0.4002	14.1119	124.8580	2.4985	35.2580	0.0709	0.0284	8.847	22
23	0.3839	14.4958	133.3044	2.6047	37.7565	0.0690	0.0265	9.196	23
24	0.3683	14.8641	141.7748	2.7153	40.3611	0.0673	0.0248	9.538	24
25	0.3533	15.2173	150.2531	2.8308	43.0765	0.0657	0.0232	9.873	25
26	0.3389	15.5562	158.7246	2.9511	45.9072	0.0643	0.0218	10.203	26
27	0.3250	15.8812	167.1758	3.0765	48.8583	0.0630	0.0205	10.526	27
28	0.3118	16.1930	175.5943	3.2072	51.9348	0.0618	0.0193	10.843	28
29	0.2991	16.4921	183.9687	3.3435	55.1420	0.0606	0.0181	11.154	29
30	0.2869	16.7790	192.2886	3.4856	58.4855	0.0596	0.0171	11.460	30
31	0.2752	17.0542	200.5444	3.6338	61.9712	0.0586	0.0161	11.759	31
32	0.2640	17.3182	208.7277	3.7882	65.6049	0.0577	0.0152	12.052	32
33	0.2532	17.5714	216.8306	3.9492	69.3931	0.0569	0.0144	12.340	33
34	0.2429	17.8143	224.8461	4.1171	73.3424	0.0561	0.0136	12.621	34
35	0.2330	18.0473	232.7677	4.2920	77.4594	0.0554	0.0129	12.897	35
36	0.2235	18.2708	240.5899	4.4744	81.7514	0.0547	0.0122	13.168	36
37	0.2144	18.4852	248.3077	4.6646	86.2259	0.0541	0.0116	13.432	37
38	0.2056	18.6908	255.9164	4.8628	90.8905	0.0535	0.0110	13.692	38
39	0.1973	18.8881	263.4122	5.0695	95.7533	0.0529	0.0104	13.946	39
40	0.1892	19.0773	270.7916	5.2850	100.8228	0.0524	0.0099	14.194	40
41	0.1815	19.2588	278.0517	5.5096	106.1078	0.0519	0.0094	14.437	41
42	0.1741	19.4329	285.1899	5.7437	111.6174	0.0515	0.0090	14.675	42
43	0.1670	19.5999	292.2041	5.9878	117.3611	0.0510	0.0085	14.908	43
44	0.1602	19.7601	299.0925	6.2423	123.3490	0.0506	0.0081	15.136	44
45	0.1537	19.9137	305.8538	6.5076	129.5913	0.0502	0.0077	15.358	45
46	0.1474	20.0611	312.4869	6.7842	136.0989	0.0498	0.0073	15.576	46
47	0.1414	20.2025	318.9909	7.0725	142.8831	0.0495	0.0070	15.789	47
48	0.1356	20.3382	325.3654	7.3731	149.9557	0.0492	0.0067	15.997	48
49	0.1301	20.4683	331.6101	7.6865	157.3288	0.0489	0.0064	16.201	49
50	0.1248	20.5931	337.7251	8.0131	165.0153	0.0486	0.0061	16.399	50
51	0.1197	20.7128	343.7105	8.3537	173.0284	0.0483	0.0058	16.594	51
52	0.1148	20.8276	349.5666	8.7087	181.3821	0.0480	0.0055	16.783	52
53	0.1101	20.9377	355.2942	9.0789	190.0909	0.0478	0.0053	16.969	53
54	0.1057	21.0434	360.8940	9.4647	199.1697	0.0475	0.0050	17.150	54
55	0.1013	21.1447	366.3668	9.8670	208.6344	0.0473	0.0048	17.326	55
60	0.0823	21.5928	391.8674	12.1497	262.3447	0.0463	0.0038	18.148	60
65	0.0668	21.9566	414.3963	14.9604	328.4808	0.0455	0.0030	18.873	65
70	0.0543	22.2521	434.1698	18.4215	409.9171	0.0449	0.0024	19.511	70
75	0.0441	22.4921	451.4282	22.6832	510.1935	0.0445	0.0020	20.070	75
80	0.0358	22.6870	466.4185	27.9309	633.6685	0.0441	0.0016	20.558	80
85	0.0291	22.8453	479.3838	34.3926	785.7090	0.0438	0.0013	20.983	85
90	0.0236	22.9738	490.5558	42.3493	972.9235	0.0435	0.0010	21.352	90
95	0.0192	23.0782	500.1508	52.1466	1203.4496	0.0433	0.0008	21.672	95
100	0.0156	23.1630	508.3669	64.2105	1487.3070	0.0432	0.0007	21.947	100

EXPANDED INTEREST TABLES

$I = 4.50\%$

n	(P/F)	(P/A)	(P/G)	(F/P)	(F/A)	(A/P)	(A/F)	(A/G)	n
1	0.9569	0.9569	0.0000	1.0450	1.0000	1.0450	1.0000	0.000	1
2	0.9157	1.8727	0.9157	1.0920	2.0450	0.5340	0.4890	0.489	2
3	0.8763	2.7490	2.6683	1.1412	3.1370	0.3638	0.3188	0.970	3
4	0.8386	3.5875	5.1840	1.1925	4.2782	0.2787	0.2337	1.445	4
5	0.8025	4.3900	8.3938	1.2462	5.4707	0.2278	0.1828	1.912	5
6	0.7679	5.1579	12.2333	1.3023	6.7169	0.1939	0.1489	2.371	6
7	0.7348	5.8927	16.6423	1.3609	8.0192	0.1697	0.1247	2.824	7
8	0.7032	6.5959	21.5646	1.4221	9.3800	0.1516	0.1066	3.269	8
9	0.6729	7.2688	26.9478	1.4861	10.8021	0.1376	0.0926	3.707	9
10	0.6439	7.9127	32.7431	1.5530	12.2882	0.1264	0.0814	4.138	10
11	0.6162	8.5289	38.9051	1.6229	13.8412	0.1172	0.0722	4.561	11
12	0.5897	9.1186	45.3914	1.6959	15.4640	0.1097	0.0647	4.977	12
13	0.5643	9.6829	52.1627	1.7722	17.1599	0.1033	0.0583	5.387	13
14	0.5400	10.2228	59.1823	1.8519	18.9321	0.0978	0.0528	5.789	14
15	0.5167	10.7395	66.4164	1.9353	20.7841	0.0931	0.0481	6.184	15
16	0.4945	11.2340	73.8335	2.0224	22.7193	0.0890	0.0440	6.572	16
17	0.4732	11.7072	81.4043	2.1134	24.7417	0.0854	0.0404	6.953	17
18	0.4528	12.1600	89.1019	2.2085	26.8551	0.0822	0.0372	7.327	18
19	0.4333	12.5933	96.9013	2.3079	29.0636	0.0794	0.0344	7.694	19
20	0.4146	13.0079	104.7795	2.4117	31.3714	0.0769	0.0319	8.055	20
21	0.3968	13.4047	112.7153	2.5202	33.7831	0.0746	0.0296	8.408	21
22	0.3797	13.7844	120.6890	2.6337	36.3034	0.0725	0.0275	8.755	22
23	0.3634	14.1478	128.6827	2.7522	38.9370	0.0707	0.0257	9.095	23
24	0.3477	14.4955	136.6799	2.8760	41.6892	0.0690	0.0240	9.429	24
25	0.3327	14.8282	144.6654	3.0054	44.5652	0.0674	0.0224	9.756	25
26	0.3184	15.1466	152.6255	3.1407	47.5706	0.0660	0.0210	10.076	26
27	0.3047	15.4513	160.5475	3.2820	50.7113	0.0647	0.0197	10.390	27
28	0.2916	15.7429	168.4199	3.4297	53.9933	0.0635	0.0185	10.698	28
29	0.2790	16.0219	176.2323	3.5840	57.4230	0.0624	0.0174	10.999	29
30	0.2670	16.2889	183.9753	3.7453	61.0071	0.0614	0.0164	11.294	30
31	0.2555	16.5444	191.6404	3.9139	64.7524	0.0604	0.0154	11.583	31
32	0.2445	16.7889	199.2199	4.0900	68.6662	0.0596	0.0146	11.866	32
33	0.2340	17.0229	206.7069	4.2740	72.7562	0.0587	0.0137	12.142	33
34	0.2239	17.2468	214.0955	4.4664	77.0303	0.0580	0.0130	12.413	34
35	0.2143	17.4610	221.3802	4.6673	81.4966	0.0573	0.0123	12.678	35
36	0.2050	17.6660	228.5561	4.8774	86.1640	0.0566	0.0116	12.937	36
37	0.1962	17.8622	235.6193	5.0969	91.0413	0.0560	0.0110	13.190	37
38	0.1878	18.0500	242.5661	5.3262	96.1382	0.0554	0.0104	13.438	38
39	0.1797	18.2297	249.3934	5.5659	101.4644	0.0549	0.0099	13.680	39
40	0.1719	18.4016	256.0986	5.8164	107.0303	0.0543	0.0093	13.917	40
41	0.1645	18.5661	262.6796	6.0781	112.8467	0.0539	0.0089	14.148	41
42	0.1574	18.7235	269.1346	6.3516	118.9248	0.0534	0.0084	14.374	42
43	0.1507	18.8742	275.4624	6.6374	125.2764	0.0530	0.0080	14.594	43
44	0.1442	19.0184	281.6618	6.9361	131.9138	0.0526	0.0076	14.810	44
45	0.1380	19.1563	287.7322	7.2482	138.8500	0.0522	0.0072	15.020	45
46	0.1320	19.2884	293.6733	7.5744	146.0982	0.0518	0.0068	15.225	46
47	0.1263	19.4147	299.4848	7.9153	153.6726	0.0515	0.0065	15.425	47
48	0.1209	19.5356	305.1670	8.2715	161.5879	0.0512	0.0062	15.621	48
49	0.1157	19.6513	310.7202	8.6437	169.8594	0.0509	0.0059	15.811	49
50	0.1107	19.7620	316.1450	9.0326	178.5030	0.0506	0.0056	15.997	50
51	0.1059	19.8680	321.4421	9.4391	187.5357	0.0503	0.0053	16.178	51
52	0.1014	19.9693	326.6125	9.8639	196.9748	0.0501	0.0051	16.355	52
53	0.0970	20.0663	331.6573	10.3077	206.8386	0.0498	0.0048	16.528	53
54	0.0928	20.1592	336.5776	10.7716	217.1464	0.0496	0.0046	16.696	54
55	0.0888	20.2480	341.3749	11.2563	227.9180	0.0494	0.0044	16.859	55
60	0.0713	20.6380	363.5707	14.0274	289.4980	0.0485	0.0035	17.616	60
65	0.0572	20.9510	382.9465	17.4807	366.2378	0.0477	0.0027	18.278	65
70	0.0459	21.2021	399.7503	21.7841	461.8697	0.0472	0.0022	18.854	70
75	0.0368	21.4036	414.2422	27.1470	581.0444	0.0467	0.0017	19.353	75
80	0.0296	21.5653	426.6797	33.8301	729.5577	0.0464	0.0014	19.785	80
85	0.0237	21.6951	437.3091	42.1585	914.6323	0.0461	0.0011	20.157	85
90	0.0190	21.7992	446.3592	52.5371	1145.2690	0.0459	0.0009	20.475	90
95	0.0153	21.8828	454.0394	65.4708	1432.6843	0.0457	0.0007	20.748	95
100	0.0123	21.9499	460.5376	81.5885	1790.8560	0.0456	0.0006	20.981	100

$I = 4.75\ \%$

n	(P/F)	(P/A)	(P/G)	(F/P)	(F/A)	(A/P)	(A/F)	(A/G)	n
1	0.9547	0.9547	0.0000	1.0475	1.0000	1.0475	1.0000	0.000	1
2	0.9114	1.8660	0.9114	1.0973	2.0475	0.5359	0.4884	0.488	2
3	0.8700	2.7361	2.6514	1.1494	3.1448	0.3655	0.3180	0.969	3
4	0.8306	3.5666	5.1432	1.2040	4.2941	0.2804	0.2329	1.442	4
5	0.7929	4.3596	8.3149	1.2612	5.4981	0.2294	0.1819	1.907	5
6	0.7570	5.1165	12.0997	1.3211	6.7593	0.1954	0.1479	2.364	6
7	0.7226	5.8392	16.4355	1.3838	8.0803	0.1713	0.1238	2.814	7
8	0.6899	6.5290	21.2646	1.4495	9.4641	0.1532	0.1057	3.256	8
9	0.6586	7.1876	26.5333	1.5184	10.9137	0.1391	0.0916	3.691	9
10	0.6287	7.8163	32.1918	1.5905	12.4321	0.1279	0.0804	4.118	10
11	0.6002	8.4166	38.1940	1.6661	14.0226	0.1188	0.0713	4.538	11
12	0.5730	8.9896	44.4969	1.7452	15.6887	0.1112	0.0637	4.949	12
13	0.5470	9.5366	51.0611	1.8281	17.4339	0.1049	0.0574	5.354	13
14	0.5222	10.0588	57.8498	1.9149	19.2620	0.0994	0.0519	5.751	14
15	0.4985	10.5573	64.8292	2.0059	21.1770	0.0947	0.0472	6.140	15
16	0.4759	11.0332	71.9680	2.1012	23.1829	0.0906	0.0431	6.522	16
17	0.4543	11.4876	79.2375	2.2010	25.2840	0.0871	0.0396	6.897	17
18	0.4337	11.9213	86.6110	2.3055	27.4850	0.0839	0.0364	7.265	18
19	0.4141	12.3354	94.0643	2.4151	29.7906	0.0811	0.0336	7.625	19
20	0.3953	12.7307	101.5748	2.5298	32.2056	0.0786	0.0311	7.978	20
21	0.3774	13.1080	109.1222	2.6499	34.7354	0.0763	0.0288	8.324	21
22	0.3603	13.4683	116.6876	2.7758	37.3853	0.0742	0.0267	8.663	22
23	0.3439	13.8122	124.2538	2.9077	40.1611	0.0724	0.0249	8.995	23
24	0.3283	14.1405	131.8053	3.0458	43.0688	0.0707	0.0232	9.321	24
25	0.3134	14.4540	139.3277	3.1904	46.1146	0.0692	0.0217	9.639	25
26	0.2992	14.7532	146.8083	3.3420	49.3050	0.0678	0.0203	9.950	26
27	0.2857	15.0389	154.2353	3.5007	52.6470	0.0665	0.0190	10.255	27
28	0.2727	15.3116	161.5983	3.6670	56.1477	0.0653	0.0178	10.554	28
29	0.2603	15.5719	168.8877	3.8412	59.8147	0.0642	0.0167	10.845	29
30	0.2485	15.8204	176.0950	4.0237	63.6559	0.0632	0.0157	11.130	30
31	0.2373	16.0577	183.2128	4.2148	67.6796	0.0623	0.0148	11.409	31
32	0.2265	16.2842	190.2344	4.4150	71.8944	0.0614	0.0139	11.682	32
33	0.2162	16.5004	197.1538	4.6247	76.3094	0.0606	0.0131	11.948	33
34	0.2064	16.7068	203.9658	4.8444	80.9341	0.0599	0.0124	12.208	34
35	0.1971	16.9039	210.6660	5.0745	85.7784	0.0592	0.0117	12.462	35
36	0.1881	17.0920	217.2505	5.3155	90.8529	0.0585	0.0110	12.710	36
37	0.1796	17.2716	223.7160	5.5680	96.1684	0.0579	0.0104	12.952	37
38	0.1715	17.4431	230.0598	5.8325	101.7364	0.0573	0.0098	13.189	38
39	0.1637	17.6068	236.2796	6.1095	107.5689	0.0568	0.0093	13.419	39
40	0.1563	17.7630	242.3736	6.3997	113.6784	0.0563	0.0088	13.644	40
41	0.1492	17.9122	248.3405	6.7037	120.0781	0.0558	0.0083	13.864	41
42	0.1424	18.0546	254.1791	7.0221	126.7818	0.0554	0.0079	14.078	42
43	0.1359	18.1905	259.8890	7.3557	133.8040	0.0550	0.0075	14.287	43
44	0.1298	18.3203	265.4697	7.7051	141.1597	0.0546	0.0071	14.490	44
45	0.1239	18.4442	270.9213	8.0711	148.8648	0.0542	0.0067	14.688	45
46	0.1183	18.5625	276.2439	8.4545	156.9358	0.0539	0.0064	14.881	46
47	0.1129	18.6754	281.4381	8.8560	165.3903	0.0535	0.0060	15.070	47
48	0.1078	18.7832	286.5046	9.2767	174.2463	0.0532	0.0057	15.253	48
49	0.1029	18.8861	291.4442	9.7173	183.5230	0.0529	0.0054	15.431	49
50	0.0982	18.9844	296.2581	10.1789	193.2404	0.0527	0.0052	15.605	50
51	0.0938	19.0782	300.9475	10.6624	203.4193	0.0524	0.0049	15.774	51
52	0.0895	19.1677	305.5137	11.1689	214.0817	0.0522	0.0047	15.939	52
53	0.0855	19.2532	309.9584	11.6994	225.2506	0.0519	0.0044	16.099	53
54	0.0816	19.3348	314.2831	12.2551	236.9500	0.0517	0.0042	16.254	54
55	0.0779	19.4127	318.4896	12.8372	249.2051	0.0515	0.0040	16.406	55
60	0.0618	19.7523	337.8155	16.1898	319.7856	0.0506	0.0031	17.102	60
65	0.0490	20.0215	354.4857	20.4179	408.7989	0.0499	0.0024	17.705	65
70	0.0388	20.2351	368.7715	25.7503	521.0588	0.0494	0.0019	18.224	70
75	0.0308	20.4044	380.9455	32.4752	662.6366	0.0490	0.0015	18.669	75
80	0.0244	20.5386	391.2698	40.9565	841.1889	0.0487	0.0012	19.050	80
85	0.0194	20.6451	399.9883	51.6527	1066.3718	0.0484	0.0009	19.374	85
90	0.0154	20.7295	407.3234	65.1423	1350.3635	0.0482	0.0007	19.649	90
95	0.0122	20.7964	413.4742	82.1548	1708.5224	0.0481	0.0006	19.882	95
100	0.0097	20.8494	418.6166	103.6104	2160.2180	0.0480	0.0005	20.078	100

EXPANDED INTEREST TABLES

$I = 5.00\ \%$

n	(P/F)	(P/A)	(P/G)	(F/P)	(F/A)	(A/P)	(A/F)	(A/G)	n
1	0.9524	0.9524	0.0000	1.0500	1.0000	1.0500	1.0000	0.000	1
2	0.9070	1.8594	0.9070	1.1025	2.0500	0.5378	0.4878	0.487	2
3	0.8638	2.7232	2.6347	1.1576	3.1525	0.3672	0.3172	0.967	3
4	0.8227	3.5460	5.1028	1.2155	4.3101	0.2820	0.2320	1.439	4
5	0.7835	4.3295	8.2369	1.2763	5.5256	0.2310	0.1810	1.902	5
6	0.7462	5.0757	11.9680	1.3401	6.8019	0.1970	0.1470	2.357	6
7	0.7107	5.7864	16.2321	1.4071	8.1420	0.1728	0.1228	2.805	7
8	0.6768	6.4632	20.9700	1.4775	9.5491	0.1547	0.1047	3.244	8
9	0.6446	7.1078	26.1268	1.5513	11.0266	0.1407	0.0907	3.675	9
10	0.6139	7.7217	31.6520	1.6289	12.5779	0.1295	0.0795	4.099	10
11	0.5847	8.3064	37.4988	1.7103	14.2068	0.1204	0.0704	4.514	11
12	0.5568	8.8633	43.6241	1.7959	15.9171	0.1128	0.0628	4.921	12
13	0.5303	9.3936	49.9879	1.8856	17.7130	0.1065	0.0565	5.321	13
14	0.5051	9.8986	56.5538	1.9799	19.5986	0.1010	0.0510	5.713	14
15	0.4810	10.3797	63.2880	2.0789	21.5786	0.0963	0.0463	6.097	15
16	0.4581	10.8378	70.1597	2.1829	23.6575	0.0923	0.0423	6.473	16
17	0.4363	11.2741	77.1405	2.2920	25.8404	0.0887	0.0387	6.842	17
18	0.4155	11.6896	84.2043	2.4066	28.1324	0.0855	0.0355	7.203	18
19	0.3957	12.0853	91.3275	2.5270	30.5390	0.0827	0.0327	7.556	19
20	0.3769	12.4622	98.4884	2.6533	33.0660	0.0802	0.0302	7.903	20
21	0.3589	12.8212	105.6673	2.7860	35.7193	0.0780	0.0280	8.241	21
22	0.3418	13.1630	112.8461	2.9253	38.5052	0.0760	0.0260	8.573	22
23	0.3256	13.4886	120.0087	3.0715	41.4305	0.0741	0.0241	8.897	23
24	0.3101	13.7986	127.1402	3.2251	44.5020	0.0725	0.0225	9.214	24
25	0.2953	14.0939	134.2275	3.3864	47.7271	0.0710	0.0210	9.523	25
26	0.2812	14.3752	141.2585	3.5557	51.1135	0.0696	0.0196	9.826	26
27	0.2678	14.6430	148.2226	3.7335	54.6691	0.0683	0.0183	10.122	27
28	0.2551	14.8981	155.1101	3.9201	58.4026	0.0671	0.0171	10.411	28
29	0.2429	15.1411	161.9126	4.1161	62.3227	0.0660	0.0160	10.693	29
30	0.2314	15.3725	168.6226	4.3219	66.4388	0.0651	0.0151	10.969	30
31	0.2204	15.5928	175.2333	4.5380	70.7608	0.0641	0.0141	11.238	31
32	0.2099	15.8027	181.7392	4.7649	75.2988	0.0633	0.0133	11.500	32
33	0.1999	16.0025	188.1351	5.0032	80.0638	0.0625	0.0125	11.756	33
34	0.1904	16.1929	194.4168	5.2533	85.0670	0.0618	0.0118	12.006	34
35	0.1813	16.3742	200.5807	5.5160	90.3203	0.0611	0.0111	12.249	35
36	0.1727	16.5469	206.6237	5.7918	95.8363	0.0604	0.0104	12.487	36
37	0.1644	16.7113	212.5434	6.0814	101.6281	0.0598	0.0098	12.718	37
38	0.1566	16.8679	218.3378	6.3855	107.7095	0.0593	0.0093	12.944	38
39	0.1491	17.0170	224.0054	6.7048	114.0950	0.0588	0.0088	13.163	39
40	0.1420	17.1591	229.5452	7.0400	120.7998	0.0583	0.0083	13.377	40
41	0.1353	17.2944	234.9564	7.3920	127.8398	0.0578	0.0078	13.585	41
42	0.1288	17.4232	240.2389	7.7616	135.2318	0.0574	0.0074	13.788	42
43	0.1227	17.5459	245.3925	8.1497	142.9933	0.0570	0.0070	13.985	43
44	0.1169	17.6628	250.4175	8.5572	151.1430	0.0566	0.0066	14.177	44
45	0.1113	17.7741	255.3145	8.9850	159.7002	0.0563	0.0063	14.364	45
46	0.1060	17.8801	260.0844	9.4343	168.6852	0.0559	0.0059	14.546	46
47	0.1009	17.9810	264.7281	9.9060	178.1194	0.0556	0.0056	14.722	47
48	0.0961	18.0772	269.2467	10.4013	188.0254	0.0553	0.0053	14.894	48
49	0.0916	18.1687	273.6418	10.9213	198.4267	0.0550	0.0050	15.061	49
50	0.0872	18.2559	277.9148	11.4674	209.3480	0.0548	0.0048	15.223	50
51	0.0831	18.3390	282.0673	12.0408	220.8154	0.0545	0.0045	15.380	51
52	0.0791	18.4181	286.1013	12.6428	232.8562	0.0543	0.0043	15.533	52
53	0.0753	18.4934	290.0184	13.2749	245.4990	0.0541	0.0041	15.682	53
54	0.0717	18.5651	293.8208	13.9387	258.7739	0.0539	0.0039	15.826	54
55	0.0683	18.6335	297.5104	14.6356	272.7126	0.0537	0.0037	15.966	55
60	0.0535	18.9293	314.3432	18.6792	353.5837	0.0528	0.0028	16.606	60
65	0.0419	19.1611	328.6910	23.8399	456.7980	0.0522	0.0022	17.154	65
70	0.0329	19.3427	340.8409	30.4264	588.5285	0.0517	0.0017	17.621	70
75	0.0258	19.4850	351.0721	38.8327	756.6537	0.0513	0.0013	18.017	75
80	0.0202	19.5965	359.6460	49.5614	971.2288	0.0510	0.0010	18.352	80
85	0.0158	19.6838	366.8007	63.2544	1245.0871	0.0508	0.0008	18.634	85
90	0.0124	19.7523	372.7488	80.7304	1594.6073	0.0506	0.0006	18.871	90
95	0.0097	19.8059	377.6774	103.0347	2040.6935	0.0505	0.0005	19.068	95
100	0.0076	19.8479	381.7492	131.5013	2610.0252	0.0504	0.0004	19.233	100

$I = 5.25\%$

n	(P/F)	(P/A)	(P/G)	(F/P)	(F/A)	(A/P)	(A/F)	(A/G)	n
1	0.9501	0.9501	0.0000	1.0525	1.0000	1.0525	1.0000	0.000	1
2	0.9027	1.8528	0.9027	1.1078	2.0525	0.5397	0.4872	0.487	2
3	0.8577	2.7105	2.6181	1.1659	3.1603	0.3689	0.3164	0.965	3
4	0.8149	3.5255	5.0629	1.2271	4.3262	0.2837	0.2312	1.436	4
5	0.7743	4.2997	8.1599	1.2915	5.5533	0.2326	0.1801	1.897	5
6	0.7356	5.0354	11.8381	1.3594	6.8448	0.1986	0.1461	2.351	6
7	0.6989	5.7343	16.0318	1.4307	8.2042	0.1744	0.1219	2.795	7
8	0.6641	6.3984	20.6804	1.5058	9.6349	0.1563	0.1038	3.232	8
9	0.6310	7.0294	25.7281	1.5849	11.1407	0.1423	0.0898	3.660	9
10	0.5995	7.6288	31.1235	1.6681	12.7256	0.1311	0.0786	4.079	10
11	0.5696	8.1984	36.8193	1.7557	14.3937	0.1220	0.0695	4.491	11
12	0.5412	8.7396	42.7722	1.8478	16.1494	0.1144	0.0619	4.894	12
13	0.5142	9.2538	48.9423	1.9449	17.9972	0.1081	0.0556	5.288	13
14	0.4885	9.7423	55.2932	2.0470	19.9421	0.1026	0.0501	5.675	14
15	0.4642	10.2065	61.7914	2.1544	21.9891	0.0980	0.0455	6.054	15
16	0.4410	10.6475	68.4065	2.2675	24.1435	0.0939	0.0414	6.424	16
17	0.4190	11.0665	75.1107	2.3866	26.4110	0.0904	0.0379	6.787	17
18	0.3981	11.4646	81.8786	2.5119	28.7976	0.0872	0.0347	7.141	18
19	0.3783	11.8428	88.6871	2.6437	31.3095	0.0844	0.0319	7.488	19
20	0.3594	12.2022	95.5154	2.7825	33.9532	0.0820	0.0295	7.827	20
21	0.3415	12.5437	102.3445	2.9286	36.7358	0.0797	0.0272	8.159	21
22	0.3244	12.8681	109.1574	3.0824	39.6644	0.0777	0.0252	8.482	22
23	0.3082	13.1763	115.9387	3.2442	42.7468	0.0759	0.0234	8.799	23
24	0.2929	13.4692	122.6747	3.4145	45.9910	0.0742	0.0217	9.107	24
25	0.2783	13.7475	129.3528	3.5938	49.4055	0.0727	0.0202	9.409	25
26	0.2644	14.0118	135.9623	3.7825	52.9993	0.0714	0.0189	9.703	26
27	0.2512	14.2630	142.4932	3.9810	56.7818	0.0701	0.0176	9.990	27
28	0.2387	14.5017	148.9371	4.1900	60.7628	0.0690	0.0165	10.270	28
29	0.2268	14.7285	155.2863	4.4100	64.9529	0.0679	0.0154	10.543	29
30	0.2154	14.9439	161.5342	4.6416	69.3629	0.0669	0.0144	10.809	30
31	0.2047	15.1486	167.6751	4.8852	74.0044	0.0660	0.0135	11.068	31
32	0.1945	15.3431	173.7043	5.1417	78.8897	0.0652	0.0127	11.321	32
33	0.1848	15.5279	179.6174	5.4116	84.0314	0.0644	0.0119	11.567	33
34	0.1756	15.7034	185.4112	5.6958	89.4430	0.0637	0.0112	11.807	34
35	0.1668	15.8703	191.0828	5.9948	95.1388	0.0630	0.0105	12.040	35
36	0.1585	16.0287	196.6300	6.3095	101.1336	0.0624	0.0099	12.267	36
37	0.1506	16.1793	202.0511	6.6408	107.4431	0.0618	0.0093	12.488	37
38	0.1431	16.3224	207.3448	6.9894	114.0838	0.0613	0.0088	12.703	38
39	0.1359	16.4583	212.5104	7.3563	121.0732	0.0608	0.0083	12.912	39
40	0.1292	16.5875	217.5475	7.7426	128.4296	0.0603	0.0078	13.115	40
41	0.1227	16.7102	222.4560	8.1490	136.1721	0.0598	0.0073	13.312	41
42	0.1166	16.8268	227.2363	8.5769	144.3212	0.0594	0.0069	13.504	42
43	0.1108	16.9376	231.8890	9.0271	152.8980	0.0590	0.0065	13.690	43
44	0.1053	17.0428	236.4148	9.5011	161.9252	0.0587	0.0062	13.871	44
45	0.1000	17.1428	240.8148	9.9999	171.4262	0.0583	0.0058	14.047	45
46	0.0950	17.2378	245.0904	10.5249	181.4261	0.0580	0.0055	14.218	46
47	0.0903	17.3281	249.2430	11.0774	191.9510	0.0577	0.0052	14.383	47
48	0.0858	17.4139	253.2742	11.6590	203.0284	0.0574	0.0049	14.544	48
49	0.0815	17.4954	257.1859	12.2711	214.6874	0.0572	0.0047	14.700	49
50	0.0774	17.5728	260.9798	12.9153	226.9585	0.0569	0.0044	14.851	50
51	0.0736	17.6464	264.6581	13.5934	239.8738	0.0567	0.0042	14.997	51
52	0.0699	17.7163	268.2228	14.3070	253.4672	0.0564	0.0039	15.139	52
53	0.0664	17.7827	271.6760	15.0581	267.7742	0.0562	0.0037	15.277	53
54	0.0631	17.8458	275.0202	15.8487	282.8324	0.0560	0.0035	15.410	54
55	0.0599	17.9057	278.2574	16.6808	298.6811	0.0558	0.0033	15.540	55
60	0.0464	18.1635	292.9237	21.5440	391.3142	0.0551	0.0026	16.127	60
65	0.0359	18.3631	305.2772	27.8251	510.9544	0.0545	0.0020	16.624	65
70	0.0278	18.5176	315.6147	35.9375	665.4753	0.0540	0.0015	17.044	70
75	0.0215	18.6372	324.2168	46.4149	865.0466	0.0537	0.0012	17.396	75
80	0.0167	18.7299	331.3404	59.9471	1122.8024	0.0534	0.0009	17.690	80
85	0.0129	18.8016	337.2145	77.4246	1455.7064	0.0532	0.0007	17.935	85
90	0.0100	18.8571	342.0403	99.9976	1885.6678	0.0530	0.0005	18.138	90
95	0.0077	18.9001	345.9918	129.1516	2440.9836	0.0529	0.0004	18.306	95
100	0.0060	18.9334	349.2177	166.8055	3158.2006	0.0528	0.0003	18.444	100

EXPANDED INTEREST TABLES

$I = 5.50$ %

n	(P/F)	(P/A)	(P/G)	(F/P)	(F/A)	(A/P)	(A/F)	(A/G)	n
1	0.9479	0.9479	0.0000	1.0550	1.0000	1.0550	1.0000	0.000	1
2	0.8985	1.8463	0.8985	1.1130	2.0550	0.5416	0.4866	0.486	2
3	0.8516	2.6979	2.6017	1.1742	3.1680	0.3707	0.3157	0.964	3
4	0.8072	3.5052	5.0233	1.2388	4.3423	0.2853	0.2303	1.433	4
5	0.7651	4.2703	8.0839	1.3070	5.5811	0.2342	0.1792	1.893	5
6	0.7252	4.9955	11.7101	1.3788	6.8881	0.2002	0.1452	2.344	6
7	0.6874	5.6830	15.8347	1.4547	8.2669	0.1760	0.1210	2.786	7
8	0.6516	6.3346	20.3959	1.5347	9.7216	0.1579	0.1029	3.219	8
9	0.6176	6.9522	25.3369	1.6191	11.2563	0.1438	0.0888	3.644	9
10	0.5854	7.5376	30.6058	1.7081	12.8754	0.1327	0.0777	4.060	10
11	0.5549	8.0925	36.1549	1.8021	14.5835	0.1236	0.0686	4.467	11
12	0.5260	8.6185	41.9407	1.9012	16.3856	0.1160	0.0610	4.866	12
13	0.4986	9.1171	47.9234	2.0058	18.2868	0.1097	0.0547	5.256	13
14	0.4726	9.5896	54.0669	2.1161	20.2926	0.1043	0.0493	5.638	14
15	0.4479	10.0376	60.3379	2.2325	22.4087	0.0996	0.0446	6.011	15
16	0.4246	10.4622	66.7066	2.3553	24.6411	0.0956	0.0406	6.376	16
17	0.4024	10.8646	73.1458	2.4848	26.9964	0.0920	0.0370	6.732	17
18	0.3815	11.2461	79.6307	2.6215	29.4812	0.0889	0.0339	7.080	18
19	0.3616	11.6077	86.1391	2.7656	32.1027	0.0862	0.0312	7.420	19
20	0.3427	11.9504	92.6510	2.9178	34.8683	0.0837	0.0287	7.753	20
21	0.3249	12.2752	99.1482	3.0782	37.7861	0.0815	0.0265	8.077	21
22	0.3079	12.5832	105.6146	3.2475	40.8643	0.0795	0.0245	8.393	22
23	0.2919	12.8750	112.0358	3.4262	44.1118	0.0777	0.0227	8.701	23
24	0.2767	13.1517	118.3989	3.6146	47.5380	0.0760	0.0210	9.002	24
25	0.2622	13.4139	124.6925	3.8134	51.1526	0.0745	0.0195	9.295	25
26	0.2486	13.6625	130.9066	4.0231	54.9660	0.0732	0.0182	9.581	26
27	0.2356	13.8981	137.0323	4.2444	58.9891	0.0720	0.0170	9.859	27
28	0.2233	14.1214	143.0620	4.4778	63.2335	0.0708	0.0158	10.130	28
29	0.2117	14.3331	148.9890	4.7241	67.7114	0.0698	0.0148	10.394	29
30	0.2006	14.5337	154.8077	4.9840	72.4355	0.0688	0.0138	10.651	30
31	0.1902	14.7239	160.5132	5.2581	77.4194	0.0679	0.0129	10.901	31
32	0.1803	14.9042	166.1016	5.5473	82.6775	0.0671	0.0121	11.144	32
33	0.1709	15.0751	171.5695	5.8524	88.2248	0.0663	0.0113	11.381	33
34	0.1620	15.2370	176.9142	6.1742	94.0771	0.0656	0.0106	11.610	34
35	0.1535	15.3906	182.1339	6.5138	100.2514	0.0650	0.0100	11.834	35
36	0.1455	15.5361	187.2270	6.8721	106.7652	0.0644	0.0094	12.051	36
37	0.1379	15.6740	192.1925	7.2501	113.6373	0.0638	0.0088	12.261	37
38	0.1307	15.8047	197.0298	7.6488	120.8873	0.0633	0.0083	12.466	38
39	0.1239	15.9287	201.7389	8.0695	128.5361	0.0628	0.0078	12.665	39
40	0.1175	16.0461	206.3200	8.5133	136.6056	0.0623	0.0073	12.857	40
41	0.1113	16.1575	210.7736	8.9815	145.1189	0.0619	0.0069	13.045	41
42	0.1055	16.2630	215.1005	9.4755	154.1005	0.0615	0.0065	13.226	42
43	0.1000	16.3630	219.3019	9.9967	163.5760	0.0611	0.0061	13.402	43
44	0.0948	16.4579	223.3791	10.5465	173.5727	0.0608	0.0058	13.572	44
45	0.0899	16.5477	227.3336	11.1266	184.1192	0.0604	0.0054	13.738	45
46	0.0852	16.6329	231.1671	11.7385	195.2457	0.0601	0.0051	13.898	46
47	0.0807	16.7137	234.8815	12.3841	206.9842	0.0598	0.0048	14.053	47
48	0.0765	16.7902	238.4789	13.0653	219.3684	0.0596	0.0046	14.203	48
49	0.0725	16.8628	241.9612	13.7838	232.4336	0.0593	0.0043	14.348	49
50	0.0688	16.9315	245.3308	14.5420	246.2175	0.0591	0.0041	14.489	50
51	0.0652	16.9967	248.5898	15.3418	260.7594	0.0588	0.0038	14.625	51
52	0.0618	17.0585	251.7408	16.1856	276.1012	0.0586	0.0036	14.757	52
53	0.0586	17.1170	254.7860	17.0758	292.2868	0.0584	0.0034	14.884	53
54	0.0555	17.1726	257.7281	18.0149	309.3625	0.0582	0.0032	15.008	54
55	0.0526	17.2252	260.5693	19.0058	327.3775	0.0581	0.0031	15.127	55
60	0.0403	17.4499	273.3522	24.8398	433.4504	0.0573	0.0023	15.665	60
65	0.0308	17.6218	283.9925	32.4646	572.0834	0.0567	0.0017	16.116	65
70	0.0236	17.7533	292.7914	42.4299	753.2712	0.0563	0.0013	16.492	70
75	0.0180	17.8539	300.0269	55.4542	990.0764	0.0560	0.0010	16.804	75
80	0.0138	17.9310	305.9481	72.4764	1299.5714	0.0558	0.0008	17.062	80
85	0.0106	17.9899	310.7732	94.7238	1704.0689	0.0556	0.0006	17.274	85
90	0.0081	18.0350	314.6905	123.8002	2232.7310	0.0554	0.0004	17.448	90
95	0.0062	18.0694	317.8602	161.8019	2923.6712	0.0553	0.0003	17.591	95
100	0.0047	18.0958	320.4174	211.4686	3826.7025	0.0553	0.0003	17.706	100

$I = 5.75\%$

n	(P/F)	(P/A)	(P/G)	(F/P)	(F/A)	(A/P)	(A/F)	(A/G)	n
1	0.9456	0.9456	0.0000	1.0575	1.0000	1.0575	1.0000	0.000	1
2	0.8942	1.8398	0.8942	1.1183	2.0575	0.5435	0.4860	0.486	2
3	0.8456	2.6854	2.5854	1.1826	3.1758	0.3724	0.3149	0.962	3
4	0.7996	3.4850	4.9842	1.2506	4.3584	0.2869	0.2294	1.430	4
5	0.7561	4.2412	8.0087	1.3225	5.6090	0.2358	0.1783	1.888	5
6	0.7150	4.9562	11.5838	1.3986	6.9315	0.2018	0.1443	2.337	6
7	0.6761	5.6323	15.6407	1.4790	8.3301	0.1775	0.1200	2.776	7
8	0.6394	6.2717	20.1163	1.5640	9.8091	0.1594	0.1019	3.207	8
9	0.6046	6.8763	24.9532	1.6540	11.3731	0.1454	0.0879	3.628	9
10	0.5717	7.4481	30.0989	1.7491	13.0271	0.1343	0.0768	4.041	10
11	0.5406	7.9887	35.5054	1.8496	14.7761	0.1252	0.0677	4.444	11
12	0.5113	8.5000	41.1291	1.9560	16.6257	0.1176	0.0601	4.838	12
13	0.4835	8.9834	46.9306	2.0684	18.5817	0.1113	0.0538	5.224	13
14	0.4572	9.4406	52.8737	2.1874	20.6502	0.1059	0.0484	5.600	14
15	0.4323	9.8729	58.9261	2.3132	22.8376	0.1013	0.0438	5.968	15
16	0.4088	10.2817	65.0581	2.4462	25.1507	0.0973	0.0398	6.327	16
17	0.3866	10.6683	71.2433	2.5868	27.5969	0.0937	0.0362	6.678	17
18	0.3656	11.0338	77.4578	2.7356	30.1837	0.0906	0.0331	7.020	18
19	0.3457	11.3795	83.6800	2.8929	32.9193	0.0879	0.0304	7.353	19
20	0.3269	11.7064	89.8908	3.0592	35.8121	0.0854	0.0279	7.678	20
21	0.3091	12.0155	96.0729	3.2351	38.8713	0.0832	0.0257	7.995	21
22	0.2923	12.3078	102.2113	3.4211	42.1064	0.0812	0.0237	8.304	22
23	0.2764	12.5842	108.2923	3.6178	45.5275	0.0795	0.0220	8.605	23
24	0.2614	12.8456	114.3040	3.8259	49.1454	0.0778	0.0203	8.898	24
25	0.2472	13.0927	120.2360	4.0458	52.9712	0.0764	0.0189	9.183	25
26	0.2337	13.3265	126.0792	4.2785	57.0171	0.0750	0.0175	9.460	26
27	0.2210	13.5475	131.8257	4.5245	61.2956	0.0738	0.0163	9.730	27
28	0.2090	13.7565	137.4687	4.7847	65.8201	0.0727	0.0152	9.993	28
29	0.1976	13.9541	143.0026	5.0598	70.6047	0.0717	0.0142	10.248	29
30	0.1869	14.1410	148.4224	5.3507	75.6645	0.0707	0.0132	10.495	30
31	0.1767	14.3178	153.7243	5.6584	81.0152	0.0698	0.0123	10.736	31
32	0.1671	14.4849	158.9050	5.9837	86.6736	0.0690	0.0115	10.970	32
33	0.1580	14.6429	163.9621	6.3278	92.6573	0.0683	0.0108	11.197	33
34	0.1494	14.7923	168.8936	6.6916	98.9851	0.0676	0.0101	11.417	34
35	0.1413	14.9337	173.6983	7.0764	105.6767	0.0670	0.0095	11.631	35
36	0.1336	15.0673	178.3754	7.4833	112.7532	0.0664	0.0089	11.838	36
37	0.1264	15.1937	182.9245	7.9136	120.2365	0.0658	0.0083	12.039	37
38	0.1195	15.3131	187.3458	8.3686	128.1501	0.0653	0.0078	12.234	38
39	0.1130	15.4261	191.6396	8.8498	136.5187	0.0648	0.0073	12.423	39
40	0.1069	15.5330	195.8069	9.3587	145.3685	0.0644	0.0069	12.605	40
41	0.1010	15.6340	199.8486	9.8968	154.7272	0.0640	0.0065	12.782	41
42	0.0955	15.7296	203.7661	10.4659	164.6240	0.0636	0.0061	12.954	42
43	0.0904	15.8199	207.5609	11.0677	175.0899	0.0632	0.0057	13.120	43
44	0.0854	15.9054	211.2349	11.7041	186.1576	0.0629	0.0054	13.280	44
45	0.0808	15.9862	214.7898	12.3770	197.8616	0.0626	0.0051	13.436	45
46	0.0764	16.0626	218.2279	13.0887	210.2387	0.0623	0.0048	13.586	46
47	0.0722	16.1348	221.5513	13.8413	223.3274	0.0620	0.0045	13.731	47
48	0.0683	16.2031	224.7623	14.6372	237.1687	0.0617	0.0042	13.871	48
49	0.0646	16.2678	227.8633	15.4788	251.8059	0.0615	0.0040	14.007	49
50	0.0611	16.3288	230.8568	16.3689	267.2848	0.0612	0.0037	14.138	50
51	0.0578	16.3866	233.7453	17.3101	283.6536	0.0610	0.0035	14.264	51
52	0.0546	16.4412	236.5313	18.3054	300.9637	0.0608	0.0033	14.386	52
53	0.0517	16.4929	239.2176	19.3580	319.2691	0.0606	0.0031	14.504	53
54	0.0488	16.5417	241.8066	20.4711	338.6271	0.0605	0.0030	14.618	54
55	0.0462	16.5879	244.3010	21.6481	359.0982	0.0603	0.0028	14.727	55
60	0.0349	16.7839	255.4462	28.6301	480.5231	0.0596	0.0021	15.219	60
65	0.0264	16.9320	264.6142	37.8638	641.1099	0.0591	0.0016	15.628	65
70	0.0200	17.0440	272.1064	50.0756	853.4890	0.0587	0.0012	15.964	70
75	0.0151	17.1287	278.1950	66.2260	1134.3644	0.0584	0.0009	16.241	75
80	0.0114	17.1927	283.1190	87.5851	1505.8273	0.0582	0.0007	16.467	80
85	0.0086	17.2412	287.0843	115.8329	1997.0941	0.0580	0.0005	16.651	85
90	0.0065	17.2778	290.2657	153.1912	2646.8036	0.0579	0.0004	16.799	90
95	0.0049	17.3055	292.8096	202.5983	3506.0568	0.0578	0.0003	16.920	95
100	0.0037	17.3264	294.8379	267.9400	4642.4353	0.0577	0.0002	17.016	100

EXPANDED INTEREST TABLES

$I = 6.00 \%$

n	(P/F)	(P/A)	(P/G)	(F/P)	(F/A)	(A/P)	(A/F)	(A/G)	n
1	0.9434	0.9434	0.0000	1.0600	1.0000	1.0600	1.0000	0.000	1
2	0.8900	1.8334	0.8900	1.1236	2.0600	0.5454	0.4854	0.485	2
3	0.8396	2.6730	2.5692	1.1910	3.1836	0.3741	0.3141	0.961	3
4	0.7921	3.4651	4.9455	1.2625	4.3746	0.2886	0.2286	1.427	4
5	0.7473	4.2124	7.9345	1.3382	5.6371	0.2374	0.1774	1.883	5
6	0.7050	4.9173	11.4594	1.4185	6.9753	0.2034	0.1434	2.330	6
7	0.6651	5.5824	15.4497	1.5036	8.3938	0.1791	0.1191	2.767	7
8	0.6274	6.2098	19.8416	1.5938	9.8975	0.1610	0.1010	3.195	8
9	0.5919	6.8017	24.5768	1.6895	11.4913	0.1470	0.0870	3.613	9
10	0.5584	7.3601	29.6023	1.7908	13.1808	0.1359	0.0759	4.022	10
11	0.5268	7.8869	34.8702	1.8983	14.9716	0.1268	0.0668	4.421	11
12	0.4970	8.3838	40.3369	2.0122	16.8699	0.1193	0.0593	4.811	12
13	0.4688	8.8527	45.9629	2.1329	18.8821	0.1130	0.0530	5.192	13
14	0.4423	9.2950	51.7128	2.2609	21.0151	0.1076	0.0476	5.563	14
15	0.4173	9.7122	57.5546	2.3966	23.2760	0.1030	0.0430	5.926	15
16	0.3936	10.1059	63.4592	2.5404	25.6725	0.0990	0.0390	6.279	16
17	0.3714	10.4773	69.4011	2.6928	28.2129	0.0954	0.0354	6.624	17
18	0.3503	10.8276	75.3569	2.8543	30.9057	0.0924	0.0324	6.959	18
19	0.3305	11.1581	81.3062	3.0256	33.7600	0.0896	0.0296	7.286	19
20	0.3118	11.4699	87.2304	3.2071	36.7856	0.0872	0.0272	7.605	20
21	0.2942	11.7641	93.1136	3.3996	39.9927	0.0850	0.0250	7.915	21
22	0.2775	12.0416	98.9412	3.6035	43.3923	0.0830	0.0230	8.216	22
23	0.2618	12.3034	104.7007	3.8197	46.9958	0.0813	0.0213	8.509	23
24	0.2470	12.5504	110.3812	4.0489	50.8156	0.0797	0.0197	8.795	24
25	0.2330	12.7834	115.9732	4.2919	54.8645	0.0782	0.0182	9.072	25
26	0.2198	13.0032	121.4684	4.5494	59.1564	0.0769	0.0169	9.341	26
27	0.2074	13.2105	ˋ126.8600	4.8223	63.7058	0.0757	0.0157	9.602	27
28	0.1956	13.4062	132.1420	5.1117	68.5281	0.0746	0.0146	9.856	28
29	0.1846	13.5907	137.3096	5.4184	73.6398	0.0736	0.0136	10.103	29
30	0.1741	13.7648	142.3588	5.7435	79.0582	0.0726	0.0126	10.342	30
31	0.1643	13.9291	147.2864	6.0881	84.8017	0.0718	0.0118	10.574	31
32	0.1550	14.0840	152.0901	6.4534	90.8898	0.0710	0.0110	10.798	32
33	0.1462	14.2302	156.7681	6.8406	97.3432	0.0703	0.0103	11.016	33
34	0.1379	14.3681	161.3192	7.2510	104.1838	0.0696	0.0096	11.227	34
35	0.1301	14.4982	165.7427	7.6861	111.4348	0.0690	0.0090	11.431	35
36	0.1227	14.6210	170.0387	8.1473	119.1209	0.0684	0.0084	11.629	36
37	0.1158	14.7368	174.2070	8.6361	127.2681	0.0679	0.0079	11.821	37
38	0.1092	14.8460	178.2490	9.1543	135.9042	0.0674	0.0074	12.006	38
39	0.1031	14.9491	182.1652	9.7035	145.0585	0.0669	0.0069	12.185	39
40	0.0972	15.0463	185.9568	10.2857	154.7620	0.0665	0.0065	12.359	40
41	0.0917	15.1380	189.6256	10.9029	165.0477	0.0661	0.0061	12.526	41
42	0.0865	15.2245	193.1732	11.5570	175.9505	0.0657	0.0057	12.688	42
43	0.0816	15.3062	196.6017	12.2505	187.5076	0.0653	0.0053	12.844	43
44	0.0770	15.3832	199.9130	12.9855	199.7580	0.0650	0.0050	12.995	44
45	0.0727	15.4558	203.1096	13.7646	212.7435	0.0647	0.0047	13.141	45
46	0.0685	15.5244	206.1938	14.5905	226.5081	0.0644	0.0044	13.281	46
47	0.0647	15.5890	209.1681	15.4659	241.0986	0.0641	0.0041	13.417	47
48	0.0610	15.6500	212.0351	16.3939	256.5645	0.0639	0.0039	13.548	48
49	0.0575	15.7076	214.7972	17.3775	272.9584	0.0637	0.0037	13.674	49
50	0.0543	15.7619	217.4574	18.4202	290.3359	0.0634	0.0034	13.796	50
51	0.0512	15.8131	220.0181	19.5254	308.7561	0.0632	0.0032	13.913	51
52	0.0483	15.8614	222.4823	20.6969	328.2814	0.0630	0.0030	14.026	52
53	0.0456	15.9070	224.8525	21.9387	348.9783	0.0629	0.0029	14.135	53
54	0.0430	15.9500	227.1316	23.2550	370.9170	0.0627	0.0027	14.240	54
55	0.0406	15.9905	229.3222	24.6503	394.1720	0.0625	0.0025	14.341	55
60	0.0303	16.1614	239.0428	32.9877	533.1282	0.0619	0.0019	14.790	60
65	0.0227	16.2891	246.9450	44.1450	719.0829	0.0614	0.0014	15.160	65
70	0.0169	16.3845	253.3271	59.0759	967.9322	0.0610	0.0010	15.461	70
75	0.0126	16.4558	258.4527	79.0569	1300.9487	0.0608	0.0008	15.705	75
80	0.0095	16.5091	262.5493	105.7960	1746.5999	0.0606	0.0006	15.903	80
85	0.0071	16.5489	265.8096	141.5789	2342.9817	0.0604	0.0004	16.062	85
90	0.0053	16.5787	268.3946	189.4645	3141.0752	0.0603	0.0003	16.189	90
95	0.0039	16.6009	270.4375	253.5463	4209.1042	0.0602	0.0002	16.290	95
100	0.0029	16.6175	272.0471	339.3021	5638.3681	0.0602	0.0002	16.371	100

I = 6.25 %

n	(P/F)	(P/A)	(P/G)	(F/P)	(F/A)	(A/P)	(A/F)	(A/G)	n
1	0.9412	0.9412	0.0000	1.0625	1.0000	1.0625	1.0000	0.000	1
2	0.8858	1.8270	0.8858	1.1289	2.0625	0.5473	0.4848	0.484	2
3	0.8337	2.6607	2.5532	1.1995	3.1914	0.3758	0.3133	0.959	3
4	0.7847	3.4454	4.9072	1.2744	4.3909	0.2902	0.2277	1.424	4
5	0.7385	4.1839	7.8613	1.3541	5.6653	0.2390	0.1765	1.878	5
6	0.6951	4.8789	11.3366	1.4387	7.0194	0.2050	0.1425	2.323	6
7	0.6542	5.5331	15.2617	1.5286	8.4581	0.1807	0.1182	2.758	7
8	0.6157	6.1488	19.5716	1.6242	9.9867	0.1626	0.1001	3.183	8
9	0.5795	6.7283	24.2074	1.7257	11.6109	0.1486	0.0861	3.597	9
10	0.5454	7.2737	29.1160	1.8335	13.3366	0.1375	0.0750	4.002	10
11	0.5133	7.7870	34.2491	1.9481	15.1701	0.1284	0.0659	4.398	11
12	0.4831	8.2701	39.5634	2.0699	17.1182	0.1209	0.0584	4.783	12
13	0.4547	8.7248	45.0198	2.1993	19.1881	0.1146	0.0521	5.160	13
14	0.4280	9.1528	50.5831	2.3367	21.3874	0.1093	0.0468	5.526	14
15	0.4028	9.5555	56.2220	2.4828	23.7241	0.1047	0.0422	5.883	15
16	0.3791	9.9346	61.9083	2.6379	26.2069	0.1007	0.0382	6.231	16
17	0.3568	10.2914	67.6169	2.8028	28.8448	0.0972	0.0347	6.570	17
18	0.3358	10.6272	73.3255	2.9780	31.6476	0.0941	0.0316	6.899	18
19	0.3160	10.9433	79.0143	3.1641	34.6256	0.0914	0.0289	7.220	19
20	0.2975	11.2407	84.6659	3.3619	37.7897	0.0890	0.0265	7.532	20
21	0.2800	11.5207	90.2651	3.5720	41.1515	0.0868	0.0243	7.835	21
22	0.2635	11.7842	95.7984	3.7952	44.7235	0.0849	0.0224	8.129	22
23	0.2480	12.0322	101.2542	4.0324	48.5187	0.0831	0.0206	8.415	23
24	0.2334	12.2656	106.6224	4.2844	52.5511	0.0815	0.0190	8.692	24
25	0.2197	12.4852	111.8946	4.5522	56.8356	0.0801	0.0176	8.962	25
26	0.2068	12.6920	117.0633	4.8367	61.3878	0.0788	0.0163	9.223	26
27	0.1946	12.8866	122.1227	5.1390	66.2245	0.0776	0.0151	9.476	27
28	0.1831	13.0697	127.0675	5.4602	71.3635	0.0765	0.0140	9.722	28
29	0.1724	13.2421	131.8939	5.8015	76.8238	0.0755	0.0130	9.960	29
30	0.1622	13.4043	136.5985	6.1641	82.6253	0.0746	0.0121	10.190	30
31	0.1527	13.5570	141.1792	6.5493	88.7893	0.0738	0.0113	10.413	31
32	0.1437	13.7007	145.6340	6.9587	95.3387	0.0730	0.0105	10.629	32
33	0.1353	13.8360	149.9621	7.3936	102.2973	0.0723	0.0098	10.838	33
34	0.1273	13.9633	154.1629	7.8557	109.6909	0.0716	0.0091	11.040	34
35	0.1198	14.0831	158.2364	8.3467	117.5466	0.0710	0.0085	11.235	35
36	0.1128	14.1958	162.1830	8.8683	125.8933	0.0704	0.0079	11.424	36
37	0.1061	14.3020	166.0036	9.4226	134.7616	0.0699	0.0074	11.607	37
38	0.0999	14.4018	169.6993	10.0115	144.1842	0.0694	0.0069	11.783	38
39	0.0940	14.4958	173.2717	10.6372	154.1957	0.0690	0.0065	11.953	39
40	0.0885	14.5843	176.7224	11.3021	164.8329	0.0686	0.0061	12.117	40
41	0.0833	14.6676	180.0534	12.0084	176.1350	0.0682	0.0057	12.275	41
42	0.0784	14.7460	183.2668	12.7590	188.1434	0.0678	0.0053	12.428	42
43	0.0738	14.8197	186.3650	13.5564	200.9024	0.0675	0.0050	12.575	43
44	0.0694	14.8892	189.3503	14.4037	214.4588	0.0672	0.0047	12.717	44
45	0.0653	14.9545	192.2254	15.3039	228.8625	0.0669	0.0044	12.854	45
46	0.0615	15.0160	194.9929	16.2604	244.1664	0.0666	0.0041	12.985	46
47	0.0579	15.0739	197.6554	17.2767	260.4268	0.0663	0.0038	13.112	47
48	0.0545	15.1284	200.2158	18.3565	277.7034	0.0661	0.0036	13.234	48
49	0.0513	15.1796	202.6769	19.5037	296.0599	0.0659	0.0034	13.351	49
50	0.0483	15.2279	205.0415	20.7227	315.5637	0.0657	0.0032	13.464	50
51	0.0454	15.2733	207.3123	22.0179	336.2864	0.0655	0.0030	13.573	51
52	0.0427	15.3161	209.4924	23.3940	358.3043	0.0653	0.0028	13.678	52
53	0.0402	15.3563	211.5844	24.8561	381.6983	0.0651	0.0026	13.778	53
54	0.0379	15.3942	213.5913	26.4097	406.5544	0.0650	0.0025	13.874	54
55	0.0356	15.4298	215.5157	28.0603	432.9641	0.0648	0.0023	13.967	55
60	0.0263	15.5789	223.9965	37.9959	591.9338	0.0642	0.0017	14.378	60
65	0.0194	15.6890	230.8102	51.4495	807.1917	0.0637	0.0012	14.711	65
70	0.0144	15.7703	236.2488	69.6668	1098.6684	0.0634	0.0009	14.980	70
75	0.0106	15.8304	240.5656	94.3345	1493.3515	0.0632	0.0007	15.196	75
80	0.0078	15.8747	243.9752	127.7365	2027.7844	0.0630	0.0005	15.368	80
85	0.0058	15.9075	246.6571	172.9656	2751.4499	0.0629	0.0004	15.505	85
90	0.0043	15.9317	248.7586	234.2095	3731.3518	0.0628	0.0003	15.614	90
95	0.0032	15.9495	250.3999	317.1387	5058.2185	0.0627	0.0002	15.699	95
100	0.0023	15.9627	251.6780	429.4315	6854.9036	0.0626	0.0001	15.766	100

$I = 6.50 \%$

n	(P/F)	(P/A)	(P/G)	(F/P)	(F/A)	(A/P)	(A/F)	(A/G)	n
1	0.9390	0.9390	0.0000	1.0650	1.0000	1.0650	1.0000	0.000	1
2	0.8817	1.8206	0.8817	1.1342	2.0650	0.5493	0.4843	0.484	2
3	0.8278	2.6485	2.5374	1.2079	3.1992	0.3776	0.3126	0.958	3
4	0.7773	3.4258	4.8693	1.2865	4.4072	0.2919	0.2269	1.421	4
5	0.7299	4.1557	7.7889	1.3701	5.6936	0.2406	0.1756	1.874	5
6	0.6853	4.8410	11.2155	1.4591	7.0637	0.2066	0.1416	2.316	6
7	0.6435	5.4845	15.0766	1.5540	8.5229	0.1823	0.1173	2.748	7
8	0.6042	6.0888	19.3062	1.6550	10.0769	0.1642	0.0992	3.170	8
9	0.5674	6.6561	23.8450	1.7626	11.7319	0.1502	0.0852	3.582	9
10	0.5327	7.1888	28.6395	1.8771	13.4944	0.1391	0.0741	3.983	10
11	0.5002	7.6890	33.6417	1.9992	15.3716	0.1301	0.0651	4.375	11
12	0.4697	8.1587	38.8082	2.1291	17.3707	0.1226	0.0576	4.756	12
13	0.4410	8.5997	44.1004	2.2675	19.4998	0.1163	0.0513	5.128	13
14	0.4141	9.0138	49.4837	2.4149	21.7673	0.1109	0.0459	5.489	14
15	0.3888	9.4027	54.9272	2.5718	24.1822	0.1064	0.0414	5.841	15
16	0.3651	9.7678	60.4037	2.7390	26.7540	0.1024	0.0374	6.184	16
17	0.3428	10.1106	65.8887	2.9170	29.4930	0.0989	0.0339	6.516	17
18	0.3219	10.4325	71.3608	3.1067	32.4101	0.0959	0.0309	6.840	18
19	0.3022	10.7347	76.8012	3.3086	35.5167	0.0932	0.0282	7.154	19
20	0.2838	11.0185	82.1933	3.5236	38.8253	0.0908	0.0258	7.459	20
21	0.2665	11.2850	87.5229	3.7527	42.3490	0.0886	0.0236	7.755	21
22	0.2502	11.5352	92.7773	3.9966	46.1016	0.0867	0.0217	8.043	22
23	0.2349	11.7701	97.9460	4.2564	50.0982	0.0850	0.0200	8.321	23
24	0.2206	11.9907	103.0199	4.5331	54.3546	0.0834	0.0184	8.591	24
25	0.2071	12.1979	107.9912	4.8277	58.8877	0.0820	0.0170	8.853	25
26	0.1945	12.3924	112.8536	5.1415	63.7154	0.0807	0.0157	9.106	26
27	0.1826	12.5750	117.6018	5.4757	68.8569	0.0795	0.0145	9.352	27
28	0.1715	12.7465	122.2318	5.8316	74.3326	0.0785	0.0135	9.589	28
29	0.1610	12.9075	126.7401	6.2107	80.1642	0.0775	0.0125	9.819	29
30	0.1512	13.0587	131.1245	6.6144	86.3749	0.0766	0.0116	10.041	30
31	0.1420	13.2006	135.3833	7.0443	92.9892	0.0758	0.0108	10.255	31
32	0.1333	13.3339	139.5154	7.5022	100.0335	0.0750	0.0100	10.463	32
33	0.1252	13.4591	143.5205	7.9898	107.5357	0.0743	0.0093	10.663	33
34	0.1175	13.5766	147.3987	8.5092	115.5255	0.0737	0.0087	10.856	34
35	0.1103	13.6870	151.1505	9.0623	124.0347	0.0731	0.0081	11.043	35
36	0.1036	13.7906	154.7770	9.6513	133.0969	0.0725	0.0075	11.223	36
37	0.0973	13.8879	158.2794	10.2786	142.7482	0.0720	0.0070	11.397	37
38	0.0914	13.9792	161.6594	10.9467	153.0269	0.0715	0.0065	11.564	38
39	0.0858	14.0650	164.9189	11.6583	163.9736	0.0711	0.0061	11.725	39
40	0.0805	14.1455	168.0599	12.4161	175.6319	0.0707	0.0057	11.880	40
41	0.0756	14.2212	171.0850	13.2231	188.0480	0.0703	0.0053	12.030	41
42	0.0710	14.2922	173.9963	14.0826	201.2711	0.0700	0.0050	12.174	42
43	0.0667	14.3588	176.7967	14.9980	215.3537	0.0696	0.0046	12.312	43
44	0.0626	14.4214	179.4888	15.9729	230.3517	0.0693	0.0043	12.446	44
45	0.0588	14.4802	182.0753	17.0111	246.3246	0.0691	0.0041	12.574	45
46	0.0552	14.5354	184.5592	18.1168	263.3357	0.0688	0.0038	12.697	46
47	0.0518	14.5873	186.9433	19.2944	281.4525	0.0686	0.0036	12.815	47
48	0.0487	14.6359	189.2306	20.5485	300.7469	0.0683	0.0033	12.929	48
49	0.0457	14.6816	191.4239	21.8842	321.2955	0.0681	0.0031	13.038	49
50	0.0429	14.7245	193.5264	23.3067	343.1797	0.0679	0.0029	13.143	50
51	0.0403	14.7648	195.5407	24.8216	366.4864	0.0677	0.0027	13.243	51
52	0.0378	14.8026	197.4700	26.4350	391.3080	0.0676	0.0026	13.340	52
53	0.0355	14.8382	199.3170	28.1533	417.7430	0.0674	0.0024	13.432	53
54	0.0334	14.8715	201.0847	29.9833	445.8963	0.0672	0.0022	13.521	54
55	0.0313	14.9028	202.7758	31.9322	475.8795	0.0671	0.0021	13.606	55
60	0.0229	15.0330	210.1774	43.7498	657.6898	0.0665	0.0015	13.981	60
65	0.0167	15.1280	216.0547	59.9411	906.7857	0.0661	0.0011	14.281	65
70	0.0122	15.1973	220.6910	82.1245	1248.0687	0.0658	0.0008	14.521	70
75	0.0089	15.2479	224.3280	112.5176	1715.6559	0.0656	0.0006	14.712	75
80	0.0065	15.2848	227.1673	154.1589	2356.2909	0.0654	0.0004	14.862	80
85	0.0047	15.3118	229.3744	211.2111	3234.0163	0.0653	0.0003	14.980	85
90	0.0035	15.3315	231.0837	289.3775	4436.5763	0.0652	0.0002	15.072	90
95	0.0025	15.3458	232.4031	396.4722	6084.1877	0.0652	0.0002	15.144	95
100	0.0018	15.3563	233.4185	543.2013	8341.5580	0.0651	0.0001	15.200	100

PROFESSIONAL PUBLICATIONS, INC. • Belmont, CA

$I = 6.75\%$

n	(P/F)	(P/A)	(P/G)	(F/P)	(F/A)	(A/P)	(A/F)	(A/G)	n
1	0.9368	0.9368	0.0000	1.0675	1.0000	1.0675	1.0000	0.000	1
2	0.8775	1.8143	0.8775	1.1396	2.0675	0.5512	0.4837	0.483	2
3	0.8220	2.6363	2.5216	1.2165	3.2071	0.3793	0.3118	0.956	3
4	0.7701	3.4064	4.8318	1.2986	4.4235	0.2936	0.2261	1.418	4
5	0.7214	4.1278	7.7173	1.3862	5.7221	0.2423	0.1748	1.869	5
6	0.6758	4.8036	11.0961	1.4798	7.1084	0.2082	0.1407	2.310	6
7	0.6330	5.4366	14.8943	1.5797	8.5882	0.1839	0.1164	2.739	7
8	0.5930	6.0296	19.0453	1.6863	10.1679	0.1658	0.0983	3.158	8
9	0.5555	6.5851	23.4894	1.8002	11.8542	0.1519	0.0844	3.567	9
10	0.5204	7.1055	28.1728	1.9217	13.6544	0.1407	0.0732	3.964	10
11	0.4875	7.5929	33.0476	2.0514	15.5760	0.1317	0.0642	4.352	11
12	0.4567	8.0496	38.0707	2.1899	17.6274	0.1242	0.0567	4.729	12
13	0.4278	8.4774	43.2041	2.3377	19.8173	0.1180	0.0505	5.096	13
14	0.4007	8.8781	48.4135	2.4955	22.1549	0.1126	0.0451	5.453	14
15	0.3754	9.2535	53.6690	2.6639	24.6504	0.1081	0.0406	5.799	15
16	0.3517	9.6051	58.9438	2.8437	27.3143	0.1041	0.0366	6.136	16
17	0.3294	9.9346	64.2144	3.0357	30.1580	0.1007	0.0332	6.463	17
18	0.3086	10.2432	69.4604	3.2406	33.1937	0.0976	0.0301	6.781	18
19	0.2891	10.5322	74.6638	3.4593	36.4343	0.0949	0.0274	7.089	19
20	0.2708	10.8030	79.8089	3.6928	39.8936	0.0926	0.0251	7.387	20
21	0.2537	11.0567	84.8824	3.9421	43.5864	0.0904	0.0229	7.677	21
22	0.2376	11.2943	89.8726	4.2082	47.5285	0.0885	0.0210	7.957	22
23	0.2226	11.5169	94.7700	4.4922	51.7366	0.0868	0.0193	8.228	23
24	0.2085	11.7255	99.5662	4.7954	56.2289	0.0853	0.0178	8.491	24
25	0.1953	11.9208	104.2545	5.1191	61.0243	0.0839	0.0164	8.745	25
26	0.1830	12.1038	108.8293	5.4647	66.1435	0.0826	0.0151	8.991	26
27	0.1714	12.2752	113.2863	5.8335	71.6081	0.0815	0.0140	9.228	27
28	0.1606	12.4358	117.6220	6.2273	77.4417	0.0804	0.0129	9.458	28
29	0.1504	12.5862	121.8341	6.6477	83.6690	0.0795	0.0120	9.679	29
30	0.1409	12.7272	125.9207	7.0964	90.3167	0.0786	0.0111	9.893	30
31	0.1320	12.8592	129.8809	7.5754	97.4130	0.0778	0.0103	10.100	31
32	0.1237	12.9828	133.7143	8.0867	104.9884	0.0770	0.0095	10.299	32
33	0.1158	13.0987	137.4212	8.6326	113.0751	0.0763	0.0088	10.491	33
34	0.1085	13.2072	141.0022	9.2153	121.7077	0.0757	0.0082	10.676	34
35	0.1017	13.3088	144.4584	9.8373	130.9230	0.0751	0.0076	10.854	35
36	0.0952	13.4041	147.7913	10.5013	140.7603	0.0746	0.0071	11.025	36
37	0.0892	13.4933	151.0027	11.2102	151.2616	0.0741	0.0066	11.191	37
38	0.0836	13.5768	154.0946	11.9668	162.4717	0.0737	0.0062	11.349	38
39	0.0783	13.6551	157.0693	12.7746	174.4386	0.0732	0.0057	11.502	39
40	0.0733	13.7284	159.9291	13.6369	187.2132	0.0728	0.0053	11.649	40
41	0.0687	13.7971	162.6769	14.5574	200.8501	0.0725	0.0050	11.790	41
42	0.0644	13.8615	165.3152	15.5400	215.4075	0.0721	0.0046	11.926	42
43	0.0603	13.9218	167.8470	16.5890	230.9475	0.0718	0.0043	12.056	43
44	0.0565	13.9782	170.2752	17.7087	247.5364	0.0715	0.0040	12.181	44
45	0.0529	14.0311	172.6028	18.9040	265.2451	0.0713	0.0038	12.301	45
46	0.0496	14.0807	174.8327	20.1801	284.1492	0.0710	0.0035	12.416	46
47	0.0464	14.1271	176.9680	21.5422	304.3292	0.0708	0.0033	12.526	47
48	0.0435	14.1706	179.0118	22.9963	325.8715	0.0706	0.0031	12.632	48
49	0.0407	14.2113	180.9671	24.5486	348.8678	0.0704	0.0029	12.734	49
50	0.0382	14.2495	182.8370	26.2056	373.4164	0.0702	0.0027	12.831	50
51	0.0357	14.2852	184.6243	27.9745	399.6220	0.0700	0.0025	12.924	51
52	0.0335	14.3187	186.3321	29.8628	427.5965	0.0698	0.0023	13.013	52
53	0.0314	14.3501	187.9633	31.8785	457.4592	0.0697	0.0022	13.098	53
54	0.0294	14.3795	189.5208	34.0303	489.3377	0.0695	0.0020	13.180	54
55	0.0275	14.4070	191.0072	36.3273	523.3680	0.0694	0.0019	13.257	55
60	0.0199	14.5206	197.4692	50.3585	731.2374	0.0689	0.0014	13.599	60
65	0.0143	14.6026	202.5405	69.8092	1019.3950	0.0685	0.0010	13.870	65
70	0.0103	14.6617	206.4945	96.7725	1418.8515	0.0682	0.0007	14.083	70
75	0.0075	14.7044	209.5601	134.1502	1972.5953	0.0680	0.0005	14.251	75
80	0.0054	14.7352	211.9254	185.9648	2740.2189	0.0679	0.0004	14.382	80
85	0.0039	14.7573	213.7426	257.7924	3804.3319	0.0678	0.0003	14.483	85
90	0.0028	14.7734	215.1335	357.3630	5279.4512	0.0677	0.0002	14.562	90
95	0.0020	14.7849	216.1947	495.3920	7324.3253	0.0676	0.0001	14.622	95
100	0.0015	14.7932	217.0019	686.7337	10159.0180	0.0676	0.0001	14.669	100

EXPANDED INTEREST TABLES

$I = 7.00\%$

n	(P/F)	(P/A)	(P/G)	(F/P)	(F/A)	(A/P)	(A/F)	(A/G)	n
1	0.9346	0.9346	0.0000	1.0700	1.0000	1.0700	1.0000	0.000	1
2	0.8734	1.8080	0.8734	1.1449	2.0700	0.5531	0.4831	0.483	2
3	0.8163	2.6243	2.5060	1.2250	3.2149	0.3811	0.3111	0.954	3
4	0.7629	3.3872	4.7947	1.3108	4.4399	0.2952	0.2252	1.415	4
5	0.7130	4.1002	7.6467	1.4026	5.7507	0.2439	0.1739	1.865	5
6	0.6663	4.7665	10.9784	1.5007	7.1533	0.2098	0.1398	2.303	6
7	0.6227	5.3893	14.7149	1.6058	8.6540	0.1856	0.1156	2.730	7
8	0.5820	5.9713	18.7889	1.7182	10.2598	0.1675	0.0975	3.146	8
9	0.5439	6.5152	23.1404	1.8385	11.9780	0.1535	0.0835	3.551	9
10	0.5083	7.0236	27.7156	1.9672	13.8164	0.1424	0.0724	3.946	10
11	0.4751	7.4987	32.4665	2.1049	15.7836	0.1334	0.0634	4.329	11
12	0.4440	7.9427	37.3506	2.2522	17.8885	0.1259	0.0559	4.702	12
13	0.4150	8.3577	42.3302	2.4098	20.1406	0.1197	0.0497	5.064	13
14	0.3878	8.7455	47.3718	2.5785	22.5505	0.1143	0.0443	5.416	14
15	0.3624	9.1079	52.4461	2.7590	25.1290	0.1098	0.0398	5.758	15
16	0.3387	9.4466	57.5271	2.9522	27.8881	0.1059	0.0359	6.089	16
17	0.3166	9.7632	62.5923	3.1588	30.8402	0.1024	0.0324	6.411	17
18	0.2959	10.0591	67.6219	3.3799	33.9990	0.0994	0.0294	6.722	18
19	0.2765	10.3356	72.5991	3.6165	37.3790	0.0968	0.0268	7.024	19
20	0.2584	10.5940	77.5091	3.8697	40.9955	0.0944	0.0244	7.316	20
21	0.2415	10.8355	82.3393	4.1406	44.8652	0.0923	0.0223	7.599	21
22	0.2257	11.0612	87.0793	4.4304	49.0057	0.0904	0.0204	7.872	22
23	0.2109	11.2722	91.7201	4.7405	53.4361	0.0887	0.0187	8.136	23
24	0.1971	11.4693	96.2545	5.0724	58.1767	0.0872	0.0172	8.392	24
25	0.1842	11.6536	100.6765	5.4274	63.2490	0.0858	0.0158	8.639	25
26	0.1722	11.8258	104.9814	5.8074	68.6765	0.0846	0.0146	8.877	26
27	0.1609	11.9867	109.1656	6.2139	74.4838	0.0834	0.0134	9.107	27
28	0.1504	12.1371	113.2264	6.6488	80.6977	0.0824	0.0124	9.328	28
29	0.1406	12.2777	117.1622	7.1143	87.3465	0.0814	0.0114	9.542	29
30	0.1314	12.4090	120.9718	7.6123	94.4608	0.0806	0.0106	9.748	30
31	0.1228	12.5318	124.6550	8.1451	102.0730	0.0798	0.0098	9.947	31
32	0.1147	12.6466	128.2120	8.7153	110.2182	0.0791	0.0091	10.138	32
33	0.1072	12.7538	131.6435	9.3253	118.9334	0.0784	0.0084	10.321	33
34	0.1002	12.8540	134.9507	9.9781	128.2588	0.0778	0.0078	10.498	34
35	0.0937	12.9477	138.1353	10.6766	138.2369	0.0772	0.0072	10.668	35
36	0.0875	13.0352	141.1990	11.4239	148.9135	0.0767	0.0067	10.832	36
37	0.0818	13.1170	144.1441	12.2236	160.3374	0.0762	0.0062	10.989	37
38	0.0765	13.1935	146.9730	13.0793	172.5610	0.0758	0.0058	11.139	38
39	0.0715	13.2649	149.6883	13.9948	185.6403	0.0754	0.0054	11.284	39
40	0.0668	13.3317	152.2928	14.9745	199.6351	0.0750	0.0050	11.423	40
41	0.0624	13.3941	154.7892	16.0227	214.6096	0.0747	0.0047	11.556	41
42	0.0583	13.4524	157.1807	17.1443	230.6322	0.0743	0.0043	11.684	42
43	0.0545	13.5070	159.4702	18.3444	247.7765	0.0740	0.0040	11.806	43
44	0.0509	13.5579	161.6609	19.6285	266.1209	0.0738	0.0038	11.923	44
45	0.0476	13.6055	163.7559	21.0025	285.7493	0.0735	0.0035	12.036	45
46	0.0445	13.6500	165.7584	22.4726	306.7518	0.0733	0.0033	12.143	46
47	0.0416	13.6916	167.6714	24.0457	329.2244	0.0730	0.0030	12.246	47
48	0.0389	13.7305	169.4981	25.7289	353.2701	0.0728	0.0028	12.344	48
49	0.0363	13.7668	171.2417	27.5299	378.9990	0.0726	0.0026	12.438	49
50	0.0339	13.8007	172.9051	29.4570	406.5289	0.0725	0.0025	12.528	50
51	0.0317	13.8325	174.4915	31.5190	435.9860	0.0723	0.0023	12.614	51
52	0.0297	13.8621	176.0037	33.7253	467.5050	0.0721	0.0021	12.696	52
53	0.0277	13.8898	177.4447	36.0861	501.2303	0.0720	0.0020	12.775	53
54	0.0259	13.9157	178.8173	38.6122	537.3164	0.0719	0.0019	12.850	54
55	0.0242	13.9399	180.1243	41.3150	575.9286	0.0717	0.0017	12.921	55
60	0.0173	14.0392	185.7677	57.9464	813.5204	0.0712	0.0012	13.232	60
65	0.0123	14.1099	190.1452	81.2729	1146.7552	0.0709	0.0009	13.476	65
70	0.0088	14.1604	193.5185	113.9894	1614.1342	0.0706	0.0006	13.666	70
75	0.0063	14.1964	196.1035	159.8760	2269.6574	0.0704	0.0004	13.813	75
80	0.0045	14.2220	198.0748	224.2344	3189.0627	0.0703	0.0003	13.927	80
85	0.0032	14.2403	199.5717	314.5003	4478.5761	0.0702	0.0002	14.014	85
90	0.0023	14.2533	200.7042	441.1030	6287.1854	0.0702	0.0002	14.081	90
95	0.0016	14.2626	201.5581	618.6697	8823.8535	0.0701	0.0001	14.131	95
100	0.0012	14.2693	202.2001	867.7163	12381.6618	0.0701	0.0001	14.170	100

$I = 7.25 \%$

n	(P/F)	(P/A)	(P/G)	(F/P)	(F/A)	(A/P)	(A/F)	(A/G)	n
1	0.9324	0.9324	0.0000	1.0725	1.0000	1.0725	1.0000	0.000	1
2	0.8694	1.8018	0.8694	1.1503	2.0725	0.5550	0.4825	0.482	2
3	0.8106	2.6124	2.4906	1.2336	3.2228	0.3828	0.3103	0.953	3
4	0.7558	3.3682	4.7580	1.3231	4.4564	0.2969	0.2244	1.412	4
5	0.7047	4.0729	7.5769	1.4190	5.7795	0.2455	0.1730	1.860	5
6	0.6571	4.7300	10.8622	1.5219	7.1985	0.2114	0.1389	2.296	6
7	0.6127	5.3426	14.5382	1.6322	8.7204	0.1872	0.1147	2.721	7
8	0.5712	5.9139	18.5369	1.7506	10.3526	0.1691	0.0966	3.134	8
9	0.5326	6.4465	22.7979	1.8775	12.1032	0.1551	0.0826	3.536	9
10	0.4966	6.9431	27.2675	2.0136	13.9807	0.1440	0.0715	3.927	10
11	0.4631	7.4062	31.8981	2.1596	15.9943	0.1350	0.0625	4.307	11
12	0.4318	7.8379	36.6473	2.3162	18.1539	0.1276	0.0551	4.675	12
13	0.4026	8.2405	41.4781	2.4841	20.4700	0.1214	0.0489	5.033	13
14	0.3754	8.6158	46.3576	2.6642	22.9541	0.1161	0.0436	5.380	14
15	0.3500	8.9658	51.2573	2.8573	25.6183	0.1115	0.0390	5.717	15
16	0.3263	9.2921	56.1521	3.0645	28.4756	0.1076	0.0351	6.043	16
17	0.3043	9.5964	61.0203	3.2867	31.5401	0.1042	0.0317	6.358	17
18	0.2837	9.8801	65.8431	3.5249	34.8267	0.1012	0.0287	6.664	18
19	0.2645	10.1446	70.6044	3.7805	38.3517	0.0986	0.0261	6.959	19
20	0.2466	10.3912	75.2904	4.0546	42.1322	0.0962	0.0237	7.245	20
21	0.2300	10.6212	79.8897	4.3485	46.1867	0.0942	0.0217	7.521	21
22	0.2144	10.8356	84.3924	4.6638	50.5353	0.0923	0.0198	7.788	22
23	0.1999	11.0355	88.7907	5.0019	55.1991	0.0906	0.0181	8.045	23
24	0.1864	11.2220	93.0781	5.3646	60.2010	0.0891	0.0166	8.294	24
25	0.1738	11.3958	97.2495	5.7535	65.5656	0.0878	0.0153	8.533	25
26	0.1621	11.5578	101.3009	6.1706	71.3191	0.0865	0.0140	8.764	26
27	0.1511	11.7089	105.2296	6.6180	77.4897	0.0854	0.0129	8.987	27
28	0.1409	11.8498	109.0336	7.0978	84.1077	0.0844	0.0119	9.201	28
29	0.1314	11.9812	112.7118	7.6124	91.2055	0.0835	0.0110	9.407	29
30	0.1225	12.1037	116.2638	8.1643	98.8179	0.0826	0.0101	9.605	30
31	0.1142	12.2179	119.6900	8.7562	106.9823	0.0818	0.0093	9.796	31
32	0.1065	12.3244	122.9910	9.3910	115.7385	0.0811	0.0086	9.979	32
33	0.0993	12.4236	126.1682	10.0719	125.1295	0.0805	0.0080	10.155	33
34	0.0926	12.5162	129.2231	10.8021	135.2014	0.0799	0.0074	10.324	34
35	0.0863	12.6025	132.1579	11.5853	146.0035	0.0793	0.0068	10.486	35
36	0.0805	12.6830	134.9748	12.4252	157.5887	0.0788	0.0063	10.642	36
37	0.0750	12.7581	137.6762	13.3260	170.0139	0.0784	0.0059	10.791	37
38	0.0700	12.8280	140.2651	14.2921	183.3399	0.0780	0.0055	10.934	38
39	0.0652	12.8933	142.7441	15.3283	197.6321	0.0776	0.0051	11.071	39
40	0.0608	12.9541	145.1165	16.4396	212.9604	0.0772	0.0047	11.202	40
41	0.0567	13.0108	147.3851	17.6315	229.4000	0.0769	0.0044	11.327	41
42	0.0529	13.0637	149.5533	18.9098	247.0315	0.0765	0.0040	11.448	42
43	0.0493	13.1130	151.6242	20.2807	265.9413	0.0763	0.0038	11.562	43
44	0.0460	13.1590	153.6012	21.7511	286.2221	0.0760	0.0035	11.672	44
45	0.0429	13.2018	155.4873	23.3281	307.9732	0.0757	0.0032	11.777	45
46	0.0400	13.2418	157.2859	25.0193	331.3012	0.0755	0.0030	11.878	46
47	0.0373	13.2791	159.0002	26.8332	356.3206	0.0753	0.0028	11.973	47
48	0.0347	13.3138	160.6334	28.7787	383.1538	0.0751	0.0026	12.065	48
49	0.0324	13.3462	162.1885	30.8651	411.9325	0.0749	0.0024	12.152	49
50	0.0302	13.3764	163.6687	33.1028	442.7976	0.0748	0.0023	12.235	50
51	0.0282	13.4046	165.0771	35.5028	475.9004	0.0746	0.0021	12.315	51
52	0.0263	13.4309	166.4165	38.0767	511.4032	0.0745	0.0020	12.390	52
53	0.0245	13.4553	167.6898	40.8373	549.4799	0.0743	0.0018	12.462	53
54	0.0228	13.4782	168.8999	43.7980	590.3172	0.0742	0.0017	12.531	54
55	0.0213	13.4995	170.0495	46.9734	634.1152	0.0741	0.0016	12.596	55
60	0.0150	13.5862	174.9797	66.6558	905.5975	0.0736	0.0011	12.879	60
65	0.0106	13.6473	178.7596	94.5855	1290.8345	0.0733	0.0008	13.098	65
70	0.0075	13.6903	181.6386	134.2181	1837.4909	0.0730	0.0005	13.267	70
75	0.0053	13.7207	183.8192	190.4573	2613.2038	0.0729	0.0004	13.397	75
80	0.0037	13.7421	185.4629	270.2614	3713.9507	0.0728	0.0003	13.496	80
85	0.0026	13.7571	186.6965	383.5046	5275.9255	0.0727	0.0002	13.570	85
90	0.0018	13.7678	187.6190	544.1982	7492.3886	0.0726	0.0001	13.627	90
95	0.0013	13.7752	188.3065	772.2245	10637.5794	0.0726	0.0001	13.669	95
100	0.0009	13.7805	188.8174	1095.7969	15100.6475	0.0726	0.0001	13.701	100

EXPANDED INTEREST TABLES

I = 7.50 %

n	(P/F)	(P/A)	(P/G)	(F/P)	(F/A)	(A/P)	(A/F)	(A/G)	n
1	0.9302	0.9302	0.0000	1.0750	1.0000	1.0750	1.0000	0.000	1
2	0.8653	1.7956	0.8653	1.1556	2.0750	0.5569	0.4819	0.481	2
3	0.8050	2.6005	2.4753	1.2423	3.2306	0.3845	0.3095	0.951	3
4	0.7488	3.3493	4.7217	1.3355	4.4729	0.2986	0.2236	1.409	4
5	0.6966	4.0459	7.5079	1.4356	5.8084	0.2472	0.1722	1.855	5
6	0.6480	4.6938	10.7477	1.5433	7.2440	0.2130	0.1380	2.289	6
7	0.6028	5.2966	14.3642	1.6590	8.7873	0.1888	0.1138	2.712	7
8	0.5607	5.8573	18.2891	1.7835	10.4464	0.1707	0.0957	3.122	8
9	0.5216	6.3789	22.4618	1.9172	12.2298	0.1568	0.0818	3.521	9
10	0.4852	6.8641	26.8286	2.0610	14.1471	0.1457	0.0707	3.908	10
11	0.4513	7.3154	31.3420	2.2156	16.2081	0.1367	0.0617	4.284	11
12	0.4199	7.7353	35.9604	2.3818	18.4237	0.1293	0.0543	4.648	12
13	0.3906	8.1258	40.6471	2.5604	20.8055	0.1231	0.0481	5.002	13
14	0.3633	8.4892	45.3702	2.7524	23.3659	0.1178	0.0428	5.344	14
15	0.3380	8.8271	50.1017	2.9589	26.1184	0.1133	0.0383	5.675	15
16	0.3144	9.1415	54.8175	3.1808	29.0772	0.1094	0.0344	5.996	16
17	0.2925	9.4340	59.4968	3.4194	32.2580	0.1060	0.0310	6.306	17
18	0.2720	9.7060	64.1216	3.6758	35.6774	0.1030	0.0280	6.606	18
19	0.2531	9.9591	68.6769	3.9515	39.3532	0.1004	0.0254	6.895	19
20	0.2354	10.1945	73.1497	4.2479	43.3047	0.0981	0.0231	7.175	20
21	0.2190	10.4135	77.5295	4.5664	47.5525	0.0960	0.0210	7.445	21
22	0.2037	10.6172	81.8074	4.9089	52.1190	0.0942	0.0192	7.705	22
23	0.1895	10.8067	85.9764	5.2771	57.0279	0.0925	0.0175	7.955	23
24	0.1763	10.9830	90.0308	5.6729	62.3050	0.0911	0.0161	8.197	24
25	0.1640	11.1469	93.9663	6.0983	67.9779	0.0897	0.0147	8.429	25
26	0.1525	11.2995	97.7797	6.5557	74.0762	0.0885	0.0135	8.653	26
27	0.1419	11.4414	101.4690	7.0474	80.6319	0.0874	0.0124	8.868	27
28	0.1320	11.5734	105.0329	7.5759	87.6793	0.0864	0.0114	9.075	28
29	0.1228	11.6962	108.4710	8.1441	95.2553	0.0855	0.0105	9.274	29
30	0.1142	11.8104	111.7834	8.7550	103.3994	0.0847	0.0097	9.464	30
31	0.1063	11.9166	114.9710	9.4116	112.1544	0.0839	0.0089	9.647	31
32	0.0988	12.0155	118.0350	10.1174	121.5659	0.0832	0.0082	9.823	32
33	0.0919	12.1074	120.9772	10.8763	131.6834	0.0826	0.0076	9.992	33
34	0.0855	12.1929	123.7996	11.6920	142.5596	0.0820	0.0070	10.153	34
35	0.0796	12.2725	126.5047	12.5689	154.2516	0.0815	0.0065	10.308	35
36	0.0740	12.3465	129.0951	13.5115	166.8205	0.0810	0.0060	10.456	36
37	0.0688	12.4154	131.5736	14.5249	180.3320	0.0805	0.0055	10.597	37
38	0.0640	12.4794	133.9432	15.6143	194.8569	0.0801	0.0051	10.733	38
39	0.0596	12.5390	136.2071	16.7853	210.4712	0.0798	0.0048	10.862	39
40	0.0554	12.5944	138.3685	18.0442	227.2565	0.0794	0.0044	10.986	40
41	0.0516	12.6460	140.4306	19.3976	245.3008	0.0791	0.0041	11.104	41
42	0.0480	12.6939	142.3968	20.8524	264.6983	0.0788	0.0038	11.217	42
43	0.0446	12.7385	144.2704	22.4163	285.5507	0.0785	0.0035	11.325	43
44	0.0415	12.7800	146.0548	24.0975	307.9670	0.0782	0.0032	11.428	44
45	0.0386	12.8186	147.7534	25.9048	332.0645	0.0780	0.0030	11.526	45
46	0.0359	12.8545	149.3693	27.8477	357.9694	0.0778	0.0028	11.620	46
47	0.0334	12.8879	150.9059	29.9363	385.8171	0.0776	0.0026	11.709	47
48	0.0311	12.9190	152.3664	32.1815	415.7533	0.0774	0.0024	11.794	48
49	0.0289	12.9479	153.7538	34.5951	447.9348	0.0772	0.0022	11.874	49
50	0.0269	12.9748	155.0714	37.1897	482.5299	0.0771	0.0021	11.951	50
51	0.0250	12.9998	156.3221	39.9790	519.7197	0.0769	0.0019	12.024	51
52	0.0233	13.0231	157.5087	42.9774	559.6987	0.0768	0.0018	12.094	52
53	0.0216	13.0447	158.6343	46.2007	602.6761	0.0767	0.0017	12.160	53
54	0.0201	13.0649	159.7014	49.6658	648.8768	0.0765	0.0015	12.223	54
55	0.0187	13.0836	160.7128	53.3907	698.5425	0.0764	0.0014	12.283	55
60	0.0130	13.1594	165.0213	76.6492	1008.6565	0.0760	0.0010	12.540	60
65	0.0091	13.2122	168.2863	110.0399	1453.8653	0.0757	0.0007	12.737	65
70	0.0063	13.2489	170.7444	157.9765	2093.0200	0.0755	0.0005	12.887	70
75	0.0044	13.2745	172.5847	226.7957	3010.6094	0.0753	0.0003	13.001	75
80	0.0031	13.2924	173.9557	325.5946	4327.9275	0.0752	0.0002	13.086	80
85	0.0021	13.3048	174.9729	467.4331	6219.1080	0.0752	0.0002	13.151	85
90	0.0015	13.3135	175.7246	671.0607	8934.1422	0.0751	0.0001	13.199	90
95	0.0010	13.3195	176.2784	963.3944	12831.9249	0.0751	0.0001	13.234	95
100	0.0007	13.3237	176.6852	1383.0772	18427.6961	0.0751	0.0001	13.261	100

$I = 7.75\ \%$

n	(P/F)	(P/A)	(P/G)	(F/P)	(F/A)	(A/P)	(A/F)	(A/G)	n
1	0.9281	0.9281	0.0000	1.0775	1.0000	1.0775	1.0000	0.000	1
2	0.8613	1.7894	0.8613	1.1610	2.0775	0.5588	0.4813	0.481	2
3	0.7994	2.5888	2.4601	1.2510	3.2385	0.3863	0.3088	0.950	3
4	0.7419	3.3306	4.6857	1.3479	4.4895	0.3002	0.2227	1.406	4
5	0.6885	4.0192	7.4398	1.4524	5.8374	0.2488	0.1713	1.851	5
6	0.6390	4.6582	10.6347	1.5650	7.2898	0.2147	0.1372	2.283	6
7	0.5930	5.2512	14.1929	1.6862	8.8548	0.1904	0.1129	2.702	7
8	0.5504	5.8016	18.0456	1.8169	10.5410	0.1724	0.0949	3.110	8
9	0.5108	6.3124	22.1319	1.9577	12.3580	0.1584	0.0809	3.506	9
10	0.4741	6.7864	26.3984	2.1095	14.3157	0.1474	0.0699	3.889	10
11	0.4400	7.2264	30.7980	2.2730	16.4252	0.1384	0.0609	4.261	11
12	0.4083	7.6347	35.2894	2.4491	18.6981	0.1310	0.0535	4.622	12
13	0.3789	8.0136	39.8367	2.6389	21.1472	0.1248	0.0473	4.971	13
14	0.3517	8.3653	44.4087	2.8434	23.7861	0.1195	0.0420	5.308	14
15	0.3264	8.6917	48.9782	3.0638	26.6296	0.1151	0.0376	5.635	15
16	0.3029	8.9946	53.5219	3.3012	29.6934	0.1112	0.0337	5.950	16
17	0.2811	9.2757	58.0200	3.5571	32.9946	0.1078	0.0303	6.255	17
18	0.2609	9.5367	62.4555	3.8328	36.5517	0.1049	0.0274	6.549	18
19	0.2421	9.7788	66.8140	4.1298	40.3844	0.1023	0.0248	6.832	19
20	0.2247	10.0035	71.0838	4.4499	44.5142	0.1000	0.0225	7.105	20
21	0.2086	10.2121	75.2551	4.7947	48.9641	0.0979	0.0204	7.369	21
22	0.1936	10.4057	79.3199	5.1663	53.7588	0.0961	0.0186	7.622	22
23	0.1796	10.5853	83.2720	5.5667	58.9251	0.0945	0.0170	7.866	23
24	0.1667	10.7520	87.1065	5.9981	64.4918	0.0930	0.0155	8.101	24
25	0.1547	10.9067	90.8200	6.4630	70.4899	0.0917	0.0142	8.327	25
26	0.1436	11.0503	94.4099	6.9638	76.9529	0.0905	0.0130	8.543	26
27	0.1333	11.1836	97.8750	7.5035	83.9167	0.0894	0.0119	8.751	27
28	0.1237	11.3073	101.2145	8.0851	91.4203	0.0884	0.0109	8.951	28
29	0.1148	11.4221	104.4285	8.7117	99.5053	0.0875	0.0100	9.142	29
30	0.1065	11.5286	107.5180	9.3868	108.2170	0.0867	0.0092	9.326	30
31	0.0989	11.6275	110.4841	10.1143	117.6038	0.0860	0.0085	9.502	31
32	0.0918	11.7192	113.3286	10.8982	127.7181	0.0853	0.0078	9.670	32
33	0.0852	11.8044	116.0537	11.7428	138.6163	0.0847	0.0072	9.831	33
34	0.0790	11.8834	118.6618	12.6528	150.3590	0.0842	0.0067	9.985	34
35	0.0733	11.9568	121.1557	13.6334	163.0118	0.0836	0.0061	10.132	35
36	0.0681	12.0249	123.5382	14.6900	176.6453	0.0832	0.0057	10.273	36
37	0.0632	12.0880	125.8126	15.8285	191.3353	0.0827	0.0052	10.408	37
38	0.0586	12.1467	127.9820	17.0552	207.1638	0.0823	0.0048	10.536	38
39	0.0544	12.2011	130.0498	18.3770	224.2190	0.0820	0.0045	10.658	39
40	0.0505	12.2516	132.0194	19.8012	242.5959	0.0816	0.0041	10.775	40
41	0.0469	12.2985	133.8942	21.3358	262.3971	0.0813	0.0038	10.887	41
42	0.0435	12.3420	135.6776	22.9893	283.7329	0.0810	0.0035	10.993	42
43	0.0404	12.3823	137.3732	24.7710	306.7222	0.0808	0.0033	11.094	43
44	0.0375	12.4198	138.9842	26.6907	331.4931	0.0805	0.0030	11.190	44
45	0.0348	12.4546	140.5142	28.7592	358.1839	0.0803	0.0028	11.282	45
46	0.0323	12.4868	141.9663	30.9881	386.9431	0.0801	0.0026	11.369	46
47	0.0299	12.5168	143.3440	33.3897	417.9312	0.0799	0.0024	11.452	47
48	0.0278	12.5446	144.6504	35.9774	451.3209	0.0797	0.0022	11.530	48
49	0.0258	12.5704	145.8886	38.7656	487.2982	0.0796	0.0021	11.605	49
50	0.0239	12.5943	147.0617	41.7699	526.0639	0.0794	0.0019	11.676	50
51	0.0222	12.6165	148.1726	45.0071	567.8338	0.0793	0.0018	11.744	51
52	0.0206	12.6372	149.2243	48.4952	612.8409	0.0791	0.0016	11.808	52
53	0.0191	12.6563	150.2194	52.2535	661.3361	0.0790	0.0015	11.869	53
54	0.0178	12.6741	151.1608	56.3032	713.5896	0.0789	0.0014	11.926	54
55	0.0165	12.6905	152.0509	60.6667	769.8928	0.0788	0.0013	11.981	55
60	0.0113	12.7568	155.8172	88.1123	1124.0302	0.0784	0.0009	12.214	60
65	0.0078	12.8024	158.6385	127.9744	1638.3794	0.0781	0.0006	12.391	65
70	0.0054	12.8338	160.7380	185.8701	2385.4206	0.0779	0.0004	12.524	70
75	0.0037	12.8554	162.2917	269.9578	3470.4235	0.0778	0.0003	12.624	75
80	0.0026	12.8703	163.4359	392.0869	5046.2823	0.0777	0.0002	12.698	80
85	0.0018	12.8806	164.2749	569.4672	7335.0604	0.0776	0.0001	12.753	85
90	0.0012	12.8876	164.8879	827.0944	10659.2829	0.0776	0.0001	12.794	90
95	0.0008	12.8925	165.3342	1201.2724	15487.3855	0.0776	0.0001	12.824	95
100	0.0006	12.8958	165.6583	1744.7286	22499.7240	0.0775	0.0000	12.845	100

$I = 8.00\%$

n	(P/F)	(P/A)	(P/G)	(F/P)	(F/A)	(A/P)	(A/F)	(A/G)	n
1	0.9259	0.9259	0.0000	1.0800	1.0000	1.0800	1.0000	0.000	1
2	0.8573	1.7833	0.8573	1.1664	2.0800	0.5608	0.4808	0.480	2
3	0.7938	2.5771	2.4450	1.2597	3.2464	0.3880	0.3080	0.948	3
4	0.7350	3.3121	4.6501	1.3605	4.5061	0.3019	0.2219	1.404	4
5	0.6806	3.9927	7.3724	1.4693	5.8666	0.2505	0.1705	1.846	5
6	0.6302	4.6229	10.5233	1.5869	7.3359	0.2163	0.1363	2.276	6
7	0.5835	5.2064	14.0242	1.7138	8.9228	0.1921	0.1121	2.693	7
8	0.5403	5.7466	17.8061	1.8509	10.6366	0.1740	0.0940	3.098	8
9	0.5002	6.2469	21.8081	1.9990	12.4876	0.1601	0.0801	3.491	9
10	0.4632	6.7101	25.9768	2.1589	14.4866	0.1490	0.0690	3.871	10
11	0.4289	7.1390	30.2657	2.3316	16.6455	0.1401	0.0601	4.239	11
12	0.3971	7.5361	34.6339	2.5182	18.9771	0.1327	0.0527	4.595	12
13	0.3677	7.9038	39.0463	2.7196	21.4953	0.1265	0.0465	4.940	13
14	0.3405	8.2442	43.4723	2.9372	24.2149	0.1213	0.0413	5.273	14
15	0.3152	8.5595	47.8857	3.1722	27.1521	0.1168	0.0368	5.594	15
16	0.2919	8.8514	52.2640	3.4259	30.3243	0.1130	0.0330	5.904	16
17	0.2703	9.1216	56.5883	3.7000	33.7502	0.1096	0.0296	6.203	17
18	0.2502	9.3719	60.8426	3.9960	37.4502	0.1067	0.0267	6.492	18
19	0.2317	9.6036	65.0134	4.3157	41.4463	0.1041	0.0241	6.769	19
20	0.2145	9.8181	69.0898	4.6610	45.7620	0.1019	0.0219	7.036	20
21	0.1987	10.0168	73.0629	5.0338	50.4229	0.0998	0.0198	7.294	21
22	0.1839	10.2007	76.9257	5.4365	55.4568	0.0980	0.0180	7.541	22
23	0.1703	10.3711	80.6726	5.8715	60.8933	0.0964	0.0164	7.778	23
24	0.1577	10.5288	84.2997	6.3412	66.7648	0.0950	0.0150	8.006	24
25	0.1460	10.6748	87.8041	6.8485	73.1059	0.0937	0.0137	8.225	25
26	0.1352	10.8100	91.1842	7.3964	79.9544	0.0925	0.0125	8.435	26
27	0.1252	10.9352	94.4390	7.9881	87.3508	0.0914	0.0114	8.636	27
28	0.1159	11.0511	97.5687	8.6271	95.3388	0.0905	0.0105	8.828	28
29	0.1073	11.1584	100.5738	9.3173	103.9659	0.0896	0.0096	9.013	29
30	0.0994	11.2578	103.4558	10.0627	113.2832	0.0888	0.0088	9.189	30
31	0.0920	11.3498	106.2163	10.8677	123.3459	0.0881	0.0081	9.358	31
32	0.0852	11.4350	108.8575	11.7371	134.2135	0.0875	0.0075	9.519	32
33	0.0789	11.5139	111.3819	12.6760	145.9506	0.0869	0.0069	9.673	33
34	0.0730	11.5869	113.7924	13.6901	158.6267	0.0863	0.0063	9.820	34
35	0.0676	11.6546	116.0920	14.7853	172.3168	0.0858	0.0058	9.961	35
36	0.0626	11.7172	118.2839	15.9682	187.1021	0.0853	0.0053	10.094	36
37	0.0580	11.7752	120.3713	17.2456	203.0703	0.0849	0.0049	10.222	37
38	0.0537	11.8289	122.3579	18.6253	220.3159	0.0845	0.0045	10.344	38
39	0.0497	11.8786	124.2470	20.1153	238.9412	0.0842	0.0042	10.459	39
40	0.0460	11.9246	126.0422	21.7245	259.0565	0.0839	0.0039	10.569	40
41	0.0426	11.9672	127.7470	23.4625	280.7810	0.0836	0.0036	10.674	41
42	0.0395	12.0067	129.3651	25.3395	304.2435	0.0833	0.0033	10.774	42
43	0.0365	12.0432	130.8998	27.3666	329.5830	0.0830	0.0030	10.869	43
44	0.0338	12.0771	132.3547	29.5560	356.9496	0.0828	0.0028	10.959	44
45	0.0313	12.1084	133.7331	31.9204	386.5056	0.0826	0.0026	11.044	45
46	0.0290	12.1374	135.0384	34.4741	418.4261	0.0824	0.0024	11.125	46
47	0.0269	12.1643	136.2739	37.2320	452.9002	0.0822	0.0022	11.202	47
48	0.0249	12.1891	137.4428	40.2106	490.1322	0.0820	0.0020	11.275	48
49	0.0230	12.2122	138.5480	43.4274	530.3427	0.0819	0.0019	11.345	49
50	0.0213	12.2335	139.5928	46.9016	573.7702	0.0817	0.0017	11.410	50
51	0.0197	12.2532	140.5799	50.6537	620.6718	0.0816	0.0016	11.472	51
52	0.0183	12.2715	141.5121	54.7060	671.3255	0.0815	0.0015	11.531	52
53	0.0169	12.2884	142.3923	59.0825	726.0316	0.0814	0.0014	11.587	53
54	0.0157	12.3041	143.2229	63.8091	785.1141	0.0813	0.0013	11.640	54
55	0.0145	12.3186	144.0065	68.9139	848.9232	0.0812	0.0012	11.690	55
60	0.0099	12.3766	147.3000	101.2571	1253.2133	0.0808	0.0008	11.901	60
65	0.0067	12.4160	149.7387	148.7798	1847.2481	0.0805	0.0005	12.060	65
70	0.0046	12.4428	151.5326	218.6064	2720.0801	0.0804	0.0004	12.178	70
75	0.0031	12.4611	152.8448	321.2045	4002.5566	0.0802	0.0002	12.265	75
80	0.0021	12.4735	153.8001	471.9548	5886.9354	0.0802	0.0002	12.330	80
85	0.0014	12.4820	154.4925	693.4565	8655.7061	0.0801	0.0001	12.377	85
90	0.0010	12.4877	154.9925	1018.9151	12723.9386	0.0801	0.0001	12.411	90
95	0.0007	12.4917	155.3524	1497.1205	18701.5069	0.0801	0.0001	12.436	95
100	0.0005	12.4943	155.6107	2199.7613	27484.5157	0.0800	0.0000	12.454	100

I = 8.25 %

n	(P/F)	(P/A)	(P/G)	(F/P)	(F/A)	(A/P)	(A/F)	(A/G)	n
1	0.9238	0.9238	0.0000	1.0825	1.0000	1.0825	1.0000	0.000	1
2	0.8534	1.7772	0.8534	1.1718	2.0825	0.5627	0.4802	0.480	2
3	0.7883	2.5655	2.4301	1.2685	3.2543	0.3898	0.3073	0.947	3
4	0.7283	3.2938	4.6149	1.3731	4.5228	0.3036	0.2211	1.401	4
5	0.6728	3.9665	7.3059	1.4864	5.8959	0.2521	0.1696	1.841	5
6	0.6215	4.5880	10.4133	1.6090	7.3823	0.2180	0.1355	2.269	6
7	0.5741	5.1621	13.8581	1.7418	8.9914	0.1937	0.1112	2.684	7
8	0.5304	5.6925	17.5707	1.8855	10.7332	0.1757	0.0932	3.086	8
9	0.4899	6.1825	21.4902	2.0410	12.6186	0.1617	0.0792	3.476	9
10	0.4526	6.6351	25.5637	2.2094	14.6597	0.1507	0.0682	3.852	10
11	0.4181	7.0532	29.7448	2.3917	16.8691	0.1418	0.0593	4.217	11
12	0.3862	7.4394	33.9935	2.5890	19.2608	0.1344	0.0519	4.569	12
13	0.3568	7.7962	38.2752	2.8026	21.8498	0.1283	0.0458	4.909	13
14	0.3296	8.1259	42.5603	3.0338	24.6524	0.1231	0.0406	5.237	14
15	0.3045	8.4304	46.8232	3.2841	27.6863	0.1186	0.0361	5.554	15
16	0.2813	8.7116	51.0426	3.5551	30.9704	0.1148	0.0323	5.859	16
17	0.2599	8.9715	55.2002	3.8483	34.5254	0.1115	0.0290	6.152	17
18	0.2400	9.2115	59.2810	4.1658	38.3738	0.1086	0.0261	6.435	18
19	0.2218	9.4333	63.2725	4.5095	42.5396	0.1060	0.0235	6.707	19
20	0.2049	9.6381	67.1648	4.8816	47.0491	0.1038	0.0213	6.968	20
21	0.1892	9.8274	70.9496	5.2843	51.9307	0.1018	0.0193	7.219	21
22	0.1748	10.0022	74.6207	5.7202	57.2150	0.1000	0.0175	7.460	22
23	0.1615	10.1637	78.1736	6.1922	62.9352	0.0984	0.0159	7.691	23
24	0.1492	10.3129	81.6049	6.7030	69.1274	0.0970	0.0145	7.912	24
25	0.1378	10.4507	84.9125	7.2560	75.8304	0.0957	0.0132	8.125	25
26	0.1273	10.5780	88.0954	7.8546	83.0864	0.0945	0.0120	8.328	26
27	0.1176	10.6956	91.1532	8.5026	90.9410	0.0935	0.0110	8.522	27
28	0.1086	10.8043	94.0867	9.2041	99.4436	0.0926	0.0101	8.708	28
29	0.1004	10.9046	96.8970	9.9634	108.6477	0.0917	0.0092	8.885	29
30	0.0927	10.9974	99.5858	10.7854	118.6112	0.0909	0.0084	9.055	30
31	0.0857	11.0830	102.1553	11.6752	129.3966	0.0902	0.0077	9.217	31
32	0.0791	11.1621	104.6082	12.6384	141.0718	0.0896	0.0071	9.371	32
33	0.0731	11.2352	106.9472	13.6811	153.7102	0.0890	0.0065	9.518	33
34	0.0675	11.3028	109.1754	14.8098	167.3913	0.0885	0.0060	9.659	34
35	0.0624	11.3651	111.2962	16.0316	182.2011	0.0880	0.0055	9.792	35
36	0.0576	11.4228	113.3130	17.3542	198.2327	0.0875	0.0050	9.919	36
37	0.0532	11.4760	115.2294	18.7859	215.5869	0.0871	0.0046	10.040	37
38	0.0492	11.5252	117.0488	20.3358	234.3728	0.0868	0.0043	10.155	38
39	0.0454	11.5706	118.7750	22.0135	254.7086	0.0864	0.0039	10.265	39
40	0.0420	11.6125	120.4117	23.8296	276.7221	0.0861	0.0036	10.369	40
41	0.0388	11.6513	121.9623	25.7955	300.5516	0.0858	0.0033	10.467	41
42	0.0358	11.6871	123.4306	27.9236	326.3471	0.0856	0.0031	10.561	42
43	0.0331	11.7202	124.8201	30.2273	354.2708	0.0853	0.0028	10.650	43
44	0.0306	11.7508	126.1342	32.7211	384.4981	0.0851	0.0026	10.734	44
45	0.0282	11.7790	127.3764	35.4206	417.2192	0.0849	0.0024	10.813	45
46	0.0261	11.8051	128.5501	38.3428	452.6398	0.0847	0.0022	10.889	46
47	0.0241	11.8292	129.6583	41.5061	490.9826	0.0845	0.0020	10.960	47
48	0.0223	11.8514	130.7044	44.9303	532.4886	0.0844	0.0019	11.028	48
49	0.0206	11.8720	131.6913	48.6371	577.4190	0.0842	0.0017	11.092	49
50	0.0190	11.8910	132.6220	52.6496	626.0560	0.0841	0.0016	11.153	50
51	0.0175	11.9085	133.4993	56.9932	678.7056	0.0840	0.0015	11.210	51
52	0.0162	11.9247	134.3259	61.6952	735.6989	0.0839	0.0014	11.264	52
53	0.0150	11.9397	135.1045	66.7850	797.3940	0.0838	0.0013	11.315	53
54	0.0138	11.9535	135.8377	72.2948	864.1790	0.0837	0.0012	11.363	54
55	0.0128	11.9663	136.5277	78.2591	936.4738	0.0836	0.0011	11.409	55
60	0.0086	12.0170	139.4087	116.3253	1397.8828	0.0832	0.0007	11.600	60
65	0.0058	12.0511	141.5174	172.9075	2083.7272	0.0830	0.0005	11.743	65
70	0.0039	12.0741	143.0508	257.0120	3103.1754	0.0828	0.0003	11.847	70
75	0.0026	12.0895	144.1595	382.0260	4618.4965	0.0827	0.0002	11.924	75
80	0.0018	12.0999	144.9574	567.8484	6870.8896	0.0826	0.0001	11.980	80
85	0.0012	12.1069	145.5291	844.0573	10218.8763	0.0826	0.0001	12.020	85
90	0.0008	12.1116	145.9372	1254.6178	15195.3675	0.0826	0.0001	12.049	90
95	0.0005	12.1147	146.2275	1864.8804	22592.4893	0.0825	0.0000	12.070	95
100	0.0004	12.1168	146.4335	2771.9826	33587.6681	0.0825	0.0000	12.085	100

EXPANDED INTEREST TABLES

I = **8.50 %**

n	(P/F)	(P/A)	(P/G)	(F/P)	(F/A)	(A/P)	(A/F)	(A/G)	n
1	0.9217	0.9217	0.0000	1.0850	1.0000	1.0850	1.0000	0.000	1
2	0.8495	1.7711	0.8495	1.1772	2.0850	0.5646	0.4796	0.479	2
3	0.7829	2.5540	2.4153	1.2773	3.2622	0.3915	0.3065	0.945	3
4	0.7216	3.2756	4.5800	1.3859	4.5395	0.3053	0.2203	1.398	4
5	0.6650	3.9406	7.2402	1.5037	5.9254	0.2538	0.1688	1.837	5
6	0.6129	4.5536	10.3049	1.6315	7.4290	0.2196	0.1346	2.263	6
7	0.5649	5.1185	13.6945	1.7701	9.0605	0.1954	0.1104	2.675	7
8	0.5207	5.6392	17.3391	1.9206	10.8306	0.1773	0.0923	3.074	8
9	0.4799	6.1191	21.1782	2.0839	12.7512	0.1634	0.0784	3.461	9
10	0.4423	6.5613	25.1588	2.2610	14.8351	0.1524	0.0674	3.834	10
11	0.4076	6.9690	29.2351	2.4532	17.0961	0.1435	0.0585	4.195	11
12	0.3757	7.3447	33.3678	2.6617	19.5492	0.1362	0.0512	4.543	12
13	0.3463	7.6910	37.5231	2.8879	22.2109	0.1300	0.0450	4.878	13
14	0.3191	8.0101	41.6719	3.1334	25.0989	0.1248	0.0398	5.202	14
15	0.2941	8.3042	45.7899	3.3997	28.2323	0.1204	0.0354	5.514	15
16	0.2711	8.5753	49.8563	3.6887	31.6320	0.1166	0.0316	5.813	16
17	0.2499	8.8252	53.8541	4.0023	35.3207	0.1133	0.0283	6.102	17
18	0.2303	9.0555	57.7689	4.3425	39.3230	0.1104	0.0254	6.379	18
19	0.2122	9.2677	61.5893	4.7116	43.6654	0.1079	0.0229	6.645	19
20	0.1956	9.4633	65.3060	5.1120	48.3770	0.1057	0.0207	6.900	20
21	0.1803	9.6436	68.9118	5.5466	53.4891	0.1037	0.0187	7.145	21
22	0.1662	9.8098	72.4013	6.0180	59.0356	0.1019	0.0169	7.380	22
23	0.1531	9.9629	75.7706	6.5296	65.0537	0.1004	0.0154	7.605	23
24	0.1412	10.1041	79.0171	7.0846	71.5832	0.0990	0.0140	7.820	24
25	0.1301	10.2342	82.1394	7.6868	78.6678	0.0977	0.0127	8.026	25
26	0.1199	10.3541	85.1369	8.3401	86.3546	0.0966	0.0116	8.222	26
27	0.1105	10.4646	88.0101	9.0490	94.6947	0.0956	0.0106	8.410	27
28	0.1019	10.5665	90.7601	9.8182	103.7437	0.0946	0.0096	8.589	28
29	0.0939	10.6603	93.3886	10.6528	113.5620	0.0938	0.0088	8.760	29
30	0.0865	10.7468	95.8976	11.5583	124.2147	0.0931	0.0081	8.923	30
31	0.0797	10.8266	98.2898	12.5407	135.7730	0.0924	0.0074	9.078	31
32	0.0735	10.9001	100.5681	13.6067	148.3137	0.0917	0.0067	9.226	32
33	0.0677	10.9678	102.7356	14.7632	161.9203	0.0912	0.0062	9.367	33
34	0.0624	11.0302	104.7958	16.0181	176.6836	0.0907	0.0057	9.500	34
35	0.0575	11.0878	106.7521	17.3796	192.7017	0.0902	0.0052	9.627	35
36	0.0530	11.1408	108.6082	18.8569	210.0813	0.0898	0.0048	9.748	36
37	0.0489	11.1897	110.3678	20.4597	228.9382	0.0894	0.0044	9.863	37
38	0.0450	11.2347	112.0345	22.1988	249.3980	0.0890	0.0040	9.972	38
39	0.0415	11.2763	113.6122	24.0857	271.5968	0.0887	0.0037	10.075	39
40	0.0383	11.3145	115.1046	26.1330	295.6825	0.0884	0.0034	10.173	40
41	0.0353	11.3498	116.5153	28.3543	321.8156	0.0881	0.0031	10.265	41
42	0.0325	11.3823	117.8480	30.7644	350.1699	0.0879	0.0029	10.353	42
43	0.0300	11.4123	119.1063	33.3794	380.9343	0.0876	0.0026	10.436	43
44	0.0276	11.4399	120.2936	36.2167	414.3137	0.0874	0.0024	10.515	44
45	0.0254	11.4653	121.4133	39.2951	450.5304	0.0872	0.0022	10.589	45
46	0.0235	11.4888	122.4688	42.6352	489.8255	0.0870	0.0020	10.659	46
47	0.0216	11.5104	123.4632	46.2592	532.4606	0.0869	0.0019	10.726	47
48	0.0199	11.5303	124.3996	50.1912	578.7198	0.0867	0.0017	10.788	48
49	0.0184	11.5487	125.2810	54.4574	628.9110	0.0866	0.0016	10.848	49
50	0.0169	11.5656	126.1103	59.0863	683.3684	0.0865	0.0015	10.903	50
51	0.0156	11.5812	126.8902	64.1087	742.4547	0.0863	0.0013	10.956	51
52	0.0144	11.5956	127.6234	69.5579	806.5634	0.0862	0.0012	11.006	52
53	0.0133	11.6088	128.3124	75.4703	876.1213	0.0861	0.0011	11.053	53
54	0.0122	11.6210	128.9597	81.8853	951.5916	0.0861	0.0011	11.097	54
55	0.0113	11.6323	129.5675	88.8455	1033.4769	0.0860	0.0010	11.138	55
60	0.0075	11.6766	132.0884	133.5932	1559.9198	0.0856	0.0006	11.312	60
65	0.0050	11.7061	133.9125	200.8783	2351.5092	0.0854	0.0004	11.439	65
70	0.0033	11.7258	135.2236	302.0520	3541.7879	0.0853	0.0003	11.532	70
75	0.0022	11.7388	136.1608	454.1825	5331.5584	0.0852	0.0002	11.599	75
80	0.0015	11.7475	136.8275	682.9345	8022.7589	0.0851	0.0001	11.647	80
85	0.0010	11.7532	137.2997	1026.8990	12069.4004	0.0851	0.0001	11.681	85
90	0.0006	11.7571	137.6329	1544.1036	18154.1600	0.0851	0.0001	11.706	90
95	0.0004	11.7596	137.8673	2321.8017	27303.5496	0.0850	0.0000	11.723	95
100	0.0003	11.7613	138.0317	3491.1927	41061.0904	0.0850	0.0000	11.736	100

$I = 8.75\%$

n	(P/F)	(P/A)	(P/G)	(F/P)	(F/A)	(A/P)	(A/F)	(A/G)	n
1	0.9195	0.9195	0.0000	1.0875	1.0000	1.0875	1.0000	0.000	1
2	0.8456	1.7651	0.8456	1.1827	2.0875	0.5665	0.4790	0.479	2
3	0.7775	2.5426	2.4006	1.2861	3.2702	0.3933	0.3058	0.944	3
4	0.7150	3.2576	4.5455	1.3987	4.5563	0.3070	0.2195	1.395	4
5	0.6574	3.9150	7.1752	1.5211	5.9550	0.2554	0.1679	1.832	5
6	0.6045	4.5196	10.1979	1.6542	7.4760	0.2213	0.1338	2.256	6
7	0.5559	5.0755	13.5333	1.7989	9.1302	0.1970	0.1095	2.666	7
8	0.5112	5.5866	17.1115	1.9563	10.9291	0.1790	0.0915	3.062	8
9	0.4700	6.0567	20.8718	2.1275	12.8854	0.1651	0.0776	3.446	9
10	0.4322	6.4889	24.7618	2.3136	15.0128	0.1541	0.0666	3.816	10
11	0.3974	6.8863	28.7363	2.5161	17.3265	0.1452	0.0577	4.172	11
12	0.3655	7.2518	32.7564	2.7362	19.8425	0.1379	0.0504	4.517	12
13	0.3361	7.5879	36.7892	2.9756	22.5787	0.1318	0.0443	4.848	13
14	0.3090	7.8969	40.8065	3.2360	25.5544	0.1266	0.0391	5.167	14
15	0.2842	8.1810	44.7847	3.5192	28.7904	0.1222	0.0347	5.474	15
16	0.2613	8.4423	48.7041	3.8271	32.3096	0.1185	0.0310	5.769	16
17	0.2403	8.6826	52.5485	4.1620	36.1366	0.1152	0.0277	6.052	17
18	0.2209	8.9035	56.3045	4.5261	40.2986	0.1123	0.0248	6.323	18
19	0.2032	9.1067	59.9614	4.9222	44.8247	0.1098	0.0223	6.584	19
20	0.1868	9.2935	63.5109	5.3529	49.7469	0.1076	0.0201	6.833	20
21	0.1718	9.4653	66.9466	5.8212	55.0997	0.1056	0.0181	7.072	21
22	0.1580	9.6233	70.2638	6.3306	60.9210	0.1039	0.0164	7.301	22
23	0.1453	9.7685	73.4594	6.8845	67.2516	0.1024	0.0149	7.520	23
24	0.1336	9.9021	76.5314	7.4869	74.1361	0.1010	0.0135	7.728	24
25	0.1228	10.0249	79.4791	8.1420	81.6230	0.0998	0.0123	7.928	25
26	0.1129	10.1379	82.3026	8.8544	89.7650	0.0986	0.0111	8.118	26
27	0.1039	10.2417	85.0027	9.6292	98.6194	0.0976	0.0101	8.299	27
28	0.0955	10.3372	87.5810	10.4718	108.2486	0.0967	0.0092	8.472	28
29	0.0878	10.4250	90.0398	11.3880	118.7204	0.0959	0.0084	8.636	29
30	0.0807	10.5058	92.3814	12.3845	130.1084	0.0952	0.0077	8.793	30
31	0.0742	10.5800	94.6089	13.4681	142.4929	0.0945	0.0070	8.942	31
32	0.0683	10.6483	96.7254	14.6466	155.9610	0.0939	0.0064	9.083	32
33	0.0628	10.7111	98.7344	15.9282	170.6076	0.0934	0.0059	9.218	33
34	0.0577	10.7688	100.6395	17.3219	186.5358	0.0929	0.0054	9.345	34
35	0.0531	10.8219	102.4444	18.8375	203.8577	0.0924	0.0049	9.466	35
36	0.0488	10.8707	104.1529	20.4858	222.6952	0.0920	0.0045	9.581	36
37	0.0449	10.9156	105.7689	22.2783	243.1810	0.0916	0.0041	9.689	37
38	0.0413	10.9569	107.2960	24.2277	265.4594	0.0913	0.0038	9.792	38
39	0.0380	10.9948	108.7383	26.3476	289.6871	0.0910	0.0035	9.890	39
40	0.0349	11.0297	110.0994	28.6530	316.0347	0.0907	0.0032	9.982	40
41	0.0321	11.0618	111.3831	31.1602	344.6877	0.0904	0.0029	10.069	41
42	0.0295	11.0913	112.5930	33.8867	375.8479	0.0902	0.0027	10.151	42
43	0.0271	11.1184	113.7327	36.8518	409.7346	0.0899	0.0024	10.229	43
44	0.0250	11.1434	114.8057	40.0763	446.5864	0.0897	0.0022	10.302	44
45	0.0229	11.1663	115.8152	43.5830	486.6627	0.0896	0.0021	10.371	45
46	0.0211	11.1874	116.7647	47.3965	530.2456	0.0894	0.0019	10.437	46
47	0.0194	11.2068	117.6571	51.5437	577.6421	0.0892	0.0017	10.498	47
48	0.0178	11.2247	118.4956	56.0538	629.1858	0.0891	0.0016	10.556	48
49	0.0164	11.2411	119.2830	60.9585	685.2396	0.0890	0.0015	10.611	49
50	0.0151	11.2562	120.0222	66.2923	746.1981	0.0888	0.0013	10.662	50
51	0.0139	11.2700	120.7157	72.0929	812.4904	0.0887	0.0012	10.711	51
52	0.0128	11.2828	121.3662	78.4010	884.5833	0.0886	0.0011	10.756	52
53	0.0117	11.2945	121.9761	85.2611	962.9843	0.0885	0.0010	10.799	53
54	0.0108	11.3053	122.5477	92.7215	1048.2455	0.0885	0.0010	10.839	54
55	0.0099	11.3152	123.0832	100.8346	1140.9669	0.0884	0.0009	10.877	55
60	0.0065	11.3541	125.2898	153.3755	1741.4341	0.0881	0.0006	11.034	60
65	0.0043	11.3796	126.8682	233.2933	2654.7806	0.0879	0.0004	11.148	65
70	0.0028	11.3964	127.9897	354.8531	4044.0353	0.0877	0.0002	11.230	70
75	0.0019	11.4074	128.7822	539.7528	6157.1751	0.0877	0.0002	11.289	75
80	0.0012	11.4147	129.3395	820.9964	9371.3874	0.0876	0.0001	11.331	80
85	0.0008	11.4194	129.7298	1248.7847	14260.3969	0.0876	0.0001	11.360	85
90	0.0005	11.4226	130.0020	1899.4764	21696.8734	0.0875	0.0000	11.381	90
95	0.0003	11.4246	130.1913	2889.2175	33008.1998	0.0875	0.0000	11.395	95
100	0.0002	11.4260	130.3225	4394.6730	50213.4054	0.0875	0.0000	11.405	100

EXPANDED INTEREST TABLES

I = 9.00 %

n	(P/F)	(P/A)	(P/G)	(F/P)	(F/A)	(A/P)	(A/F)	(A/G)	n
1	0.9174	0.9174	0.0000	1.0900	1.0000	1.0900	1.0000	0.000	1
2	0.8417	1.7591	0.8417	1.1881	2.0900	0.5685	0.4785	0.478	2
3	0.7722	2.5313	2.3860	1.2950	3.2781	0.3951	0.3051	0.942	3
4	0.7084	3.2397	4.5113	1.4116	4.5731	0.3087	0.2187	1.392	4
5	0.6499	3.8897	7.1110	1.5386	5.9847	0.2571	0.1671	1.828	5
6	0.5963	4.4859	10.0924	1.6771	7.5233	0.2229	0.1329	2.249	6
7	0.5470	5.0330	13.3746	1.8280	9.2004	0.1987	0.1087	2.657	7
8	0.5019	5.5348	16.8877	1.9926	11.0285	0.1807	0.0907	3.051	8
9	0.4604	5.9952	20.5711	2.1719	13.0210	0.1668	0.0768	3.431	9
10	0.4224	6.4177	24.3728	2.3674	15.1929	0.1558	0.0658	3.797	10
11	0.3875	6.8052	28.2481	2.5804	17.5603	0.1469	0.0569	4.151	11
12	0.3555	7.1607	32.1590	2.8127	20.1407	0.1397	0.0497	4.491	12
13	0.3262	7.4869	36.0731	3.0658	22.9534	0.1336	0.0436	4.818	13
14	0.2992	7.7862	39.9633	3.3417	26.0192	0.1284	0.0384	5.132	14
15	0.2745	8.0607	43.8069	3.6425	29.3609	0.1241	0.0341	5.434	15
16	0.2519	8.3126	47.5849	3.9703	33.0034	0.1203	0.0303	5.724	16
17	0.2311	8.5436	51.2821	4.3276	36.9737	0.1170	0.0270	6.002	17
18	0.2120	8.7556	54.8860	4.7171	41.3013	0.1142	0.0242	6.268	18
19	0.1945	8.9501	58.3868	5.1417	46.0185	0.1117	0.0217	6.523	19
20	0.1784	9.1285	61.7770	5.6044	51.1601	0.1095	0.0195	6.767	20
21	0.1637	9.2922	65.0509	6.1088	56.7645	0.1076	0.0176	7.000	21
22	0.1502	9.4424	68.2048	6.6586	62.8733	0.1059	0.0159	7.223	22
23	0.1378	9.5802	71.2359	7.2579	69.5319	0.1044	0.0144	7.435	23
24	0.1264	9.7066	74.1433	7.9111	76.7898	0.1030	0.0130	7.638	24
25	0.1160	9.8226	76.9265	8.6231	84.7009	0.1018	0.0118	7.831	25
26	0.1064	9.9290	79.5863	9.3992	93.3240	0.1007	0.0107	8.015	26
27	0.0976	10.0266	82.1241	10.2451	102.7231	0.0997	0.0097	8.190	27
28	0.0895	10.1161	84.5419	11.1671	112.9682	0.0989	0.0089	8.357	28
29	0.0822	10.1983	86.8422	12.1722	124.1354	0.0981	0.0081	8.515	29
30	0.0754	10.2737	89.0280	13.2677	136.3075	0.0973	0.0073	8.665	30
31	0.0691	10.3428	91.1024	14.4618	149.5752	0.0967	0.0067	8.808	31
32	0.0634	10.4062	93.0690	15.7633	164.0370	0.0961	0.0061	8.943	32
33	0.0582	10.4644	94.9314	17.1820	179.8003	0.0956	0.0056	9.071	33
34	0.0534	10.5178	96.6935	18.7284	196.9823	0.0951	0.0051	9.193	34
35	0.0490	10.5668	98.3590	20.4140	215.7108	0.0946	0.0046	9.308	35
36	0.0449	10.6118	99.9319	22.2512	236.1247	0.0942	0.0042	9.417	36
37	0.0412	10.6530	101.4162	24.2538	258.3759	0.0939	0.0039	9.520	37
38	0.0378	10.6908	102.8158	26.4367	282.6298	0.0935	0.0035	9.617	38
39	0.0347	10.7255	104.1345	28.8160	309.0665	0.0932	0.0032	9.709	39
40	0.0318	10.7574	105.3762	31.4094	337.8824	0.0930	0.0030	9.795	40
41	0.0292	10.7866	106.5445	34.2363	369.2919	0.0927	0.0027	9.877	41
42	0.0268	10.8134	107.6432	37.3175	403.5281	0.0925	0.0025	9.954	42
43	0.0246	10.8380	108.6758	40.6761	440.8457	0.0923	0.0023	10.027	43
44	0.0226	10.8605	109.6456	44.3370	481.5218	0.0921	0.0021	10.095	44
45	0.0207	10.8812	110.5561	48.3273	525.8587	0.0919	0.0019	10.160	45
46	0.0190	10.9002	111.4103	52.6767	574.1860	0.0917	0.0017	10.221	46
47	0.0174	10.9176	112.2115	57.4176	626.8628	0.0916	0.0016	10.278	47
48	0.0160	10.9336	112.9625	62.5852	684.2804	0.0915	0.0015	10.331	48
49	0.0147	10.9482	113.6661	68.2179	746.8656	0.0913	0.0013	10.382	49
50	0.0134	10.9617	114.3251	74.3575	815.0836	0.0912	0.0012	10.429	50
51	0.0123	10.9740	114.9420	81.0497	889.4411	0.0911	0.0011	10.474	51
52	0.0113	10.9853	115.5193	88.3442	970.4908	0.0910	0.0010	10.515	52
53	0.0104	10.9957	116.0593	96.2951	1058.8349	0.0909	0.0009	10.554	53
54	0.0095	11.0053	116.5642	104.9617	1155.1301	0.0909	0.0009	10.591	54
55	0.0087	11.0140	117.0362	114.4083	1260.0918	0.0908	0.0008	10.626	55
60	0.0057	11.0480	118.9683	176.0313	1944.7921	0.0905	0.0005	10.768	60
65	0.0037	11.0701	120.3344	270.8460	2998.2885	0.0903	0.0003	10.870	65
70	0.0024	11.0844	121.2942	416.7301	4619.2232	0.0902	0.0002	10.942	70
75	0.0016	11.0938	121.9646	641.1909	7113.2321	0.0901	0.0001	10.994	75
80	0.0010	11.0998	122.4306	986.5517	10950.5741	0.0901	0.0001	11.029	80
85	0.0007	11.1038	122.7533	1517.9320	16854.8003	0.0901	0.0001	11.055	85
90	0.0004	11.1064	122.9758	2335.5266	25939.1842	0.0900	0.0000	11.072	90
95	0.0003	11.1080	123.1287	3593.4971	39916.6350	0.0900	0.0000	11.084	95
100	0.0002	11.1091	123.2335	5529.0408	61422.6755	0.0900	0.0000	11.093	100

PROFESSIONAL PUBLICATIONS, INC. • Belmont, CA

$I = 9.25\%$

n	(P/F)	(P/A)	(P/G)	(F/P)	(F/A)	(A/P)	(A/F)	(A/G)	n
1	0.9153	0.9153	0.0000	1.0925	1.0000	1.0925	1.0000	0.000	1
2	0.8378	1.7532	0.8378	1.1936	2.0925	0.5704	0.4779	0.477	2
3	0.7669	2.5201	2.3716	1.3040	3.2861	0.3968	0.3043	0.941	3
4	0.7020	3.2220	4.4775	1.4246	4.5900	0.3104	0.2179	1.389	4
5	0.6425	3.8646	7.0476	1.5563	6.0146	0.2588	0.1663	1.823	5
6	0.5881	4.4527	9.9883	1.7003	7.5709	0.2246	0.1321	2.243	6
7	0.5383	4.9910	13.2183	1.8576	9.2713	0.2004	0.1079	2.648	7
8	0.4928	5.4838	16.6675	2.0294	11.1288	0.1824	0.0899	3.039	8
9	0.4510	5.9348	20.2758	2.2171	13.1583	0.1685	0.0760	3.416	9
10	0.4128	6.3476	23.9914	2.4222	15.3754	0.1575	0.0650	3.779	10
11	0.3779	6.7255	27.7703	2.6463	17.7976	0.1487	0.0562	4.129	11
12	0.3459	7.0714	31.5751	2.8911	20.4439	0.1414	0.0489	4.465	12
13	0.3166	7.3880	35.3744	3.1585	23.3350	0.1354	0.0429	4.788	13
14	0.2898	7.6778	39.1418	3.4506	26.4935	0.1302	0.0377	5.098	14
15	0.2653	7.9431	42.8555	3.7698	29.9441	0.1259	0.0334	5.395	15
16	0.2428	8.1859	46.4975	4.1185	33.7139	0.1222	0.0297	5.680	16
17	0.2222	8.4081	50.0535	4.4995	37.8325	0.1189	0.0264	5.953	17
18	0.2034	8.6116	53.5118	4.9157	42.3320	0.1161	0.0236	6.213	18
19	0.1862	8.7978	56.8635	5.3704	47.2477	0.1137	0.0212	6.463	19
20	0.1704	8.9682	60.1019	5.8672	52.6181	0.1115	0.0190	6.701	20
21	0.1560	9.1242	63.2220	6.4099	58.4853	0.1096	0.0171	6.929	21
22	0.1428	9.2670	66.2208	7.0028	64.8951	0.1079	0.0154	7.145	22
23	0.1307	9.3977	69.0964	7.6506	71.8980	0.1064	0.0139	7.352	23
24	0.1196	9.5174	71.8482	8.3582	79.5485	0.1051	0.0126	7.549	24
25	0.1095	9.6269	74.4765	9.1314	87.9067	0.1039	0.0114	7.736	25
26	0.1002	9.7271	76.9825	9.9760	97.0381	0.1028	0.0103	7.914	26
27	0.0918	9.8189	79.3681	10.8988	107.0141	0.1018	0.0093	8.083	27
28	0.0840	9.9029	81.6357	11.9069	117.9130	0.1010	0.0085	8.243	28
29	0.0769	9.9797	83.7882	13.0083	129.8199	0.1002	0.0077	8.395	29
30	0.0704	10.0501	85.8287	14.2116	142.8282	0.0995	0.0070	8.540	30
31	0.0644	10.1145	87.7610	15.5262	157.0399	0.0989	0.0064	8.676	31
32	0.0590	10.1735	89.5885	16.9624	172.5660	0.0983	0.0058	8.806	32
33	0.0540	10.2274	91.3153	18.5314	189.5284	0.0978	0.0053	8.928	33
34	0.0494	10.2768	92.9453	20.2455	208.0598	0.0973	0.0048	9.044	34
35	0.0452	10.3220	94.4825	22.1182	228.3053	0.0969	0.0044	9.153	35
36	0.0414	10.3634	95.9309	24.1642	250.4236	0.0965	0.0040	9.256	36
37	0.0379	10.4013	97.2946	26.3994	274.5877	0.0961	0.0036	9.354	37
38	0.0347	10.4360	98.5775	28.8413	300.9871	0.0958	0.0033	9.445	38
39	0.0317	10.4677	99.7835	31.5091	329.8284	0.0955	0.0030	9.532	39
40	0.0290	10.4968	100.9164	34.4237	361.3375	0.0953	0.0028	9.614	40
41	0.0266	10.5233	101.9800	37.6079	395.7613	0.0950	0.0025	9.690	41
42	0.0243	10.5477	102.9779	41.0866	433.3692	0.0948	0.0023	9.763	42
43	0.0223	10.5700	103.9136	44.8872	474.4558	0.0946	0.0021	9.831	43
44	0.0204	10.5904	104.7905	49.0392	519.3430	0.0944	0.0019	9.894	44
45	0.0187	10.6090	105.6117	53.5754	568.3822	0.0943	0.0018	9.954	45
46	0.0171	10.6261	106.3806	58.5311	621.9576	0.0941	0.0016	10.011	46
47	0.0156	10.6417	107.0999	63.9452	680.4886	0.0940	0.0015	10.064	47
48	0.0143	10.6561	107.7727	69.8601	744.4338	0.0938	0.0013	10.113	48
49	0.0131	10.6692	108.4016	76.3222	814.2940	0.0937	0.0012	10.160	49
50	0.0120	10.6812	108.9893	83.3820	890.6162	0.0936	0.0011	10.203	50
51	0.0110	10.6921	109.5381	91.0948	973.9982	0.0935	0.0010	10.244	51
52	0.0100	10.7022	110.0506	99.5211	1065.0930	0.0934	0.0009	10.283	52
53	0.0092	10.7114	110.5289	108.7268	1164.6141	0.0934	0.0009	10.318	53
54	0.0084	10.7198	110.9750	118.7840	1273.3409	0.0933	0.0008	10.352	54
55	0.0077	10.7275	111.3912	129.7716	1392.1249	0.0932	0.0007	10.383	55
60	0.0050	10.7573	113.0834	201.9699	2172.6480	0.0930	0.0005	10.512	60
65	0.0032	10.7764	114.2663	314.3359	3387.4150	0.0928	0.0003	10.603	65
70	0.0020	10.7887	115.0879	489.2166	5278.0174	0.0927	0.0002	10.667	70
75	0.0013	10.7966	115.6552	761.3922	8220.4562	0.0926	0.0001	10.712	75
80	0.0008	10.8017	116.0452	1184.9926	12799.9204	0.0926	0.0001	10.743	80
85	0.0005	10.8049	116.3120	1844.2631	19927.1688	0.0926	0.0001	10.764	85
90	0.0003	10.8070	116.4939	2870.3186	31019.6607	0.0925	0.0000	10.779	90
95	0.0002	10.8084	116.6176	4467.2199	48283.4589	0.0925	0.0000	10.789	95
100	0.0001	10.8093	116.7013	6952.5571	75151.9686	0.0925	0.0000	10.796	100

EXPANDED INTEREST TABLES

I = 9.50 %

n	(P/F)	(P/A)	(P/G)	(F/P)	(F/A)	(A/P)	(A/F)	(A/G)	n
1	0.9132	0.9132	0.0000	1.0950	1.0000	1.0950	1.0000	0.000	1
2	0.8340	1.7473	0.8340	1.1990	2.0950	0.5723	0.4773	0.477	2
3	0.7617	2.5089	2.3573	1.3129	3.2940	0.3986	0.3036	0.939	3
4	0.6956	3.2045	4.4440	1.4377	4.6070	0.3121	0.2171	1.386	4
5	0.6352	3.8397	6.9850	1.5742	6.0446	0.2604	0.1654	1.819	5
6	0.5801	4.4198	9.8855	1.7238	7.6189	0.2263	0.1313	2.236	6
7	0.5298	4.9496	13.0643	1.8876	9.3426	0.2020	0.1070	2.639	7
8	0.4838	5.4334	16.4510	2.0669	11.2302	0.1840	0.0890	3.027	8
9	0.4418	5.8753	19.9858	2.2632	13.2971	0.1702	0.0752	3.401	9
10	0.4035	6.2788	23.6174	2.4782	15.5603	0.1593	0.0643	3.761	10
11	0.3685	6.6473	27.3025	2.7137	18.0385	0.1504	0.0554	4.107	11
12	0.3365	6.9838	31.0044	2.9715	20.7522	0.1432	0.0482	4.439	12
13	0.3073	7.2912	34.6924	3.2537	23.7236	0.1372	0.0422	4.758	13
14	0.2807	7.5719	38.3412	3.5629	26.9774	0.1321	0.0371	5.063	14
15	0.2563	7.8282	41.9297	3.9013	30.5402	0.1277	0.0327	5.356	15
16	0.2341	8.0623	45.4410	4.2719	34.4416	0.1240	0.0290	5.636	16
17	0.2138	8.2760	48.8614	4.6778	38.7135	0.1208	0.0258	5.904	17
18	0.1952	8.4713	52.1803	5.1222	43.3913	0.1180	0.0230	6.159	18
19	0.1783	8.6496	55.3896	5.6088	48.5135	0.1156	0.0206	6.403	19
20	0.1628	8.8124	58.4832	6.1416	54.1222	0.1135	0.0185	6.636	20
21	0.1487	8.9611	61.4572	6.7251	60.2638	0.1116	0.0166	6.858	21
22	0.1358	9.0969	64.3089	7.3639	66.9889	0.1099	0.0149	7.069	22
23	0.1240	9.2209	67.0373	8.0635	74.3529	0.1084	0.0134	7.270	23
24	0.1133	9.3341	69.6421	8.8296	82.4164	0.1071	0.0121	7.461	24
25	0.1034	9.4376	72.1245	9.6684	91.2459	0.1060	0.0110	7.642	25
26	0.0945	9.5320	74.4859	10.5869	100.9143	0.1049	0.0099	7.814	26
27	0.0863	9.6183	76.7287	11.5926	111.5012	0.1040	0.0090	7.977	27
28	0.0788	9.6971	78.8557	12.6939	123.0938	0.1031	0.0081	8.131	28
29	0.0719	9.7690	80.8701	13.8998	135.7877	0.1024	0.0074	8.278	29
30	0.0657	9.8347	82.7755	15.2203	149.6875	0.1017	0.0067	8.416	30
31	0.0600	9.8947	84.5755	16.6662	164.9078	0.1011	0.0061	8.547	31
32	0.0548	9.9495	86.2742	18.2495	181.5741	0.1005	0.0055	8.671	32
33	0.0500	9.9996	87.8755	19.9832	199.8236	0.1000	0.0050	8.787	33
34	0.0457	10.0453	89.3836	21.8816	219.8068	0.0995	0.0045	8.898	34
35	0.0417	10.0870	90.8026	23.9604	241.6885	0.0991	0.0041	9.002	35
36	0.0381	10.1251	92.1367	26.2366	265.6489	0.0988	0.0038	9.099	36
37	0.0348	10.1599	93.3897	28.7291	291.8855	0.0984	0.0034	9.192	37
38	0.0318	10.1917	94.5659	31.4584	320.6147	0.0981	0.0031	9.278	38
39	0.0290	10.2207	95.6690	34.4469	352.0731	0.0978	0.0028	9.360	39
40	0.0265	10.2472	96.7030	37.7194	386.5200	0.0976	0.0026	9.437	40
41	0.0242	10.2715	97.6715	41.3027	424.2394	0.0974	0.0024	9.509	41
42	0.0221	10.2936	98.5780	45.2265	465.5421	0.0971	0.0021	9.576	42
43	0.0202	10.3138	99.4261	49.5230	510.7686	0.0970	0.0020	9.640	43
44	0.0184	10.3322	100.2190	54.2277	560.2917	0.0968	0.0018	9.699	44
45	0.0168	10.3490	100.9600	59.3793	614.5194	0.0966	0.0016	9.755	45
46	0.0154	10.3644	101.6521	65.0204	673.8987	0.0965	0.0015	9.807	46
47	0.0140	10.3785	102.2982	71.1973	738.9191	0.0964	0.0014	9.856	47
48	0.0128	10.3913	102.9011	77.9611	810.1164	0.0962	0.0012	9.902	48
49	0.0117	10.4030	103.4634	85.3674	888.0775	0.0961	0.0011	9.945	49
50	0.0107	10.4137	103.9876	93.4773	973.4448	0.0960	0.0010	9.985	50
51	0.0098	10.4235	104.4760	102.3576	1066.9221	0.0959	0.0009	10.023	51
52	0.0089	10.4324	104.9311	112.0816	1169.2797	0.0959	0.0009	10.058	52
53	0.0081	10.4405	105.3548	122.7293	1281.3612	0.0958	0.0008	10.090	53
54	0.0074	10.4480	105.7491	134.3886	1404.0905	0.0957	0.0007	10.121	54
55	0.0068	10.4548	106.1161	147.1555	1538.4791	0.0956	0.0006	10.150	55
60	0.0043	10.4809	107.5987	231.6579	2427.9781	0.0954	0.0004	10.266	60
65	0.0027	10.4975	108.6233	364.6849	3828.2618	0.0953	0.0003	10.347	65
70	0.0017	10.5080	109.3268	574.1011	6032.6426	0.0952	0.0002	10.404	70
75	0.0011	10.5147	109.8072	903.7721	9502.8644	0.0951	0.0001	10.443	75
80	0.0007	10.5189	110.1336	1422.7531	14965.8219	0.0951	0.0001	10.470	80
85	0.0004	10.5216	110.3544	2239.7530	23565.8212	0.0950	0.0000	10.488	85
90	0.0003	10.5233	110.5032	3525.9060	37104.2733	0.0950	0.0000	10.500	90
95	0.0002	10.5244	110.6032	5550.6178	58417.0292	0.0950	0.0000	10.509	95
100	0.0001	10.5251	110.6702	8737.9975	91968.3951	0.0950	0.0000	10.514	100

$I = 9.75\%$

n	(P/F)	(P/A)	(P/G)	(F/P)	(F/A)	(A/P)	(A/F)	(A/G)	n
1	0.9112	0.9112	0.0000	1.0975	1.0000	1.0975	1.0000	0.000	1
2	0.8302	1.7414	0.8302	1.2045	2.0975	0.5743	0.4768	0.476	2
3	0.7565	2.4978	2.3431	1.3219	3.3020	0.4003	0.3028	0.938	3
4	0.6893	3.1871	4.4109	1.4508	4.6240	0.3138	0.2163	1.384	4
5	0.6280	3.8151	6.9230	1.5923	6.0748	0.2621	0.1646	1.814	5
6	0.5722	4.3874	9.7842	1.7475	7.6671	0.2279	0.1304	2.230	6
7	0.5214	4.9088	12.9126	1.9179	9.4146	0.2037	0.1062	2.630	7
8	0.4751	5.3838	16.2381	2.1049	11.3325	0.1857	0.0882	3.016	8
9	0.4329	5.8167	19.7011	2.3102	13.4375	0.1719	0.0744	3.387	9
10	0.3944	6.2111	23.2508	2.5354	15.7476	0.1610	0.0635	3.743	10
11	0.3594	6.5705	26.8446	2.7826	18.2830	0.1522	0.0547	4.085	11
12	0.3275	6.8979	30.4465	3.0539	21.0656	0.1450	0.0475	4.413	12
13	0.2984	7.1963	34.0269	3.3517	24.1195	0.1390	0.0415	4.728	13
14	0.2719	7.4682	37.5610	3.6784	27.4712	0.1339	0.0364	5.029	14
15	0.2477	7.7159	41.0288	4.0371	31.1496	0.1296	0.0321	5.317	15
16	0.2257	7.9416	44.4143	4.4307	35.1867	0.1259	0.0284	5.592	16
17	0.2056	8.1472	47.7046	4.8627	39.6174	0.1227	0.0252	5.855	17
18	0.1874	8.3346	50.8901	5.3368	44.4801	0.1200	0.0225	6.105	18
19	0.1707	8.5053	53.9632	5.8571	49.8169	0.1176	0.0201	6.344	19
20	0.1556	8.6609	56.9190	6.4282	55.6740	0.1155	0.0180	6.572	20
21	0.1417	8.8026	59.7538	7.0550	62.1022	0.1136	0.0161	6.788	21
22	0.1292	8.9318	62.4660	7.7428	69.1572	0.1120	0.0145	6.993	22
23	0.1177	9.0495	65.0549	8.4978	76.9000	0.1105	0.0130	7.188	23
24	0.1072	9.1567	67.5211	9.3263	85.3978	0.1092	0.0117	7.374	24
25	0.0977	9.2544	69.8659	10.2356	94.7241	0.1081	0.0106	7.549	25
26	0.0890	9.3434	72.0913	11.2336	104.9597	0.1070	0.0095	7.715	26
27	0.0811	9.4245	74.2002	12.3288	116.1932	0.1061	0.0086	7.873	27
28	0.0739	9.4984	76.1956	13.5309	128.5221	0.1053	0.0078	8.021	28
29	0.0673	9.5658	78.0811	14.8502	142.0530	0.1045	0.0070	8.162	29
30	0.0614	9.6271	79.8605	16.2981	156.9032	0.1039	0.0064	8.295	30
31	0.0559	9.6830	81.5377	17.8871	173.2012	0.1033	0.0058	8.420	31
32	0.0509	9.7340	83.1168	19.6311	191.0883	0.1027	0.0052	8.538	32
33	0.0464	9.7804	84.6021	21.5451	210.7195	0.1022	0.0047	8.650	33
34	0.0423	9.8227	85.9976	23.6458	232.2646	0.1018	0.0043	8.755	34
35	0.0385	9.8612	87.3078	25.9513	255.9104	0.1014	0.0039	8.853	35
36	0.0351	9.8963	88.5367	28.4815	281.8617	0.1010	0.0035	8.946	36
37	0.0320	9.9283	89.6884	31.2585	310.3432	0.1007	0.0032	9.033	37
38	0.0291	9.9574	90.7669	34.3062	341.6016	0.1004	0.0029	9.115	38
39	0.0266	9.9840	91.7761	37.6510	375.9078	0.1002	0.0027	9.192	39
40	0.0242	10.0082	92.7200	41.3220	413.5588	0.0999	0.0024	9.264	40
41	0.0221	10.0303	93.6020	45.3509	454.8808	0.0997	0.0022	9.332	41
42	0.0201	10.0503	94.4257	49.7726	500.2317	0.0995	0.0020	9.395	42
43	0.0183	10.0687	95.1946	54.6254	550.0042	0.0993	0.0018	9.454	43
44	0.0167	10.0853	95.9118	59.9514	604.6297	0.0992	0.0017	9.510	44
45	0.0152	10.1005	96.5806	65.7967	664.5811	0.0990	0.0015	9.561	45
46	0.0138	10.1144	97.2037	72.2118	730.3777	0.0989	0.0014	9.610	46
47	0.0126	10.1270	97.7841	79.2525	802.5895	0.0987	0.0012	9.655	47
48	0.0115	10.1385	98.3245	86.9796	881.8420	0.0986	0.0011	9.698	48
49	0.0105	10.1490	98.8273	95.4601	968.8216	0.0985	0.0010	9.737	49
50	0.0095	10.1585	99.2950	104.7675	1064.2817	0.0984	0.0009	9.774	50
51	0.0087	10.1672	99.7299	114.9823	1169.0492	0.0984	0.0009	9.809	51
52	0.0079	10.1751	100.1340	126.1931	1284.0315	0.0983	0.0008	9.841	52
53	0.0072	10.1824	100.5095	138.4969	1410.2245	0.0982	0.0007	9.870	53
54	0.0066	10.1889	100.8582	152.0003	1548.7214	0.0981	0.0006	9.898	54
55	0.0060	10.1949	101.1819	166.8204	1700.7218	0.0981	0.0006	9.924	55
60	0.0038	10.2178	102.4812	265.6267	2714.1201	0.0979	0.0004	10.029	60
65	0.0024	10.2322	103.3690	422.9552	4327.7457	0.0977	0.0002	10.102	65
70	0.0015	10.2412	103.9717	673.4681	6897.1086	0.0976	0.0001	10.152	70
75	0.0009	10.2468	104.3785	1072.3577	10988.2840	0.0976	0.0001	10.186	75
80	0.0006	10.2504	104.6518	1707.5063	17502.6287	0.0976	0.0001	10.209	80
85	0.0004	10.2526	104.8346	2718.8482	27875.3660	0.0975	0.0000	10.225	85
90	0.0002	10.2540	104.9564	4329.1995	44391.7900	0.0975	0.0000	10.235	90
95	0.0001	10.2549	105.0373	6893.3487	70690.7557	0.0975	0.0000	10.242	95
100	0.0001	10.2555	105.0909	10976.2222	112566.3819	0.0975	0.0000	10.247	100

$I = 10.00\ \%$

n	(P/F)	(P/A)	(P/G)	(F/P)	(F/A)	(A/P)	(A/F)	(A/G)	n
1	0.9091	0.9091	0.0000	1.1000	1.0000	1.1000	1.0000	0.000	1
2	0.8264	1.7355	0.8264	1.2100	2.1000	0.5762	0.4762	0.476	2
3	0.7513	2.4869	2.3291	1.3310	3.3100	0.4021	0.3021	0.936	3
4	0.6830	3.1699	4.3781	1.4641	4.6410	0.3155	0.2155	1.381	4
5	0.6209	3.7908	6.8618	1.6105	6.1051	0.2638	0.1638	1.810	5
6	0.5645	4.3553	9.6842	1.7716	7.7156	0.2296	0.1296	2.223	6
7	0.5132	4.8684	12.7631	1.9487	9.4872	0.2054	0.1054	2.621	7
8	0.4665	5.3349	16.0287	2.1436	11.4359	0.1874	0.0874	3.004	8
9	0.4241	5.7590	19.4215	2.3579	13.5795	0.1736	0.0736	3.372	9
10	0.3855	6.1446	22.8913	2.5937	15.9374	0.1627	0.0627	3.725	10
11	0.3505	6.4951	26.3963	2.8531	18.5312	0.1540	0.0540	4.064	11
12	0.3186	6.8137	29.9012	3.1384	21.3843	0.1468	0.0468	4.388	12
13	0.2897	7.1034	33.3772	3.4523	24.5227	0.1408	0.0408	4.698	13
14	0.2633	7.3667	36.8005	3.7975	27.9750	0.1357	0.0357	4.995	14
15	0.2394	7.6061	40.1520	4.1772	31.7725	0.1315	0.0315	5.278	15
16	0.2176	7.8237	43.4164	4.5950	35.9497	0.1278	0.0278	5.549	16
17	0.1978	8.0216	46.5819	5.0545	40.5447	0.1247	0.0247	5.807	17
18	0.1799	8.2014	49.6395	5.5599	45.5992	0.1219	0.0219	6.052	18
19	0.1635	8.3649	52.5827	6.1159	51.1591	0.1195	0.0195	6.286	19
20	0.1486	8.5136	55.4069	6.7275	57.2750	0.1175	0.0175	6.508	20
21	0.1351	8.6487	58.1095	7.4002	64.0025	0.1156	0.0156	6.718	21
22	0.1228	8.7715	60.6893	8.1403	71.4027	0.1140	0.0140	6.918	22
23	0.1117	8.8832	63.1462	8.9543	79.5430	0.1126	0.0126	7.108	23
24	0.1015	8.9847	65.4813	9.8497	88.4973	0.1113	0.0113	7.288	24
25	0.0923	9.0770	67.6964	10.8347	98.3471	0.1102	0.0102	7.458	25
26	0.0839	9.1609	69.7940	11.9182	109.1818	0.1092	0.0092	7.618	26
27	0.0763	9.2372	71.7773	13.1100	121.0999	0.1083	0.0083	7.770	27
28	0.0693	9.3066	73.6495	14.4210	134.2099	0.1075	0.0075	7.913	28
29	0.0630	9.3696	75.4146	15.8631	148.6309	0.1067	0.0067	8.048	29
30	0.0573	9.4269	77.0766	17.4494	164.4940	0.1061	0.0061	8.176	30
31	0.0521	9.4790	78.6395	19.1943	181.9434	0.1055	0.0055	8.296	31
32	0.0474	9.5264	80.1078	21.1138	201.1378	0.1050	0.0050	8.409	32
33	0.0431	9.5694	81.4856	23.2252	222.2515	0.1045	0.0045	8.515	33
34	0.0391	9.6086	82.7773	25.5477	245.4767	0.1041	0.0041	8.614	34
35	0.0356	9.6442	83.9872	28.1024	271.0244	0.1037	0.0037	8.708	35
36	0.0323	9.6765	85.1194	30.9127	299.1268	0.1033	0.0033	8.796	36
37	0.0294	9.7059	86.1781	34.0039	330.0395	0.1030	0.0030	8.878	37
38	0.0267	9.7327	87.1673	37.4043	364.0434	0.1027	0.0027	8.956	38
39	0.0243	9.7570	88.0908	41.1448	401.4478	0.1025	0.0025	9.028	39
40	0.0221	9.7791	88.9525	45.2593	442.5926	0.1023	0.0023	9.096	40
41	0.0201	9.7991	89.7560	49.7852	487.8518	0.1020	0.0020	9.159	41
42	0.0183	9.8174	90.5047	54.7637	537.6370	0.1019	0.0019	9.218	42
43	0.0166	9.8340	91.2019	60.2401	592.4007	0.1017	0.0017	9.274	43
44	0.0151	9.8491	91.8508	66.2641	652.6408	0.1015	0.0015	9.325	44
45	0.0137	9.8628	92.4544	72.8905	718.9048	0.1014	0.0014	9.374	45
46	0.0125	9.8753	93.0157	80.1795	791.7953	0.1013	0.0013	9.419	46
47	0.0113	9.8866	93.5372	88.1975	871.9749	0.1011	0.0011	9.461	47
48	0.0103	9.8969	94.0217	97.0172	960.1723	0.1010	0.0010	9.500	48
49	0.0094	9.9063	94.4715	106.7190	1057.1896	0.1009	0.0009	9.536	49
50	0.0085	9.9148	94.8889	117.3909	1163.9085	0.1009	0.0009	9.570	50
51	0.0077	9.9226	95.2761	129.1299	1281.2994	0.1008	0.0008	9.602	51
52	0.0070	9.9296	95.6351	142.0429	1410.4293	0.1007	0.0007	9.631	52
53	0.0064	9.9360	95.9679	156.2472	1552.4723	0.1006	0.0006	9.658	53
54	0.0058	9.9418	96.2763	171.8719	1708.7195	0.1006	0.0006	9.684	54
55	0.0053	9.9471	96.5619	189.0591	1880.5914	0.1005	0.0005	9.707	55
60	0.0033	9.9672	97.7010	304.4816	3034.8164	0.1003	0.0003	9.802	60
65	0.0020	9.9796	98.4705	490.3707	4893.7073	0.1002	0.0002	9.867	65
70	0.0013	9.9873	98.9870	789.7470	7887.4696	0.1001	0.0001	9.911	70
75	0.0008	9.9921	99.3317	1271.8954	12708.9537	0.1001	0.0001	9.941	75
80	0.0005	9.9951	99.5606	2048.4002	20474.0021	0.1000	0.0000	9.960	80
85	0.0003	9.9970	99.7120	3298.9690	32979.6903	0.1000	0.0000	9.974	85
90	0.0002	9.9981	99.8118	5313.0226	53120.2261	0.1000	0.0000	9.983	90
95	0.0001	9.9988	99.8773	8556.6760	85556.7605	0.1000	0.0000	9.988	95
100	0.0001	9.9993	99.9202	13780.6123	137796.1234	0.1000	0.0000	9.992	100

$I = 10.25\%$

n	(P/F)	(P/A)	(P/G)	(F/P)	(F/A)	(A/P)	(A/F)	(A/G)	n
1	0.9070	0.9070	0.0000	1.1025	1.0000	1.1025	1.0000	0.000	1
2	0.8227	1.7297	0.8227	1.2155	2.1025	0.5781	0.4756	0.475	2
3	0.7462	2.4759	2.3151	1.3401	3.3180	0.4039	0.3014	0.935	3
4	0.6768	3.1528	4.3457	1.4775	4.6581	0.3172	0.2147	1.378	4
5	0.6139	3.7667	6.8013	1.6289	6.1356	0.2655	0.1630	1.805	5
6	0.5568	4.3235	9.5855	1.7959	7.7645	0.2313	0.1288	2.217	6
7	0.5051	4.8286	12.6159	1.9799	9.5603	0.2071	0.1046	2.612	7
8	0.4581	5.2867	15.8227	2.1829	11.5402	0.1892	0.0867	2.992	8
9	0.4155	5.7022	19.1468	2.4066	13.7231	0.1754	0.0729	3.357	9
10	0.3769	6.0791	22.5389	2.6533	16.1297	0.1645	0.0620	3.707	10
11	0.3418	6.4210	25.9573	2.9253	18.7830	0.1557	0.0532	4.042	11
12	0.3101	6.7310	29.3681	3.2251	21.7083	0.1486	0.0461	4.363	12
13	0.2812	7.0123	32.7430	3.5557	24.9334	0.1426	0.0401	4.669	13
14	0.2551	7.2674	36.0592	3.9201	28.4891	0.1376	0.0351	4.961	14
15	0.2314	7.4988	39.2985	4.3219	32.4092	0.1334	0.0309	5.240	15
16	0.2099	7.7086	42.4465	4.7649	36.7311	0.1297	0.0272	5.506	16
17	0.1904	7.8990	45.4922	5.2533	41.4961	0.1266	0.0241	5.759	17
18	0.1727	8.0716	48.4273	5.7918	46.7494	0.1239	0.0214	5.999	18
19	0.1566	8.2282	51.2462	6.3855	52.5412	0.1215	0.0190	6.228	19
20	0.1420	8.3703	53.9451	7.0400	58.9267	0.1195	0.0170	6.444	20
21	0.1288	8.4991	56.5219	7.7616	65.9667	0.1177	0.0152	6.650	21
22	0.1169	8.6160	58.9760	8.5572	73.7283	0.1161	0.0136	6.844	22
23	0.1060	8.7220	61.3079	9.4343	82.2854	0.1147	0.0122	7.029	23
24	0.0961	8.8181	63.5192	10.4013	91.7197	0.1134	0.0109	7.203	24
25	0.0872	8.9053	65.6121	11.4674	102.1210	0.1123	0.0098	7.367	25
26	0.0791	8.9844	67.5895	12.6428	113.5884	0.1113	0.0088	7.523	26
27	0.0717	9.0562	69.4548	13.9387	126.2312	0.1104	0.0079	7.669	27
28	0.0651	9.1212	71.2117	15.3674	140.1699	0.1096	0.0071	7.807	28
29	0.0590	9.1803	72.8644	16.9426	155.5373	0.1089	0.0064	7.937	29
30	0.0535	9.2338	74.4169	18.6792	172.4799	0.1083	0.0058	8.059	30
31	0.0486	9.2824	75.8737	20.5938	191.1590	0.1077	0.0052	8.174	31
32	0.0440	9.3264	77.2390	22.7047	211.7529	0.1072	0.0047	8.281	32
33	0.0399	9.3664	78.5174	25.0319	234.4575	0.1068	0.0043	8.382	33
34	0.0362	9.4026	79.7131	27.5977	259.4894	0.1064	0.0039	8.477	34
35	0.0329	9.4355	80.8306	30.4264	287.0871	0.1060	0.0035	8.566	35
36	0.0298	9.4653	81.8740	33.5451	317.5135	0.1056	0.0031	8.649	36
37	0.0270	9.4923	82.8474	36.9835	351.0586	0.1053	0.0028	8.727	37
38	0.0245	9.5168	83.7548	40.7743	388.0421	0.1051	0.0026	8.800	38
39	0.0222	9.5391	84.6001	44.9537	428.8165	0.1048	0.0023	8.868	39
40	0.0202	9.5592	85.3870	49.5614	473.7702	0.1046	0.0021	8.932	40
41	0.0183	9.5776	86.1191	54.6415	523.3316	0.1044	0.0019	8.991	41
42	0.0166	9.5941	86.7997	60.2422	577.9731	0.1042	0.0017	9.047	42
43	0.0151	9.6092	87.4320	66.4171	638.2153	0.1041	0.0016	9.098	43
44	0.0137	9.6229	88.0193	73.2248	704.6324	0.1039	0.0014	9.146	44
45	0.0124	9.6352	88.5643	80.7304	777.8572	0.1038	0.0013	9.191	45
46	0.0112	9.6465	89.0699	89.0052	858.5876	0.1037	0.0012	9.233	46
47	0.0102	9.6567	89.5386	98.1283	947.5928	0.1036	0.0011	9.272	47
48	0.0092	9.6659	89.9731	108.1864	1045.7211	0.1035	0.0010	9.308	48
49	0.0084	9.6743	90.3755	119.2755	1153.9075	0.1034	0.0009	9.341	49
50	0.0076	9.6819	90.7481	131.5013	1273.1830	0.1033	0.0008	9.373	50
51	0.0069	9.6888	91.0930	144.9801	1404.6843	0.1032	0.0007	9.401	51
52	0.0063	9.6951	91.4121	159.8406	1549.6644	0.1031	0.0006	9.428	52
53	0.0057	9.7007	91.7071	176.2243	1709.5050	0.1031	0.0006	9.453	53
54	0.0051	9.7059	91.9799	194.2872	1885.7293	0.1030	0.0005	9.476	54
55	0.0047	9.7106	92.2320	214.2017	2080.0165	0.1030	0.0005	9.498	55
60	0.0029	9.7281	93.2310	348.9120	3394.2633	0.1028	0.0003	9.583	60
65	0.0018	9.7389	93.8982	568.3409	5535.0328	0.1027	0.0002	9.641	65
70	0.0011	9.7456	94.3409	925.7674	9022.1207	0.1026	0.0001	9.680	70
75	0.0007	9.7496	94.6331	1507.9775	14702.2195	0.1026	0.0001	9.706	75
80	0.0004	9.7521	94.8249	2456.3364	23954.5019	0.1025	0.0000	9.723	80
85	0.0002	9.7537	94.9504	4001.1132	39025.4949	0.1025	0.0000	9.734	85
90	0.0002	9.7546	95.0321	6517.3918	63574.5545	0.1025	0.0000	9.742	90
95	0.0001	9.7552	95.0852	10616.1446	103562.3859	0.1025	0.0000	9.747	95
100	0.0001	9.7555	95.1195	17292.5808	168698.3494	0.1025	0.0000	9.750	100

PROFESSIONAL PUBLICATIONS, INC. ● Belmont, CA

EXPANDED INTEREST TABLES

I = 10.50 %

n	(P/F)	(P/A)	(P/G)	(F/P)	(F/A)	(A/P)	(A/F)	(A/G)	n
1	0.9050	0.9050	0.0000	1.1050	1.0000	1.1050	1.0000	0.000	1
2	0.8190	1.7240	0.8190	1.2210	2.1050	0.5801	0.4751	0.475	2
3	0.7412	2.4651	2.3013	1.3492	3.3260	0.4057	0.3007	0.933	3
4	0.6707	3.1359	4.3135	1.4909	4.6753	0.3189	0.2139	1.375	4
5	0.6070	3.7429	6.7415	1.6474	6.1662	0.2672	0.1622	1.801	5
6	0.5493	4.2922	9.4881	1.8204	7.8136	0.2330	0.1280	2.210	6
7	0.4971	4.7893	12.4709	2.0116	9.6340	0.2088	0.1038	2.603	7
8	0.4499	5.2392	15.6201	2.2228	11.6456	0.1909	0.0859	2.981	8
9	0.4071	5.6463	18.8771	2.4562	13.8684	0.1771	0.0721	3.343	9
10	0.3684	6.0148	22.1932	2.7141	16.3246	0.1663	0.0613	3.689	10
11	0.3334	6.3482	25.5276	2.9991	19.0387	0.1575	0.0525	4.021	11
12	0.3018	6.6500	28.8469	3.3140	22.0377	0.1504	0.0454	4.337	12
13	0.2731	6.9230	32.1238	3.6619	25.3517	0.1444	0.0394	4.640	13
14	0.2471	7.1702	35.3365	4.0464	29.0136	0.1395	0.0345	4.928	14
15	0.2236	7.3938	38.4676	4.4713	33.0600	0.1352	0.0302	5.202	15
16	0.2024	7.5962	41.5036	4.9408	37.5313	0.1316	0.0266	5.463	16
17	0.1832	7.7794	44.4342	5.4596	42.4721	0.1285	0.0235	5.711	17
18	0.1658	7.9451	47.2521	6.0328	47.9317	0.1259	0.0209	5.947	18
19	0.1500	8.0952	49.9523	6.6663	53.9645	0.1235	0.0185	6.170	19
20	0.1358	8.2309	52.5316	7.3662	60.6308	0.1215	0.0165	6.382	20
21	0.1229	8.3538	54.9887	8.1397	67.9970	0.1197	0.0147	6.582	21
22	0.1112	8.4649	57.3235	8.9944	76.1367	0.1181	0.0131	6.771	22
23	0.1006	8.5656	59.5370	9.9388	85.1311	0.1167	0.0117	6.950	23
24	0.0911	8.6566	61.6313	10.9823	95.0699	0.1155	0.0105	7.119	24
25	0.0824	8.7390	63.6090	12.1355	106.0522	0.1144	0.0094	7.278	25
26	0.0746	8.8136	65.4733	13.4097	118.1877	0.1135	0.0085	7.428	26
27	0.0675	8.8811	67.2280	14.8177	131.5974	0.1126	0.0076	7.569	27
28	0.0611	8.9422	68.8770	16.3736	146.4151	0.1118	0.0068	7.702	28
29	0.0553	8.9974	70.4245	18.0928	162.7887	0.1111	0.0061	7.827	29
30	0.0500	9.0474	71.8751	19.9926	180.8815	0.1105	0.0055	7.944	30
31	0.0453	9.0927	73.2331	22.0918	200.8741	0.1100	0.0050	8.054	31
32	0.0410	9.1337	74.5029	24.4114	222.9658	0.1095	0.0045	8.157	32
33	0.0371	9.1707	75.6892	26.9746	247.3772	0.1090	0.0040	8.253	33
34	0.0335	9.2043	76.7964	29.8069	274.3518	0.1086	0.0036	8.343	34
35	0.0304	9.2347	77.8287	32.9367	304.1588	0.1083	0.0033	8.427	35
36	0.0275	9.2621	78.7903	36.3950	337.0955	0.1080	0.0030	8.506	36
37	0.0249	9.2870	79.6855	40.2165	373.4905	0.1077	0.0027	8.580	37
38	0.0225	9.3095	80.5181	44.4392	413.7070	0.1074	0.0024	8.649	38
39	0.0204	9.3299	81.2919	49.1054	458.1462	0.1072	0.0022	8.713	39
40	0.0184	9.3483	82.0107	54.2614	507.2516	0.1070	0.0020	8.772	40
41	0.0167	9.3650	82.6778	59.9589	561.5130	0.1068	0.0018	8.828	41
42	0.0151	9.3801	83.2966	66.2545	621.4719	0.1066	0.0016	8.880	42
43	0.0137	9.3937	83.8703	73.2113	687.7264	0.1065	0.0015	8.928	43
44	0.0124	9.4061	84.4018	80.8985	760.9377	0.1063	0.0013	8.973	44
45	0.0112	9.4173	84.8940	89.3928	841.8361	0.1062	0.0012	9.014	45
46	0.0101	9.4274	85.3496	98.7790	931.2289	0.1061	0.0011	9.053	46
47	0.0092	9.4366	85.7710	109.1508	1030.0080	0.1060	0.0010	9.089	47
48	0.0083	9.4448	86.1607	120.6117	1139.1588	0.1059	0.0009	9.122	48
49	0.0075	9.4524	86.5209	133.2759	1259.7705	0.1058	0.0008	9.153	49
50	0.0068	9.4591	86.8536	147.2699	1393.0464	0.1057	0.0007	9.182	50
51	0.0061	9.4653	87.1608	162.7332	1540.3162	0.1056	0.0006	9.208	51
52	0.0056	9.4708	87.4445	179.8202	1703.0494	0.1056	0.0006	9.233	52
53	0.0050	9.4759	87.7062	198.7013	1882.8696	0.1055	0.0005	9.255	53
54	0.0046	9.4804	87.9476	219.5649	2081.5710	0.1055	0.0005	9.276	54
55	0.0041	9.4846	88.1701	242.6193	2301.1359	0.1054	0.0004	9.296	55
60	0.0025	9.5000	89.0464	399.7023	3797.1651	0.1053	0.0003	9.373	60
65	0.0015	9.5093	89.6251	658.4883	6261.7935	0.1052	0.0002	9.424	65
70	0.0009	9.5150	90.0048	1084.8244	10322.1375	0.1051	0.0001	9.459	70
75	0.0006	9.5185	90.2525	1787.1905	17011.3383	0.1051	0.0001	9.481	75
80	0.0003	9.5206	90.4134	2944.3012	28031.4404	0.1050	0.0000	9.496	80
85	0.0002	9.5218	90.5174	4850.5796	46186.4719	0.1050	0.0000	9.506	85
90	0.0001	9.5226	90.5843	7991.0716	76095.9200	0.1050	0.0000	9.512	90
95	0.0001	9.5231	90.6273	13164.8651	125370.1434	0.1050	0.0000	9.516	95
100	0.0000	9.5234	90.6549	21688.4144	206546.8035	0.1050	0.0000	9.519	100

$$I = 10.75\ \%$$

n	(P/F)	(P/A)	(P/G)	(F/P)	(F/A)	(A/P)	(A/F)	(A/G)	n
1	0.9029	0.9029	0.0000	1.1075	1.0000	1.1075	1.0000	0.000	1
2	0.8153	1.7182	0.8153	1.2266	2.1075	0.5820	0.4745	0.474	2
3	0.7362	2.4544	2.2876	1.3584	3.3341	0.4074	0.2999	0.932	3
4	0.6647	3.1191	4.2817	1.5044	4.6925	0.3206	0.2131	1.372	4
5	0.6002	3.7193	6.6824	1.6662	6.1969	0.2689	0.1614	1.796	5
6	0.5419	4.2612	9.3920	1.8453	7.8631	0.2347	0.1272	2.204	6
7	0.4893	4.7505	12.3280	2.0436	9.7084	0.2105	0.1030	2.595	7
8	0.4418	5.1923	15.4207	2.2633	11.7520	0.1926	0.0851	2.969	8
9	0.3989	5.5913	18.6122	2.5066	14.0153	0.1789	0.0714	3.328	9
10	0.3602	5.9515	21.8542	2.7761	16.5220	0.1680	0.0605	3.672	10
11	0.3253	6.2767	25.1067	3.0745	19.2981	0.1593	0.0518	4.000	11
12	0.2937	6.5704	28.3372	3.4051	22.3727	0.1522	0.0447	4.312	12
13	0.2652	6.8356	31.5193	3.7711	25.7777	0.1463	0.0388	4.611	13
14	0.2394	7.0750	34.6319	4.1765	29.5488	0.1413	0.0338	4.895	14
15	0.2162	7.2912	37.6586	4.6255	33.7253	0.1372	0.0297	5.164	15
16	0.1952	7.4864	40.5868	5.1227	38.3508	0.1336	0.0261	5.421	16
17	0.1763	7.6627	43.4070	5.6734	43.4735	0.1305	0.0230	5.664	17
18	0.1592	7.8218	46.1126	6.2833	49.1469	0.1278	0.0203	5.895	18
19	0.1437	7.9655	48.6992	6.9587	55.4302	0.1255	0.0180	6.113	19
20	0.1298	8.0953	51.1646	7.7068	62.3889	0.1235	0.0160	6.320	20
21	0.1172	8.2125	53.5078	8.5353	70.0957	0.1218	0.0143	6.515	21
22	0.1058	8.3182	55.7293	9.4528	78.6310	0.1202	0.0127	6.699	22
23	0.0955	8.4138	57.8308	10.4690	88.0839	0.1189	0.0114	6.873	23
24	0.0862	8.5000	59.8145	11.5944	98.5529	0.1176	0.0101	7.037	24
25	0.0779	8.5779	61.6835	12.8408	110.1473	0.1166	0.0091	7.191	25
26	0.0703	8.6482	63.4415	14.2212	122.9882	0.1156	0.0081	7.335	26
27	0.0635	8.7117	65.0923	15.7500	137.2094	0.1148	0.0073	7.471	27
28	0.0573	8.7690	66.6401	17.4431	152.9594	0.1140	0.0065	7.599	28
29	0.0518	8.8208	68.0895	19.3183	170.4025	0.1134	0.0059	7.719	29
30	0.0467	8.8675	69.4450	21.3950	189.7208	0.1128	0.0053	7.831	30
31	0.0422	8.9097	70.7111	23.6949	211.1158	0.1122	0.0047	7.936	31
32	0.0381	8.9478	71.8924	26.2422	234.8108	0.1118	0.0043	8.034	32
33	0.0344	8.9823	72.9935	29.0632	261.0529	0.1113	0.0038	8.126	33
34	0.0311	9.0133	74.0187	32.1875	290.1161	0.1109	0.0034	8.212	34
35	0.0281	9.0414	74.9725	35.6476	322.3036	0.1106	0.0031	8.292	35
36	0.0253	9.0667	75.8590	39.4798	357.9512	0.1103	0.0028	8.366	36
37	0.0229	9.0896	76.6824	43.7238	397.4310	0.1100	0.0025	8.436	37
38	0.0207	9.1102	77.4464	48.4241	441.1548	0.1098	0.0023	8.501	38
39	0.0186	9.1289	78.1550	53.6297	489.5789	0.1095	0.0020	8.561	39
40	0.0168	9.1457	78.8116	59.3949	543.2087	0.1093	0.0018	8.617	40
41	0.0152	9.1609	79.4197	65.7799	602.6036	0.1092	0.0017	8.669	41
42	0.0137	9.1746	79.9825	72.8512	668.3835	0.1090	0.0015	8.717	42
43	0.0124	9.1870	80.5031	80.6827	741.2347	0.1088	0.0013	8.762	43
44	0.0112	9.1982	80.9843	89.3561	821.9175	0.1087	0.0012	8.804	44
45	0.0101	9.2083	81.4289	98.9619	911.2736	0.1086	0.0011	8.843	45
46	0.0091	9.2175	81.8395	109.6003	1010.2355	0.1085	0.0010	8.878	46
47	0.0082	9.2257	82.2184	121.3823	1119.8358	0.1084	0.0009	8.911	47
48	0.0074	9.2331	82.5681	134.4310	1241.2182	0.1083	0.0008	8.942	48
49	0.0067	9.2398	82.8905	148.8823	1375.6491	0.1082	0.0007	8.971	49
50	0.0061	9.2459	83.1876	164.8871	1524.5314	0.1082	0.0007	8.997	50
51	0.0055	9.2514	83.4614	182.6125	1689.4185	0.1081	0.0006	9.021	51
52	0.0049	9.2563	83.7136	202.2433	1872.0310	0.1080	0.0005	9.043	52
53	0.0045	9.2608	83.9458	223.9845	2074.2743	0.1080	0.0005	9.064	53
54	0.0040	9.2648	84.1594	248.0628	2298.2588	0.1079	0.0004	9.083	54
55	0.0036	9.2685	84.3560	274.7296	2546.3217	0.1079	0.0004	9.101	55
60	0.0022	9.2820	85.1249	457.7455	4248.7954	0.1077	0.0002	9.171	60
65	0.0013	9.2901	85.6270	762.6807	7085.4021	0.1076	0.0001	9.217	65
70	0.0008	9.2950	85.9527	1270.7539	11811.6640	0.1076	0.0001	9.247	70
75	0.0005	9.2979	86.1629	2117.2889	19686.4082	0.1076	0.0001	9.266	75
80	0.0003	9.2997	86.2978	3527.7581	32807.0516	0.1075	0.0000	9.279	80
85	0.0002	9.3007	86.3840	5877.8360	54668.2421	0.1075	0.0000	9.287	85
90	0.0001	9.3014	86.4389	9793.4597	91092.6484	0.1075	0.0000	9.293	90
95	0.0001	9.3018	86.4738	16317.5448	151781.8125	0.1075	0.0000	9.296	95
100	0.0000	9.3020	86.4959	27187.7639	252900.1291	0.1075	0.0000	9.298	100

EXPANDED INTEREST TABLES

I = 11.00 %

n	(P/F)	(P/A)	(P/G)	(F/P)	(F/A)	(A/P)	(A/F)	(A/G)	n
1	0.9009	0.9009	0.0000	1.1100	1.0000	1.1100	1.0000	0.000	1
2	0.8116	1.7125	0.8116	1.2321	2.1100	0.5839	0.4739	0.473	2
3	0.7312	2.4437	2.2740	1.3676	3.3421	0.4092	0.2992	0.930	3
4	0.6587	3.1024	4.2502	1.5181	4.7097	0.3223	0.2123	1.370	4
5	0.5935	3.6959	6.6240	1.6851	6.2278	0.2706	0.1606	1.792	5
6	0.5346	4.2305	9.2972	1.8704	7.9129	0.2364	0.1264	2.197	6
7	0.4817	4.7122	12.1872	2.0762	9.7833	0.2122	0.1022	2.586	7
8	0.4339	5.1461	15.2246	2.3045	11.8594	0.1943	0.0843	2.958	8
9	0.3909	5.5370	18.3520	2.5580	14.1640	0.1806	0.0706	3.314	9
10	0.3522	5.8892	21.5217	2.8394	16.7220	0.1698	0.0598	3.654	10
11	0.3173	6.2065	24.6945	3.1518	19.5614	0.1611	0.0511	3.978	11
12	0.2858	6.4924	27.8388	3.4985	22.7132	0.1540	0.0440	4.287	12
13	0.2575	6.7499	30.9290	3.8833	26.2116	0.1482	0.0382	4.582	13
14	0.2320	6.9819	33.9449	4.3104	30.0949	0.1432	0.0332	4.861	14
15	0.2090	7.1909	36.8709	4.7846	34.4054	0.1391	0.0291	5.127	15
16	0.1883	7.3792	39.6953	5.3109	39.1899	0.1355	0.0255	5.379	16
17	0.1696	7.5488	42.4095	5.8951	44.5008	0.1325	0.0225	5.618	17
18	0.1528	7.7016	45.0074	6.5436	50.3959	0.1298	0.0198	5.843	18
19	0.1377	7.8393	47.4856	7.2633	56.9395	0.1276	0.0176	6.057	19
20	0.1240	7.9633	49.8423	8.0623	64.2028	0.1256	0.0156	6.259	20
21	0.1117	8.0751	52.0771	8.9492	72.2651	0.1238	0.0138	6.449	21
22	0.1007	8.1757	54.1912	9.9336	81.2143	0.1223	0.0123	6.628	22
23	0.0907	8.2664	56.1864	11.0263	91.1479	0.1210	0.0110	6.796	23
24	0.0817	8.3481	58.0656	12.2392	102.1742	0.1198	0.0098	6.955	24
25	0.0736	8.4217	59.8322	13.5855	114.4133	0.1187	0.0087	7.104	25
26	0.0663	8.4881	61.4900	15.0799	127.9988	0.1178	0.0078	7.244	26
27	0.0597	8.5478	63.0433	16.7386	143.0786	0.1170	0.0070	7.375	27
28	0.0538	8.6016	64.4965	18.5799	159.8173	0.1163	0.0063	7.498	28
29	0.0485	8.6501	65.8542	20.6237	178.3972	0.1156	0.0056	7.613	29
30	0.0437	8.6938	67.1210	22.8923	199.0209	0.1150	0.0050	7.720	30
31	0.0394	8.7331	68.3016	25.4104	221.9132	0.1145	0.0045	7.821	31
32	0.0355	8.7686	69.4007	28.2056	247.3236	0.1140	0.0040	7.914	32
33	0.0319	8.8005	70.4228	31.3082	275.5292	0.1136	0.0036	8.002	33
34	0.0288	8.8293	71.3724	34.7521	306.8374	0.1133	0.0033	8.083	34
35	0.0259	8.8552	72.2538	38.5749	341.5896	0.1129	0.0029	8.159	35
36	0.0234	8.8786	73.0712	42.8181	380.1644	0.1126	0.0026	8.230	36
37	0.0210	8.8996	73.8286	47.5281	422.9825	0.1124	0.0024	8.295	37
38	0.0190	8.9186	74.5300	52.7562	470.5106	0.1121	0.0021	8.356	38
39	0.0171	8.9357	75.1789	58.5593	523.2667	0.1119	0.0019	8.413	39
40	0.0154	8.9511	75.7789	65.0009	581.8261	0.1117	0.0017	8.465	40
41	0.0139	8.9649	76.3333	72.1510	646.8269	0.1115	0.0015	8.514	41
42	0.0125	8.9774	76.8452	80.0876	718.9779	0.1114	0.0014	8.559	42
43	0.0112	8.9886	77.3176	88.8972	799.0655	0.1113	0.0013	8.601	43
44	0.0101	8.9988	77.7534	98.6759	887.9627	0.1111	0.0011	8.640	44
45	0.0091	9.0079	78.1551	109.5302	986.6386	0.1110	0.0010	8.676	45
46	0.0082	9.0161	78.5253	121.5786	1096.1688	0.1109	0.0009	8.709	46
47	0.0074	9.0235	78.8661	134.9522	1217.7474	0.1108	0.0008	8.740	47
48	0.0067	9.0302	79.1799	149.7970	1352.6996	0.1107	0.0007	8.768	48
49	0.0060	9.0362	79.4686	166.2746	1502.4965	0.1107	0.0007	8.794	49
50	0.0054	9.0417	79.7341	184.5648	1668.7712	0.1106	0.0006	8.818	50
51	0.0049	9.0465	79.9781	204.8670	1853.3360	0.1105	0.0005	8.840	51
52	0.0044	9.0509	80.2024	227.4023	2058.2029	0.1105	0.0005	8.861	52
53	0.0040	9.0549	80.4084	252.4166	2285.6053	0.1104	0.0004	8.880	53
54	0.0036	9.0585	80.5976	280.1824	2538.0218	0.1104	0.0004	8.897	54
55	0.0032	9.0617	80.7712	311.0025	2818.2042	0.1104	0.0004	8.913	55
60	0.0019	9.0736	81.4461	524.0572	4755.0658	0.1102	0.0002	8.976	60
65	0.0011	9.0806	81.8819	883.0669	8018.7903	0.1101	0.0001	9.017	65
70	0.0007	9.0848	82.1614	1488.0191	13518.3557	0.1101	0.0001	9.043	70
75	0.0004	9.0873	82.3397	2507.3988	22785.4434	0.1100	0.0000	9.061	75
80	0.0002	9.0888	82.4529	4225.1128	38401.0250	0.1100	0.0000	9.072	80
85	0.0001	9.0896	82.5245	7119.5607	64714.1881	0.1100	0.0000	9.079	85
90	0.0001	9.0902	82.5695	11996.8738	109053.3983	0.1100	0.0000	9.083	90
95	0.0000	9.0905	82.5978	20215.4301	183767.5459	0.1100	0.0000	9.086	95
100	0.0000	9.0906	82.6155	34064.1753	309665.2297	0.1100	0.0000	9.088	100

$I = 11.25\%$

n	(P/F)	(P/A)	(P/G)	(F/P)	(F/A)	(A/P)	(A/F)	(A/G)	n
1	0.8989	0.8989	0.0000	1.1125	1.0000	1.1125	1.0000	0.000	1
2	0.8080	1.7069	0.8080	1.2377	2.1125	0.5859	0.4734	0.473	2
3	0.7263	2.4331	2.2605	1.3769	3.3502	0.4110	0.2985	0.929	3
4	0.6528	3.0860	4.2190	1.5318	4.7270	0.3240	0.2115	1.367	4
5	0.5868	3.6728	6.5663	1.7041	6.2588	0.2723	0.1598	1.787	5
6	0.5275	4.2002	9.2036	1.8958	7.9630	0.2381	0.1256	2.191	6
7	0.4741	4.6744	12.0484	2.1091	9.8588	0.2139	0.1014	2.577	7
8	0.4262	5.1006	15.0317	2.3464	11.9679	0.1961	0.0836	2.947	8
9	0.3831	5.4837	18.0964	2.6104	14.3143	0.1824	0.0699	3.300	9
10	0.3443	5.8280	21.1956	2.9040	16.9247	0.1716	0.0591	3.636	10
11	0.3095	6.1375	24.2909	3.2307	19.8287	0.1629	0.0504	3.957	11
12	0.2782	6.4158	27.3514	3.5942	23.0594	0.1559	0.0434	4.263	12
13	0.2501	6.6658	30.3525	3.9985	26.6536	0.1500	0.0375	4.553	13
14	0.2248	6.8907	33.2749	4.4484	30.6521	0.1451	0.0326	4.829	14
15	0.2021	7.0927	36.1039	4.9488	35.1005	0.1410	0.0285	5.090	15
16	0.1816	7.2744	38.8284	5.5055	40.0493	0.1375	0.0250	5.337	16
17	0.1633	7.4376	41.4407	6.1249	45.5548	0.1345	0.0220	5.571	17
18	0.1468	7.5844	43.9355	6.8140	51.6798	0.1318	0.0193	5.792	18
19	0.1319	7.7163	46.3100	7.5805	58.4937	0.1296	0.0171	6.001	19
20	0.1186	7.8349	48.5630	8.4334	66.0743	0.1276	0.0151	6.198	20
21	0.1066	7.9415	50.6947	9.3821	74.5076	0.1259	0.0134	6.383	21
22	0.0958	8.0373	52.7067	10.4376	83.8897	0.1244	0.0119	6.557	22
23	0.0861	8.1234	54.6013	11.6118	94.3273	0.1231	0.0106	6.721	23
24	0.0774	8.2008	56.3817	12.9182	105.9392	0.1219	0.0094	6.875	24
25	0.0696	8.2704	58.0517	14.3714	118.8573	0.1209	0.0084	7.019	25
26	0.0625	8.3329	59.6154	15.9882	133.2288	0.1200	0.0075	7.154	26
27	0.0562	8.3891	61.0771	17.7869	149.2170	0.1192	0.0067	7.280	27
28	0.0505	8.4397	62.4416	19.7879	167.0039	0.1185	0.0060	7.398	28
29	0.0454	8.4851	63.7135	22.0141	186.7918	0.1179	0.0054	7.508	29
30	0.0408	8.5259	64.8976	24.4907	208.8059	0.1173	0.0048	7.611	30
31	0.0367	8.5626	65.9987	27.2459	233.2966	0.1168	0.0043	7.707	31
32	0.0330	8.5956	67.0214	30.3110	260.5424	0.1163	0.0038	7.797	32
33	0.0297	8.6253	67.9704	33.7210	290.8535	0.1159	0.0034	7.880	33
34	0.0267	8.6519	68.8501	37.5146	324.5745	0.1156	0.0031	7.957	34
35	0.0240	8.6759	69.6647	41.7350	362.0891	0.1153	0.0028	8.029	35
36	0.0215	8.6974	70.4185	46.4302	403.8241	0.1150	0.0025	8.096	36
37	0.0194	8.7168	71.1155	51.6536	450.2544	0.1147	0.0022	8.158	37
38	0.0174	8.7342	71.7594	57.4646	501.9080	0.1145	0.0020	8.215	38
39	0.0156	8.7498	72.3538	63.9294	559.3726	0.1143	0.0018	8.269	39
40	0.0141	8.7639	72.9021	71.1215	623.3020	0.1141	0.0016	8.318	40
41	0.0126	8.7765	73.4077	79.1226	694.4235	0.1139	0.0014	8.364	41
42	0.0114	8.7879	73.8735	88.0239	773.5462	0.1138	0.0013	8.406	42
43	0.0102	8.7981	74.3023	97.9266	861.5701	0.1137	0.0012	8.445	43
44	0.0092	8.8073	74.6970	108.9434	959.4968	0.1135	0.0010	8.481	44
45	0.0083	8.8155	75.0601	121.1995	1068.4401	0.1134	0.0009	8.514	45
46	0.0074	8.8230	75.3938	134.8345	1189.6397	0.1133	0.0008	8.545	46
47	0.0067	8.8296	75.7005	150.0033	1324.4741	0.1133	0.0008	8.573	47
48	0.0060	8.8356	75.9821	166.8787	1474.4775	0.1132	0.0007	8.599	48
49	0.0054	8.8410	76.2407	185.6526	1641.3562	0.1131	0.0006	8.623	49
50	0.0048	8.8459	76.4779	206.5385	1827.0087	0.1130	0.0005	8.645	50
51	0.0044	8.8502	76.6955	229.7741	2033.5472	0.1130	0.0005	8.666	51
52	0.0039	8.8541	76.8950	255.6236	2263.3213	0.1129	0.0004	8.684	52
53	0.0035	8.8576	77.0779	284.3813	2518.9449	0.1129	0.0004	8.701	53
54	0.0032	8.8608	77.2454	316.3742	2803.3262	0.1129	0.0004	8.717	54
55	0.0028	8.8636	77.3988	351.9663	3119.7004	0.1128	0.0003	8.732	55
60	0.0017	8.8741	77.9914	599.7927	5322.6018	0.1127	0.0002	8.788	60
65	0.0010	8.8802	78.3698	1022.1186	9076.6095	0.1126	0.0001	8.825	65
70	0.0006	8.8838	78.6098	1741.8124	15473.8879	0.1126	0.0001	8.848	70
75	0.0003	8.8859	78.7611	2968.2568	26375.6162	0.1125	0.0000	8.863	75
80	0.0002	8.8871	78.8561	5058.2649	44953.4661	0.1125	0.0000	8.873	80
85	0.0001	8.8879	78.9155	8619.8889	76612.3462	0.1125	0.0000	8.879	85
90	0.0001	8.8883	78.9525	14689.3226	130562.8676	0.1125	0.0000	8.882	90
95	0.0000	8.8885	78.9755	25032.3641	222501.0142	0.1125	0.0000	8.885	95
100	0.0000	8.8887	78.9897	42658.1449	379174.6215	0.1125	0.0000	8.886	100

EXPANDED INTEREST TABLES

$I = 11.50 \%$

n	(P/F)	(P/A)	(P/G)	(F/P)	(F/A)	(A/P)	(A/F)	(A/G)	n
1	0.8969	0.8969	0.0000	1.1150	1.0000	1.1150	1.0000	0.000	1
2	0.8044	1.7012	0.8044	1.2432	2.1150	0.5878	0.4728	0.472	2
3	0.7214	2.4226	2.2472	1.3862	3.3582	0.4128	0.2978	0.927	3
4	0.6470	3.0696	4.1881	1.5456	4.7444	0.3258	0.2108	1.364	4
5	0.5803	3.6499	6.5092	1.7234	6.2900	0.2740	0.1590	1.783	5
6	0.5204	4.1703	9.1113	1.9215	8.0134	0.2398	0.1248	2.184	6
7	0.4667	4.6370	11.9117	2.1425	9.9349	0.2157	0.1007	2.568	7
8	0.4186	5.0556	14.8419	2.3889	12.0774	0.1978	0.0828	2.935	8
9	0.3754	5.4311	17.8454	2.6636	14.4663	0.1841	0.0691	3.285	9
10	0.3367	5.7678	20.8757	2.9699	17.1300	0.1734	0.0584	3.619	10
11	0.3020	6.0697	23.8955	3.3115	20.0999	0.1648	0.0498	3.936	11
12	0.2708	6.3406	26.8747	3.6923	23.4114	0.1577	0.0427	4.238	12
13	0.2429	6.5835	29.7895	4.1169	27.1037	0.1519	0.0369	4.524	13
14	0.2178	6.8013	32.6215	4.5904	31.2207	0.1470	0.0320	4.796	14
15	0.1954	6.9967	35.3568	5.1183	35.8110	0.1429	0.0279	5.053	15
16	0.1752	7.1719	37.9852	5.7069	40.9293	0.1394	0.0244	5.296	16
17	0.1572	7.3291	40.4997	6.3632	46.6362	0.1364	0.0214	5.525	17
18	0.1409	7.4700	42.8957	7.0949	52.9993	0.1339	0.0189	5.742	18
19	0.1264	7.5964	45.1711	7.9108	60.0942	0.1316	0.0166	5.946	19
20	0.1134	7.7098	47.3252	8.8206	68.0051	0.1297	0.0147	6.138	20
21	0.1017	7.8115	49.3587	9.8350	76.8257	0.1280	0.0130	6.318	21
22	0.0912	7.9027	51.2737	10.9660	86.6606	0.1265	0.0115	6.488	22
23	0.0818	7.9845	53.0730	12.2271	97.6266	0.1252	0.0102	6.647	23
24	0.0734	8.0578	54.7601	13.6332	109.8536	0.1241	0.0091	6.795	24
25	0.0658	8.1236	56.3389	15.2010	123.4868	0.1231	0.0081	6.935	25
26	0.0590	8.1826	57.8139	16.9491	138.6878	0.1222	0.0072	7.065	26
27	0.0529	8.2355	59.1897	18.8982	155.6369	0.1214	0.0064	7.187	27
28	0.0475	8.2830	60.4711	21.0715	174.5351	0.1207	0.0057	7.300	28
29	0.0426	8.3255	61.6628	23.4948	195.6067	0.1201	0.0051	7.406	29
30	0.0382	8.3637	62.7698	26.1967	219.1014	0.1196	0.0046	7.505	30
31	0.0342	8.3980	63.7969	29.2093	245.2981	0.1191	0.0041	7.596	31
32	0.0307	8.4287	64.7487	32.5683	274.5074	0.1186	0.0036	7.682	32
33	0.0275	8.4562	65.6300	36.3137	307.0757	0.1183	0.0033	7.761	33
34	0.0247	8.4809	66.4450	40.4898	343.3895	0.1179	0.0029	7.834	34
35	0.0222	8.5030	67.1981	45.1461	383.8792	0.1176	0.0026	7.902	35
36	0.0199	8.5229	67.8934	50.3379	429.0254	0.1173	0.0023	7.966	36
37	0.0178	8.5407	68.5348	56.1268	479.3633	0.1171	0.0021	8.024	37
38	0.0160	8.5567	69.1260	62.5814	535.4900	0.1169	0.0019	8.078	38
39	0.0143	8.5710	69.6706	69.7782	598.0714	0.1167	0.0017	8.128	39
40	0.0129	8.5839	70.1719	77.8027	667.8496	0.1165	0.0015	8.174	40
41	0.0115	8.5954	70.6330	86.7500	745.6523	0.1163	0.0013	8.217	41
42	0.0103	8.6058	71.0568	96.7263	832.4023	0.1162	0.0012	8.256	42
43	0.0093	8.6150	71.4463	107.8498	929.1286	0.1161	0.0011	8.293	43
44	0.0083	8.6233	71.8039	120.2525	1036.9784	0.1160	0.0010	8.326	44
45	0.0075	8.6308	72.1320	134.0816	1157.2309	0.1159	0.0009	8.357	45
46	0.0067	8.6375	72.4330	149.5009	1291.3125	0.1158	0.0008	8.385	46
47	0.0060	8.6435	72.7090	166.6935	1440.8134	0.1157	0.0007	8.412	47
48	0.0054	8.6489	72.9618	185.8633	1607.5069	0.1156	0.0006	8.436	48
49	0.0048	8.6537	73.1935	207.2376	1793.3702	0.1156	0.0006	8.458	49
50	0.0043	8.6580	73.4055	231.0699	2000.6078	0.1155	0.0005	8.478	50
51	0.0039	8.6619	73.5996	257.6429	2231.6777	0.1154	0.0004	8.496	51
52	0.0035	8.6654	73.7771	287.2719	2489.3206	0.1154	0.0004	8.514	52
53	0.0031	8.6685	73.9395	320.3081	2776.5925	0.1154	0.0004	8.529	53
54	0.0028	8.6713	74.0879	357.1436	3096.9006	0.1153	0.0003	8.544	54
55	0.0025	8.6738	74.2235	398.2151	3454.0442	0.1153	0.0003	8.557	55
60	0.0015	8.6830	74.7439	686.2653	5958.8287	0.1152	0.0002	8.608	60
65	0.0008	8.6883	75.0725	1182.6776	10275.4576	0.1151	0.0001	8.640	65
70	0.0005	8.6914	75.2786	2038.1715	17714.5345	0.1151	0.0001	8.661	70
75	0.0003	8.6932	75.4072	3512.4897	30534.6927	0.1150	0.0000	8.674	75
80	0.0002	8.6942	75.4870	6053.2609	52628.3554	0.1150	0.0000	8.682	80
85	0.0001	8.6948	75.5363	10431.9075	90703.5435	0.1150	0.0000	8.687	85
90	0.0001	8.6952	75.5666	17977.8629	156320.5471	0.1150	0.0000	8.690	90
95	0.0000	8.6954	75.5853	30982.2106	269401.8312	0.1150	0.0000	8.692	95
100	0.0000	8.6955	75.5967	53393.2969	464280.8428	0.1150	0.0000	8.693	100

I = 11.75 %

n	(P/F)	(P/A)	(P/G)	(F/P)	(F/A)	(A/P)	(A/F)	(A/G)	n
1	0.8949	0.8949	0.0000	1.1175	1.0000	1.1175	1.0000	0.000	1
2	0.8008	1.6956	0.8008	1.2488	2.1175	0.5898	0.4723	0.472	2
3	0.7166	2.4122	2.2339	1.3955	3.3663	0.4146	0.2971	0.926	3
4	0.6412	3.0534	4.1576	1.5595	4.7618	0.3275	0.2100	1.361	4
5	0.5738	3.6272	6.4528	1.7428	6.3214	0.2757	0.1582	1.779	5
6	0.5135	4.1407	9.0201	1.9475	8.0641	0.2415	0.1240	2.178	6
7	0.4595	4.6002	11.7770	2.1764	10.0117	0.2174	0.0999	2.560	7
8	0.4112	5.0113	14.6552	2.4321	12.1880	0.1995	0.0820	2.924	8
9	0.3679	5.3793	17.5987	2.7179	14.6201	0.1859	0.0684	3.271	9
10	0.3292	5.7085	20.5619	3.0372	17.3380	0.1752	0.0577	3.602	10
11	0.2946	6.0031	23.5082	3.3941	20.3752	0.1666	0.0491	3.916	11
12	0.2637	6.2668	26.4084	3.7929	23.7693	0.1596	0.0421	4.214	12
13	0.2359	6.5027	29.2395	4.2386	27.5622	0.1538	0.0363	4.496	13
14	0.2111	6.7139	31.9841	4.7366	31.8007	0.1489	0.0314	4.763	14
15	0.1889	6.9028	34.6291	5.2931	36.5373	0.1449	0.0274	5.016	15
16	0.1691	7.0718	37.1650	5.9151	41.8305	0.1414	0.0239	5.255	16
17	0.1513	7.2231	39.5855	6.6101	47.7455	0.1384	0.0209	5.480	17
18	0.1354	7.3585	41.8869	7.3868	54.3556	0.1359	0.0184	5.692	18
19	0.1211	7.4796	44.0675	8.2547	61.7424	0.1337	0.0162	5.891	19
20	0.1084	7.5880	46.1272	9.2247	69.9972	0.1318	0.0143	6.078	20
21	0.0970	7.6850	48.0673	10.3086	79.2218	0.1301	0.0126	6.254	21
22	0.0868	7.7719	49.8902	11.5198	89.5304	0.1287	0.0112	6.419	22
23	0.0777	7.8495	51.5992	12.8734	101.0502	0.1274	0.0099	6.573	23
24	0.0695	7.9190	53.1980	14.3860	113.9236	0.1263	0.0088	6.717	24
25	0.0622	7.9813	54.6908	16.0764	128.3096	0.1253	0.0078	6.852	25
26	0.0557	8.0369	56.0824	17.9654	144.3860	0.1244	0.0069	6.978	26
27	0.0498	8.0867	57.3775	20.0763	162.3514	0.1237	0.0062	7.095	27
28	0.0446	8.1313	58.5809	22.4352	182.4276	0.1230	0.0055	7.204	28
29	0.0399	8.1712	59.6977	25.0714	204.8629	0.1224	0.0049	7.305	29
30	0.0357	8.2069	60.7328	28.0173	229.9343	0.1218	0.0043	7.400	30
31	0.0319	8.2388	61.6910	31.3093	257.9516	0.1214	0.0039	7.487	31
32	0.0286	8.2674	62.5770	34.9882	289.2609	0.1210	0.0035	7.569	32
33	0.0256	8.2930	63.3954	39.0993	324.2490	0.1206	0.0031	7.644	33
34	0.0229	8.3159	64.1507	43.6934	363.3483	0.1203	0.0028	7.714	34
35	0.0205	8.3363	64.8470	48.8274	407.0417	0.1200	0.0025	7.778	35
36	0.0183	8.3547	65.4885	54.5646	455.8691	0.1197	0.0022	7.838	36
37	0.0164	8.3711	66.0789	60.9760	510.4337	0.1195	0.0020	7.893	37
38	0.0147	8.3857	66.6219	68.1406	571.4097	0.1193	0.0018	7.944	38
39	0.0131	8.3989	67.1209	76.1472	639.5503	0.1191	0.0016	7.991	39
40	0.0118	8.4106	67.5792	85.0945	715.6975	0.1189	0.0014	8.035	40
41	0.0105	8.4211	67.9999	95.0931	800.7920	0.1187	0.0012	8.074	41
42	0.0094	8.4306	68.3857	106.2665	895.8850	0.1186	0.0011	8.111	42
43	0.0084	8.4390	68.7394	118.7528	1002.1515	0.1185	0.0010	8.145	43
44	0.0075	8.4465	69.0634	132.7063	1120.9043	0.1184	0.0009	8.176	44
45	0.0067	8.4533	69.3601	148.2992	1253.6106	0.1183	0.0008	8.205	45
46	0.0060	8.4593	69.6316	165.7244	1401.9098	0.1182	0.0007	8.231	46
47	0.0054	8.4647	69.8800	185.1970	1567.6342	0.1181	0.0006	8.255	47
48	0.0048	8.4695	70.1071	206.9577	1752.8312	0.1181	0.0006	8.277	48
49	0.0043	8.4738	70.3146	231.2752	1959.7889	0.1180	0.0005	8.297	49
50	0.0039	8.4777	70.5042	258.4500	2191.0641	0.1180	0.0005	8.316	50
51	0.0035	8.4812	70.6774	288.8179	2449.5141	0.1179	0.0004	8.333	51
52	0.0031	8.4843	70.8354	322.7540	2738.3320	0.1179	0.0004	8.349	52
53	0.0028	8.4870	70.9795	360.6776	3061.0861	0.1178	0.0003	8.363	53
54	0.0025	8.4895	71.1110	403.0572	3421.7637	0.1178	0.0003	8.376	54
55	0.0022	8.4917	71.2309	450.4165	3824.8209	0.1178	0.0003	8.388	55
60	0.0013	8.4998	71.6882	784.9679	6672.0674	0.1176	0.0001	8.434	60
65	0.0007	8.5044	71.9736	1368.0109	11634.1356	0.1176	0.0001	8.463	65
70	0.0004	8.5071	72.1507	2384.1151	20281.8310	0.1175	0.0000	8.481	70
75	0.0002	8.5086	72.2599	4154.9412	35352.6913	0.1175	0.0000	8.492	75
80	0.0001	8.5095	72.3269	7241.0666	61617.5884	0.1175	0.0000	8.499	80
85	0.0001	8.5100	72.3679	12619.4435	107391.0085	0.1175	0.0000	8.503	85
90	0.0000	8.5103	72.3928	21992.6652	187163.1079	0.1175	0.0000	8.506	90
95	0.0000	8.5104	72.4080	38327.9438	326186.7560	0.1175	0.0000	8.508	95
100	0.0000	8.5105	72.4171	66796.4190	568471.6512	0.1175	0.0000	8.509	100

EXPANDED INTEREST TABLES

I = 12.00 %

n	(P/F)	(P/A)	(P/G)	(F/P)	(F/A)	(A/P)	(A/F)	(A/G)	n
1	0.8929	0.8929	0.0000	1.1200	1.0000	1.1200	1.0000	0.000	1
2	0.7972	1.6901	0.7972	1.2544	2.1200	0.5917	0.4717	0.471	2
3	0.7118	2.4018	2.2208	1.4049	3.3744	0.4163	0.2963	0.924	3
4	0.6355	3.0373	4.1273	1.5735	4.7793	0.3292	0.2092	1.358	4
5	0.5674	3.6048	6.3970	1.7623	6.3528	0.2774	0.1574	1.774	5
6	0.5066	4.1114	8.9302	1.9738	8.1152	0.2432	0.1232	2.172	6
7	0.4523	4.5638	11.6443	2.2107	10.0890	0.2191	0.0991	2.551	7
8	0.4039	4.9676	14.4714	2.4760	12.2997	0.2013	0.0813	2.913	8
9	0.3606	5.3282	17.3563	2.7731	14.7757	0.1877	0.0677	3.257	9
10	0.3220	5.6502	20.2541	3.1058	17.5487	0.1770	0.0570	3.584	10
11	0.2875	5.9377	23.1288	3.4785	20.6546	0.1684	0.0484	3.895	11
12	0.2567	6.1944	25.9523	3.8960	24.1331	0.1614	0.0414	4.189	12
13	0.2292	6.4235	28.7024	4.3635	28.0291	0.1557	0.0357	4.468	13
14	0.2046	6.6282	31.3624	4.8871	32.3926	0.1509	0.0309	4.731	14
15	0.1827	6.8109	33.9202	5.4736	37.2797	0.1468	0.0268	4.980	15
16	0.1631	6.9740	36.3670	6.1304	42.7533	0.1434	0.0234	5.214	16
17	0.1456	7.1196	38.6973	6.8660	48.8837	0.1405	0.0205	5.435	17
18	0.1300	7.2497	40.9080	7.6900	55.7497	0.1379	0.0179	5.642	18
19	0.1161	7.3658	42.9979	8.6128	63.4397	0.1358	0.0158	5.837	19
20	0.1037	7.4694	44.9676	9.6463	72.0524	0.1339	0.0139	6.020	20
21	0.0926	7.5620	46.8188	10.8038	81.6987	0.1322	0.0122	6.191	21
22	0.0826	7.6446	48.5543	12.1003	92.5026	0.1308	0.0108	6.351	22
23	0.0738	7.7184	50.1776	13.5523	104.6029	0.1296	0.0096	6.501	23
24	0.0659	7.7843	51.6929	15.1786	118.1552	0.1285	0.0085	6.640	24
25	0.0588	7.8431	53.1046	17.0001	133.3339	0.1275	0.0075	6.770	25
26	0.0525	7.8957	54.4177	19.0401	150.3339	0.1267	0.0067	6.892	26
27	0.0469	7.9426	55.6369	21.3249	169.3740	0.1259	0.0059	7.004	27
28	0.0419	7.9844	56.7674	23.8839	190.6989	0.1252	0.0052	7.109	28
29	0.0374	8.0218	57.8141	26.7499	214.5828	0.1247	0.0047	7.207	29
30	0.0334	8.0552	58.7821	29.9599	241.3327	0.1241	0.0041	7.297	30
31	0.0298	8.0850	59.6761	33.5551	271.2926	0.1237	0.0037	7.381	31
32	0.0266	8.1116	60.5010	37.5817	304.8477	0.1233	0.0033	7.458	32
33	0.0238	8.1354	61.2612	42.0915	342.4294	0.1229	0.0029	7.530	33
34	0.0212	8.1566	61.9612	47.1425	384.5210	0.1226	0.0026	7.596	34
35	0.0189	8.1755	62.6052	52.7996	431.6635	0.1223	0.0023	7.657	35
36	0.0169	8.1924	63.1970	59.1356	484.4631	0.1221	0.0021	7.714	36
37	0.0151	8.2075	63.7406	66.2318	543.5987	0.1218	0.0018	7.766	37
38	0.0135	8.2210	64.2394	74.1797	609.8305	0.1216	0.0016	7.814	38
39	0.0120	8.2330	64.6967	83.0812	684.0102	0.1215	0.0015	7.858	39
40	0.0107	8.2438	65.1159	93.0510	767.0914	0.1213	0.0013	7.898	40
41	0.0096	8.2534	65.4997	104.2171	860.1424	0.1212	0.0012	7.936	41
42	0.0086	8.2619	65.8509	116.7231	964.3595	0.1210	0.0010	7.970	42
43	0.0076	8.2696	66.1722	130.7299	1081.0826	0.1209	0.0009	8.001	43
44	0.0068	8.2764	66.4659	146.4175	1211.8125	0.1208	0.0008	8.030	44
45	0.0061	8.2825	66.7342	163.9876	1358.2300	0.1207	0.0007	8.057	45
46	0.0054	8.2880	66.9792	183.6661	1522.2176	0.1207	0.0007	8.081	46
47	0.0049	8.2928	67.2028	205.7061	1705.8838	0.1206	0.0006	8.103	47
48	0.0043	8.2972	67.4068	230.3908	1911.5898	0.1205	0.0005	8.124	48
49	0.0039	8.3010	67.5929	258.0377	2141.9806	0.1205	0.0005	8.142	49
50	0.0035	8.3045	67.7624	289.0022	2400.0182	0.1204	0.0004	8.159	50
51	0.0031	8.3076	67.9169	323.6825	2689.0204	0.1204	0.0004	8.175	51
52	0.0028	8.3103	68.0576	362.5243	3012.7029	0.1203	0.0003	8.189	52
53	0.0025	8.3128	68.1856	406.0273	3375.2272	0.1203	0.0003	8.202	53
54	0.0022	8.3150	68.3022	454.7505	3781.2545	0.1203	0.0003	8.214	54
55	0.0020	8.3170	68.4082	509.3206	4236.0500	0.1202	0.0002	8.225	55
60	0.0011	8.3240	68.8100	897.5969	7471.6411	0.1201	0.0001	8.266	60
65	0.0006	8.3281	69.0581	1581.8725	13173.9374	0.1201	0.0001	8.292	65
70	0.0004	8.3303	69.2103	2787.7998	23223.3319	0.1200	0.0000	8.308	70
75	0.0002	8.3316	69.3031	4913.0558	40933.7987	0.1200	0.0000	8.318	75
80	0.0001	8.3324	69.3594	8658.4831	72145.6925	0.1200	0.0000	8.324	80
85	0.0001	8.3328	69.3935	15259.2057	127151.7140	0.1200	0.0000	8.327	85
90	0.0000	8.3330	69.4140	26891.9342	224091.1185	0.1200	0.0000	8.330	90
95	0.0000	8.3332	69.4263	47392.7766	394931.4719	0.1200	0.0000	8.331	95
100	0.0000	8.3332	69.4336	83522.2657	696010.5477	0.1200	0.0000	8.332	100

I = 12.25 %

n	(P/F)	(P/A)	(P/G)	(F/P)	(F/A)	(A/P)	(A/F)	(A/G)	n
1	0.8909	0.8909	0.0000	1.1225	1.0000	1.1225	1.0000	0.000	1
2	0.7936	1.6845	0.7936	1.2600	2.1225	0.5936	0.4711	0.471	2
3	0.7070	2.3916	2.2077	1.4144	3.3825	0.4181	0.2956	0.923	3
4	0.6299	3.0214	4.0973	1.5876	4.7969	0.3310	0.2085	1.356	4
5	0.5611	3.5826	6.3419	1.7821	6.3845	0.2791	0.1566	1.770	5
6	0.4999	4.0825	8.8414	2.0004	8.1666	0.2450	0.1225	2.165	6
7	0.4453	4.5278	11.5134	2.2455	10.1670	0.2209	0.0984	2.542	7
8	0.3967	4.9245	14.2906	2.5205	12.4124	0.2031	0.0806	2.901	8
9	0.3534	5.2780	17.1182	2.8293	14.9330	0.1895	0.0670	3.243	9
10	0.3149	5.5929	19.9521	3.1759	17.7623	0.1788	0.0563	3.567	10
11	0.2805	5.8734	22.7572	3.5649	20.9381	0.1703	0.0478	3.874	11
12	0.2499	6.1233	25.5061	4.0016	24.5030	0.1633	0.0408	4.165	12
13	0.2226	6.3459	28.1776	4.4918	28.5047	0.1576	0.0351	4.440	13
14	0.1983	6.5442	30.7559	5.0421	32.9965	0.1528	0.0303	4.699	14
15	0.1767	6.7209	33.2295	5.6597	38.0386	0.1488	0.0263	4.944	15
16	0.1574	6.8783	35.5906	6.3530	43.6983	0.1454	0.0229	5.174	16
17	0.1402	7.0186	37.8342	7.1313	50.0513	0.1425	0.0200	5.390	17
18	0.1249	7.1435	39.9579	8.0049	57.1826	0.1400	0.0175	5.593	18
19	0.1113	7.2548	41.9612	8.9855	65.1875	0.1378	0.0153	5.783	19
20	0.0991	7.3539	43.8449	10.0862	74.1730	0.1360	0.0135	5.962	20
21	0.0883	7.4422	45.6114	11.3217	84.2591	0.1344	0.0119	6.128	21
22	0.0787	7.5209	47.2639	12.7087	95.5809	0.1330	0.0105	6.284	22
23	0.0701	7.5910	48.8060	14.2655	108.2895	0.1317	0.0092	6.429	23
24	0.0624	7.6535	50.2424	16.0130	122.5550	0.1307	0.0082	6.564	24
25	0.0556	7.7091	51.5776	17.9746	138.5680	0.1297	0.0072	6.690	25
26	0.0496	7.7587	52.8167	20.1765	156.5426	0.1289	0.0064	6.807	26
27	0.0442	7.8028	53.9647	22.6481	176.7190	0.1282	0.0057	6.916	27
28	0.0393	7.8422	55.0267	25.4225	199.3671	0.1275	0.0050	7.016	28
29	0.0350	7.8772	56.0079	28.5367	224.7896	0.1269	0.0044	7.110	29
30	0.0312	7.9084	56.9132	32.0325	253.3263	0.1264	0.0039	7.196	30
31	0.0278	7.9362	57.7476	35.9565	285.3588	0.1260	0.0035	7.276	31
32	0.0248	7.9610	58.5157	40.3611	321.3153	0.1256	0.0031	7.350	32
33	0.0221	7.9831	59.2220	45.3054	361.6764	0.1253	0.0028	7.418	33
34	0.0197	8.0027	59.8709	50.8553	406.9817	0.1250	0.0025	7.481	34
35	0.0175	8.0203	60.4665	57.0850	457.8370	0.1247	0.0022	7.539	35
36	0.0156	8.0359	61.0127	64.0779	514.9220	0.1244	0.0019	7.592	36
37	0.0139	8.0498	61.5132	71.9275	579.0000	0.1242	0.0017	7.641	37
38	0.0124	8.0622	61.9715	80.7386	650.9275	0.1240	0.0015	7.686	38
39	0.0110	8.0732	62.3907	90.6291	731.6661	0.1239	0.0014	7.728	39
40	0.0098	8.0830	62.7741	101.7312	822.2952	0.1237	0.0012	7.766	40
41	0.0088	8.0918	63.1244	114.1932	924.0263	0.1236	0.0011	7.801	41
42	0.0078	8.0996	63.4443	128.1819	1038.2195	0.1235	0.0010	7.833	42
43	0.0070	8.1065	63.7362	143.8842	1166.4014	0.1234	0.0009	7.862	43
44	0.0062	8.1127	64.0024	161.5100	1310.2856	0.1233	0.0008	7.889	44
45	0.0055	8.1182	64.2451	181.2950	1471.7956	0.1232	0.0007	7.913	45
46	0.0049	8.1232	64.4662	203.5036	1653.0906	0.1231	0.0006	7.936	46
47	0.0044	8.1275	64.6676	228.4328	1856.5942	0.1230	0.0005	7.956	47
48	0.0039	8.1314	64.8509	256.4158	2085.0269	0.1230	0.0005	7.975	48
49	0.0035	8.1349	65.0177	287.8267	2341.4428	0.1229	0.0004	7.992	49
50	0.0031	8.1380	65.1693	323.0855	2629.2695	0.1229	0.0004	8.008	50
51	0.0028	8.1408	65.3072	362.6635	2952.3550	0.1228	0.0003	8.022	51
52	0.0025	8.1432	65.4325	407.0898	3315.0185	0.1228	0.0003	8.035	52
53	0.0022	8.1454	65.5463	456.9583	3722.1083	0.1228	0.0003	8.047	53
54	0.0019	8.1474	65.6496	512.9356	4179.0665	0.1227	0.0002	8.057	54
55	0.0017	8.1491	65.7434	575.7703	4692.0022	0.1227	0.0002	8.067	55
60	0.0010	8.1553	66.0966	1026.0794	8367.9953	0.1226	0.0001	8.104	60
65	0.0005	8.1588	66.3123	1828.5748	14918.9779	0.1226	0.0001	8.127	65
70	0.0003	8.1608	66.4431	3258.7007	26593.4753	0.1225	0.0000	8.141	70
75	0.0002	8.1619	66.5220	5807.3263	47398.5817	0.1225	0.0000	8.150	75
80	0.0001	8.1625	66.5694	10349.2285	84475.3343	0.1225	0.0000	8.155	80
85	0.0001	8.1628	66.5977	18443.3464	150549.7663	0.1225	0.0000	8.158	85
90	0.0000	8.1630	66.6145	32867.8632	268300.9241	0.1225	0.0000	8.160	90
95	0.0000	8.1631	66.6245	58573.7756	478145.1070	0.1225	0.0000	8.161	95
100	0.0000	8.1632	66.6304	104384.2482	852108.1483	0.1225	0.0000	8.162	100

EXPANDED INTEREST TABLES

I = 12.50 %

n	(P/F)	(P/A)	(P/G)	(F/P)	(F/A)	(A/P)	(A/F)	(A/G)	n
1	0.8889	0.8889	0.0000	1.1250	1.0000	1.1250	1.0000	0.000	1
2	0.7901	1.6790	0.7901	1.2656	2.1250	0.5956	0.4706	0.470	2
3	0.7023	2.3813	2.1948	1.4238	3.3906	0.4199	0.2949	0.921	3
4	0.6243	3.0056	4.0677	1.6018	4.8145	0.3327	0.2077	1.353	4
5	0.5549	3.5606	6.2874	1.8020	6.4163	0.2809	0.1559	1.765	5
6	0.4933	4.0538	8.7537	2.0273	8.2183	0.2467	0.1217	2.159	6
7	0.4385	4.4923	11.3845	2.2807	10.2456	0.2226	0.0976	2.534	7
8	0.3897	4.8820	14.1127	2.5658	12.5263	0.2048	0.0798	2.890	8
9	0.3464	5.2285	16.8842	2.8865	15.0921	0.1913	0.0663	3.229	9
10	0.3079	5.5364	19.6558	3.2473	17.9786	0.1806	0.0556	3.550	10
11	0.2737	5.8102	22.3931	3.6532	21.2259	0.1721	0.0471	3.854	11
12	0.2433	6.0535	25.0695	4.1099	24.8791	0.1652	0.0402	4.141	12
13	0.2163	6.2698	27.6649	4.6236	28.9890	0.1595	0.0345	4.412	13
14	0.1922	6.4620	30.1641	5.2016	33.6126	0.1548	0.0298	4.667	14
15	0.1709	6.6329	32.5566	5.8518	38.8142	0.1508	0.0258	4.908	15
16	0.1519	6.7848	34.8351	6.5833	44.6660	0.1474	0.0224	5.134	16
17	0.1350	6.9198	36.9954	7.4062	51.2493	0.1445	0.0195	5.346	17
18	0.1200	7.0398	39.0358	8.3319	58.6554	0.1420	0.0170	5.545	18
19	0.1067	7.1465	40.9561	9.3734	66.9873	0.1399	0.0149	5.730	19
20	0.0948	7.2414	42.7579	10.5451	76.3608	0.1381	0.0131	5.904	20
21	0.0843	7.3256	44.4438	11.8632	86.9058	0.1365	0.0115	6.066	21
22	0.0749	7.4006	46.0173	13.3461	98.7691	0.1351	0.0101	6.218	22
23	0.0666	7.4672	47.4825	15.0144	112.1152	0.1339	0.0089	6.358	23
24	0.0592	7.5264	48.8442	16.8912	127.1296	0.1329	0.0079	6.489	24
25	0.0526	7.5790	50.1072	19.0026	144.0208	0.1319	0.0069	6.611	25
26	0.0468	7.6258	51.2766	21.3779	163.0234	0.1311	0.0061	6.724	26
27	0.0416	7.6674	52.3577	24.0502	184.4013	0.1304	0.0054	6.828	27
28	0.0370	7.7043	53.3556	27.0564	208.4515	0.1298	0.0048	6.925	28
29	0.0329	7.7372	54.2755	30.4385	235.5079	0.1292	0.0042	7.014	29
30	0.0292	7.7664	55.1224	34.2433	265.9464	0.1288	0.0038	7.097	30
31	0.0260	7.7923	55.9011	38.5237	300.1897	0.1283	0.0033	7.173	31
32	0.0231	7.8154	56.6164	43.3392	338.7135	0.1280	0.0030	7.244	32
33	0.0205	7.8359	57.2727	48.7566	382.0526	0.1276	0.0026	7.309	33
34	0.0182	7.8542	57.8743	54.8512	430.8092	0.1273	0.0023	7.368	34
35	0.0162	7.8704	58.4253	61.7075	485.6604	0.1271	0.0021	7.423	35
36	0.0144	7.8848	58.9295	69.4210	547.3679	0.1268	0.0018	7.473	36
37	0.0128	7.8976	59.3904	78.0986	616.7889	0.1266	0.0016	7.520	37
38	0.0114	7.9089	59.8116	87.8609	694.8875	0.1264	0.0014	7.562	38
39	0.0101	7.9191	60.1960	98.8436	782.7485	0.1263	0.0013	7.601	39
40	0.0090	7.9281	60.5467	111.1990	881.5920	0.1261	0.0011	7.637	40
41	0.0080	7.9361	60.8665	125.0989	992.7910	0.1260	0.0010	7.669	41
42	0.0071	7.9432	61.1578	140.7362	1117.8899	0.1259	0.0009	7.699	42
43	0.0063	7.9495	61.4231	158.3283	1258.6262	0.1258	0.0008	7.726	43
44	0.0056	7.9551	61.6645	178.1193	1416.9544	0.1257	0.0007	7.751	44
45	0.0050	7.9601	61.8841	200.3842	1595.0737	0.1256	0.0006	7.774	45
46	0.0044	7.9645	62.0837	225.4322	1795.4579	0.1256	0.0006	7.795	46
47	0.0039	7.9685	62.2651	253.6113	2020.8902	0.1255	0.0005	7.813	47
48	0.0035	7.9720	62.4298	285.3127	2274.5015	0.1254	0.0004	7.831	48
49	0.0031	7.9751	62.5793	320.9768	2559.8141	0.1254	0.0004	7.846	49
50	0.0028	7.9778	62.7150	361.0989	2880.7909	0.1253	0.0003	7.861	50
51	0.0025	7.9803	62.8381	406.2362	3241.8898	0.1253	0.0003	7.874	51
52	0.0022	7.9825	62.9497	457.0157	3648.1260	0.1253	0.0003	7.886	52
53	0.0019	7.9844	63.0508	514.1427	4105.1417	0.1252	0.0002	7.896	53
54	0.0017	7.9862	63.1425	578.4106	4619.2845	0.1252	0.0002	7.906	54
55	0.0015	7.9877	63.2255	650.7119	5197.6950	0.1252	0.0002	7.915	55
60	0.0009	7.9932	63.5361	1172.6039	9372.8315	0.1251	0.0001	7.948	60
65	0.0005	7.9962	63.7236	2113.0704	16896.5629	0.1251	0.0001	7.969	65
70	0.0003	7.9979	63.8361	3807.8214	30454.5713	0.1250	0.0000	7.981	70
75	0.0001	7.9988	63.9032	6861.8178	54886.5426	0.1250	0.0000	7.989	75
80	0.0001	7.9994	63.9431	12365.2185	98913.7482	0.1250	0.0000	7.993	80
85	0.0000	7.9996	63.9666	22282.5253	178252.2023	0.1250	0.0000	7.996	85
90	0.0000	7.9998	63.9805	40153.8341	321222.6728	0.1250	0.0000	7.997	90
95	0.0000	7.9999	63.9886	72358.5129	578860.1029	0.1250	0.0000	7.998	95
100	0.0000	7.9999	63.9934	130392.3897	1043131.1177	0.1250	0.0000	7.999	100

$I = 12.75\%$

n	(P/F)	(P/A)	(P/G)	(F/P)	(F/A)	(A/P)	(A/F)	(A/G)	n
1	0.8869	0.8869	0.0000	1.1275	1.0000	1.1275	1.0000	0.000	1
2	0.7866	1.6735	0.7866	1.2713	2.1275	0.5975	0.4700	0.470	2
3	0.6977	2.3712	2.1820	1.4333	3.3988	0.4217	0.2942	0.920	3
4	0.6188	2.9900	4.0383	1.6161	4.8321	0.3344	0.2069	1.350	4
5	0.5488	3.5388	6.2335	1.8221	6.4482	0.2826	0.1551	1.761	5
6	0.4867	4.0255	8.6672	2.0545	8.2703	0.2484	0.1209	2.153	6
7	0.4317	4.4572	11.2574	2.3164	10.3248	0.2244	0.0969	2.525	7
8	0.3829	4.8401	13.9376	2.6118	12.6412	0.2066	0.0791	2.879	8
9	0.3396	5.1797	16.6543	2.9448	15.2530	0.1931	0.0656	3.215	9
10	0.3012	5.4809	19.3650	3.3202	18.1977	0.1825	0.0550	3.533	10
11	0.2671	5.7480	22.0363	3.7435	21.5179	0.1740	0.0465	3.833	11
12	0.2369	5.9849	24.6424	4.2208	25.2615	0.1671	0.0396	4.117	12
13	0.2101	6.1951	27.1639	4.7590	29.4823	0.1614	0.0339	4.384	13
14	0.1864	6.3814	29.5867	5.3658	34.2413	0.1567	0.0292	4.636	14
15	0.1653	6.5467	31.9008	6.0499	39.6071	0.1527	0.0252	4.872	15
16	0.1466	6.6933	34.0998	6.8213	45.6570	0.1494	0.0219	5.094	16
17	0.1300	6.8234	36.1802	7.6910	52.4782	0.1466	0.0191	5.302	17
18	0.1153	6.9387	38.1406	8.6716	60.1692	0.1441	0.0166	5.496	18
19	0.1023	7.0410	39.9816	9.7772	68.8408	0.1420	0.0145	5.678	19
20	0.0907	7.1317	41.7051	11.0238	78.6180	0.1402	0.0127	5.847	20
21	0.0805	7.2121	43.3142	12.4293	89.6418	0.1387	0.0112	6.005	21
22	0.0714	7.2835	44.8127	14.0141	102.0711	0.1373	0.0098	6.152	22
23	0.0633	7.3468	46.2051	15.8009	116.0852	0.1361	0.0086	6.289	23
24	0.0561	7.4029	47.4961	17.8155	131.8860	0.1351	0.0076	6.415	24
25	0.0498	7.4527	48.6909	20.0869	149.7015	0.1342	0.0067	6.533	25
26	0.0442	7.4968	49.7947	22.6480	169.7884	0.1334	0.0059	6.642	26
27	0.0392	7.5360	50.8129	25.5356	192.4364	0.1327	0.0052	6.742	27
28	0.0347	7.5707	51.7507	28.7914	217.9721	0.1321	0.0046	6.835	28
29	0.0308	7.6015	52.6132	32.4624	246.7635	0.1316	0.0041	6.921	29
30	0.0273	7.6289	53.4056	36.6013	279.2259	0.1311	0.0036	7.000	30
31	0.0242	7.6531	54.1325	41.2680	315.8272	0.1307	0.0032	7.073	31
32	0.0215	7.6746	54.7988	46.5296	357.0952	0.1303	0.0028	7.140	32
33	0.0191	7.6936	55.4087	52.4622	403.6248	0.1300	0.0025	7.201	33
34	0.0169	7.7105	55.9666	59.1511	456.0869	0.1297	0.0022	7.258	34
35	0.0150	7.7255	56.4764	66.6928	515.2380	0.1294	0.0019	7.310	35
36	0.0133	7.7388	56.9419	75.1962	581.9309	0.1292	0.0017	7.357	36
37	0.0118	7.7506	57.3665	84.7837	657.1271	0.1290	0.0015	7.401	37
38	0.0105	7.7611	57.7535	95.5936	741.9108	0.1288	0.0013	7.441	38
39	0.0093	7.7704	58.1061	107.7818	837.5044	0.1287	0.0012	7.477	39
40	0.0082	7.7786	58.4270	121.5240	945.2862	0.1286	0.0011	7.511	40
41	0.0073	7.7859	58.7189	137.0183	1066.8102	0.1284	0.0009	7.541	41
42	0.0065	7.7924	58.9843	154.4881	1203.8285	0.1283	0.0008	7.569	42
43	0.0057	7.7981	59.2255	174.1854	1358.3166	0.1282	0.0007	7.594	43
44	0.0051	7.8032	59.4444	196.3940	1532.5020	0.1282	0.0007	7.618	44
45	0.0045	7.8077	59.6431	221.4342	1728.8960	0.1281	0.0006	7.639	45
46	0.0040	7.8117	59.8234	249.6671	1950.3302	0.1280	0.0005	7.658	46
47	0.0036	7.8153	59.9868	281.4997	2199.9973	0.1280	0.0005	7.675	47
48	0.0032	7.8184	60.1348	317.3909	2481.4970	0.1279	0.0004	7.691	48
49	0.0028	7.8212	60.2690	357.8582	2798.8879	0.1279	0.0004	7.705	49
50	0.0025	7.8237	60.3904	403.4851	3156.7461	0.1278	0.0003	7.718	50
51	0.0022	7.8259	60.5003	454.9295	3560.2312	0.1278	0.0003	7.730	51
52	0.0019	7.8278	60.5998	512.9330	4015.1607	0.1277	0.0002	7.741	52
53	0.0017	7.8296	60.6897	578.3319	4528.0937	0.1277	0.0002	7.751	53
54	0.0015	7.8311	60.7709	652.0693	5106.4256	0.1277	0.0002	7.760	54
55	0.0014	7.8325	60.8444	735.2081	5758.4949	0.1277	0.0002	7.768	55
60	0.0007	7.8373	61.1176	1339.6552	10499.2564	0.1276	0.0001	7.798	60
65	0.0004	7.8399	61.2808	2441.0450	19137.6079	0.1276	0.0001	7.816	65
70	0.0002	7.8414	61.3775	4447.9361	34877.9301	0.1275	0.0000	7.827	70
75	0.0001	7.8422	61.4346	8104.7811	63559.0677	0.1275	0.0000	7.833	75
80	0.0001	7.8426	61.4681	14768.0803	115820.2373	0.1275	0.0000	7.837	80
85	0.0000	7.8428	61.4877	26909.5724	211047.6267	0.1275	0.0000	7.840	85
90	0.0000	7.8430	61.4992	49033.1224	384565.6657	0.1275	0.0000	7.841	90
95	0.0000	7.8430	61.5058	89345.4215	700740.5612	0.1275	0.0000	7.842	95
100	0.0000	7.8431	61.5096	162800.2453	1276856.8261	0.1275	0.0000	7.842	100

$$I = 13.00\ \%$$

n	(P/F)	(P/A)	(P/G)	(F/P)	(F/A)	(A/P)	(A/F)	(A/G)	n
1	0.8850	0.8850	0.0000	1.1300	1.0000	1.1300	1.0000	0.000	1
2	0.7831	1.6681	0.7831	1.2769	2.1300	0.5995	0.4695	0.469	2
3	0.6931	2.3612	2.1692	1.4429	3.4069	0.4235	0.2935	0.918	3
4	0.6133	2.9745	4.0092	1.6305	4.8498	0.3362	0.2062	1.347	4
5	0.5428	3.5172	6.1802	1.8424	6.4803	0.2843	0.1543	1.757	5
6	0.4803	3.9975	8.5818	2.0820	8.3227	0.2502	0.1202	2.146	6
7	0.4251	4.4226	11.1322	2.3526	10.4047	0.2261	0.0961	2.517	7
8	0.3762	4.7988	13.7653	2.6584	12.7573	0.2084	0.0784	2.868	8
9	0.3329	5.1317	16.4284	3.0040	15.4157	0.1949	0.0649	3.201	9
10	0.2946	5.4262	19.0797	3.3946	18.4197	0.1843	0.0543	3.516	10
11	0.2607	5.6869	21.6867	3.8359	21.8143	0.1758	0.0458	3.813	11
12	0.2307	5.9176	24.2244	4.3345	25.6502	0.1690	0.0390	4.093	12
13	0.2042	6.1218	26.6744	4.8980	29.9847	0.1634	0.0334	4.357	13
14	0.1807	6.3025	29.0232	5.5348	34.8827	0.1587	0.0287	4.605	14
15	0.1599	6.4624	31.2617	6.2543	40.4175	0.1547	0.0247	4.837	15
16	0.1415	6.6039	33.3841	7.0673	46.6717	0.1514	0.0214	5.055	16
17	0.1252	6.7291	35.3876	7.9861	53.7391	0.1486	0.0186	5.258	17
18	0.1108	6.8399	37.2714	9.0243	61.7251	0.1462	0.0162	5.449	18
19	0.0981	6.9380	39.0366	10.1974	70.7494	0.1441	0.0141	5.626	19
20	0.0868	7.0248	40.6854	11.5231	80.9468	0.1424	0.0124	5.791	20
21	0.0768	7.1016	42.2214	13.0211	92.4699	0.1408	0.0108	5.945	21
22	0.0680	7.1695	43.6486	14.7138	105.4910	0.1395	0.0095	6.088	22
23	0.0601	7.2297	44.9718	16.6266	120.2048	0.1383	0.0083	6.220	23
24	0.0532	7.2829	46.1960	18.7881	136.8315	0.1373	0.0073	6.343	24
25	0.0471	7.3300	47.3264	21.2305	155.6196	0.1364	0.0064	6.456	25
26	0.0417	7.3717	48.3685	23.9905	176.8501	0.1357	0.0057	6.561	26
27	0.0369	7.4086	49.3276	27.1093	200.8406	0.1350	0.0050	6.658	27
28	0.0326	7.4412	50.2090	30.6335	227.9499	0.1344	0.0044	6.747	28
29	0.0289	7.4701	51.0179	34.6158	258.5834	0.1339	0.0039	6.829	29
30	0.0256	7.4957	51.7592	39.1159	293.1992	0.1334	0.0034	6.905	30
31	0.0226	7.5183	52.4380	44.2010	332.3151	0.1330	0.0030	6.974	31
32	0.0200	7.5383	53.0586	49.9471	376.5161	0.1327	0.0027	7.038	32
33	0.0177	7.5560	53.6256	56.4402	426.4632	0.1323	0.0023	7.097	33
34	0.0157	7.5717	54.1430	63.7774	482.9034	0.1321	0.0021	7.150	34
35	0.0139	7.5856	54.6148	72.0685	546.6808	0.1318	0.0018	7.199	35
36	0.0123	7.5979	55.0446	81.4374	618.7493	0.1316	0.0016	7.244	36
37	0.0109	7.6087	55.4358	92.0243	700.1867	0.1314	0.0014	7.285	37
38	0.0096	7.6183	55.7916	103.9874	792.2110	0.1313	0.0013	7.323	38
39	0.0085	7.6268	56.1150	117.5058	896.1984	0.1311	0.0011	7.357	39
40	0.0075	7.6344	56.4087	132.7816	1013.7042	0.1310	0.0010	7.388	40
41	0.0067	7.6410	56.6753	150.0432	1146.4858	0.1309	0.0009	7.417	41
42	0.0059	7.6469	56.9171	169.5488	1296.5289	0.1308	0.0008	7.443	42
43	0.0052	7.6522	57.1363	191.5901	1466.0777	0.1307	0.0007	7.466	43
44	0.0046	7.6568	57.3349	216.4968	1657.6678	0.1306	0.0006	7.488	44
45	0.0041	7.6609	57.5148	244.6414	1874.1646	0.1305	0.0005	7.507	45
46	0.0036	7.6645	57.6776	276.4448	2118.8060	0.1305	0.0005	7.525	46
47	0.0032	7.6677	57.8248	312.3826	2395.2508	0.1304	0.0004	7.541	47
48	0.0028	7.6705	57.9580	352.9923	2707.6334	0.1304	0.0004	7.555	48
49	0.0025	7.6730	58.0783	398.8813	3060.6258	0.1303	0.0003	7.569	49
50	0.0022	7.6752	58.1870	450.7359	3459.5071	0.1303	0.0003	7.581	50
51	0.0020	7.6772	58.2852	509.3316	3910.2430	0.1303	0.0003	7.592	51
52	0.0017	7.6789	58.3738	575.5447	4419.5746	0.1302	0.0002	7.601	52
53	0.0015	7.6805	58.4537	650.3655	4995.1193	0.1302	0.0002	7.610	53
54	0.0014	7.6818	58.5259	734.9130	5645.4849	0.1302	0.0002	7.618	54
55	0.0012	7.6830	58.5909	830.4517	6380.3979	0.1302	0.0002	7.626	55
60	0.0007	7.6873	58.8313	1530.0535	11761.9498	0.1301	0.0001	7.653	60
65	0.0004	7.6896	58.9732	2819.0243	21677.1103	0.1300	0.0000	7.669	65
70	0.0002	7.6908	59.0565	5193.8696	39945.1510	0.1300	0.0000	7.678	70
75	0.0001	7.6915	59.1051	9569.3681	73602.8316	0.1300	0.0000	7.684	75
80	0.0001	7.6919	59.1333	17630.9405	135614.9266	0.1300	0.0000	7.687	80
85	0.0000	7.6921	59.1496	32483.8649	249868.1918	0.1300	0.0000	7.689	85
90	0.0000	7.6922	59.1590	59849.4155	460372.4271	0.1300	0.0000	7.690	90
95	0.0000	7.6922	59.1644	110268.6686	848212.8355	0.1300	0.0000	7.691	95
100	0.0000	7.6923	59.1675	203162.8742	1562783.6479	0.1300	0.0000	7.691	100

$I = 13.25\ \%$

n	(P/F)	(P/A)	(P/G)	(F/P)	(F/A)	(A/P)	(A/F)	(A/G)	n
1	0.8830	0.8830	0.0000	1.1325	1.0000	1.1325	1.0000	0.000	1
2	0.7797	1.6627	0.7797	1.2826	2.1325	0.6014	0.4689	0.468	2
3	0.6885	2.3512	2.1566	1.4525	3.4151	0.4253	0.2928	0.917	3
4	0.6079	2.9591	3.9804	1.6450	4.8676	0.3379	0.2054	1.345	4
5	0.5368	3.4959	6.1276	1.8629	6.5125	0.2861	0.1536	1.752	5
6	0.4740	3.9699	8.4975	2.1097	8.3754	0.2519	0.1194	2.140	6
7	0.4185	4.3884	11.0088	2.3893	10.4851	0.2279	0.0954	2.508	7
8	0.3696	4.7580	13.5957	2.7059	12.8744	0.2102	0.0777	2.857	8
9	0.3263	5.0843	16.2064	3.0644	15.5803	0.1967	0.0642	3.187	9
10	0.2881	5.3725	18.7997	3.4704	18.6447	0.1861	0.0536	3.499	10
11	0.2544	5.6269	21.3441	3.9303	22.1151	0.1777	0.0452	3.793	11
12	0.2247	5.8516	23.8154	4.4510	26.0454	0.1709	0.0384	4.069	12
13	0.1984	6.0499	26.1960	5.0408	30.4964	0.1653	0.0328	4.330	13
14	0.1752	6.2251	28.4733	5.7087	35.5371	0.1606	0.0281	4.573	14
15	0.1547	6.3798	30.6387	6.4651	41.2458	0.1567	0.0242	4.802	15
16	0.1366	6.5164	32.6874	7.3217	47.7109	0.1535	0.0210	5.016	16
17	0.1206	6.6370	34.6171	8.2918	55.0326	0.1507	0.0182	5.215	17
18	0.1065	6.7435	36.4274	9.3905	63.3244	0.1483	0.0158	5.401	18
19	0.0940	6.8375	38.1200	10.6347	72.7149	0.1463	0.0138	5.575	19
20	0.0830	6.9205	39.6975	12.0438	83.3496	0.1445	0.0120	5.736	20
21	0.0733	6.9938	41.1639	13.6396	95.3934	0.1430	0.0105	5.885	21
22	0.0647	7.0586	42.5234	15.4469	109.0330	0.1417	0.0092	6.024	22
23	0.0572	7.1157	43.7810	17.4936	124.4799	0.1405	0.0080	6.152	23
24	0.0505	7.1662	44.9419	19.8115	141.9735	0.1395	0.0070	6.271	24
25	0.0446	7.2108	46.0116	22.4365	161.7850	0.1387	0.0062	6.380	25
26	0.0394	7.2501	46.9955	25.4093	184.2215	0.1379	0.0054	6.482	26
27	0.0348	7.2849	47.8990	28.7761	209.6308	0.1373	0.0048	6.575	27
28	0.0307	7.3156	48.7275	32.5889	238.4069	0.1367	0.0042	6.660	28
29	0.0271	7.3427	49.4862	36.9069	270.9958	0.1362	0.0037	6.739	29
30	0.0239	7.3666	50.1800	41.7971	307.9028	0.1357	0.0032	6.811	30
31	0.0211	7.3877	50.8138	47.3352	349.6999	0.1354	0.0029	6.878	31
32	0.0187	7.4064	51.3921	53.6072	397.0351	0.1350	0.0025	6.938	32
33	0.0165	7.4229	51.9192	60.7101	450.6423	0.1347	0.0022	6.994	33
34	0.0145	7.4374	52.3991	68.7542	511.3524	0.1345	0.0020	7.045	34
35	0.0128	7.4502	52.8358	77.8641	580.1066	0.1342	0.0017	7.091	35
36	0.0113	7.4616	53.2327	88.1811	657.9707	0.1340	0.0015	7.134	36
37	0.0100	7.4716	53.5932	99.8651	746.1518	0.1338	0.0013	7.172	37
38	0.0088	7.4804	53.9203	113.0972	846.0169	0.1337	0.0012	7.208	38
39	0.0078	7.4882	54.2170	128.0826	959.1141	0.1335	0.0010	7.240	39
40	0.0069	7.4951	54.4859	145.0536	1087.1968	0.1334	0.0009	7.269	40
41	0.0061	7.5012	54.7294	164.2732	1232.2503	0.1333	0.0008	7.296	41
42	0.0054	7.5066	54.9498	186.0394	1396.5235	0.1332	0.0007	7.320	42
43	0.0047	7.5113	55.1491	210.6896	1582.5629	0.1331	0.0006	7.342	43
44	0.0042	7.5155	55.3293	238.6060	1793.2525	0.1331	0.0006	7.362	44
45	0.0037	7.5192	55.4922	270.2212	2031.8584	0.1330	0.0005	7.380	45
46	0.0033	7.5225	55.6392	306.0256	2302.0796	0.1329	0.0004	7.396	46
47	0.0029	7.5254	55.7719	346.5739	2608.1052	0.1329	0.0004	7.411	47
48	0.0025	7.5279	55.8917	392.4950	2954.6791	0.1328	0.0003	7.424	48
49	0.0022	7.5302	55.9997	444.5006	3347.1741	0.1328	0.0003	7.436	49
50	0.0020	7.5322	56.0970	503.3969	3791.6747	0.1328	0.0003	7.447	50
51	0.0018	7.5339	56.1847	570.0970	4295.0716	0.1327	0.0002	7.457	51
52	0.0015	7.5355	56.2637	645.6348	4865.1686	0.1327	0.0002	7.466	52
53	0.0014	7.5368	56.3348	731.1815	5510.8034	0.1327	0.0002	7.474	53
54	0.0012	7.5381	56.3988	828.0630	6241.9849	0.1327	0.0002	7.481	54
55	0.0011	7.5391	56.4564	937.7813	7070.0479	0.1326	0.0001	7.488	55
60	0.0006	7.5428	56.6680	1746.9989	13177.3505	0.1326	0.0001	7.512	60
65	0.0003	7.5449	56.7915	3254.4956	24554.6841	0.1325	0.0000	7.527	65
70	0.0002	7.5459	56.8632	6062.8210	45749.5926	0.1325	0.0000	7.535	70
75	0.0001	7.5465	56.9046	11294.4686	85233.7251	0.1325	0.0000	7.540	75
80	0.0000	7.5468	56.9284	21040.5387	158788.9713	0.1325	0.0000	7.543	80
85	0.0000	7.5470	56.9420	39196.5559	295815.5161	0.1325	0.0000	7.545	85
90	0.0000	7.5471	56.9497	73019.5180	551083.1544	0.1325	0.0000	7.545	90
95	0.0000	7.5471	56.9541	136028.5332	1026622.8921	0.1325	0.0000	7.546	95
100	0.0000	7.5471	56.9566	253408.4360	1912508.9508	0.1325	0.0000	7.546	100

EXPANDED INTEREST TABLES

$I = 13.50\ \%$

n	(P/F)	(P/A)	(P/G)	(F/P)	(F/A)	(A/P)	(A/F)	(A/G)	n
1	0.8811	0.8811	0.0000	1.1350	1.0000	1.1350	1.0000	0.000	1
2	0.7763	1.6573	0.7763	1.2882	2.1350	0.6034	0.4684	0.468	2
3	0.6839	2.3413	2.1441	1.4621	3.4232	0.4271	0.2921	0.915	3
4	0.6026	2.9438	3.9519	1.6595	4.8854	0.3397	0.2047	1.342	4
5	0.5309	3.4747	6.0755	1.8836	6.5449	0.2878	0.1528	1.748	5
6	0.4678	3.9425	8.4143	2.1378	8.4284	0.2536	0.1186	2.134	6
7	0.4121	4.3546	10.8871	2.4264	10.5663	0.2296	0.0946	2.500	7
8	0.3631	4.7177	13.4288	2.7540	12.9927	0.2120	0.0770	2.846	8
9	0.3199	5.0377	15.9881	3.1258	15.7468	0.1985	0.0635	3.173	9
10	0.2819	5.3195	18.5249	3.5478	18.8726	0.1880	0.0530	3.482	10
11	0.2483	5.5679	21.0083	4.0267	22.4204	0.1796	0.0446	3.773	11
12	0.2188	5.7867	23.4151	4.5704	26.4471	0.1728	0.0378	4.046	12
13	0.1928	5.9794	25.7285	5.1874	31.0175	0.1672	0.0322	4.302	13
14	0.1698	6.1493	27.9365	5.8877	36.2048	0.1626	0.0276	4.543	14
15	0.1496	6.2989	30.0315	6.6825	42.0925	0.1588	0.0238	4.767	15
16	0.1318	6.4308	32.0092	7.5846	48.7750	0.1555	0.0205	4.977	16
17	0.1162	6.5469	33.8678	8.6085	56.3596	0.1527	0.0177	5.173	17
18	0.1023	6.6493	35.6077	9.7707	64.9681	0.1504	0.0154	5.355	18
19	0.0902	6.7395	37.2308	11.0897	74.7388	0.1484	0.0134	5.524	19
20	0.0794	6.8189	38.7403	12.5869	85.8286	0.1467	0.0117	5.681	20
21	0.0700	6.8889	40.1403	14.2861	98.4154	0.1452	0.0102	5.826	21
22	0.0617	6.9506	41.4354	16.2147	112.7015	0.1439	0.0089	5.961	22
23	0.0543	7.0049	42.6308	18.4037	128.9162	0.1428	0.0078	6.085	23
24	0.0479	7.0528	43.7319	20.8882	147.3199	0.1418	0.0068	6.200	24
25	0.0422	7.0950	44.7442	23.7081	168.2081	0.1409	0.0059	6.306	25
26	0.0372	7.1321	45.6733	26.9087	191.9162	0.1402	0.0052	6.403	26
27	0.0327	7.1649	46.5246	30.5414	218.8248	0.1396	0.0046	6.493	27
28	0.0288	7.1937	47.3035	34.6644	249.3662	0.1390	0.0040	6.575	28
29	0.0254	7.2191	48.0152	39.3441	284.0306	0.1385	0.0035	6.651	29
30	0.0224	7.2415	48.6646	44.6556	323.3748	0.1381	0.0031	6.720	30
31	0.0197	7.2613	49.2565	50.6841	368.0303	0.1377	0.0027	6.783	31
32	0.0174	7.2786	49.7954	57.5264	418.7144	0.1374	0.0024	6.841	32
33	0.0153	7.2940	50.2855	65.2925	476.2409	0.1371	0.0021	6.894	33
34	0.0135	7.3075	50.7308	74.1070	541.5334	0.1368	0.0018	6.942	34
35	0.0119	7.3193	51.1350	84.1115	615.6404	0.1366	0.0016	6.986	35
36	0.0105	7.3298	51.5016	95.4665	699.7519	0.1364	0.0014	7.026	36
37	0.0092	7.3390	51.8339	108.3545	795.2184	0.1363	0.0013	7.062	37
38	0.0081	7.3472	52.1347	122.9823	903.5729	0.1361	0.0011	7.095	38
39	0.0072	7.3543	52.4070	139.5850	1026.5552	0.1360	0.0010	7.126	39
40	0.0063	7.3607	52.6531	158.4289	1166.1401	0.1359	0.0009	7.153	40
41	0.0056	7.3662	52.8756	179.8168	1324.5691	0.1358	0.0008	7.178	41
42	0.0049	7.3711	53.0765	204.0921	1504.3859	0.1357	0.0007	7.200	42
43	0.0043	7.3754	53.2578	231.6445	1708.4780	0.1356	0.0006	7.221	43
44	0.0038	7.3792	53.4213	262.9165	1940.1225	0.1355	0.0005	7.239	44
45	0.0034	7.3826	53.5688	298.4103	2203.0391	0.1355	0.0005	7.256	45
46	0.0030	7.3855	53.7016	338.6957	2501.4493	0.1354	0.0004	7.271	46
47	0.0026	7.3881	53.8213	384.4196	2840.1450	0.1354	0.0004	7.284	47
48	0.0023	7.3904	53.9290	436.3162	3224.5646	0.1353	0.0003	7.297	48
49	0.0020	7.3924	54.0260	495.2189	3660.8808	0.1353	0.0003	7.308	49
50	0.0018	7.3942	54.1131	562.0735	4156.0997	0.1352	0.0002	7.318	50
51	0.0016	7.3958	54.1915	637.9534	4718.1731	0.1352	0.0002	7.327	51
52	0.0014	7.3972	54.2619	724.0771	5356.1265	0.1352	0.0002	7.335	52
53	0.0012	7.3984	54.3252	821.8275	6080.2036	0.1352	0.0002	7.342	53
54	0.0011	7.3995	54.3820	932.7742	6902.0311	0.1351	0.0001	7.349	54
55	0.0009	7.4004	54.4330	1058.6987	7834.8053	0.1351	0.0001	7.355	55
60	0.0005	7.4037	54.6193	1994.1218	14763.8655	0.1351	0.0001	7.377	60
65	0.0003	7.4054	54.7269	3756.0468	27815.1618	0.1350	0.0000	7.390	65
70	0.0001	7.4064	54.7886	7074.7371	52398.0527	0.1350	0.0000	7.397	70
75	0.0001	7.4069	54.8239	13325.6872	98701.3867	0.1350	0.0000	7.401	75
80	0.0000	7.4071	54.8439	25099.7226	185916.4640	0.1350	0.0000	7.404	80
85	0.0000	7.4073	54.8552	47276.8171	350191.2377	0.1350	0.0000	7.405	85
90	0.0000	7.4073	54.8616	89048.6906	659612.5226	0.1350	0.0000	7.406	90
95	0.0000	7.4074	54.8652	167728.4931	1242425.8749	0.1350	0.0000	7.406	95
100	0.0000	7.4074	54.8672	315926.5704	2340189.4102	0.1350	0.0000	7.407	100

$$I = 13.75\ \%$$

n	(P/F)	(P/A)	(P/G)	(F/P)	(F/A)	(A/P)	(A/F)	(A/G)	n
1	0.8791	0.8791	0.0000	1.1375	1.0000	1.1375	1.0000	0.000	1
2	0.7729	1.6520	0.7729	1.2939	2.1375	0.6053	0.4678	0.467	2
3	0.6794	2.3314	2.1317	1.4718	3.4314	0.4289	0.2914	0.914	3
4	0.5973	2.9287	3.9236	1.6742	4.9032	0.3414	0.2039	1.339	4
5	0.5251	3.4538	6.0240	1.9044	6.5774	0.2895	0.1520	1.744	5
6	0.4616	3.9154	8.3322	2.1662	8.4818	0.2554	0.1179	2.128	6
7	0.4058	4.3213	10.7671	2.4641	10.6481	0.2314	0.0939	2.491	7
8	0.3568	4.6780	13.2645	2.8029	13.1122	0.2138	0.0763	2.835	8
9	0.3136	4.9917	15.7737	3.1883	15.9151	0.2003	0.0628	3.160	9
10	0.2757	5.2674	18.2553	3.6267	19.1034	0.1898	0.0523	3.465	10
11	0.2424	5.5098	20.6793	4.1254	22.7301	0.1815	0.0440	3.753	11
12	0.2131	5.7229	23.0234	4.6926	26.8555	0.1747	0.0372	4.023	12
13	0.1873	5.9103	25.2714	5.3379	31.5482	0.1692	0.0317	4.275	13
14	0.1647	6.0749	27.4125	6.0718	36.8860	0.1646	0.0271	4.512	14
15	0.1448	6.2197	29.4395	6.9067	42.9579	0.1608	0.0233	4.733	15
16	0.1273	6.3470	31.3488	7.8564	49.8646	0.1576	0.0201	4.939	16
17	0.1119	6.4589	33.1392	8.9366	57.7210	0.1548	0.0173	5.130	17
18	0.0984	6.5573	34.8115	10.1654	66.6576	0.1525	0.0150	5.308	18
19	0.0865	6.6438	36.3682	11.5632	76.8230	0.1505	0.0130	5.474	19
20	0.0760	6.7198	37.8127	13.1531	88.3862	0.1488	0.0113	5.627	20
21	0.0668	6.7866	39.1494	14.9617	101.5393	0.1473	0.0098	5.768	21
22	0.0588	6.8454	40.3834	17.0189	116.5009	0.1461	0.0086	5.899	22
23	0.0517	6.8970	41.5198	19.3590	133.5198	0.1450	0.0075	6.019	23
24	0.0454	6.9425	42.5643	22.0208	152.8788	0.1440	0.0065	6.131	24
25	0.0399	6.9824	43.5224	25.0487	174.8996	0.1432	0.0057	6.233	25
26	0.0351	7.0175	44.3998	28.4929	199.9483	0.1425	0.0050	6.327	26
27	0.0309	7.0483	45.2020	32.4107	228.4412	0.1419	0.0044	6.413	27
28	0.0271	7.0755	45.9344	36.8671	260.8519	0.1413	0.0038	6.492	28
29	0.0238	7.0993	46.6020	41.9364	297.7190	0.1409	0.0034	6.564	29
30	0.0210	7.1203	47.2100	47.7026	339.6554	0.1404	0.0029	6.630	30
31	0.0184	7.1387	47.7628	54.2617	387.3580	0.1401	0.0026	6.690	31
32	0.0162	7.1549	48.2651	61.7227	441.6197	0.1398	0.0023	6.745	32
33	0.0142	7.1691	48.7209	70.2096	503.3424	0.1395	0.0020	6.795	33
34	0.0125	7.1817	49.1341	79.8634	573.5520	0.1392	0.0017	6.841	34
35	0.0110	7.1927	49.5083	90.8446	653.4154	0.1390	0.0015	6.883	35
36	0.0097	7.2023	49.8470	103.3357	744.2600	0.1388	0.0013	6.920	36
37	0.0085	7.2109	50.1533	117.5444	847.5957	0.1387	0.0012	6.955	37
38	0.0075	7.2183	50.4300	133.7068	965.1402	0.1385	0.0010	6.986	38
39	0.0066	7.2249	50.6799	152.0915	1098.8469	0.1384	0.0009	7.014	39
40	0.0058	7.2307	50.9053	173.0040	1250.9384	0.1383	0.0008	7.040	40
41	0.0051	7.2358	51.1086	196.7921	1423.9424	0.1382	0.0007	7.063	41
42	0.0045	7.2402	51.2917	223.8510	1620.7345	0.1381	0.0006	7.084	42
43	0.0039	7.2442	51.4567	254.6305	1844.5855	0.1380	0.0005	7.103	43
44	0.0035	7.2476	51.6051	289.6422	2099.2160	0.1380	0.0005	7.120	44
45	0.0030	7.2507	51.7387	329.4680	2388.8582	0.1379	0.0004	7.135	45
46	0.0027	7.2533	51.8588	374.7699	2718.3262	0.1379	0.0004	7.149	46
47	0.0023	7.2557	51.9667	426.3007	3093.0960	0.1378	0.0003	7.162	47
48	0.0021	7.2577	52.0636	484.9171	3519.3967	0.1378	0.0003	7.173	48
49	0.0018	7.2595	52.1506	551.5931	4004.3138	0.1377	0.0002	7.183	49
50	0.0016	7.2611	52.2287	627.4372	4555.9069	0.1377	0.0002	7.192	50
51	0.0014	7.2625	52.2988	713.7098	5183.3441	0.1377	0.0002	7.201	51
52	0.0012	7.2638	52.3616	811.8449	5897.0540	0.1377	0.0002	7.208	52
53	0.0011	7.2649	52.4179	923.4736	6708.8989	0.1376	0.0001	7.215	53
54	0.0010	7.2658	52.4683	1050.4512	7632.3725	0.1376	0.0001	7.221	54
55	0.0008	7.2666	52.5135	1194.8883	8682.8237	0.1376	0.0001	7.226	55
60	0.0004	7.2695	52.6776	2275.5392	16542.1032	0.1376	0.0001	7.246	60
65	0.0002	7.2710	52.7713	4333.5254	31509.2756	0.1375	0.0000	7.257	65
70	0.0001	7.2718	52.8245	8252.7440	60012.6836	0.1375	0.0000	7.264	70
75	0.0001	7.2723	52.8545	15716.4842	114294.4304	0.1375	0.0000	7.268	75
80	0.0000	7.2725	52.8714	29930.3935	217668.3162	0.1375	0.0000	7.270	80
85	0.0000	7.2726	52.8808	56999.2909	414533.0248	0.1375	0.0000	7.271	85
90	0.0000	7.2727	52.8860	108549.1631	789441.1865	0.1375	0.0000	7.271	90
95	0.0000	7.2727	52.8890	206720.4807	1503414.4053	0.1375	0.0000	7.272	95
100	0.0000	7.2727	52.8906	393677.4445	2863101.4148	0.1375	0.0000	7.272	100

I = 14.00 %

n	(P/F)	(P/A)	(P/G)	(F/P)	(F/A)	(A/P)	(A/F)	(A/G)	n
1	0.8772	0.8772	0.0000	1.1400	1.0000	1.1400	1.0000	0.000	1
2	0.7695	1.6467	0.7695	1.2996	2.1400	0.6073	0.4673	0.467	2
3	0.6750	2.3216	2.1194	1.4815	3.4396	0.4307	0.2907	0.912	3
4	0.5921	2.9137	3.8957	1.6890	4.9211	0.3432	0.2032	1.337	4
5	0.5194	3.4331	5.9731	1.9254	6.6101	0.2913	0.1513	1.739	5
6	0.4556	3.8887	8.2511	2.1950	8.5355	0.2572	0.1172	2.121	6
7	0.3996	4.2883	10.6489	2.5023	10.7305	0.2332	0.0932	2.483	7
8	0.3506	4.6389	13.1028	2.8526	13.2328	0.2156	0.0756	2.824	8
9	0.3075	4.9464	15.5629	3.2519	16.0853	0.2022	0.0622	3.146	9
10	0.2697	5.2161	17.9906	3.7072	19.3373	0.1917	0.0517	3.449	10
11	0.2366	5.4527	20.3567	4.2262	23.0445	0.1834	0.0434	3.733	11
12	0.2076	5.6603	22.6399	4.8179	27.2707	0.1767	0.0367	3.999	12
13	0.1821	5.8424	24.8247	5.4924	32.0887	0.1712	0.0312	4.249	13
14	0.1597	6.0021	26.9009	6.2613	37.5811	0.1666	0.0266	4.481	14
15	0.1401	6.1422	28.8623	7.1379	43.8424	0.1628	0.0228	4.699	15
16	0.1229	6.2651	30.7057	8.1372	50.9804	0.1596	0.0196	4.901	16
17	0.1078	6.3729	32.4305	9.2765	59.1176	0.1569	0.0169	5.088	17
18	0.0946	6.4674	34.0380	10.5752	68.3941	0.1546	0.0146	5.263	18
19	0.0829	6.5504	35.5311	12.0557	78.9692	0.1527	0.0127	5.424	19
20	0.0728	6.6231	36.9135	13.7435	91.0249	0.1510	0.0110	5.573	20
21	0.0638	6.6870	38.1901	15.6676	104.7684	0.1495	0.0095	5.711	21
22	0.0560	6.7429	39.3658	17.8610	120.4360	0.1483	0.0083	5.838	22
23	0.0491	6.7921	40.4463	20.3616	138.2970	0.1472	0.0072	5.954	23
24	0.0431	6.8351	41.4371	23.2122	158.6586	0.1463	0.0063	6.062	24
25	0.0378	6.8729	42.3441	26.4619	181.8708	0.1455	0.0055	6.161	25
26	0.0331	6.9061	43.1728	30.1666	208.3327	0.1448	0.0048	6.251	26
27	0.0291	6.9352	43.9289	34.3899	238.4993	0.1442	0.0042	6.334	27
28	0.0255	6.9607	44.6176	39.2045	272.8892	0.1437	0.0037	6.410	28
29	0.0224	6.9830	45.2441	44.6931	312.0937	0.1432	0.0032	6.479	29
30	0.0196	7.0027	45.8132	50.9502	356.7868	0.1428	0.0028	6.542	30
31	0.0172	7.0199	46.3297	58.0832	407.7370	0.1425	0.0025	6.599	31
32	0.0151	7.0350	46.7979	66.2148	465.8202	0.1421	0.0021	6.652	32
33	0.0132	7.0482	47.2218	75.4849	532.0350	0.1419	0.0019	6.699	33
34	0.0116	7.0599	47.6053	86.0528	607.5199	0.1416	0.0016	6.743	34
35	0.0102	7.0700	47.9519	98.1002	693.5727	0.1414	0.0014	6.782	35
36	0.0089	7.0790	48.2649	111.8342	791.6729	0.1413	0.0013	6.818	36
37	0.0078	7.0868	48.5472	127.4910	903.5071	0.1411	0.0011	6.850	37
38	0.0069	7.0937	48.8018	145.3397	1030.9981	0.1410	0.0010	6.879	38
39	0.0060	7.0997	49.0312	165.6873	1176.3378	0.1409	0.0009	6.906	39
40	0.0053	7.1050	49.2376	188.8835	1342.0251	0.1407	0.0007	6.930	40
41	0.0046	7.1097	49.4234	215.3272	1530.9086	0.1407	0.0007	6.951	41
42	0.0041	7.1138	49.5904	245.4730	1746.2358	0.1406	0.0006	6.971	42
43	0.0036	7.1173	49.7405	279.8392	1991.7088	0.1405	0.0005	6.988	43
44	0.0031	7.1205	49.8753	319.0167	2271.5481	0.1404	0.0004	7.004	44
45	0.0027	7.1232	49.9963	363.6791	2590.5648	0.1404	0.0004	7.018	45
46	0.0024	7.1256	50.1048	414.5941	2954.2439	0.1403	0.0003	7.031	46
47	0.0021	7.1277	50.2022	472.6373	3368.8380	0.1403	0.0003	7.043	47
48	0.0019	7.1296	50.2894	538.8065	3841.4753	0.1403	0.0003	7.053	48
49	0.0016	7.1312	50.3675	614.2395	4380.2819	0.1402	0.0002	7.063	49
50	0.0014	7.1327	50.4375	700.2330	4994.5213	0.1402	0.0002	7.071	50
51	0.0013	7.1339	50.5001	798.2656	5694.7543	0.1402	0.0002	7.078	51
52	0.0011	7.1350	50.5562	910.0228	6493.0199	0.1402	0.0002	7.085	52
53	0.0010	7.1360	50.6063	1037.4260	7403.0427	0.1401	0.0001	7.091	53
54	0.0008	7.1368	50.6511	1182.6656	8440.4687	0.1401	0.0001	7.097	54
55	0.0007	7.1376	50.6912	1348.2388	9623.1343	0.1401	0.0001	7.102	55
60	0.0004	7.1401	50.8357	2595.9187	18535.1333	0.1401	0.0001	7.119	60
65	0.0002	7.1414	50.9173	4998.2196	35694.4260	0.1400	0.0000	7.129	65
70	0.0001	7.1421	50.9632	9623.6450	68733.1785	0.1400	0.0000	7.135	70
75	0.0001	7.1425	50.9887	18529.5064	132346.4742	0.1400	0.0000	7.138	75
80	0.0000	7.1427	51.0030	35676.9818	254828.4415	0.1400	0.0000	7.140	80
85	0.0000	7.1428	51.0108	68692.9810	490657.0073	0.1400	0.0000	7.141	85
90	0.0000	7.1428	51.0152	132262.4674	944724.7670	0.1400	0.0000	7.142	90
95	0.0000	7.1428	51.0175	254660.0834	1818993.4528	0.1400	0.0000	7.142	95
100	0.0000	7.1428	51.0188	490326.2381	3502323.1295	0.1400	0.0000	7.142	100

I = 14.25 %

n	(P/F)	(P/A)	(P/G)	(F/P)	(F/A)	(A/P)	(A/F)	(A/G)	n
1	0.8753	0.8753	0.0000	1.1425	1.0000	1.1425	1.0000	0.000	1
2	0.7661	1.6414	0.7661	1.3053	2.1425	0.6092	0.4667	0.466	2
3	0.6706	2.3119	2.1072	1.4913	3.4478	0.4325	0.2900	0.911	3
4	0.5869	2.8988	3.8679	1.7038	4.9391	0.3450	0.2025	1.334	4
5	0.5137	3.4126	5.9228	1.9466	6.6429	0.2930	0.1505	1.735	5
6	0.4496	3.8622	8.1710	2.2240	8.5896	0.2589	0.1164	2.115	6
7	0.3936	4.2557	10.5323	2.5409	10.8136	0.2350	0.0925	2.474	7
8	0.3445	4.6002	12.9436	2.9030	13.3545	0.2174	0.0749	2.813	8
9	0.3015	4.9017	15.3556	3.3167	16.2575	0.2040	0.0615	3.132	9
10	0.2639	5.1656	17.7307	3.7893	19.5742	0.1936	0.0511	3.432	10
11	0.2310	5.3966	20.0406	4.3293	23.3636	0.1853	0.0428	3.713	11
12	0.2022	5.5988	22.2645	4.9462	27.6929	0.1786	0.0361	3.976	12
13	0.1770	5.7757	24.3880	5.6511	32.6391	0.1731	0.0306	4.222	13
14	0.1549	5.9306	26.4015	6.4563	38.2902	0.1686	0.0261	4.451	14
15	0.1356	6.0662	28.2995	7.3764	44.7465	0.1648	0.0223	4.665	15
16	0.1187	6.1848	30.0793	8.4275	52.1229	0.1617	0.0192	4.863	16
17	0.1039	6.2887	31.7411	9.6284	60.5504	0.1590	0.0165	5.047	17
18	0.0909	6.3796	33.2865	11.0005	70.1788	0.1567	0.0142	5.217	18
19	0.0796	6.4592	34.7187	12.5681	81.1793	0.1548	0.0123	5.375	19
20	0.0696	6.5288	36.0419	14.3590	93.7474	0.1532	0.0107	5.520	20
21	0.0610	6.5898	37.2610	16.4052	108.1064	0.1518	0.0093	5.654	21
22	0.0534	6.6431	38.3814	18.7429	124.5115	0.1505	0.0080	5.777	22
23	0.0467	6.6898	39.4088	21.4138	143.2544	0.1495	0.0070	5.890	23
24	0.0409	6.7307	40.3489	24.4652	164.6682	0.1486	0.0061	5.994	24
25	0.0358	6.7665	41.2076	27.9515	189.1334	0.1478	0.0053	6.090	25
26	0.0313	6.7978	41.9904	31.9346	217.0849	0.1471	0.0046	6.177	26
27	0.0274	6.8252	42.7030	36.4853	249.0195	0.1465	0.0040	6.256	27
28	0.0240	6.8492	43.3507	41.6844	285.5048	0.1460	0.0035	6.329	28
29	0.0210	6.8702	43.9387	47.6245	327.1892	0.1456	0.0031	6.395	29
30	0.0184	6.8886	44.4717	54.4109	374.8136	0.1452	0.0027	6.455	30
31	0.0161	6.9047	44.9542	62.1645	429.2246	0.1448	0.0023	6.510	31
32	0.0141	6.9187	45.3907	71.0229	491.3891	0.1445	0.0020	6.560	32
33	0.0123	6.9311	45.7851	81.1437	562.4120	0.1443	0.0018	6.605	33
34	0.0108	6.9418	46.1410	92.7067	643.5558	0.1441	0.0016	6.646	34
35	0.0094	6.9513	46.4621	105.9174	736.2624	0.1439	0.0014	6.683	35
36	0.0083	6.9596	46.7513	121.0106	842.1798	0.1437	0.0012	6.717	36
37	0.0072	6.9668	47.0117	138.2546	963.1905	0.1435	0.0010	6.748	37
38	0.0063	6.9731	47.2459	157.9559	1101.4451	0.1434	0.0009	6.775	38
39	0.0055	6.9787	47.4565	180.4646	1259.4010	0.1433	0.0008	6.800	39
40	0.0049	6.9835	47.6456	206.1809	1439.8657	0.1432	0.0007	6.822	40
41	0.0042	6.9878	47.8154	235.5616	1646.0466	0.1431	0.0006	6.842	41
42	0.0037	6.9915	47.9678	269.1292	1881.6082	0.1430	0.0005	6.860	42
43	0.0033	6.9947	48.1044	307.4801	2150.7374	0.1430	0.0005	6.877	43
44	0.0028	6.9976	48.2268	351.2960	2458.2174	0.1429	0.0004	6.891	44
45	0.0025	7.0001	48.3364	401.3557	2809.5134	0.1429	0.0004	6.905	45
46	0.0022	7.0022	48.4346	458.5488	3210.8691	0.1428	0.0003	6.917	46
47	0.0019	7.0041	48.5224	523.8921	3669.4179	0.1428	0.0003	6.927	47
48	0.0017	7.0058	48.6009	598.5467	4193.3100	0.1427	0.0002	6.937	48
49	0.0015	7.0073	48.6711	683.8396	4791.8566	0.1427	0.0002	6.945	49
50	0.0013	7.0086	48.7338	781.2867	5475.6962	0.1427	0.0002	6.953	50
51	0.0011	7.0097	48.7898	892.6201	6256.9829	0.1427	0.0002	6.960	51
52	0.0010	7.0107	48.8398	1019.8184	7149.6030	0.1426	0.0001	6.966	52
53	0.0009	7.0115	48.8844	1165.1426	8169.4214	0.1426	0.0001	6.972	53
54	0.0008	7.0123	48.9243	1331.1754	9334.5640	0.1426	0.0001	6.976	54
55	0.0007	7.0129	48.9598	1520.8679	10665.7393	0.1426	0.0001	6.981	55
60	0.0003	7.0152	49.0871	2960.5508	20768.7779	0.1425	0.0000	6.997	60
65	0.0002	7.0163	49.1582	5763.0657	40435.5485	0.1425	0.0000	7.006	65
70	0.0001	7.0169	49.1977	11218.4953	78719.2656	0.1425	0.0000	7.011	70
75	0.0000	7.0172	49.2196	21838.1405	153243.0912	0.1425	0.0000	7.014	75
80	0.0000	7.0174	49.2316	42510.5476	298312.6147	0.1425	0.0000	7.015	80
85	0.0000	7.0175	49.2381	82751.8560	580707.7613	0.1425	0.0000	7.016	85
90	0.0000	7.0175	49.2417	161086.3669	1130423.6277	0.1425	0.0000	7.017	90
95	0.0000	7.0175	49.2436	313573.8444	2200511.1889	0.1425	0.0000	7.017	95
100	0.0000	7.0175	49.2447	610408.9239	4283564.3783	0.1425	0.0000	7.017	100

EXPANDED INTEREST TABLES

I = 14.50 %

n	(P/F)	(P/A)	(P/G)	(F/P)	(F/A)	(A/P)	(A/F)	(A/G)	n
1	0.8734	0.8734	0.0000	1.1450	1.0000	1.1450	1.0000	0.000	1
2	0.7628	1.6361	0.7628	1.3110	2.1450	0.6112	0.4662	0.466	2
3	0.6662	2.3023	2.0951	1.5011	3.4560	0.4343	0.2893	0.910	3
4	0.5818	2.8841	3.8405	1.7188	4.9571	0.3467	0.2017	1.331	4
5	0.5081	3.3922	5.8730	1.9680	6.6759	0.2948	0.1498	1.731	5
6	0.4438	3.8360	8.0919	2.2534	8.6439	0.2607	0.1157	2.109	6
7	0.3876	4.2236	10.4174	2.5801	10.8973	0.2368	0.0918	2.466	7
8	0.3385	4.5621	12.7869	2.9542	13.4774	0.2192	0.0742	2.802	8
9	0.2956	4.8577	15.1519	3.3826	16.4317	0.2059	0.0609	3.119	9
10	0.2582	5.1159	17.4757	3.8731	19.8142	0.1955	0.0505	3.415	10
11	0.2255	5.3414	19.7306	4.4347	23.6873	0.1872	0.0422	3.693	11
12	0.1969	5.5383	21.8970	5.0777	28.1220	0.1806	0.0356	3.953	12
13	0.1720	5.7103	23.9610	5.8140	33.1997	0.1751	0.0301	4.196	13
14	0.1502	5.8606	25.9138	6.6570	39.0136	0.1706	0.0256	4.421	14
15	0.1312	5.9918	27.7506	7.6222	45.6706	0.1669	0.0219	4.631	15
16	0.1146	6.1063	29.4693	8.7275	53.2928	0.1638	0.0188	4.826	16
17	0.1001	6.2064	31.0704	9.9929	62.0203	0.1611	0.0161	5.006	17
18	0.0874	6.2938	32.5562	11.4419	72.0132	0.1589	0.0139	5.172	18
19	0.0763	6.3701	33.9301	13.1010	83.4551	0.1570	0.0120	5.326	19
20	0.0667	6.4368	35.1967	15.0006	96.5561	0.1554	0.0104	5.468	20
21	0.0582	6.4950	36.3612	17.1757	111.5568	0.1540	0.0090	5.598	21
22	0.0508	6.5459	37.4290	19.6662	128.7325	0.1528	0.0078	5.718	22
23	0.0444	6.5903	38.4060	22.5178	148.3987	0.1517	0.0067	5.827	23
24	0.0388	6.6291	39.2980	25.7829	170.9165	0.1509	0.0059	5.928	24
25	0.0339	6.6629	40.1110	29.5214	196.6994	0.1501	0.0051	6.020	25
26	0.0296	6.6925	40.8506	33.8020	226.2208	0.1494	0.0044	6.103	26
27	0.0258	6.7184	41.5224	38.7033	260.0228	0.1488	0.0038	6.180	27
28	0.0226	6.7409	42.1317	44.3153	298.7262	0.1483	0.0033	6.250	28
29	0.0197	6.7606	42.6835	50.7410	343.0415	0.1479	0.0029	6.313	29
30	0.0172	6.7778	43.1826	58.0985	393.7825	0.1475	0.0025	6.371	30
31	0.0150	6.7929	43.6336	66.5227	451.8809	0.1472	0.0022	6.423	31
32	0.0131	6.8060	44.0406	76.1685	518.4037	0.1469	0.0019	6.470	32
33	0.0115	6.8175	44.4075	87.2130	594.5722	0.1467	0.0017	6.513	33
34	0.0100	6.8275	44.7380	99.8588	681.7852	0.1465	0.0015	6.552	34
35	0.0087	6.8362	45.0354	114.3384	781.6440	0.1463	0.0013	6.587	35
36	0.0076	6.8439	45.3027	130.9174	895.9824	0.1461	0.0011	6.619	36
37	0.0067	6.8505	45.5429	149.9005	1026.8998	0.1460	0.0010	6.648	37
38	0.0058	6.8564	45.7584	171.6360	1176.8003	0.1458	0.0008	6.673	38
39	0.0051	6.8615	45.9518	196.5233	1348.4363	0.1457	0.0007	6.697	39
40	0.0044	6.8659	46.1251	225.0191	1544.9596	0.1456	0.0006	6.718	40
41	0.0039	6.8698	46.2804	257.6469	1769.9788	0.1456	0.0006	6.736	41
42	0.0034	6.8732	46.4193	295.0057	2027.6257	0.1455	0.0005	6.753	42
43	0.0030	6.8761	46.5437	337.7816	2322.6314	0.1454	0.0004	6.768	43
44	0.0026	6.8787	46.6549	386.7599	2660.4129	0.1454	0.0004	6.782	44
45	0.0023	6.8810	46.7542	442.8401	3047.1728	0.1453	0.0003	6.794	45
46	0.0020	6.8830	46.8430	507.0519	3490.0129	0.1453	0.0003	6.805	46
47	0.0017	6.8847	46.9222	580.5744	3997.0648	0.1453	0.0003	6.815	47
48	0.0015	6.8862	46.9929	664.7577	4577.6391	0.1452	0.0002	6.824	48
49	0.0013	6.8875	47.0560	761.1475	5242.3968	0.1452	0.0002	6.832	49
50	0.0011	6.8886	47.1122	871.5139	6003.5444	0.1452	0.0002	6.839	50
51	0.0010	6.8896	47.1623	997.8835	6875.0583	0.1451	0.0001	6.845	51
52	0.0009	6.8905	47.2069	1142.5766	7872.9417	0.1451	0.0001	6.851	52
53	0.0008	6.8913	47.2467	1308.2502	9015.5183	0.1451	0.0001	6.856	53
54	0.0007	6.8919	47.2821	1497.9464	10323.7684	0.1451	0.0001	6.860	54
55	0.0006	6.8925	47.3135	1715.1487	11821.7149	0.1451	0.0001	6.864	55
60	0.0003	6.8945	47.4257	3375.4307	23271.9361	0.1450	0.0000	6.878	60
65	0.0002	6.8955	47.4878	6642.8835	45806.0929	0.1450	0.0000	6.886	65
70	0.0001	6.8960	47.5219	13073.2651	90153.5523	0.1450	0.0000	6.891	70
75	0.0000	6.8963	47.5405	25728.3243	177429.8225	0.1450	0.0000	6.893	75
80	0.0000	6.8964	47.5506	50633.6149	349190.4475	0.1450	0.0000	6.895	80
85	0.0000	6.8965	47.5561	99647.4908	687217.1782	0.1450	0.0000	6.895	85
90	0.0000	6.8965	47.5590	196107.3183	1352457.3674	0.1450	0.0000	6.896	90
95	0.0000	6.8965	47.5606	385941.2812	2661657.1116	0.1450	0.0000	6.896	95
100	0.0000	6.8965	47.5615	759536.5325	5238176.0864	0.1450	0.0000	6.896	100

$I = 14.75\%$

n	(P/F)	(P/A)	(P/G)	(F/P)	(F/A)	(A/P)	(A/F)	(A/G)	n
1	0.8715	0.8715	0.0000	1.1475	1.0000	1.1475	1.0000	0.000	1
2	0.7594	1.6309	0.7594	1.3168	2.1475	0.6132	0.4657	0.465	2
3	0.6618	2.2927	2.0831	1.5110	3.4643	0.4362	0.2887	0.908	3
4	0.5768	2.8695	3.8133	1.7338	4.9752	0.3485	0.2010	1.328	4
5	0.5026	3.3721	5.8238	1.9896	6.7091	0.2966	0.1491	1.727	5
6	0.4380	3.8101	8.0139	2.2831	8.6987	0.2625	0.1150	2.103	6
7	0.3817	4.1918	10.3041	2.6198	10.9817	0.2386	0.0911	2.458	7
8	0.3326	4.5245	12.6326	3.0062	13.6015	0.2210	0.0735	2.792	8
9	0.2899	4.8143	14.9517	3.4496	16.6078	0.2077	0.0602	3.105	9
10	0.2526	5.0670	17.2253	3.9585	20.0574	0.1974	0.0499	3.399	10
11	0.2202	5.2871	19.4268	4.5423	24.0159	0.1891	0.0416	3.674	11
12	0.1919	5.4790	21.5372	5.2123	28.5582	0.1825	0.0350	3.930	12
13	0.1672	5.6462	23.5435	5.9812	33.7705	0.1771	0.0296	4.169	13
14	0.1457	5.7919	25.4376	6.8634	39.7517	0.1727	0.0252	4.392	14
15	0.1270	5.9188	27.2152	7.8757	46.6151	0.1690	0.0215	4.598	15
16	0.1107	6.0295	28.8750	9.0374	54.4908	0.1659	0.0184	4.789	16
17	0.0964	6.1259	30.4178	10.3704	63.5282	0.1632	0.0157	4.965	17
18	0.0840	6.2099	31.8464	11.9000	73.8986	0.1610	0.0135	5.128	18
19	0.0732	6.2832	33.1646	13.6553	85.7986	0.1592	0.0117	5.278	19
20	0.0638	6.3470	34.3771	15.6695	99.4539	0.1576	0.0101	5.416	20
21	0.0556	6.4026	35.4894	17.9807	115.1234	0.1562	0.0087	5.543	21
22	0.0485	6.4511	36.5072	20.6329	133.1041	0.1550	0.0075	5.659	22
23	0.0422	6.4933	37.4364	23.6762	153.7369	0.1540	0.0065	5.765	23
24	0.0368	6.5301	38.2830	27.1684	177.4131	0.1531	0.0056	5.862	24
25	0.0321	6.5622	39.0528	31.1758	204.5816	0.1524	0.0049	5.951	25
26	0.0280	6.5901	39.7516	35.7742	235.7574	0.1517	0.0042	6.032	26
27	0.0244	6.6145	40.3850	41.0509	271.5316	0.1512	0.0037	6.105	27
28	0.0212	6.6357	40.9582	47.1059	312.5825	0.1507	0.0032	6.172	28
29	0.0185	6.6542	41.4762	54.0540	359.6884	0.1503	0.0028	6.233	29
30	0.0161	6.6704	41.9437	62.0270	413.7424	0.1499	0.0024	6.288	30
31	0.0140	6.6844	42.3652	71.1760	475.7694	0.1496	0.0021	6.337	31
32	0.0122	6.6967	42.7448	81.6744	546.9454	0.1493	0.0018	6.383	32
33	0.0107	6.7073	43.0862	93.7214	628.6199	0.1491	0.0016	6.423	33
34	0.0093	6.7166	43.3931	107.5453	722.3413	0.1489	0.0014	6.460	34
35	0.0081	6.7247	43.6686	123.4083	829.8866	0.1487	0.0012	6.493	35
36	0.0071	6.7318	43.9157	141.6110	953.2949	0.1485	0.0010	6.523	36
37	0.0062	6.7379	44.1373	162.4986	1094.9059	0.1484	0.0009	6.550	37
38	0.0054	6.7433	44.3357	186.4672	1257.4045	0.1483	0.0008	6.574	38
39	0.0047	6.7480	44.5133	213.9711	1443.8717	0.1482	0.0007	6.596	39
40	0.0041	6.7520	44.6721	245.5318	1657.8428	0.1481	0.0006	6.616	40
41	0.0035	6.7556	44.8141	281.7478	1903.3746	0.1480	0.0005	6.633	41
42	0.0031	6.7587	44.9409	323.3055	2185.1224	0.1480	0.0005	6.649	42
43	0.0027	6.7614	45.0541	370.9931	2508.4279	0.1479	0.0004	6.663	43
44	0.0023	6.7637	45.1551	425.7146	2879.4210	0.1478	0.0003	6.676	44
45	0.0020	6.7658	45.2452	488.5075	3305.1356	0.1478	0.0003	6.687	45
46	0.0018	6.7676	45.3255	560.5624	3793.6431	0.1478	0.0003	6.697	46
47	0.0016	6.7691	45.3970	643.2453	4354.2055	0.1477	0.0002	6.706	47
48	0.0014	6.7705	45.4607	738.1240	4997.4508	0.1477	0.0002	6.714	48
49	0.0012	6.7717	45.5173	846.9973	5735.5748	0.1477	0.0002	6.721	49
50	0.0010	6.7727	45.5677	971.9294	6582.5721	0.1477	0.0002	6.728	50
51	0.0009	6.7736	45.6126	1115.2890	7554.5014	0.1476	0.0001	6.733	51
52	0.0008	6.7744	45.6524	1279.7941	8669.7904	0.1476	0.0001	6.739	52
53	0.0007	6.7750	45.6878	1468.5637	9949.5845	0.1476	0.0001	6.743	53
54	0.0006	6.7756	45.7193	1685.1769	11418.1482	0.1476	0.0001	6.747	54
55	0.0005	6.7762	45.7472	1933.7404	13103.3251	0.1476	0.0001	6.751	55
60	0.0003	6.7779	45.8461	3847.3496	26076.9465	0.1475	0.0000	6.764	60
65	0.0001	6.7788	45.9002	7654.6462	51889.1269	0.1475	0.0000	6.771	65
70	0.0001	6.7792	45.9296	15229.6034	103244.7690	0.1475	0.0000	6.775	70
75	0.0000	6.7794	45.9455	30300.6584	205421.4130	0.1475	0.0000	6.777	75
80	0.0000	6.7795	45.9540	60285.8706	408710.9869	0.1475	0.0000	6.778	80
85	0.0000	6.7796	45.9586	119944.1325	813173.7798	0.1475	0.0000	6.779	85
90	0.0000	6.7796	45.9611	238639.5816	1617888.6885	0.1475	0.0000	6.779	90
95	0.0000	6.7796	45.9624	474794.7956	3218940.9874	0.1475	0.0000	6.779	95
100	0.0000	6.7797	45.9630	944646.7199	6404377.7624	0.1475	0.0000	6.779	100

EXPANDED INTEREST TABLES

$I = 15.00 \%$

n	(P/F)	(P/A)	(P/G)	(F/P)	(F/A)	(A/P)	(A/F)	(A/G)	n
1	0.8696	0.8696	0.0000	1.1500	1.0000	1.1500	1.0000	0.000	1
2	0.7561	1.6257	0.7561	1.3225	2.1500	0.6151	0.4651	0.465	2
3	0.6575	2.2832	2.0712	1.5209	3.4725	0.4380	0.2880	0.907	3
4	0.5718	2.8550	3.7864	1.7490	4.9934	0.3503	0.2003	1.326	4
5	0.4972	3.3522	5.7751	2.0114	6.7424	0.2983	0.1483	1.722	5
6	0.4323	3.7845	7.9368	2.3131	8.7537	0.2642	0.1142	2.097	6
7	0.3759	4.1604	10.1924	2.6600	11.0668	0.2404	0.0904	2.449	7
8	0.3269	4.4873	12.4807	3.0590	13.7268	0.2229	0.0729	2.781	8
9	0.2843	4.7716	14.7548	3.5179	16.7858	0.2096	0.0596	3.092	9
10	0.2472	5.0188	16.9795	4.0456	20.3037	0.1993	0.0493	3.383	10
11	0.2149	5.2337	19.1289	4.6524	24.3493	0.1911	0.0411	3.654	11
12	0.1869	5.4206	21.1849	5.3503	29.0017	0.1845	0.0345	3.908	12
13	0.1625	5.5831	23.1352	6.1528	34.3519	0.1791	0.0291	4.143	13
14	0.1413	5.7245	24.9725	7.0757	40.5047	0.1747	0.0247	4.362	14
15	0.1229	5.8474	26.6930	8.1371	47.5804	0.1710	0.0210	4.565	15
16	0.1069	5.9542	28.2960	9.3576	55.7175	0.1679	0.0179	4.752	16
17	0.0929	6.0472	29.7828	10.7613	65.0751	0.1654	0.0154	4.925	17
18	0.0808	6.1280	31.1565	12.3755	75.8364	0.1632	0.0132	5.084	18
19	0.0703	6.1982	32.4213	14.2318	88.2118	0.1613	0.0113	5.230	19
20	0.0611	6.2593	33.5822	16.3665	102.4436	0.1598	0.0098	5.365	20
21	0.0531	6.3125	34.6448	18.8215	118.8101	0.1584	0.0084	5.488	21
22	0.0462	6.3587	35.6150	21.6447	137.6316	0.1573	0.0073	5.601	22
23	0.0402	6.3988	36.4988	24.8915	159.2764	0.1563	0.0063	5.704	23
24	0.0349	6.4338	37.3023	28.6252	184.1678	0.1554	0.0054	5.797	24
25	0.0304	6.4641	38.0314	32.9190	212.7930	0.1547	0.0047	5.883	25
26	0.0264	6.4906	38.6918	37.8568	245.7120	0.1541	0.0041	5.961	26
27	0.0230	6.5135	39.2890	43.5353	283.5688	0.1535	0.0035	6.031	27
28	0.0200	6.5335	39.8283	50.0656	327.1041	0.1531	0.0031	6.096	28
29	0.0174	6.5509	40.3146	57.5755	377.1697	0.1527	0.0027	6.154	29
30	0.0151	6.5660	40.7526	66.2118	434.7451	0.1523	0.0023	6.206	30
31	0.0131	6.5791	41.1446	76.1435	500.9569	0.1520	0.0020	6.254	31
32	0.0114	6.5905	41.5006	87.5651	577.1005	0.1517	0.0017	6.297	32
33	0.0099	6.6005	41.8184	100.6998	664.6655	0.1515	0.0015	6.335	33
34	0.0086	6.6091	42.1033	115.8048	765.3654	0.1513	0.0013	6.370	34
35	0.0075	6.6166	42.3586	133.1755	881.1702	0.1511	0.0011	6.401	35
36	0.0065	6.6231	42.5872	153.1519	1014.3457	0.1510	0.0010	6.430	36
37	0.0057	6.6288	42.7916	176.1246	1167.4975	0.1509	0.0009	6.455	37
38	0.0049	6.6338	42.9743	202.5433	1343.6222	0.1507	0.0007	6.478	38
39	0.0043	6.6380	43.1374	232.9248	1546.1655	0.1506	0.0006	6.498	39
40	0.0037	6.6418	43.2830	267.8635	1779.0903	0.1506	0.0006	6.516	40
41	0.0032	6.6450	43.4128	308.0431	2046.9539	0.1505	0.0005	6.533	41
42	0.0028	6.6478	43.5286	354.2495	2354.9969	0.1504	0.0004	6.547	42
43	0.0025	6.6503	43.6317	407.3870	2709.2465	0.1504	0.0004	6.560	43
44	0.0021	6.6524	43.7235	468.4950	3116.6334	0.1503	0.0003	6.572	44
45	0.0019	6.6543	43.8051	538.7693	3585.1285	0.1503	0.0003	6.583	45
46	0.0016	6.6559	43.8778	619.5847	4123.8977	0.1502	0.0002	6.592	46
47	0.0014	6.6573	43.9423	712.5224	4743.4824	0.1502	0.0002	6.600	47
48	0.0012	6.6585	43.9997	819.4007	5456.0047	0.1502	0.0002	6.608	48
49	0.0011	6.6596	44.0506	942.3108	6275.4055	0.1502	0.0002	6.614	49
50	0.0009	6.6605	44.0958	1083.6574	7217.7163	0.1501	0.0001	6.620	50
51	0.0008	6.6613	44.1360	1246.2061	8301.3737	0.1501	0.0001	6.625	51
52	0.0007	6.6620	44.1715	1433.1370	9547.5798	0.1501	0.0001	6.630	52
53	0.0006	6.6626	44.2031	1648.1075	10980.7167	0.1501	0.0001	6.634	53
54	0.0005	6.6631	44.2311	1895.3236	12628.8243	0.1501	0.0001	6.638	54
55	0.0005	6.6636	44.2558	2179.6222	14524.1479	0.1501	0.0001	6.641	55
60	0.0002	6.6651	44.3431	4383.9987	29219.9916	0.1500	0.0000	6.653	60
65	0.0001	6.6659	44.3903	8817.7874	58778.5826	0.1500	0.0000	6.659	65
70	0.0001	6.6663	44.4156	17735.7200	118231.4669	0.1500	0.0000	6.662	70
75	0.0000	6.6665	44.4292	35672.8680	237812.4532	0.1500	0.0000	6.664	75
80	0.0000	6.6666	44.4364	71750.8794	478332.5293	0.1500	0.0000	6.665	80
85	0.0000	6.6666	44.4402	144316.6470	962104.3133	0.1500	0.0000	6.666	85
90	0.0000	6.6666	44.4422	290272.3252	1935142.1680	0.1500	0.0000	6.666	90
95	0.0000	6.6667	44.4433	583841.3276	3892268.8509	0.1500	0.0000	6.666	95
100	0.0000	6.6667	44.4438	1174313.4507	7828749.6713	0.1500	0.0000	6.666	100

$I = 15.25\%$

n	(P/F)	(P/A)	(P/G)	(F/P)	(F/A)	(A/P)	(A/F)	(A/G)	n
1	0.8677	0.8677	0.0000	1.1525	1.0000	1.1525	1.0000	0.000	1
2	0.7529	1.6205	0.7529	1.3283	2.1525	0.6171	0.4646	0.464	2
3	0.6532	2.2738	2.0594	1.5308	3.4808	0.4398	0.2873	0.905	3
4	0.5668	2.8406	3.7598	1.7643	5.0116	0.3520	0.1995	1.323	4
5	0.4918	3.3324	5.7270	2.0333	6.7758	0.3001	0.1476	1.718	5
6	0.4267	3.7591	7.8607	2.3434	8.8092	0.2660	0.1135	2.091	6
7	0.3703	4.1294	10.0823	2.7008	11.1525	0.2422	0.0897	2.441	7
8	0.3213	4.4507	12.3312	3.1126	13.8533	0.2247	0.0722	2.770	8
9	0.2788	4.7294	14.5613	3.5873	16.9659	0.2114	0.0589	3.078	9
10	0.2419	4.9713	16.7381	4.1344	20.5532	0.2012	0.0487	3.366	10
11	0.2099	5.1812	18.8368	4.7649	24.6876	0.1930	0.0405	3.635	11
12	0.1821	5.3633	20.8399	5.4915	29.4525	0.1865	0.0340	3.885	12
13	0.1580	5.5213	22.7360	6.3290	34.9440	0.1811	0.0286	4.117	13
14	0.1371	5.6584	24.5182	7.2941	41.2729	0.1767	0.0242	4.333	14
15	0.1190	5.7773	26.1836	8.4065	48.5671	0.1731	0.0206	4.532	15
16	0.1032	5.8806	27.7318	9.6885	56.9735	0.1701	0.0176	4.715	16
17	0.0896	5.9701	29.1648	11.1660	66.6620	0.1675	0.0150	4.885	17
18	0.0777	6.0478	30.4858	12.8688	77.8280	0.1653	0.0128	5.040	18
19	0.0674	6.1152	31.6994	14.8312	90.6967	0.1635	0.0110	5.183	19
20	0.0585	6.1737	32.8110	17.0930	105.5280	0.1620	0.0095	5.314	20
21	0.0508	6.2245	33.8263	19.6997	122.6210	0.1607	0.0082	5.434	21
22	0.0440	6.2686	34.7512	22.7039	142.3207	0.1595	0.0070	5.543	22
23	0.0382	6.3068	35.5920	26.1662	165.0246	0.1586	0.0061	5.643	23
24	0.0332	6.3399	36.3547	30.1566	191.1908	0.1577	0.0052	5.734	24
25	0.0288	6.3687	37.0452	34.7555	221.3474	0.1570	0.0045	5.816	25
26	0.0250	6.3937	37.6693	40.0557	256.1029	0.1564	0.0039	5.891	26
27	0.0217	6.4153	38.2325	46.1642	296.1586	0.1559	0.0034	5.959	27
28	0.0188	6.4341	38.7400	53.2042	342.3228	0.1554	0.0029	6.021	28
29	0.0163	6.4504	39.1967	61.3179	395.5270	0.1550	0.0025	6.076	29
30	0.0142	6.4646	39.6070	70.6688	456.8449	0.1547	0.0022	6.126	30
31	0.0123	6.4769	39.9754	81.4458	527.5138	0.1544	0.0019	6.172	31
32	0.0107	6.4875	40.3056	93.8663	608.9596	0.1541	0.0016	6.212	32
33	0.0092	6.4968	40.6014	108.1810	702.8260	0.1539	0.0014	6.249	33
34	0.0080	6.5048	40.8661	124.6786	811.0069	0.1537	0.0012	6.282	34
35	0.0070	6.5117	41.1027	143.6920	935.6855	0.1536	0.0011	6.312	35
36	0.0060	6.5178	41.3141	165.6051	1079.3775	0.1534	0.0009	6.338	36
37	0.0052	6.5230	41.5027	190.8598	1244.9826	0.1533	0.0008	6.362	37
38	0.0045	6.5276	41.6709	219.9660	1435.8424	0.1532	0.0007	6.383	38
39	0.0039	6.5315	41.8208	253.5108	1655.8084	0.1531	0.0006	6.402	39
40	0.0034	6.5349	41.9543	292.1712	1909.3192	0.1530	0.0005	6.420	40
41	0.0030	6.5379	42.0731	336.7273	2201.4903	0.1530	0.0005	6.435	41
42	0.0026	6.5405	42.1787	388.0782	2538.2176	0.1529	0.0004	6.448	42
43	0.0022	6.5427	42.2726	447.2601	2926.2958	0.1528	0.0003	6.461	43
44	0.0019	6.5447	42.3560	515.4673	3373.5559	0.1528	0.0003	6.471	44
45	0.0017	6.5463	42.4301	594.0760	3889.0232	0.1528	0.0003	6.481	45
46	0.0015	6.5478	42.4958	684.6726	4483.0992	0.1527	0.0002	6.490	46
47	0.0013	6.5491	42.5541	789.0852	5167.7718	0.1527	0.0002	6.497	47
48	0.0011	6.5502	42.6058	909.4207	5956.8570	0.1527	0.0002	6.504	48
49	0.0010	6.5511	42.6516	1048.1074	6866.2777	0.1526	0.0001	6.510	49
50	0.0008	6.5519	42.6922	1207.9437	7914.3851	0.1526	0.0001	6.516	50
51	0.0007	6.5527	42.7281	1392.1551	9122.3288	0.1526	0.0001	6.520	51
52	0.0006	6.5533	42.7599	1604.4588	10514.4840	0.1526	0.0001	6.524	52
53	0.0005	6.5538	42.7880	1849.1388	12118.9428	0.1526	0.0001	6.528	53
54	0.0005	6.5543	42.8129	2131.1324	13968.0816	0.1526	0.0001	6.532	54
55	0.0004	6.5547	42.8348	2456.1301	16099.2140	0.1526	0.0001	6.535	55
60	0.0002	6.5561	42.9118	4994.0863	32741.5496	0.1525	0.0000	6.545	60
65	0.0001	6.5567	42.9530	10154.5507	66580.6606	0.1525	0.0000	6.551	65
70	0.0000	6.5571	42.9749	20647.4006	135386.2335	0.1525	0.0000	6.554	70
75	0.0000	6.5572	42.9865	41982.6699	275289.6390	0.1525	0.0000	6.555	75
80	0.0000	6.5573	42.9925	85363.9937	559757.3355	0.1525	0.0000	6.556	80
85	0.0000	6.5573	42.9957	173571.8911	1138169.7778	0.1525	0.0000	6.556	85
90	0.0000	6.5574	42.9974	352926.3345	2314264.4885	0.1525	0.0000	6.557	90
95	0.0000	6.5574	42.9983	717610.4194	4705635.5371	0.1525	0.0000	6.557	95
100	0.0000	6.5574	42.9987	1459128.0494	9568046.2259	0.1525	0.0000	6.557	100

$I = 15.50\%$

n	(P/F)	(P/A)	(P/G)	(F/P)	(F/A)	(A/P)	(A/F)	(A/G)	n
1	0.8658	0.8658	0.0000	1.1550	1.0000	1.1550	1.0000	0.000	1
2	0.7496	1.6154	0.7496	1.3340	2.1550	0.6190	0.4640	0.464	2
3	0.6490	2.2644	2.0476	1.5408	3.4890	0.4416	0.2866	0.904	3
4	0.5619	2.8263	3.7334	1.7796	5.0298	0.3538	0.1988	1.320	4
5	0.4865	3.3129	5.6794	2.0555	6.8094	0.3019	0.1469	1.714	5
6	0.4212	3.7341	7.7855	2.3741	8.8649	0.2678	0.1128	2.085	6
7	0.3647	4.0988	9.9737	2.7420	11.2390	0.2440	0.0890	2.433	7
8	0.3158	4.4145	12.1839	3.1671	13.9810	0.2265	0.0715	2.760	8
9	0.2734	4.6879	14.3709	3.6580	17.1481	0.2133	0.0583	3.065	9
10	0.2367	4.9246	16.5012	4.2249	20.8060	0.2031	0.0481	3.350	10
11	0.2049	5.1295	18.5504	4.8798	25.0310	0.1950	0.0400	3.616	11
12	0.1774	5.3069	20.5021	5.6362	29.9108	0.1884	0.0334	3.863	12
13	0.1536	5.4605	22.3455	6.5098	35.5469	0.1831	0.0281	4.092	13
14	0.1330	5.5935	24.0745	7.5188	42.0567	0.1788	0.0238	4.304	14
15	0.1152	5.7087	25.6866	8.6842	49.5755	0.1752	0.0202	4.499	15
16	0.0997	5.8084	27.1821	10.0302	58.2597	0.1722	0.0172	4.679	16
17	0.0863	5.8947	28.5632	11.5849	68.2899	0.1696	0.0146	4.845	17
18	0.0747	5.9695	29.8337	13.3806	79.8749	0.1675	0.0125	4.997	18
19	0.0647	6.0342	30.9984	15.4546	93.2555	0.1657	0.0107	5.137	19
20	0.0560	6.0902	32.0628	17.8501	108.7101	0.1642	0.0092	5.264	20
21	0.0485	6.1387	33.0329	20.6168	126.5601	0.1629	0.0079	5.381	21
22	0.0420	6.1807	33.9148	23.8124	147.1769	0.1618	0.0068	5.487	22
23	0.0364	6.2170	34.7147	27.5034	170.9894	0.1608	0.0058	5.583	23
24	0.0315	6.2485	35.4387	31.7664	198.4927	0.1600	0.0050	5.671	24
25	0.0273	6.2758	36.0928	36.6902	230.2591	0.1593	0.0043	5.751	25
26	0.0236	6.2994	36.6828	42.3771	266.9493	0.1587	0.0037	5.823	26
27	0.0204	6.3198	37.2140	48.9456	309.3264	0.1582	0.0032	5.888	27
28	0.0177	6.3375	37.6916	56.5322	358.2720	0.1578	0.0028	5.947	28
29	0.0153	6.3528	38.1204	65.2946	414.8041	0.1574	0.0024	6.000	29
30	0.0133	6.3661	38.5050	75.4153	480.0988	0.1571	0.0021	6.048	30
31	0.0115	6.3775	38.8494	87.1047	555.5141	0.1568	0.0018	6.091	31
32	0.0099	6.3875	39.1575	100.6059	642.6188	0.1566	0.0016	6.130	32
33	0.0086	6.3961	39.4329	116.1998	743.2247	0.1563	0.0013	6.165	33
34	0.0075	6.4035	39.6788	134.2108	859.4245	0.1562	0.0012	6.196	34
35	0.0065	6.4100	39.8981	155.0135	993.6353	0.1560	0.0010	6.224	35
36	0.0056	6.4156	40.0936	179.0406	1148.6488	0.1559	0.0009	6.249	36
37	0.0048	6.4204	40.2677	206.7918	1327.6893	0.1558	0.0008	6.271	37
38	0.0042	6.4246	40.4226	238.8446	1534.4812	0.1557	0.0007	6.291	38
39	0.0036	6.4282	40.5603	275.8655	1773.3258	0.1556	0.0006	6.309	39
40	0.0031	6.4314	40.6827	318.6246	2049.1913	0.1555	0.0005	6.325	40
41	0.0027	6.4341	40.7914	368.0115	2367.8159	0.1554	0.0004	6.339	41
42	0.0024	6.4364	40.8879	425.0532	2735.8274	0.1554	0.0004	6.352	42
43	0.0020	6.4385	40.9734	490.9365	3160.8806	0.1553	0.0003	6.363	43
44	0.0018	6.4402	41.0493	567.0317	3651.8171	0.1553	0.0003	6.373	44
45	0.0015	6.4418	41.1165	654.9216	4218.8488	0.1552	0.0002	6.382	45
46	0.0013	6.4431	41.1760	756.4344	4873.7704	0.1552	0.0002	6.390	46
47	0.0011	6.4442	41.2286	873.6817	5630.2048	0.1552	0.0002	6.397	47
48	0.0010	6.4452	41.2752	1009.1024	6503.8865	0.1552	0.0002	6.404	48
49	0.0009	6.4461	41.3164	1165.5133	7512.9889	0.1551	0.0001	6.409	49
50	0.0007	6.4468	41.3528	1346.1678	8678.5022	0.1551	0.0001	6.414	50
51	0.0006	6.4475	41.3849	1554.8239	10024.6700	0.1551	0.0001	6.418	51
52	0.0006	6.4480	41.4133	1795.8216	11579.4939	0.1551	0.0001	6.422	52
53	0.0005	6.4485	41.4384	2074.1739	13375.3155	0.1551	0.0001	6.426	53
54	0.0004	6.4489	41.4605	2395.6708	15449.4893	0.1551	0.0001	6.429	54
55	0.0004	6.4493	41.4800	2766.9998	17845.1602	0.1551	0.0001	6.431	55
60	0.0002	6.4505	41.5479	5687.4691	36686.8977	0.1550	0.0000	6.441	60
65	0.0001	6.4511	41.5839	11690.3893	75415.4150	0.1550	0.0000	6.446	65
70	0.0000	6.4513	41.6028	24029.1770	155020.4966	0.1550	0.0000	6.448	70
75	0.0000	6.4515	41.6127	49391.1135	318645.8935	0.1550	0.0000	6.450	75
80	0.0000	6.4515	41.6178	101521.6665	654972.0420	0.1550	0.0000	6.450	80
85	0.0000	6.4516	41.6205	208674.1530	1346278.4065	0.1550	0.0000	6.451	85
90	0.0000	6.4516	41.6219	428922.2550	2767233.9030	0.1550	0.0000	6.451	90
95	0.0000	6.4516	41.6226	881634.3479	5687957.0833	0.1550	0.0000	6.451	95
100	0.0000	6.4516	41.6229	1812167.8566	************	0.1550	0.0000	6.451	100

$I = 15.75\%$

n	(P/F)	(P/A)	(P/G)	(F/P)	(F/A)	(A/P)	(A/F)	(A/G)	n
1	0.8639	0.8639	0.0000	1.1575	1.0000	1.1575	1.0000	0.000	1
2	0.7464	1.6103	0.7464	1.3398	2.1575	0.6210	0.4635	0.463	2
3	0.6448	2.2551	2.0360	1.5508	3.4973	0.4434	0.2859	0.902	3
4	0.5571	2.8122	3.7072	1.7951	5.0481	0.3556	0.1981	1.318	4
5	0.4813	3.2935	5.6324	2.0778	6.8432	0.3036	0.1461	1.710	5
6	0.4158	3.7093	7.7113	2.4051	8.9210	0.2696	0.1121	2.078	6
7	0.3592	4.0685	9.8666	2.7839	11.3261	0.2458	0.0883	2.425	7
8	0.3103	4.3788	12.0389	3.2223	14.1099	0.2284	0.0709	2.749	8
9	0.2681	4.6469	14.1838	3.7298	17.3323	0.2152	0.0577	3.052	9
10	0.2316	4.8786	16.2685	4.3173	21.0621	0.2050	0.0475	3.334	10
11	0.2001	5.0787	18.2696	4.9972	25.3794	0.1969	0.0394	3.597	11
12	0.1729	5.2515	20.1712	5.7843	30.3766	0.1904	0.0329	3.841	12
13	0.1494	5.4009	21.9635	6.6953	36.1609	0.1852	0.0277	4.066	13
14	0.1290	5.5299	23.6410	7.7499	42.8563	0.1808	0.0233	4.275	14
15	0.1115	5.6414	25.2017	8.9705	50.6061	0.1773	0.0198	4.467	15
16	0.0963	5.7377	26.6463	10.3833	59.5766	0.1743	0.0168	4.644	16
17	0.0832	5.8209	27.9776	12.0187	69.9599	0.1718	0.0143	4.806	17
18	0.0719	5.8928	29.1996	13.9116	81.9786	0.1697	0.0122	4.955	18
19	0.0621	5.9549	30.3174	16.1027	95.8902	0.1679	0.0104	5.091	19
20	0.0537	6.0086	31.3367	18.6389	111.9929	0.1664	0.0089	5.215	20
21	0.0464	6.0549	32.2638	21.5745	130.6318	0.1652	0.0077	5.328	21
22	0.0400	6.0950	33.1047	24.9725	152.2063	0.1641	0.0066	5.431	22
23	0.0346	6.1296	33.8658	28.9057	177.1788	0.1631	0.0056	5.525	23
24	0.0299	6.1594	34.5532	33.4583	206.0845	0.1624	0.0049	5.609	24
25	0.0258	6.1853	35.1729	38.7280	239.5428	0.1617	0.0042	5.686	25
26	0.0223	6.2076	35.7306	44.8277	278.2708	0.1611	0.0036	5.756	26
27	0.0193	6.2268	36.2317	51.8880	323.0985	0.1606	0.0031	5.818	27
28	0.0166	6.2435	36.6812	60.0604	374.9865	0.1602	0.0027	5.875	28
29	0.0144	6.2579	37.0840	69.5199	435.0468	0.1598	0.0023	5.926	29
30	0.0124	6.2703	37.4444	80.4693	504.5667	0.1595	0.0020	5.971	30
31	0.0107	6.2810	37.7665	93.1432	585.0360	0.1592	0.0017	6.012	31
32	0.0093	6.2903	38.0540	107.8132	678.1791	0.1590	0.0015	6.049	32
33	0.0080	6.2983	38.3104	124.7938	785.9923	0.1588	0.0013	6.082	33
34	0.0069	6.3053	38.5389	144.4488	910.7861	0.1586	0.0011	6.112	34
35	0.0060	6.3112	38.7422	167.1995	1055.2350	0.1584	0.0009	6.138	35
36	0.0052	6.3164	38.9231	193.5334	1222.4345	0.1583	0.0008	6.162	36
37	0.0045	6.3209	39.0838	224.0149	1415.9679	0.1582	0.0007	6.183	37
38	0.0039	6.3247	39.2265	259.2973	1639.9828	0.1581	0.0006	6.202	38
39	0.0033	6.3281	39.3531	300.1366	1899.2801	0.1580	0.0005	6.218	39
40	0.0029	6.3309	39.4653	347.4081	2199.4167	0.1580	0.0005	6.233	40
41	0.0025	6.3334	39.5648	402.1249	2546.8249	0.1579	0.0004	6.247	41
42	0.0021	6.3356	39.6529	465.4596	2948.9498	0.1578	0.0003	6.258	42
43	0.0019	6.3374	39.7309	538.7695	3414.4094	0.1578	0.0003	6.269	43
44	0.0016	6.3390	39.7998	623.6257	3953.1789	0.1578	0.0003	6.278	44
45	0.0014	6.3404	39.8608	721.8467	4576.8046	0.1577	0.0002	6.286	45
46	0.0012	6.3416	39.9146	835.5376	5298.6513	0.1577	0.0002	6.294	46
47	0.0010	6.3426	39.9622	967.1347	6134.1889	0.1577	0.0002	6.300	47
48	0.0009	6.3435	40.0042	1119.4585	7101.3236	0.1576	0.0001	6.306	48
49	0.0008	6.3443	40.0412	1295.7732	8220.7821	0.1576	0.0001	6.311	49
50	0.0007	6.3450	40.0739	1499.8574	9516.5552	0.1576	0.0001	6.315	50
51	0.0006	6.3455	40.1027	1736.0850	11016.4127	0.1576	0.0001	6.319	51
52	0.0005	6.3460	40.1281	2009.5184	12752.4977	0.1576	0.0001	6.323	52
53	0.0004	6.3465	40.1504	2326.0175	14762.0161	0.1576	0.0001	6.326	53
54	0.0004	6.3468	40.1701	2692.3653	17088.0336	0.1576	0.0001	6.329	54
55	0.0003	6.3472	40.1874	3116.4128	19780.3989	0.1576	0.0001	6.331	55
60	0.0002	6.3482	40.2474	6475.3013	41106.6749	0.1575	0.0000	6.339	60
65	0.0001	6.3487	40.2788	13454.4200	85418.5395	0.1575	0.0000	6.344	65
70	0.0000	6.3490	40.2951	27955.6747	177489.9981	0.1575	0.0000	6.346	70
75	0.0000	6.3491	40.3035	58086.4690	368796.6283	0.1575	0.0000	6.347	75
80	0.0000	6.3492	40.3079	120692.4144	766294.6945	0.1575	0.0000	6.348	80
85	0.0000	6.3492	40.3101	250775.4242	1592218.5661	0.1575	0.0000	6.348	85
90	0.0000	6.3492	40.3112	521062.6839	3308328.1516	0.1575	0.0000	6.349	90
95	0.0000	6.3492	40.3118	1082667.1770	6874070.9649	0.1575	0.0000	6.349	95
100	0.0000	6.3492	40.3121	2249572.3688	***********	0.1575	0.0000	6.349	100

$$I = 16.00\ \%$$

n	(P/F)	(P/A)	(P/G)	(F/P)	(F/A)	(A/P)	(A/F)	(A/G)	n
1	0.8621	0.8621	0.0000	1.1600	1.0000	1.1600	1.0000	0.000	1
2	0.7432	1.6052	0.7432	1.3456	2.1600	0.6230	0.4630	0.463	2
3	0.6407	2.2459	2.0245	1.5609	3.5056	0.4453	0.2853	0.901	3
4	0.5523	2.7982	3.6814	1.8106	5.0665	0.3574	0.1974	1.315	4
5	0.4761	3.2743	5.5858	2.1003	6.8771	0.3054	0.1454	1.706	5
6	0.4104	3.6847	7.6380	2.4364	8.9775	0.2714	0.1114	2.072	6
7	0.3538	4.0386	9.7610	2.8262	11.4139	0.2476	0.0876	2.416	7
8	0.3050	4.3436	11.8962	3.2784	14.2401	0.2302	0.0702	2.738	8
9	0.2630	4.6065	13.9998	3.8030	17.5185	0.2171	0.0571	3.039	9
10	0.2267	4.8332	16.0399	4.4114	21.3215	0.2069	0.0469	3.318	10
11	0.1954	5.0286	17.9941	5.1173	25.7329	0.1989	0.0389	3.578	11
12	0.1685	5.1971	19.8472	5.9360	30.8502	0.1924	0.0324	3.818	12
13	0.1452	5.3423	21.5899	6.8858	36.7862	0.1872	0.0272	4.041	13
14	0.1252	5.4675	23.2175	7.9875	43.6720	0.1829	0.0229	4.246	14
15	0.1079	5.5755	24.7284	9.2655	51.6595	0.1794	0.0194	4.435	15
16	0.0930	5.6685	26.1241	10.7480	60.9250	0.1764	0.0164	4.608	16
17	0.0802	5.7487	27.4074	12.4677	71.6730	0.1740	0.0140	4.767	17
18	0.0691	5.8178	28.5828	14.4625	84.1407	0.1719	0.0119	4.913	18
19	0.0596	5.8775	29.6557	16.7765	98.6032	0.1701	0.0101	5.045	19
20	0.0514	5.9288	30.6321	19.4608	115.3797	0.1687	0.0087	5.166	20
21	0.0443	5.9731	31.5180	22.5745	134.8405	0.1674	0.0074	5.276	21
22	0.0382	6.0113	32.3200	26.1864	157.4150	0.1664	0.0064	5.376	22
23	0.0329	6.0442	33.0442	30.3762	183.6014	0.1654	0.0054	5.467	23
24	0.0284	6.0726	33.6970	35.2364	213.9776	0.1647	0.0047	5.549	24
25	0.0245	6.0971	34.2841	40.8742	249.2140	0.1640	0.0040	5.623	25
26	0.0211	6.1182	34.8114	47.4141	290.0883	0.1634	0.0034	5.689	26
27	0.0182	6.1364	35.2841	55.0004	337.5024	0.1630	0.0030	5.750	27
28	0.0157	6.1520	35.7073	63.8004	392.5028	0.1625	0.0025	5.804	28
29	0.0135	6.1656	36.0856	74.0085	456.3032	0.1622	0.0022	5.852	29
30	0.0116	6.1772	36.4234	85.8499	530.3117	0.1619	0.0019	5.896	30
31	0.0100	6.1872	36.7247	99.5859	616.1616	0.1616	0.0016	5.935	31
32	0.0087	6.1959	36.9930	115.5196	715.7475	0.1614	0.0014	5.970	32
33	0.0075	6.2034	37.2318	134.0027	831.2671	0.1612	0.0012	6.001	33
34	0.0064	6.2098	37.4441	155.4432	965.2698	0.1610	0.0010	6.029	34
35	0.0055	6.2153	37.6327	180.3141	1120.7130	0.1609	0.0009	6.054	35
36	0.0048	6.2201	37.8000	209.1643	1301.0270	0.1608	0.0008	6.077	36
37	0.0041	6.2242	37.9484	242.6306	1510.1914	0.1607	0.0007	6.096	37
38	0.0036	6.2278	38.0799	281.4515	1752.8220	0.1606	0.0006	6.114	38
39	0.0031	6.2309	38.1963	326.4838	2034.2735	0.1605	0.0005	6.130	39
40	0.0026	6.2335	38.2992	378.7212	2360.7572	0.1604	0.0004	6.144	40
41	0.0023	6.2358	38.3903	439.3165	2739.4784	0.1604	0.0004	6.156	41
42	0.0020	6.2377	38.4707	509.6072	3178.7949	0.1603	0.0003	6.167	42
43	0.0017	6.2394	38.5418	591.1443	3688.4021	0.1603	0.0003	6.177	43
44	0.0015	6.2409	38.6045	685.7274	4279.5465	0.1602	0.0002	6.185	44
45	0.0013	6.2421	38.6598	795.4438	4965.2739	0.1602	0.0002	6.193	45
46	0.0011	6.2432	38.7086	922.7148	5760.7177	0.1602	0.0002	6.200	46
47	0.0009	6.2442	38.7516	1070.3492	6683.4326	0.1601	0.0001	6.206	47
48	0.0008	6.2450	38.7894	1241.6051	7753.7818	0.1601	0.0001	6.211	48
49	0.0007	6.2457	38.8227	1440.2619	8995.3869	0.1601	0.0001	6.216	49
50	0.0006	6.2463	38.8521	1670.7038	10435.6488	0.1601	0.0001	6.220	50
51	0.0005	6.2468	38.8779	1938.0164	12106.3526	0.1601	0.0001	6.223	51
52	0.0004	6.2472	38.9006	2248.0990	14044.3690	0.1601	0.0001	6.226	52
53	0.0004	6.2476	38.9205	2607.7949	16292.4680	0.1601	0.0001	6.229	53
54	0.0003	6.2479	38.9380	3025.0421	18900.2629	0.1601	0.0001	6.232	54
55	0.0003	6.2482	38.9534	3509.0488	21925.3050	0.1600	0.0000	6.234	55
60	0.0001	6.2492	39.0063	7370.2014	46057.5085	0.1600	0.0000	6.241	60
65	0.0001	6.2496	39.0337	15479.9410	96743.3810	0.1600	0.0000	6.245	65
70	0.0000	6.2498	39.0478	32513.1648	203201.0302	0.1600	0.0000	6.247	70
75	0.0000	6.2499	39.0551	68288.7545	426798.4658	0.1600	0.0000	6.248	75
80	0.0000	6.2500	39.0587	143429.7159	896429.4743	0.1600	0.0000	6.249	80
85	0.0000	6.2500	39.0606	301251.4072	1882815.0451	0.1600	0.0000	6.249	85
90	0.0000	6.2500	39.0615	632730.8800	3954561.7500	0.1600	0.0000	6.249	90
95	0.0000	6.2500	39.0620	1328951.0253	8305937.6582	0.1600	0.0000	6.249	95
100	0.0000	6.2500	39.0623	2791251.1994	************	0.1600	0.0000	6.250	100

$I = 16.25 \%$

n	(P/F)	(P/A)	(P/G)	(F/P)	(F/A)	(A/P)	(A/F)	(A/G)	n
1	0.8602	0.8602	0.0000	1.1625	1.0000	1.1625	1.0000	0.000	1
2	0.7400	1.6002	0.7400	1.3514	2.1625	0.6249	0.4624	0.462	2
3	0.6365	2.2367	2.0130	1.5710	3.5139	0.4471	0.2846	0.900	3
4	0.5476	2.7843	3.6557	1.8263	5.0849	0.3592	0.1967	1.313	4
5	0.4710	3.2553	5.5398	2.1231	6.9112	0.3072	0.1447	1.701	5
6	0.4052	3.6605	7.5656	2.4681	9.0343	0.2732	0.1107	2.066	6
7	0.3485	4.0090	9.6569	2.8691	11.5024	0.2494	0.0869	2.408	7
8	0.2998	4.3088	11.7556	3.3354	14.3715	0.2321	0.0696	2.728	8
9	0.2579	4.5667	13.8188	3.8774	17.7069	0.2190	0.0565	3.026	9
10	0.2219	4.7886	15.8155	4.5074	21.5842	0.2088	0.0463	3.302	10
11	0.1908	4.9794	17.7240	5.2399	26.0917	0.2008	0.0383	3.559	11
12	0.1642	5.1436	19.5298	6.0914	31.3316	0.1944	0.0319	3.796	12
13	0.1412	5.2848	21.2244	7.0812	37.4229	0.1892	0.0267	4.016	13
14	0.1215	5.4063	22.8036	8.2319	44.5042	0.1850	0.0225	4.218	14
15	0.1045	5.5108	24.2666	9.5696	52.7361	0.1815	0.0190	4.403	15
16	0.0899	5.6007	25.6150	11.1247	62.3057	0.1785	0.0160	4.573	16
17	0.0773	5.6780	26.8522	12.9324	73.4304	0.1761	0.0136	4.729	17
18	0.0665	5.7445	27.9829	15.0340	86.3628	0.1741	0.0116	4.871	18
19	0.0572	5.8017	29.0129	17.4770	101.3968	0.1724	0.0099	5.000	19
20	0.0492	5.8510	29.9480	20.3170	118.8737	0.1709	0.0084	5.118	20
21	0.0423	5.8933	30.7948	23.6185	139.1907	0.1697	0.0072	5.225	21
22	0.0364	5.9297	31.5597	27.4565	162.8092	0.1686	0.0061	5.322	22
23	0.0313	5.9610	32.2489	31.9182	190.2657	0.1678	0.0053	5.409	23
24	0.0270	5.9880	32.8688	37.1049	222.1839	0.1670	0.0045	5.489	24
25	0.0232	6.0112	33.4252	43.1344	259.2888	0.1664	0.0039	5.560	25
26	0.0199	6.0311	33.9238	50.1438	302.4232	0.1658	0.0033	5.624	26
27	0.0172	6.0483	34.3698	58.2921	352.5670	0.1653	0.0028	5.682	27
28	0.0148	6.0630	34.7682	67.7646	410.8591	0.1649	0.0024	5.734	28
29	0.0127	6.0757	35.1237	78.7764	478.6237	0.1646	0.0021	5.781	29
30	0.0109	6.0866	35.4403	91.5775	557.4001	0.1643	0.0018	5.822	30
31	0.0094	6.0960	35.7221	106.4589	648.9776	0.1640	0.0015	5.859	31
32	0.0081	6.1041	35.9726	123.7584	755.4365	0.1638	0.0013	5.893	32
33	0.0070	6.1111	36.1951	143.8692	879.1949	0.1636	0.0011	5.922	33
34	0.0060	6.1171	36.3924	167.2479	1023.0640	0.1635	0.0010	5.949	34
35	0.0051	6.1222	36.5672	194.4257	1190.3120	0.1633	0.0008	5.972	35
36	0.0044	6.1266	36.7221	226.0199	1384.7376	0.1632	0.0007	5.993	36
37	0.0038	6.1304	36.8591	262.7481	1610.7575	0.1631	0.0006	6.012	37
38	0.0033	6.1337	36.9802	305.4447	1873.5056	0.1630	0.0005	6.029	38
39	0.0028	6.1365	37.0873	355.0794	2178.9503	0.1630	0.0005	6.043	39
40	0.0024	6.1389	37.1817	412.7798	2534.0297	0.1629	0.0004	6.056	40
41	0.0021	6.1410	37.2651	479.8665	2946.8095	0.1628	0.0003	6.068	41
42	0.0018	6.1428	37.3386	557.8332	3426.6661	0.1628	0.0003	6.078	42
43	0.0015	6.1444	37.4034	648.4811	3984.4993	0.1628	0.0003	6.087	43
44	0.0013	6.1457	37.4604	753.8593	4632.9804	0.1627	0.0002	6.095	44
45	0.0011	6.1468	37.5106	876.3615	5386.8398	0.1627	0.0002	6.102	45
46	0.0010	6.1478	37.5548	1018.7702	6263.2012	0.1627	0.0002	6.108	46
47	0.0008	6.1487	37.5936	1184.3204	7281.9714	0.1626	0.0001	6.114	47
48	0.0007	6.1494	37.6278	1376.7724	8466.2918	0.1626	0.0001	6.119	48
49	0.0006	6.1500	37.6578	1600.4979	9843.0642	0.1626	0.0001	6.123	49
50	0.0005	6.1505	37.6841	1860.5788	11443.5621	0.1626	0.0001	6.127	50
51	0.0005	6.1510	37.7072	2162.9229	13304.1410	0.1626	0.0001	6.130	51
52	0.0004	6.1514	37.7275	2514.3979	15467.0639	0.1626	0.0001	6.133	52
53	0.0003	6.1517	37.7453	2922.9875	17981.4617	0.1626	0.0001	6.135	53
54	0.0003	6.1520	37.7609	3397.9730	20904.4493	0.1625	0.0000	6.137	54
55	0.0003	6.1523	37.7746	3950.1436	24302.4223	0.1625	0.0000	6.139	55
60	0.0001	6.1531	37.8213	8386.4410	51602.7136	0.1625	0.0000	6.146	60
65	0.0001	6.1535	37.8452	17805.0215	109563.2090	0.1625	0.0000	6.150	65
70	0.0000	6.1537	37.8574	37801.3499	232617.5381	0.1625	0.0000	6.152	70
75	0.0000	6.1538	37.8636	80255.0033	493870.7898	0.1625	0.0000	6.152	75
80	0.0000	6.1538	37.8667	170387.1838	1048530.3621	0.1625	0.0000	6.153	80
85	0.0000	6.1538	37.8683	361744.3301	2226112.8004	0.1625	0.0000	6.153	85
90	0.0000	6.1538	37.8691	768009.4088	4726205.5928	0.1625	0.0000	6.153	90
95	0.0000	6.1538	37.8694	1630539.5912	************	0.1625	0.0000	6.153	95
100	0.0000	6.1538	37.8696	3461753.6294	************	0.1625	0.0000	6.153	100

EXPANDED INTEREST TABLES

I = 16.50 %

n	(P/F)	(P/A)	(P/G)	(F/P)	(F/A)	(A/P)	(A/F)	(A/G)	n
1	0.8584	0.8584	0.0000	1.1650	1.0000	1.1650	1.0000	0.000	1
2	0.7368	1.5952	0.7368	1.3572	2.1650	0.6269	0.4619	0.461	2
3	0.6324	2.2276	2.0017	1.5812	3.5222	0.4489	0.2839	0.898	3
4	0.5429	2.7705	3.6303	1.8421	5.1034	0.3609	0.1959	1.310	4
5	0.4660	3.2365	5.4942	2.1460	6.9455	0.3090	0.1440	1.697	5
6	0.4000	3.6365	7.4942	2.5001	9.0915	0.2750	0.1100	2.060	6
7	0.3433	3.9798	9.5542	2.9126	11.5915	0.2513	0.0863	2.400	7
8	0.2947	4.2745	11.6171	3.3932	14.5041	0.2339	0.0689	2.717	8
9	0.2530	4.5275	13.6409	3.9531	17.8973	0.2209	0.0559	3.012	9
10	0.2171	4.7446	15.5951	4.6053	21.8504	0.2108	0.0458	3.286	10
11	0.1864	4.9310	17.4590	5.3652	26.4557	0.2028	0.0378	3.540	11
12	0.1600	5.0910	19.2189	6.2504	31.8209	0.1964	0.0314	3.775	12
13	0.1373	5.2283	20.8668	7.2818	38.0713	0.1913	0.0263	3.991	13
14	0.1179	5.3462	22.3993	8.4833	45.3531	0.1870	0.0220	4.189	14
15	0.1012	5.4474	23.8158	9.8830	53.8364	0.1836	0.0186	4.372	15
16	0.0869	5.5342	25.1186	11.5137	63.7194	0.1807	0.0157	4.538	16
17	0.0746	5.6088	26.3115	13.4135	75.2331	0.1783	0.0133	4.691	17
18	0.0640	5.6728	27.3993	15.6267	88.6465	0.1763	0.0113	4.830	18
19	0.0549	5.7277	28.3881	18.2051	104.2732	0.1746	0.0096	4.956	19
20	0.0471	5.7748	29.2839	21.2089	122.4783	0.1732	0.0082	5.070	20
21	0.0405	5.8153	30.0934	24.7084	143.6872	0.1720	0.0070	5.174	21
22	0.0347	5.8501	30.8229	28.7853	168.3956	0.1709	0.0059	5.268	22
23	0.0298	5.8799	31.4789	33.5348	197.1809	0.1701	0.0051	5.353	23
24	0.0256	5.9055	32.0677	39.0681	230.7157	0.1693	0.0043	5.430	24
25	0.0220	5.9274	32.5950	45.5143	269.7838	0.1687	0.0037	5.499	25
26	0.0189	5.9463	33.0665	53.0242	315.2981	0.1682	0.0032	5.560	26
27	0.0162	5.9625	33.4873	61.7732	368.3223	0.1677	0.0027	5.616	27
28	0.0139	5.9764	33.8625	71.9658	430.0955	0.1673	0.0023	5.666	28
29	0.0119	5.9883	34.1965	83.8401	502.0613	0.1670	0.0020	5.710	29
30	0.0102	5.9986	34.4934	97.6737	585.9014	0.1667	0.0017	5.750	30
31	0.0088	6.0073	34.7570	113.7899	683.5751	0.1665	0.0015	5.785	31
32	0.0075	6.0149	34.9909	132.5652	797.3650	0.1663	0.0013	5.817	32
33	0.0065	6.0214	35.1981	154.4385	929.9302	0.1661	0.0011	5.845	33
34	0.0056	6.0269	35.3815	179.9208	1084.3687	0.1659	0.0009	5.870	34
35	0.0048	6.0317	35.5437	209.6078	1264.2895	0.1658	0.0008	5.892	35
36	0.0041	6.0358	35.6870	244.1931	1473.8973	0.1657	0.0007	5.912	36
37	0.0035	6.0393	35.8136	284.4849	1718.0904	0.1656	0.0006	5.930	37
38	0.0030	6.0423	35.9252	331.4249	2002.5753	0.1655	0.0005	5.945	38
39	0.0026	6.0449	36.0236	386.1100	2334.0002	0.1654	0.0004	5.959	39
40	0.0022	6.0471	36.1104	449.8182	2720.1102	0.1654	0.0004	5.971	40
41	0.0019	6.0490	36.1867	524.0382	3169.9284	0.1653	0.0003	5.982	41
42	0.0016	6.0507	36.2538	610.5045	3693.9666	0.1653	0.0003	5.991	42
43	0.0014	6.0521	36.3129	711.2377	4304.4711	0.1652	0.0002	6.000	43
44	0.0012	6.0533	36.3648	828.5920	5015.7089	0.1652	0.0002	6.007	44
45	0.0010	6.0543	36.4104	965.3096	5844.3008	0.1652	0.0002	6.013	45
46	0.0009	6.0552	36.4504	1124.5857	6809.6105	0.1651	0.0001	6.019	46
47	0.0008	6.0560	36.4855	1310.1424	7934.1962	0.1651	0.0001	6.024	47
48	0.0007	6.0566	36.5163	1526.3159	9244.3386	0.1651	0.0001	6.029	48
49	0.0006	6.0572	36.5433	1778.1580	10770.6544	0.1651	0.0001	6.033	49
50	0.0005	6.0577	36.5669	2071.5540	12548.8124	0.1651	0.0001	6.036	50
51	0.0004	6.0581	36.5877	2413.3605	14620.3664	0.1651	0.0001	6.039	51
52	0.0004	6.0585	36.6058	2811.5649	17033.7269	0.1651	0.0001	6.042	52
53	0.0003	6.0588	36.6217	3275.4732	19845.2918	0.1651	0.0001	6.044	53
54	0.0003	6.0590	36.6356	3815.9262	23120.7650	0.1650	0.0000	6.046	54
55	0.0002	6.0592	36.6477	4445.5541	26936.6912	0.1650	0.0000	6.048	55
60	0.0001	6.0600	36.6890	9540.1570	57813.0727	0.1650	0.0000	6.054	60
65	0.0000	6.0603	36.7099	20473.1726	124073.7735	0.1650	0.0000	6.057	65
70	0.0000	6.0605	36.7205	43935.4193	266269.2078	0.1650	0.0000	6.059	70
75	0.0000	6.0605	36.7257	94285.3901	571420.5459	0.1650	0.0000	6.059	75
80	0.0000	6.0606	36.7284	202336.4048	1226275.1805	0.1650	0.0000	6.060	80
85	0.0000	6.0606	36.7297	434213.8339	2631592.9325	0.1650	0.0000	6.060	85
90	0.0000	6.0606	36.7303	931822.6926	5647404.1976	0.1650	0.0000	6.060	90
95	0.0000	6.0606	36.7306	1999691.0802	************	0.1650	0.0000	6.060	95
100	0.0000	6.0606	36.7308	4291336.1606	************	0.1650	0.0000	6.060	100

$I = 16.75\%$

n	(P/F)	(P/A)	(P/G)	(F/P)	(F/A)	(A/P)	(A/F)	(A/G)	n
1	0.8565	0.8565	0.0000	1.1675	1.0000	1.1675	1.0000	0.000	1
2	0.7336	1.5902	0.7336	1.3631	2.1675	0.6289	0.4614	0.461	2
3	0.6284	2.2186	1.9904	1.5914	3.5306	0.4507	0.2832	0.897	3
4	0.5382	2.7568	3.6051	1.8579	5.1219	0.3627	0.1952	1.307	4
5	0.4610	3.2178	5.4492	2.1691	6.9798	0.3108	0.1433	1.693	5
6	0.3949	3.6127	7.4236	2.5325	9.1490	0.2768	0.1093	2.054	6
7	0.3382	3.9509	9.4529	2.9566	11.6814	0.2531	0.0856	2.392	7
8	0.2897	4.2406	11.4808	3.4519	14.6381	0.2358	0.0683	2.707	8
9	0.2481	4.4887	13.4659	4.0301	18.0899	0.2228	0.0553	2.999	9
10	0.2125	4.7013	15.3787	4.7051	22.1200	0.2127	0.0452	3.271	10
11	0.1820	4.8833	17.1991	5.4932	26.8251	0.2048	0.0373	3.522	11
12	0.1559	5.0393	18.9143	6.4133	32.3183	0.1984	0.0309	3.753	12
13	0.1336	5.1728	20.5170	7.4875	38.7316	0.1933	0.0258	3.966	13
14	0.1144	5.2872	22.0041	8.7417	46.2192	0.1891	0.0216	4.161	14
15	0.0980	5.3852	23.3758	10.2059	54.9609	0.1857	0.0182	4.340	15
16	0.0839	5.4691	24.6347	11.9154	65.1668	0.1828	0.0153	4.504	16
17	0.0719	5.5410	25.7848	13.9113	77.0823	0.1805	0.0130	4.653	17
18	0.0616	5.6026	26.8315	16.2414	90.9936	0.1785	0.0110	4.789	18
19	0.0527	5.6553	27.7808	18.9619	107.2350	0.1768	0.0093	4.912	19
20	0.0452	5.7005	28.6391	22.1380	126.1968	0.1754	0.0079	5.024	20
21	0.0387	5.7392	29.4129	25.8461	148.3348	0.1742	0.0067	5.124	21
22	0.0331	5.7723	30.1088	30.1753	174.1809	0.1732	0.0057	5.216	22
23	0.0284	5.8007	30.7333	35.2297	204.3562	0.1724	0.0049	5.298	23
24	0.0243	5.8250	31.2925	41.1306	239.5858	0.1717	0.0042	5.372	24
25	0.0208	5.8458	31.7923	48.0200	280.7165	0.1711	0.0036	5.438	25
26	0.0178	5.8637	32.2382	56.0634	328.7365	0.1705	0.0030	5.498	26
27	0.0153	5.8789	32.6354	65.4540	384.7998	0.1701	0.0026	5.551	27
28	0.0131	5.8920	32.9888	76.4175	450.2538	0.1697	0.0022	5.598	28
29	0.0112	5.9032	33.3026	89.2174	526.6713	0.1694	0.0019	5.641	29
30	0.0096	5.9128	33.5810	104.1614	615.8888	0.1691	0.0016	5.679	30
31	0.0082	5.9211	33.8277	121.6084	720.0501	0.1689	0.0014	5.713	31
32	0.0070	5.9281	34.0460	141.9778	841.6585	0.1687	0.0012	5.743	32
33	0.0060	5.9341	34.2391	165.7591	983.6363	0.1685	0.0010	5.769	33
34	0.0052	5.9393	34.4096	193.5237	1149.3954	0.1684	0.0009	5.793	34
35	0.0044	5.9437	34.5601	225.9390	1342.9192	0.1682	0.0007	5.814	35
36	0.0038	5.9475	34.6928	263.7837	1568.8581	0.1681	0.0006	5.833	36
37	0.0032	5.9508	34.8097	307.9675	1832.6419	0.1680	0.0005	5.849	37
38	0.0028	5.9535	34.9126	359.5521	2140.6094	0.1680	0.0005	5.864	38
39	0.0024	5.9559	35.0031	419.7770	2500.1614	0.1679	0.0004	5.877	39
40	0.0020	5.9580	35.0827	490.0897	2919.9385	0.1678	0.0003	5.888	40
41	0.0017	5.9597	35.1526	572.1797	3410.0282	0.1678	0.0003	5.898	41
42	0.0015	5.9612	35.2140	668.0198	3982.2079	0.1678	0.0003	5.907	42
43	0.0013	5.9625	35.2678	779.9131	4650.2277	0.1677	0.0002	5.914	43
44	0.0011	5.9636	35.3150	910.5486	5430.1408	0.1677	0.0002	5.921	44
45	0.0009	5.9645	35.3564	1063.0655	6340.6894	0.1677	0.0002	5.927	45
46	0.0008	5.9653	35.3927	1241.1289	7403.7549	0.1676	0.0001	5.933	46
47	0.0007	5.9660	35.4244	1449.0180	8644.8839	0.1676	0.0001	5.937	47
48	0.0006	5.9666	35.4522	1691.7286	10093.9019	0.1676	0.0001	5.941	48
49	0.0005	5.9671	35.4765	1975.0931	11785.6305	0.1676	0.0001	5.945	49
50	0.0004	5.9676	35.4978	2305.9124	13760.7236	0.1676	0.0001	5.948	50
51	0.0004	5.9679	35.5163	2692.1630	16066.6448	0.1676	0.0001	5.951	51
52	0.0003	5.9682	35.5326	3143.1003	18758.8078	0.1676	0.0001	5.953	52
53	0.0003	5.9685	35.5467	3669.5696	21901.9081	0.1675	0.0000	5.955	53
54	0.0002	5.9688	35.5591	4284.2225	25571.4777	0.1675	0.0000	5.957	54
55	0.0002	5.9690	35.5699	5001.8298	29855.7002	0.1675	0.0000	5.959	55
60	0.0001	5.9696	35.6064	10849.5907	64767.7056	0.1675	0.0000	5.964	60
65	0.0000	5.9699	35.6247	23534.1112	140496.1860	0.1675	0.0000	5.967	65
70	0.0000	5.9700	35.6338	51048.4132	304760.6756	0.1675	0.0000	5.968	70
75	0.0000	5.9701	35.6383	110730.3552	661070.7770	0.1675	0.0000	5.969	75
80	0.0000	5.9701	35.6405	240187.9077	1433951.6880	0.1675	0.0000	5.969	80
85	0.0000	5.9701	35.6416	520997.4351	3110426.4782	0.1675	0.0000	5.970	85
90	0.0000	5.9701	35.6422	1130108.2137	6746908.7388	0.1675	0.0000	5.970	90
95	0.0000	5.9701	35.6424	2451345.2251	************	0.1675	0.0000	5.970	95
100	0.0000	5.9701	35.6426	5317272.5756	************	0.1675	0.0000	5.970	100

EXPANDED INTEREST TABLES

I = 17.00 %

n	(P/F)	(P/A)	(P/G)	(F/P)	(F/A)	(A/P)	(A/F)	(A/G)	n
1	0.8547	0.8547	0.0000	1.1700	1.0000	1.1700	1.0000	0.000	1
2	0.7305	1.5852	0.7305	1.3689	2.1700	0.6308	0.4608	0.460	2
3	0.6244	2.2096	1.9793	1.6016	3.5389	0.4526	0.2826	0.895	3
4	0.5337	2.7432	3.5802	1.8739	5.1405	0.3645	0.1945	1.305	4
5	0.4561	3.1993	5.4046	2.1924	7.0144	0.3126	0.1426	1.689	5
6	0.3898	3.5892	7.3538	2.5652	9.2068	0.2786	0.1086	2.048	6
7	0.3332	3.9224	9.3530	3.0012	11.7720	0.2549	0.0849	2.384	7
8	0.2848	4.2072	11.3465	3.5115	14.7733	0.2377	0.0677	2.696	8
9	0.2434	4.4506	13.2937	4.1084	18.2847	0.2247	0.0547	2.987	9
10	0.2080	4.6586	15.1661	4.8068	22.3931	0.2147	0.0447	3.255	10
11	0.1778	4.8364	16.9442	5.6240	27.1999	0.2068	0.0368	3.503	11
12	0.1520	4.9884	18.6159	6.5801	32.8239	0.2005	0.0305	3.731	12
13	0.1299	5.1183	20.1746	7.6987	39.4040	0.1954	0.0254	3.941	13
14	0.1110	5.2293	21.6178	9.0075	47.1027	0.1912	0.0212	4.134	14
15	0.0949	5.3242	22.9463	10.5387	56.1101	0.1878	0.0178	4.309	15
16	0.0811	5.4053	24.1628	12.3303	66.6488	0.1850	0.0150	4.470	16
17	0.0693	5.4746	25.2719	14.4265	78.9792	0.1827	0.0127	4.616	17
18	0.0592	5.5339	26.2790	16.8790	93.4056	0.1807	0.0107	4.748	18
19	0.0506	5.5845	27.1905	19.7484	110.2846	0.1791	0.0091	4.868	19
20	0.0433	5.6278	28.0128	23.1056	130.0329	0.1777	0.0077	4.977	20
21	0.0370	5.6648	28.7526	27.0336	153.1385	0.1765	0.0065	5.075	21
22	0.0316	5.6964	29.4166	31.6293	180.1721	0.1756	0.0056	5.164	22
23	0.0270	5.7234	30.0111	37.0062	211.8013	0.1747	0.0047	5.243	23
24	0.0231	5.7465	30.5423	43.2973	248.8076	0.1740	0.0040	5.314	24
25	0.0197	5.7662	31.0160	50.6578	292.1049	0.1734	0.0034	5.378	25
26	0.0169	5.7831	31.4378	59.2697	342.7627	0.1729	0.0029	5.436	26
27	0.0144	5.7975	31.8128	69.3455	402.0323	0.1725	0.0025	5.487	27
28	0.0123	5.8099	32.1456	81.1342	471.3778	0.1721	0.0021	5.532	28
29	0.0105	5.8204	32.4405	94.9271	552.5121	0.1718	0.0018	5.573	29
30	0.0090	5.8294	32.7016	111.0647	647.4391	0.1715	0.0015	5.609	30
31	0.0077	5.8371	32.9325	129.9456	758.5038	0.1713	0.0013	5.641	31
32	0.0066	5.8437	33.1364	152.0364	888.4494	0.1711	0.0011	5.670	32
33	0.0056	5.8493	33.3163	177.8826	1040.4858	0.1710	0.0010	5.695	33
34	0.0048	5.8541	33.4748	208.1226	1218.3684	0.1708	0.0008	5.718	34
35	0.0041	5.8582	33.6145	243.5035	1426.4910	0.1707	0.0007	5.738	35
36	0.0035	5.8617	33.7373	284.8991	1669.9945	0.1706	0.0006	5.755	36
37	0.0030	5.8647	33.8453	333.3319	1954.8936	0.1705	0.0005	5.771	37
38	0.0026	5.8673	33.9402	389.9983	2288.2255	0.1704	0.0004	5.784	38
39	0.0022	5.8695	34.0235	456.2980	2678.2238	0.1704	0.0004	5.796	39
40	0.0019	5.8713	34.0965	533.8687	3134.5218	0.1703	0.0003	5.807	40
41	0.0016	5.8729	34.1606	624.6264	3668.3906	0.1703	0.0003	5.816	41
42	0.0014	5.8743	34.2167	730.8129	4293.0169	0.1702	0.0002	5.824	42
43	0.0012	5.8755	34.2658	855.0511	5023.8298	0.1702	0.0002	5.832	43
44	0.0010	5.8765	34.3088	1000.4098	5878.8809	0.1702	0.0002	5.838	44
45	0.0009	5.8773	34.3464	1170.4794	6879.2907	0.1701	0.0001	5.843	45
46	0.0007	5.8781	34.3792	1369.4609	8049.7701	0.1701	0.0001	5.848	46
47	0.0006	5.8787	34.4079	1602.2693	9419.2310	0.1701	0.0001	5.853	47
48	0.0005	5.8792	34.4330	1874.6550	11021.5002	0.1701	0.0001	5.856	48
49	0.0005	5.8797	34.4549	2193.3464	12896.1553	0.1701	0.0001	5.860	49
50	0.0004	5.8801	34.4740	2566.2153	15089.5017	0.1701	0.0001	5.862	50
51	0.0003	5.8804	34.4906	3002.4719	17655.7170	0.1701	0.0001	5.865	51
52	0.0003	5.8807	34.5052	3512.8921	20658.1888	0.1700	0.0000	5.867	52
53	0.0002	5.8809	34.5178	4110.0838	24171.0809	0.1700	0.0000	5.869	53
54	0.0002	5.8811	34.5288	4808.7980	28281.1647	0.1700	0.0000	5.871	54
55	0.0002	5.8813	34.5384	5626.2937	33089.9627	0.1700	0.0000	5.872	55
60	0.0001	5.8819	34.5707	12335.3565	72555.0381	0.1700	0.0000	5.877	60
65	0.0000	5.8821	34.5867	27044.6281	159080.1652	0.1700	0.0000	5.879	65
70	0.0000	5.8823	34.5945	59293.9417	348782.0102	0.1700	0.0000	5.881	70
75	0.0000	5.8823	34.5984	129998.8861	764693.4475	0.1700	0.0000	5.881	75
80	0.0000	5.8823	34.6003	285015.8024	1676557.6612	0.1700	0.0000	5.882	80
85	0.0000	5.8823	34.6012	624882.3361	3675772.5655	0.1700	0.0000	5.882	85
90	0.0000	5.8823	34.6017	1370022.0504	8058947.3554	0.1700	0.0000	5.882	90
95	0.0000	5.8824	34.6019	3003702.1533	************	0.1700	0.0000	5.882	95
100	0.0000	5.8824	34.6020	6585460.8858	************	0.1700	0.0000	5.882	100

$I = 17.25$ %

n	(P/F)	(P/A)	(P/G)	(F/P)	(F/A)	(A/P)	(A/F)	(A/G)	n
1	0.8529	0.8529	0.0000	1.1725	1.0000	1.1725	1.0000	0.000	1
2	0.7274	1.5803	0.7274	1.3748	2.1725	0.6328	0.4603	0.460	2
3	0.6204	2.2007	1.9682	1.6119	3.5473	0.4544	0.2819	0.894	3
4	0.5291	2.7298	3.5555	1.8900	5.1592	0.3663	0.1938	1.302	4
5	0.4513	3.1810	5.3606	2.2160	7.0491	0.3144	0.1419	1.685	5
6	0.3849	3.5659	7.2850	2.5982	9.2651	0.2804	0.1079	2.042	6
7	0.3283	3.8942	9.2545	3.0464	11.8633	0.2568	0.0843	2.376	7
8	0.2800	4.1741	11.2142	3.5719	14.9097	0.2396	0.0671	2.686	8
9	0.2388	4.4129	13.1244	4.1881	18.4817	0.2266	0.0541	2.974	9
10	0.2036	4.6166	14.9572	4.9105	22.6697	0.2166	0.0441	3.239	10
11	0.1737	4.7902	16.6940	5.7576	27.5803	0.2088	0.0363	3.485	11
12	0.1481	4.9384	18.3235	6.7508	33.3379	0.2025	0.0300	3.710	12
13	0.1263	5.0647	19.8395	7.9153	40.0887	0.1974	0.0249	3.917	13
14	0.1078	5.1725	21.2403	9.2807	48.0040	0.1933	0.0208	4.106	14
15	0.0919	5.2644	22.5269	10.8816	57.2846	0.1900	0.0175	4.279	15
16	0.0784	5.3427	23.7025	12.7587	68.1662	0.1872	0.0147	4.436	16
17	0.0668	5.4096	24.7721	14.9595	80.9249	0.1849	0.0124	4.579	17
18	0.0570	5.4666	25.7413	17.5401	95.8845	0.1829	0.0104	4.708	18
19	0.0486	5.5152	26.6165	20.5657	113.4245	0.1813	0.0088	4.826	19
20	0.0415	5.5567	27.4045	24.1133	133.9903	0.1800	0.0075	4.931	20
21	0.0354	5.5921	28.1119	28.2729	158.1036	0.1788	0.0063	5.027	21
22	0.0302	5.6222	28.7454	33.1499	186.3765	0.1779	0.0054	5.112	22
23	0.0257	5.6480	29.3114	38.8683	219.5264	0.1771	0.0046	5.189	23
24	0.0219	5.6699	29.8161	45.5731	258.3947	0.1764	0.0039	5.258	24
25	0.0187	5.6886	30.2652	53.4344	303.9678	0.1758	0.0033	5.320	25
26	0.0160	5.7046	30.6642	62.6519	357.4022	0.1753	0.0028	5.375	26
27	0.0136	5.7182	31.0182	73.4593	420.0541	0.1749	0.0024	5.424	27
28	0.0116	5.7298	31.3317	86.1311	493.5134	0.1745	0.0020	5.468	28
29	0.0099	5.7397	31.6089	100.9887	579.6445	0.1742	0.0017	5.507	29
30	0.0084	5.7481	31.8538	118.4092	680.6332	0.1740	0.0015	5.541	30
31	0.0072	5.7553	32.0699	138.8348	799.0424	0.1738	0.0013	5.572	31
32	0.0061	5.7615	32.2603	162.7838	937.8772	0.1736	0.0011	5.599	32
33	0.0052	5.7667	32.4280	190.8640	1100.6611	0.1734	0.0009	5.623	33
34	0.0045	5.7712	32.5755	223.7881	1291.5251	0.1733	0.0008	5.644	34
35	0.0038	5.7750	32.7050	262.3915	1515.3132	0.1732	0.0007	5.663	35
36	0.0033	5.7783	32.8188	307.6541	1777.7047	0.1731	0.0006	5.679	36
37	0.0028	5.7810	32.9186	360.7244	2085.3588	0.1730	0.0005	5.694	37
38	0.0024	5.7834	33.0061	422.9493	2446.0831	0.1729	0.0004	5.707	38
39	0.0020	5.7854	33.0827	495.9081	2869.0325	0.1728	0.0003	5.718	39
40	0.0017	5.7871	33.1498	581.4523	3364.9406	0.1728	0.0003	5.728	40
41	0.0015	5.7886	33.2085	681.7528	3946.3928	0.1728	0.0003	5.736	41
42	0.0013	5.7898	33.2597	799.3551	4628.1456	0.1727	0.0002	5.744	42
43	0.0011	5.7909	33.3046	937.2439	5427.5007	0.1727	0.0002	5.751	43
44	0.0009	5.7918	33.3437	1098.9184	6364.7446	0.1727	0.0002	5.757	44
45	0.0008	5.7926	33.3778	1288.4819	7463.6630	0.1726	0.0001	5.762	45
46	0.0007	5.7933	33.4076	1510.7450	8752.1449	0.1726	0.0001	5.766	46
47	0.0006	5.7938	33.4336	1771.3485	10262.8899	0.1726	0.0001	5.770	47
48	0.0005	5.7943	33.4562	2076.9061	12034.2384	0.1726	0.0001	5.774	48
49	0.0004	5.7947	33.4759	2435.1724	14111.1445	0.1726	0.0001	5.777	49
50	0.0004	5.7951	33.4931	2855.2397	16546.3169	0.1726	0.0001	5.779	50
51	0.0003	5.7954	33.5080	3347.7685	19401.5566	0.1726	0.0001	5.781	51
52	0.0003	5.7956	33.5210	3925.2586	22749.3251	0.1725	0.0000	5.783	52
53	0.0002	5.7958	33.5323	4602.3657	26674.5837	0.1725	0.0000	5.785	53
54	0.0002	5.7960	33.5421	5396.2738	31276.9494	0.1725	0.0000	5.787	54
55	0.0002	5.7962	33.5507	6327.1310	36673.2232	0.1725	0.0000	5.788	55
60	0.0001	5.7967	33.5792	14020.7448	81273.8827	0.1725	0.0000	5.792	60
65	0.0000	5.7969	33.5932	31069.5770	180107.6926	0.1725	0.0000	5.795	65
70	0.0000	5.7970	33.6000	68849.3108	399120.6422	0.1725	0.0000	5.796	70
75	0.0000	5.7971	33.6033	152568.1408	884447.1932	0.1725	0.0000	5.796	75
80	0.0000	5.7971	33.6049	338086.7191	1959917.2124	0.1725	0.0000	5.796	80
85	0.0000	5.7971	33.6057	749190.6832	4343128.5980	0.1725	0.0000	5.797	85
90	0.0000	5.7971	33.6061	1660185.5322	9624258.1574	0.1725	0.0000	5.797	90
95	0.0000	5.7971	33.6062	3678924.5557	************	0.1725	0.0000	5.797	95
100	0.0000	5.7971	33.6063	8152393.5876	************	0.1725	0.0000	5.797	100

EXPANDED INTEREST TABLES

$I = 17.50\%$

n	(P/F)	(P/A)	(P/G)	(F/P)	(F/A)	(A/P)	(A/F)	(A/G)	n
1	0.8511	0.8511	0.0000	1.1750	1.0000	1.1750	1.0000	0.000	1
2	0.7243	1.5754	0.7243	1.3806	2.1750	0.6348	0.4598	0.459	2
3	0.6164	2.1918	1.9572	1.6222	3.5556	0.4562	0.2812	0.893	3
4	0.5246	2.7164	3.5311	1.9061	5.1779	0.3681	0.1931	1.299	4
5	0.4465	3.1629	5.3170	2.2397	7.0840	0.3162	0.1412	1.681	5
6	0.3800	3.5429	7.2170	2.6316	9.3237	0.2823	0.1073	2.037	6
7	0.3234	3.8663	9.1573	3.0922	11.9553	0.2586	0.0836	2.368	7
8	0.2752	4.1415	11.0840	3.6333	15.0475	0.2415	0.0665	2.676	8
9	0.2342	4.3758	12.9579	4.2691	18.6808	0.2285	0.0535	2.961	9
10	0.1994	4.5751	14.7520	5.0162	22.9500	0.2186	0.0436	3.224	10
11	0.1697	4.7448	16.4487	5.8941	27.9662	0.2108	0.0358	3.466	11
12	0.1444	4.8892	18.0370	6.9256	33.8603	0.2045	0.0295	3.689	12
13	0.1229	5.0121	19.5116	8.1375	40.7858	0.1995	0.0245	3.892	13
14	0.1046	5.1167	20.8712	9.5616	48.9234	0.1954	0.0204	4.079	14
15	0.0890	5.2057	22.1173	11.2349	58.4850	0.1921	0.0171	4.248	15
16	0.0758	5.2814	23.2536	13.2010	69.7198	0.1893	0.0143	4.402	16
17	0.0645	5.3459	24.2851	15.5111	82.9208	0.1871	0.0121	4.542	17
18	0.0549	5.4008	25.2179	18.2256	98.4319	0.1852	0.0102	4.669	18
19	0.0467	5.4475	26.0584	21.4151	116.6575	0.1836	0.0086	4.783	19
20	0.0397	5.4872	26.8135	25.1627	138.0726	0.1822	0.0072	4.886	20
21	0.0338	5.5210	27.4900	29.5662	163.2353	0.1811	0.0061	4.979	21
22	0.0288	5.5498	28.0944	34.7403	192.8015	0.1802	0.0052	5.062	22
23	0.0245	5.5743	28.6334	40.8198	227.5417	0.1794	0.0044	5.136	23
24	0.0208	5.5951	29.1129	47.9633	268.3616	0.1787	0.0037	5.203	24
25	0.0177	5.6129	29.5388	56.3568	316.3248	0.1782	0.0032	5.262	25
26	0.0151	5.6280	29.9163	66.2193	372.6817	0.1777	0.0027	5.315	26
27	0.0129	5.6408	30.2505	77.8077	438.9010	0.1773	0.0023	5.362	27
28	0.0109	5.6518	30.5458	91.4240	516.7086	0.1769	0.0019	5.404	28
29	0.0093	5.6611	30.8065	107.4232	608.1326	0.1766	0.0016	5.441	29
30	0.0079	5.6690	31.0362	126.2223	715.5558	0.1764	0.0014	5.474	30
31	0.0067	5.6758	31.2385	148.3112	841.7781	0.1762	0.0012	5.503	31
32	0.0057	5.6815	31.4164	174.2656	990.0893	0.1760	0.0010	5.529	32
33	0.0049	5.6864	31.5727	204.7621	1164.3549	0.1759	0.0009	5.552	33
34	0.0042	5.6905	31.7098	240.5955	1369.1170	0.1757	0.0007	5.572	34
35	0.0035	5.6941	31.8301	282.6997	1609.7125	0.1756	0.0006	5.590	35
36	0.0030	5.6971	31.9355	332.1721	1892.4122	0.1755	0.0005	5.605	36
37	0.0026	5.6996	32.0277	390.3023	2224.5843	0.1754	0.0004	5.619	37
38	0.0022	5.7018	32.1084	458.6052	2614.8866	0.1754	0.0004	5.631	38
39	0.0019	5.7037	32.1789	538.8611	3073.4917	0.1753	0.0003	5.641	39
40	0.0016	5.7053	32.2405	633.1617	3612.3528	0.1753	0.0003	5.651	40
41	0.0013	5.7066	32.2943	743.9650	4245.5145	0.1752	0.0002	5.659	41
42	0.0011	5.7077	32.3412	874.1589	4989.4796	0.1752	0.0002	5.666	42
43	0.0010	5.7087	32.3820	1027.1367	5863.6385	0.1752	0.0002	5.672	43
44	0.0008	5.7096	32.4177	1206.8857	6890.7753	0.1751	0.0001	5.677	44
45	0.0007	5.7103	32.4487	1418.0907	8097.6609	0.1751	0.0001	5.682	45
46	0.0006	5.7109	32.4757	1666.2565	9515.7516	0.1751	0.0001	5.686	46
47	0.0005	5.7114	32.4992	1957.8514	11182.0081	0.1751	0.0001	5.690	47
48	0.0004	5.7118	32.5196	2300.4754	13139.8595	0.1751	0.0001	5.693	48
49	0.0004	5.7122	32.5374	2703.0586	15440.3350	0.1751	0.0001	5.696	49
50	0.0003	5.7125	32.5528	3176.0939	18143.3936	0.1751	0.0001	5.698	50
51	0.0003	5.7128	32.5662	3731.9103	21319.4875	0.1750	0.0000	5.700	51
52	0.0002	5.7130	32.5779	4384.9946	25051.3978	0.1750	0.0000	5.702	52
53	0.0002	5.7132	32.5879	5152.3687	29436.3924	0.1750	0.0000	5.704	53
54	0.0002	5.7133	32.5967	6054.0332	34588.7610	0.1750	0.0000	5.705	54
55	0.0001	5.7135	32.6043	7113.4890	40642.7942	0.1750	0.0000	5.706	55
60	0.0001	5.7139	32.6295	15932.0623	91034.6418	0.1750	0.0000	5.710	60
65	0.0000	5.7141	32.6417	35682.9975	203897.1286	0.1750	0.0000	5.712	65
70	0.0000	5.7142	32.6476	79919.1144	456674.9392	0.1750	0.0000	5.713	70
75	0.0000	5.7143	32.6505	178994.6274	1022820.7279	0.1750	0.0000	5.713	75
80	0.0000	5.7143	32.6518	400893.7897	2290815.9413	0.1750	0.0000	5.714	80
85	0.0000	5.7143	32.6525	897880.7521	5130741.4404	0.1750	0.0000	5.714	85
90	0.0000	5.7143	32.6528	2010981.1266	************	0.1750	0.0000	5.714	90
95	0.0000	5.7143	32.6529	4503989.0680	************	0.1750	0.0000	5.714	95
100	0.0000	5.7143	32.6530	************	************	0.1750	0.0000	5.714	100

$I = 17.75\ \%$

n	(P/F)	(P/A)	(P/G)	(F/P)	(F/A)	(A/P)	(A/F)	(A/G)	n
1	0.8493	0.8493	0.0000	1.1775	1.0000	1.1775	1.0000	0.000	1
2	0.7212	1.5705	0.7212	1.3865	2.1775	0.6367	0.4592	0.459	2
3	0.6125	2.1830	1.9463	1.6326	3.5640	0.4581	0.2806	0.891	3
4	0.5202	2.7032	3.5068	1.9224	5.1966	0.3699	0.1924	1.297	4
5	0.4418	3.1450	5.2739	2.2636	7.1190	0.3180	0.1405	1.676	5
6	0.3752	3.5201	7.1498	2.6654	9.3826	0.2841	0.1066	2.031	6
7	0.3186	3.8388	9.0615	3.1385	12.0481	0.2605	0.0830	2.360	7
8	0.2706	4.1093	10.9556	3.6956	15.1866	0.2433	0.0658	2.666	8
9	0.2298	4.3391	12.7940	4.3516	18.8822	0.2305	0.0530	2.948	9
10	0.1952	4.5343	14.5505	5.1240	23.2338	0.2205	0.0430	3.209	10
11	0.1657	4.7001	16.2079	6.0335	28.3578	0.2128	0.0353	3.448	11
12	0.1408	4.8408	17.7562	7.1045	34.3913	0.2066	0.0291	3.668	12
13	0.1195	4.9603	19.1907	8.3655	41.4958	0.2016	0.0241	3.868	13
14	0.1015	5.0619	20.5104	9.8504	49.8613	0.1976	0.0201	4.051	14
15	0.0862	5.1481	21.7174	11.5988	59.7117	0.1942	0.0167	4.218	15
16	0.0732	5.2213	22.8157	13.6576	71.3105	0.1915	0.0140	4.369	16
17	0.0622	5.2835	23.8106	16.0818	84.9681	0.1893	0.0118	4.506	17
18	0.0528	5.3363	24.7084	18.9364	101.0499	0.1874	0.0099	4.630	18
19	0.0448	5.3811	25.5156	22.2976	119.9863	0.1858	0.0083	4.741	19
20	0.0381	5.4192	26.2393	26.2554	142.2838	0.1845	0.0070	4.841	20
21	0.0323	5.4516	26.8862	30.9157	168.5392	0.1834	0.0059	4.931	21
22	0.0275	5.4790	27.4631	36.4032	199.4549	0.1825	0.0050	5.012	22
23	0.0233	5.5024	27.9763	42.8648	235.8582	0.1817	0.0042	5.084	23
24	0.0198	5.5222	28.4320	50.4733	278.7230	0.1811	0.0036	5.148	24
25	0.0168	5.5390	28.8358	59.4323	329.1963	0.1805	0.0030	5.206	25
26	0.0143	5.5533	29.1931	69.9816	388.6287	0.1801	0.0026	5.256	26
27	0.0121	5.5654	29.5086	82.4033	458.6103	0.1797	0.0022	5.302	27
28	0.0103	5.5757	29.7869	97.0299	541.0136	0.1793	0.0018	5.342	28
29	0.0088	5.5845	30.0319	114.2527	638.0435	0.1791	0.0016	5.377	29
30	0.0074	5.5919	30.2475	134.5326	752.2962	0.1788	0.0013	5.409	30
31	0.0063	5.5982	30.4369	158.4121	886.8288	0.1786	0.0011	5.436	31
32	0.0054	5.6036	30.6031	186.5303	1045.2409	0.1785	0.0010	5.461	32
33	0.0046	5.6082	30.7488	219.6394	1231.7712	0.1783	0.0008	5.482	33
34	0.0039	5.6120	30.8764	258.6254	1451.4106	0.1782	0.0007	5.501	34
35	0.0033	5.6153	30.9880	304.5314	1710.0360	0.1781	0.0006	5.518	35
36	0.0028	5.6181	31.0856	358.5857	2014.5673	0.1780	0.0005	5.533	36
37	0.0024	5.6205	31.1709	422.2347	2373.1530	0.1779	0.0004	5.546	37
38	0.0020	5.6225	31.2453	497.1813	2795.3877	0.1779	0.0004	5.557	38
39	0.0017	5.6242	31.3102	585.4310	3292.5690	0.1778	0.0003	5.567	39
40	0.0015	5.6256	31.3668	689.3450	3878.0000	0.1778	0.0003	5.575	40
41	0.0012	5.6269	31.4161	811.7037	4567.3450	0.1777	0.0002	5.583	41
42	0.0010	5.6279	31.4590	955.7812	5379.0488	0.1777	0.0002	5.589	42
43	0.0009	5.6288	31.4963	1125.4323	6334.8299	0.1777	0.0002	5.595	43
44	0.0008	5.6296	31.5287	1325.1965	7460.2622	0.1776	0.0001	5.600	44
45	0.0006	5.6302	31.5569	1560.4189	8785.4588	0.1776	0.0001	5.604	45
46	0.0005	5.6307	31.5814	1837.3933	10345.8777	0.1776	0.0001	5.608	46
47	0.0005	5.6312	31.6027	2163.5306	12183.2710	0.1776	0.0001	5.612	47
48	0.0004	5.6316	31.6211	2547.5573	14346.8016	0.1776	0.0001	5.615	48
49	0.0003	5.6319	31.6371	2999.7487	16894.3589	0.1776	0.0001	5.617	49
50	0.0003	5.6322	31.6510	3532.2041	19894.1076	0.1776	0.0001	5.619	50
51	0.0002	5.6324	31.6630	4159.1703	23426.3117	0.1775	0.0000	5.621	51
52	0.0002	5.6327	31.6734	4897.4231	27585.4820	0.1775	0.0000	5.623	52
53	0.0002	5.6328	31.6825	5766.7157	32482.9051	0.1775	0.0000	5.624	53
54	0.0001	5.6330	31.6903	6790.3077	38249.6207	0.1775	0.0000	5.625	54
55	0.0001	5.6331	31.6970	7995.5873	45039.9284	0.1775	0.0000	5.626	55
60	0.0001	5.6335	31.7193	18099.0153	101960.6498	0.1775	0.0000	5.630	60
65	0.0000	5.6337	31.7300	40969.3928	230807.8466	0.1775	0.0000	5.632	65
70	0.0000	5.6337	31.7351	92739.3625	522469.6477	0.1775	0.0000	5.633	70
75	0.0000	5.6338	31.7376	209927.1864	1182682.7403	0.1775	0.0000	5.633	75
80	0.0000	5.6338	31.7387	475196.5337	2677157.9365	0.1775	0.0000	5.633	80
85	0.0000	5.6338	31.7393	1075666.9946	6060090.1103	0.1775	0.0000	5.633	85
90	0.0000	5.6338	31.7395	2434907.2459	***********	0.1775	0.0000	5.633	90
95	0.0000	5.6338	31.7396	5511718.1490	***********	0.1775	0.0000	5.633	95
100	0.0000	5.6338	31.7397	***********	***********	0.1775	0.0000	5.633	100

EXPANDED INTEREST TABLES

$I = 18.00 \%$

n	(P/F)	(P/A)	(P/G)	(F/P)	(F/A)	(A/P)	(A/F)	(A/G)	n
1	0.8475	0.8475	0.0000	1.1800	1.0000	1.1800	1.0000	0.000	1
2	0.7182	1.5656	0.7182	1.3924	2.1800	0.6387	0.4587	0.458	2
3	0.6086	2.1743	1.9354	1.6430	3.5724	0.4599	0.2799	0.890	3
4	0.5158	2.6901	3.4828	1.9388	5.2154	0.3717	0.1917	1.294	4
5	0.4371	3.1272	5.2312	2.2878	7.1542	0.3198	0.1398	1.672	5
6	0.3704	3.4976	7.0834	2.6996	9.4420	0.2859	0.1059	2.025	6
7	0.3139	3.8115	8.9670	3.1855	12.1415	0.2624	0.0824	2.352	7
8	0.2660	4.0776	10.8292	3.7589	15.3270	0.2452	0.0652	2.655	8
9	0.2255	4.3030	12.6329	4.4355	19.0859	0.2324	0.0524	2.935	9
10	0.1911	4.4941	14.3525	5.2338	23.5213	0.2225	0.0425	3.193	10
11	0.1619	4.6560	15.9716	6.1759	28.7551	0.2148	0.0348	3.430	11
12	0.1372	4.7932	17.4811	7.2876	34.9311	0.2086	0.0286	3.647	12
13	0.1163	4.9095	18.8765	8.5994	42.2187	0.2037	0.0237	3.844	13
14	0.0985	5.0081	20.1576	10.1472	50.8180	0.1997	0.0197	4.025	14
15	0.0835	5.0916	21.3269	11.9737	60.9653	0.1964	0.0164	4.188	15
16	0.0708	5.1624	22.3885	14.1290	72.9390	0.1937	0.0137	4.336	16
17	0.0600	5.2223	23.3482	16.6722	87.0680	0.1915	0.0115	4.470	17
18	0.0508	5.2732	24.2123	19.6733	103.7403	0.1896	0.0096	4.591	18
19	0.0431	5.3162	24.9877	23.2144	123.4135	0.1881	0.0081	4.700	19
20	0.0365	5.3527	25.6813	27.3930	146.6280	0.1868	0.0068	4.797	20
21	0.0309	5.3837	26.3000	32.3238	174.0210	0.1857	0.0057	4.885	21
22	0.0262	5.4099	26.8506	38.1421	206.3448	0.1848	0.0048	4.963	22
23	0.0222	5.4321	27.3394	45.0076	244.4868	0.1841	0.0041	5.032	23
24	0.0188	5.4509	27.7725	53.1090	289.4945	0.1835	0.0035	5.095	24
25	0.0160	5.4669	28.1555	62.6686	342.6035	0.1829	0.0029	5.150	25
26	0.0135	5.4804	28.4935	73.9490	405.2721	0.1825	0.0025	5.199	26
27	0.0115	5.4919	28.7915	87.2598	479.2211	0.1821	0.0021	5.242	27
28	0.0097	5.5016	29.0537	102.9666	566.4809	0.1818	0.0018	5.281	28
29	0.0082	5.5098	29.2842	121.5005	669.4475	0.1815	0.0015	5.314	29
30	0.0070	5.5168	29.4864	143.3706	790.9480	0.1813	0.0013	5.344	30
31	0.0059	5.5227	29.6638	169.1774	934.3186	0.1811	0.0011	5.371	31
32	0.0050	5.5277	29.8191	199.6293	1103.4960	0.1809	0.0009	5.394	32
33	0.0042	5.5320	29.9549	235.5625	1303.1253	0.1808	0.0008	5.414	33
34	0.0036	5.5356	30.0736	277.9638	1538.6878	0.1806	0.0006	5.432	34
35	0.0030	5.5386	30.1773	327.9973	1816.6516	0.1806	0.0006	5.448	35
36	0.0026	5.5412	30.2677	387.0368	2144.6489	0.1805	0.0005	5.462	36
37	0.0022	5.5434	30.3465	456.7034	2531.6857	0.1804	0.0004	5.474	37
38	0.0019	5.5452	30.4152	538.9100	2988.3891	0.1803	0.0003	5.484	38
39	0.0016	5.5468	30.4749	635.9139	3527.2992	0.1803	0.0003	5.494	39
40	0.0013	5.5482	30.5269	750.3783	4163.2130	0.1802	0.0002	5.502	40
41	0.0011	5.5493	30.5721	885.4464	4913.5914	0.1802	0.0002	5.509	41
42	0.0010	5.5502	30.6113	1044.8268	5799.0378	0.1802	0.0002	5.515	42
43	0.0008	5.5510	30.6454	1232.8956	6843.8646	0.1801	0.0001	5.520	43
44	0.0007	5.5517	30.6750	1454.8168	8076.7603	0.1801	0.0001	5.525	44
45	0.0006	5.5523	30.7006	1716.6839	9531.5771	0.1801	0.0001	5.529	45
46	0.0005	5.5528	30.7228	2025.6870	11248.2610	0.1801	0.0001	5.532	46
47	0.0004	5.5532	30.7420	2390.3106	13273.9480	0.1801	0.0001	5.535	47
48	0.0004	5.5536	30.7587	2820.5665	15664.2586	0.1801	0.0001	5.538	48
49	0.0003	5.5539	30.7731	3328.2685	18484.8251	0.1801	0.0001	5.540	49
50	0.0003	5.5541	30.7856	3927.3569	21813.0937	0.1800	0.0000	5.542	50
51	0.0002	5.5544	30.7964	4634.2811	25740.4505	0.1800	0.0000	5.544	51
52	0.0002	5.5545	30.8057	5468.4517	30374.7316	0.1800	0.0000	5.546	52
53	0.0002	5.5547	30.8138	6452.7730	35843.1833	0.1800	0.0000	5.547	53
54	0.0001	5.5548	30.8207	7614.2721	42295.9563	0.1800	0.0000	5.548	54
55	0.0001	5.5549	30.8268	8984.8411	49910.2284	0.1800	0.0000	5.549	55
60	0.0000	5.5553	30.8465	20555.1400	114189.6665	0.1800	0.0000	5.552	60
65	0.0000	5.5554	30.8559	47025.1809	261245.4494	0.1800	0.0000	5.554	65
70	0.0000	5.5555	30.8603	107582.2224	597673.4576	0.1800	0.0000	5.554	70
75	0.0000	5.5555	30.8624	246122.0637	1367339.2429	0.1800	0.0000	5.555	75
80	0.0000	5.5555	30.8634	563067.6604	3128148.1133	0.1800	0.0000	5.555	80
85	0.0000	5.5556	30.8638	1288162.4077	7156452.2647	0.1800	0.0000	5.555	85
90	0.0000	5.5556	30.8640	2947003.5401	************	0.1800	0.0000	5.555	90
95	0.0000	5.5556	30.8641	6742030.2082	************	0.1800	0.0000	5.555	95
100	0.0000	5.5556	30.8642	************	************	0.1800	0.0000	5.555	100

$I = 18.25\ \%$

n	(P/F)	(P/A)	(P/G)	(F/P)	(F/A)	(A/P)	(A/F)	(A/G)	n
1	0.8457	0.8457	0.0000	1.1825	1.0000	1.1825	1.0000	0.000	1
2	0.7152	1.5608	0.7152	1.3983	2.1825	0.6407	0.4582	0.458	2
3	0.6048	2.1656	1.9247	1.6535	3.5808	0.4618	0.2793	0.888	3
4	0.5114	2.6770	3.4590	1.9553	5.2343	0.3735	0.1910	1.292	4
5	0.4325	3.1095	5.1891	2.3121	7.1896	0.3216	0.1391	1.668	5
6	0.3658	3.4753	7.0179	2.7341	9.5017	0.2877	0.1052	2.019	6
7	0.3093	3.7846	8.8737	3.2330	12.2357	0.2642	0.0817	2.344	7
8	0.2616	4.0462	10.7047	3.8230	15.4687	0.2471	0.0646	2.645	8
9	0.2212	4.2674	12.4743	4.5207	19.2918	0.2343	0.0518	2.923	9
10	0.1871	4.4544	14.1579	5.3458	23.8125	0.2245	0.0420	3.178	10
11	0.1582	4.6126	15.7398	6.3214	29.1583	0.2168	0.0343	3.412	11
12	0.1338	4.7464	17.2114	7.4750	35.4797	0.2107	0.0282	3.626	12
13	0.1131	4.8596	18.5690	8.8392	42.9547	0.2058	0.0233	3.821	13
14	0.0957	4.9552	19.8127	10.4524	51.7940	0.2018	0.0193	3.998	14
15	0.0809	5.0361	20.9454	12.3600	62.2464	0.1986	0.0161	4.159	15
16	0.0684	5.1045	21.9717	14.6157	74.6063	0.1959	0.0134	4.304	16
17	0.0579	5.1624	22.8975	17.2830	89.2220	0.1937	0.0112	4.435	17
18	0.0489	5.2113	23.7293	20.4372	106.5050	0.1919	0.0094	4.553	18
19	0.0414	5.2527	24.4741	24.1669	126.9422	0.1904	0.0079	4.659	19
20	0.0350	5.2877	25.1389	28.5774	151.1091	0.1891	0.0066	4.754	20
21	0.0296	5.3173	25.7308	33.7928	179.6866	0.1881	0.0056	4.839	21
22	0.0250	5.3423	26.2563	39.9600	213.4794	0.1872	0.0047	4.914	22
23	0.0212	5.3635	26.7219	47.2527	253.4393	0.1864	0.0039	4.982	23
24	0.0179	5.3814	27.1335	55.8763	300.6920	0.1858	0.0033	5.042	24
25	0.0151	5.3965	27.4968	66.0737	356.5683	0.1853	0.0028	5.095	25
26	0.0128	5.4093	27.8167	78.1322	422.6420	0.1849	0.0024	5.142	26
27	0.0108	5.4201	28.0981	92.3913	500.7742	0.1845	0.0020	5.184	27
28	0.0092	5.4293	28.3453	109.2527	593.1655	0.1842	0.0017	5.220	28
29	0.0077	5.4370	28.5620	129.1913	702.4182	0.1839	0.0014	5.253	29
30	0.0065	5.4436	28.7518	152.7687	831.6095	0.1837	0.0012	5.281	30
31	0.0055	5.4491	28.9179	180.6490	984.3782	0.1835	0.0010	5.306	31
32	0.0047	5.4538	29.0630	213.6175	1165.0273	0.1834	0.0009	5.328	32
33	0.0040	5.4578	29.1897	252.6027	1378.6447	0.1832	0.0007	5.348	33
34	0.0033	5.4611	29.3002	298.7027	1631.2474	0.1831	0.0006	5.365	34
35	0.0028	5.4639	29.3964	353.2159	1929.9501	0.1830	0.0005	5.380	35
36	0.0024	5.4663	29.4802	417.6778	2283.1660	0.1829	0.0004	5.393	36
37	0.0020	5.4684	29.5531	493.9040	2700.8437	0.1829	0.0004	5.404	37
38	0.0017	5.4701	29.6165	584.0415	3194.7477	0.1828	0.0003	5.414	38
39	0.0014	5.4715	29.6715	690.6290	3778.7892	0.1828	0.0003	5.422	39
40	0.0012	5.4727	29.7192	816.6688	4469.4182	0.1827	0.0002	5.430	40
41	0.0010	5.4738	29.7607	965.7109	5286.0870	0.1827	0.0002	5.437	41
42	0.0009	5.4747	29.7966	1141.9531	6251.7979	0.1827	0.0002	5.442	42
43	0.0007	5.4754	29.8277	1350.3596	7393.7510	0.1826	0.0001	5.447	43
44	0.0006	5.4760	29.8546	1596.8002	8744.1106	0.1826	0.0001	5.451	44
45	0.0005	5.4766	29.8779	1888.2162	10340.9108	0.1826	0.0001	5.455	45
46	0.0004	5.4770	29.8981	2232.8157	12229.1270	0.1826	0.0001	5.458	46
47	0.0004	5.4774	29.9155	2640.3045	14461.9427	0.1826	0.0001	5.461	47
48	0.0003	5.4777	29.9305	3122.1601	17102.2472	0.1826	0.0001	5.464	48
49	0.0003	5.4780	29.9435	3691.9543	20224.4073	0.1825	0.0000	5.466	49
50	0.0002	5.4782	29.9548	4365.7360	23916.3617	0.1825	0.0000	5.468	50
51	0.0002	5.4784	29.9644	5162.4828	28282.0977	0.1825	0.0000	5.469	51
52	0.0002	5.4786	29.9728	6104.6359	33444.5805	0.1825	0.0000	5.470	52
53	0.0001	5.4787	29.9800	7218.7320	39549.2164	0.1825	0.0000	5.472	53
54	0.0001	5.4788	29.9862	8536.1506	46767.9484	0.1825	0.0000	5.473	54
55	0.0001	5.4789	29.9916	10093.9981	55304.0990	0.1825	0.0000	5.474	55
60	0.0000	5.4792	30.0090	23338.2864	127875.5418	0.1825	0.0000	5.476	60
65	0.0000	5.4794	30.0172	53960.3442	295667.6397	0.1825	0.0000	5.478	65
70	0.0000	5.4794	30.0211	124761.4630	683618.9751	0.1825	0.0000	5.478	70
75	0.0000	5.4794	30.0229	288460.4029	1580599.4678	0.1825	0.0000	5.479	75
80	0.0000	5.4794	30.0237	666947.9666	3654503.9264	0.1825	0.0000	5.479	80
85	0.0000	5.4794	30.0241	1542047.3163	8449568.8563	0.1825	0.0000	5.479	85
90	0.0000	5.4795	30.0242	3565360.4851	***********	0.1825	0.0000	5.479	90
95	0.0000	5.4795	30.0243	8243453.5273	***********	0.1825	0.0000	5.479	95
100	0.0000	5.4795	30.0244	***********	***********	0.1825	0.0000	5.479	100

EXPANDED INTEREST TABLES

I = **18.50 %**

n	(P/F)	(P/A)	(P/G)	(F/P)	(F/A)	(A/P)	(A/F)	(A/G)	n
1	0.8439	0.8439	0.0000	1.1850	1.0000	1.1850	1.0000	0.000	1
2	0.7121	1.5560	0.7121	1.4042	2.1850	0.6427	0.4577	0.457	2
3	0.6010	2.1570	1.9141	1.6640	3.5892	0.4636	0.2786	0.887	3
4	0.5071	2.6641	3.4355	1.9718	5.2532	0.3754	0.1904	1.289	4
5	0.4280	3.0921	5.1473	2.3366	7.2251	0.3234	0.1384	1.664	5
6	0.3612	3.4532	6.9531	2.7689	9.5617	0.2896	0.1046	2.013	6
7	0.3048	3.7580	8.7817	3.2812	12.3306	0.2661	0.0811	2.336	7
8	0.2572	4.0152	10.5820	3.8882	15.6118	0.2491	0.0641	2.635	8
9	0.2170	4.2322	12.3183	4.6075	19.5000	0.2363	0.0513	2.910	9
10	0.1832	4.4154	13.9667	5.4599	24.1075	0.2265	0.0415	3.163	10
11	0.1546	4.5699	15.5123	6.4700	29.5674	0.2188	0.0338	3.394	11
12	0.1304	4.7004	16.9471	7.6669	36.0373	0.2127	0.0277	3.605	12
13	0.1101	4.8104	18.2679	9.0853	43.7042	0.2079	0.0229	3.797	13
14	0.0929	4.9033	19.4754	10.7661	52.7895	0.2039	0.0189	3.971	14
15	0.0784	4.9817	20.5727	12.7578	63.5556	0.2007	0.0157	4.129	15
16	0.0661	5.0479	21.5649	15.1180	76.3134	0.1981	0.0131	4.272	16
17	0.0558	5.1037	22.4581	17.9148	91.4313	0.1959	0.0109	4.400	17
18	0.0471	5.1508	23.2588	21.2290	109.3461	0.1941	0.0091	4.515	18
19	0.0398	5.1905	23.9744	25.1564	130.5752	0.1927	0.0077	4.618	19
20	0.0335	5.2241	24.6117	29.8103	155.7316	0.1914	0.0064	4.711	20
21	0.0283	5.2524	25.1779	35.3253	185.5419	0.1904	0.0054	4.793	21
22	0.0239	5.2763	25.6796	41.8604	220.8672	0.1895	0.0045	4.867	22
23	0.0202	5.2964	26.1231	49.6046	262.7276	0.1888	0.0038	4.932	23
24	0.0170	5.3134	26.5144	58.7815	312.3322	0.1882	0.0032	4.990	24
25	0.0144	5.3278	26.8589	69.6560	371.1137	0.1877	0.0027	5.041	25
26	0.0121	5.3399	27.1618	82.5424	440.7697	0.1873	0.0023	5.086	26
27	0.0102	5.3501	27.4276	97.8127	523.3122	0.1869	0.0019	5.126	27
28	0.0086	5.3588	27.6605	115.9081	621.1249	0.1866	0.0016	5.161	28
29	0.0073	5.3661	27.8644	137.3511	737.0330	0.1864	0.0014	5.192	29
30	0.0061	5.3722	28.0426	162.7611	874.3841	0.1861	0.0011	5.219	30
31	0.0052	5.3774	28.1981	192.8719	1037.1452	0.1860	0.0010	5.243	31
32	0.0044	5.3818	28.3337	228.5531	1230.0170	0.1858	0.0008	5.264	32
33	0.0037	5.3854	28.4519	270.8355	1458.5702	0.1857	0.0007	5.283	33
34	0.0031	5.3886	28.5547	320.9400	1729.4057	0.1856	0.0006	5.299	34
35	0.0026	5.3912	28.6441	380.3140	2050.3457	0.1855	0.0005	5.313	35
36	0.0022	5.3934	28.7218	450.6720	2430.6597	0.1854	0.0004	5.325	36
37	0.0019	5.3953	28.7892	534.0464	2881.3317	0.1853	0.0003	5.336	37
38	0.0016	5.3969	28.8477	632.8449	3415.3781	0.1853	0.0003	5.345	38
39	0.0013	5.3982	28.8983	749.9213	4048.2230	0.1852	0.0002	5.353	39
40	0.0011	5.3993	28.9422	888.6567	4798.1443	0.1852	0.0002	5.360	40
41	0.0009	5.4003	28.9802	1053.0582	5686.8009	0.1852	0.0002	5.366	41
42	0.0008	5.4011	29.0131	1247.8739	6739.8591	0.1851	0.0001	5.371	42
43	0.0007	5.4017	29.0415	1478.7306	7987.7331	0.1851	0.0001	5.376	43
44	0.0006	5.4023	29.0660	1752.2958	9466.4637	0.1851	0.0001	5.380	44
45	0.0005	5.4028	29.0872	2076.4705	11218.7595	0.1851	0.0001	5.383	45
46	0.0004	5.4032	29.1055	2460.6175	13295.2300	0.1851	0.0001	5.386	46
47	0.0003	5.4036	29.1213	2915.8318	15755.8475	0.1851	0.0001	5.389	47
48	0.0003	5.4038	29.1349	3455.2607	18671.6793	0.1851	0.0001	5.391	48
49	0.0002	5.4041	29.1466	4094.4839	22126.9400	0.1850	0.0000	5.393	49
50	0.0002	5.4043	29.1567	4851.9634	26221.4239	0.1850	0.0000	5.395	50
51	0.0002	5.4045	29.1654	5749.5766	31073.3873	0.1850	0.0000	5.396	51
52	0.0001	5.4046	29.1729	6813.2483	36822.9639	0.1850	0.0000	5.397	52
53	0.0001	5.4047	29.1793	8073.6993	43636.2122	0.1850	0.0000	5.398	53
54	0.0001	5.4048	29.1848	9567.3336	51709.9115	0.1850	0.0000	5.399	54
55	0.0001	5.4049	29.1896	11337.2903	61277.2451	0.1850	0.0000	5.400	55
60	0.0000	5.4052	29.2051	26491.1628	143190.0689	0.1850	0.0000	5.403	60
65	0.0000	5.4053	29.2123	61900.3027	334590.8252	0.1850	0.0000	5.404	65
70	0.0000	5.4054	29.2156	144638.7048	781825.4315	0.1850	0.0000	5.404	70
75	0.0000	5.4054	29.2171	337968.5403	1826851.5691	0.1850	0.0000	5.405	75
80	0.0000	5.4054	29.2178	789710.7096	4268701.1328	0.1850	0.0000	5.405	80
85	0.0000	5.4054	29.2181	1845269.3979	9974423.7723	0.1850	0.0000	5.405	85
90	0.0000	5.4054	29.2183	4311729.7378	************	0.1850	0.0000	5.405	90
95	0.0000	5.4054	29.2184	************	************	0.1850	0.0000	5.405	95
100	0.0000	5.4054	29.2184	************	************	0.1850	0.0000	5.405	100

I = 18.75 %

n	(P/F)	(P/A)	(P/G)	(F/P)	(F/A)	(A/P)	(A/F)	(A/G)	n
1	0.8421	0.8421	0.0000	1.1875	1.0000	1.1875	1.0000	0.000	1
2	0.7091	1.5512	0.7091	1.4102	2.1875	0.6446	0.4571	0.457	2
3	0.5972	2.1484	1.9035	1.6746	3.5977	0.4655	0.2780	0.886	3
4	0.5029	2.6513	3.4121	1.9885	5.2722	0.3772	0.1897	1.287	4
5	0.4235	3.0748	5.1060	2.3614	7.2608	0.3252	0.1377	1.660	5
6	0.3566	3.4314	6.8891	2.8042	9.6221	0.2914	0.1039	2.007	6
7	0.3003	3.7317	8.6910	3.3299	12.4263	0.2680	0.0805	2.329	7
8	0.2529	3.9846	10.4612	3.9543	15.7562	0.2510	0.0635	2.625	8
9	0.2130	4.1975	12.1649	4.6957	19.7105	0.2382	0.0507	2.898	9
10	0.1793	4.3769	13.7789	5.5762	24.4063	0.2285	0.0410	3.148	10
11	0.1510	4.5279	15.2891	6.6217	29.9824	0.2209	0.0334	3.376	11
12	0.1272	4.6551	16.6880	7.8633	36.6041	0.2148	0.0273	3.584	12
13	0.1071	4.7622	17.9731	9.3376	44.4674	0.2100	0.0225	3.774	13
14	0.0902	4.8524	19.1455	11.0884	53.8050	0.2061	0.0186	3.945	14
15	0.0759	4.9283	20.2087	13.1675	64.8935	0.2029	0.0154	4.100	15
16	0.0640	4.9922	21.1680	15.6364	78.0610	0.2003	0.0128	4.240	16
17	0.0539	5.0461	22.0297	18.5683	93.6975	0.1982	0.0107	4.365	17
18	0.0454	5.0915	22.8007	22.0498	112.2657	0.1964	0.0089	4.478	18
19	0.0382	5.1296	23.4881	26.1842	134.3156	0.1949	0.0074	4.578	19
20	0.0322	5.1618	24.0992	31.0937	160.4997	0.1937	0.0062	4.668	20
21	0.0271	5.1889	24.6408	36.9238	191.5934	0.1927	0.0052	4.748	21
22	0.0228	5.2117	25.1198	43.8470	228.5172	0.1919	0.0044	4.819	22
23	0.0192	5.2309	25.5423	52.0683	272.3642	0.1912	0.0037	4.883	23
24	0.0162	5.2471	25.9143	61.8311	324.4324	0.1906	0.0031	4.938	24
25	0.0136	5.2607	26.2411	73.4244	386.2635	0.1901	0.0026	4.988	25
26	0.0115	5.2722	26.5278	87.1915	459.6879	0.1897	0.0022	5.031	26
27	0.0097	5.2818	26.7790	103.5399	546.8794	0.1893	0.0018	5.070	27
28	0.0081	5.2900	26.9986	122.9536	650.4193	0.1890	0.0015	5.103	28
29	0.0068	5.2968	27.1903	146.0074	773.3729	0.1888	0.0013	5.133	29
30	0.0058	5.3026	27.3576	173.3838	919.3803	0.1886	0.0011	5.159	30
31	0.0049	5.3074	27.5033	205.8933	1092.7641	0.1884	0.0009	5.182	31
32	0.0041	5.3115	27.6301	244.4983	1298.6574	0.1883	0.0008	5.201	32
33	0.0034	5.3150	27.7403	290.3417	1543.1557	0.1881	0.0006	5.219	33
34	0.0029	5.3179	27.8360	344.7808	1833.4974	0.1880	0.0005	5.234	34
35	0.0024	5.3203	27.9190	409.4272	2178.2781	0.1880	0.0005	5.247	35
36	0.0021	5.3224	27.9910	486.1947	2587.7053	0.1879	0.0004	5.259	36
37	0.0017	5.3241	28.0534	577.3563	3073.9000	0.1878	0.0003	5.269	37
38	0.0015	5.3256	28.1074	685.6106	3651.2563	0.1878	0.0003	5.277	38
39	0.0012	5.3268	28.1540	814.1625	4336.8669	0.1877	0.0002	5.285	39
40	0.0010	5.3278	28.1944	966.8180	5151.0294	0.1877	0.0002	5.291	40
41	0.0009	5.3287	28.2292	1148.0964	6117.8474	0.1877	0.0002	5.297	41
42	0.0007	5.3294	28.2593	1363.3645	7265.9438	0.1876	0.0001	5.302	42
43	0.0006	5.3300	28.2852	1618.9953	8629.3082	0.1876	0.0001	5.306	43
44	0.0005	5.3306	28.3076	1922.5569	10248.3035	0.1876	0.0001	5.310	44
45	0.0004	5.3310	28.3269	2283.0363	12170.8605	0.1876	0.0001	5.313	45
46	0.0004	5.3314	28.3435	2711.1056	14453.8968	0.1876	0.0001	5.316	46
47	0.0003	5.3317	28.3577	3219.4380	17165.0024	0.1876	0.0001	5.318	47
48	0.0003	5.3319	28.3700	3823.0826	20384.4404	0.1875	0.0000	5.320	48
49	0.0002	5.3322	28.3806	4539.9106	24207.5230	0.1875	0.0000	5.322	49
50	0.0002	5.3323	28.3897	5391.1438	28747.4335	0.1875	0.0000	5.324	50
51	0.0002	5.3325	28.3975	6401.9832	34138.5773	0.1875	0.0000	5.325	51
52	0.0001	5.3326	28.4042	7602.3551	40540.5605	0.1875	0.0000	5.326	52
53	0.0001	5.3327	28.4100	9027.7967	48142.9156	0.1875	0.0000	5.327	53
54	0.0001	5.3328	28.4149	10720.5086	57170.7123	0.1875	0.0000	5.328	54
55	0.0001	5.3329	28.4192	12730.6039	67891.2209	0.1875	0.0000	5.329	55
60	0.0000	5.3332	28.4329	30061.9465	160325.0481	0.1875	0.0000	5.331	60
65	0.0000	5.3333	28.4392	70988.0406	378597.5501	0.1875	0.0000	5.332	65
70	0.0000	5.3333	28.4420	167630.5928	894024.4948	0.1875	0.0000	5.332	70
75	0.0000	5.3333	28.4434	395841.5443	2111149.5696	0.1875	0.0000	5.333	75
80	0.0000	5.3333	28.4440	934737.0644	4985259.0099	0.1875	0.0000	5.333	80
85	0.0000	5.3333	28.4442	2207280.6457	************	0.1875	0.0000	5.333	85
90	0.0000	5.3333	28.4443	5212254.9052	************	0.1875	0.0000	5.333	90
95	0.0000	5.3333	28.4444	************	************	0.1875	0.0000	5.333	95
100	0.0000	5.3333	28.4444	************	************	0.1875	0.0000	5.333	100

EXPANDED INTEREST TABLES

I = 19.00 %

n	(P/F)	(P/A)	(P/G)	(F/P)	(F/A)	(A/P)	(A/F)	(A/G)	n
1	0.8403	0.8403	0.0000	1.1900	1.0000	1.1900	1.0000	0.000	1
2	0.7062	1.5465	0.7062	1.4161	2.1900	0.6466	0.4566	0.456	2
3	0.5934	2.1399	1.8930	1.6852	3.6061	0.4673	0.2773	0.884	3
4	0.4987	2.6386	3.3890	2.0053	5.2913	0.3790	0.1890	1.284	4
5	0.4190	3.0576	5.0652	2.3864	7.2966	0.3271	0.1371	1.656	5
6	0.3521	3.4098	6.8259	2.8398	9.6830	0.2933	0.1033	2.001	6
7	0.2959	3.7057	8.6014	3.3793	12.5227	0.2699	0.0799	2.321	7
8	0.2487	3.9544	10.3421	4.0214	15.9020	0.2529	0.0629	2.615	8
9	0.2090	4.1633	12.0138	4.7854	19.9234	0.2402	0.0502	2.885	9
10	0.1756	4.3389	13.5943	5.6947	24.7089	0.2305	0.0405	3.133	10
11	0.1476	4.4865	15.0699	6.7767	30.4035	0.2229	0.0329	3.358	11
12	0.1240	4.6105	16.4340	8.0642	37.1802	0.2169	0.0269	3.564	12
13	0.1042	4.7147	17.6844	9.5964	45.2445	0.2121	0.0221	3.750	13
14	0.0876	4.8023	18.8228	11.4198	54.8409	0.2082	0.0182	3.919	14
15	0.0736	4.8759	19.8530	13.5895	66.2607	0.2051	0.0151	4.071	15
16	0.0618	4.9377	20.7806	16.1715	79.8502	0.2025	0.0125	4.208	16
17	0.0520	4.9897	21.6120	19.2441	96.0218	0.2004	0.0104	4.331	17
18	0.0437	5.0333	22.3543	22.9005	115.2659	0.1987	0.0087	4.441	18
19	0.0367	5.0700	23.0148	27.2516	138.1664	0.1972	0.0072	4.539	19
20	0.0308	5.1009	23.6007	32.4294	165.4180	0.1960	0.0060	4.626	20
21	0.0259	5.1268	24.1190	38.5910	197.8474	0.1951	0.0051	4.704	21
22	0.0218	5.1486	24.5763	45.9233	236.4385	0.1942	0.0042	4.773	22
23	0.0183	5.1668	24.9788	54.6487	282.3618	0.1935	0.0035	4.834	23
24	0.0154	5.1822	25.3325	65.0320	337.0105	0.1930	0.0030	4.888	24
25	0.0129	5.1951	25.6426	77.3881	402.0425	0.1925	0.0025	4.935	25
26	0.0109	5.2060	25.9141	92.0918	479.4306	0.1921	0.0021	4.977	26
27	0.0091	5.2151	26.1514	109.5893	571.5224	0.1917	0.0017	5.014	27
28	0.0077	5.2228	26.3584	130.4112	681.1116	0.1915	0.0015	5.046	28
29	0.0064	5.2292	26.5388	155.1893	811.5228	0.1912	0.0012	5.075	29
30	0.0054	5.2347	26.6958	184.6753	966.7122	0.1910	0.0010	5.099	30
31	0.0046	5.2392	26.8324	219.7636	1151.3875	0.1909	0.0009	5.121	31
32	0.0038	5.2430	26.9509	261.5187	1371.1511	0.1907	0.0007	5.140	32
33	0.0032	5.2462	27.0537	311.2073	1632.6698	0.1906	0.0006	5.156	33
34	0.0027	5.2489	27.1428	370.3366	1943.8771	0.1905	0.0005	5.171	34
35	0.0023	5.2512	27.2200	440.7006	2314.2137	0.1904	0.0004	5.183	35
36	0.0019	5.2531	27.2867	524.4337	2754.9143	0.1904	0.0004	5.194	36
37	0.0016	5.2547	27.3444	624.0761	3279.3481	0.1903	0.0003	5.203	37
38	0.0013	5.2561	27.3942	742.6506	3903.4242	0.1903	0.0003	5.211	38
39	0.0011	5.2572	27.4372	883.7542	4646.0748	0.1902	0.0002	5.219	39
40	0.0010	5.2582	27.4743	1051.6675	5529.8290	0.1902	0.0002	5.225	40
41	0.0008	5.2590	27.5063	1251.4843	6581.4965	0.1902	0.0002	5.230	41
42	0.0007	5.2596	27.5338	1489.2664	7832.9808	0.1901	0.0001	5.234	42
43	0.0006	5.2602	27.5575	1772.2270	9322.2472	0.1901	0.0001	5.238	43
44	0.0005	5.2607	27.5779	2108.9501	11094.4741	0.1901	0.0001	5.242	44
45	0.0004	5.2611	27.5954	2509.6506	13203.4242	0.1901	0.0001	5.245	45
46	0.0003	5.2614	27.6105	2986.4842	15713.0748	0.1901	0.0001	5.247	46
47	0.0003	5.2617	27.6234	3553.9162	18699.5590	0.1901	0.0001	5.249	47
48	0.0002	5.2619	27.6345	4229.1603	22253.4753	0.1900	0.0000	5.251	48
49	0.0002	5.2621	27.6441	5032.7008	26482.6356	0.1900	0.0000	5.253	49
50	0.0002	5.2623	27.6523	5988.9139	31515.3363	0.1900	0.0000	5.254	50
51	0.0001	5.2624	27.6593	7126.8075	37504.2502	0.1900	0.0000	5.256	51
52	0.0001	5.2625	27.6653	8480.9010	44631.0578	0.1900	0.0000	5.257	52
53	0.0001	5.2626	27.6704	10092.2722	53111.9588	0.1900	0.0000	5.257	53
54	0.0001	5.2627	27.6749	12009.8039	63204.2309	0.1900	0.0000	5.258	54
55	0.0001	5.2628	27.6786	14291.6666	75214.0348	0.1900	0.0000	5.259	55
60	0.0000	5.2630	27.6908	34104.9709	179494.5838	0.1900	0.0000	5.261	60
65	0.0000	5.2631	27.6963	81386.5222	428344.8535	0.1900	0.0000	5.262	65
70	0.0000	5.2631	27.6988	194217.0251	1022189.6056	0.1900	0.0000	5.262	70
75	0.0000	5.2631	27.6999	463470.5086	2439313.2029	0.1900	0.0000	5.263	75
80	0.0000	5.2632	27.7004	1106004.5444	5821071.2861	0.1900	0.0000	5.263	80
85	0.0000	5.2632	27.7007	2639317.9923	***********	0.1900	0.0000	5.263	85
90	0.0000	5.2632	27.7008	6298346.1505	***********	0.1900	0.0000	5.263	90
95	0.0000	5.2632	27.7008	************	***********	0.1900	0.0000	5.263	95
100	0.0000	5.2632	27.7008	************	***********	0.1900	0.0000	5.263	100

$I = 19.25\%$

n	(P/F)	(P/A)	(P/G)	(F/P)	(F/A)	(A/P)	(A/F)	(A/G)	n
1	0.8386	0.8386	0.0000	1.1925	1.0000	1.1925	1.0000	0.000	1
2	0.7032	1.5418	0.7032	1.4221	2.1925	0.6486	0.4561	0.456	2
3	0.5897	2.1315	1.8826	1.6958	3.6146	0.4692	0.2767	0.883	3
4	0.4945	2.6260	3.3661	2.0222	5.3104	0.3808	0.1883	1.281	4
5	0.4147	3.0406	5.0248	2.4115	7.3326	0.3289	0.1364	1.652	5
6	0.3477	3.3884	6.7635	2.8757	9.7441	0.2951	0.1026	1.996	6
7	0.2916	3.6800	8.5131	3.4293	12.6199	0.2717	0.0792	2.313	7
8	0.2445	3.9245	10.2248	4.0895	16.0492	0.2548	0.0623	2.605	8
9	0.2051	4.1296	11.8653	4.8767	20.1387	0.2422	0.0497	2.873	9
10	0.1720	4.3015	13.4129	5.8155	25.0154	0.2325	0.0400	3.118	10
11	0.1442	4.4457	14.8548	6.9349	30.8308	0.2249	0.0324	3.341	11
12	0.1209	4.5666	16.1850	8.2699	37.7658	0.2190	0.0265	3.544	12
13	0.1014	4.6680	17.4018	9.8619	46.0357	0.2142	0.0217	3.727	13
14	0.0850	4.7531	18.5072	11.7603	55.8975	0.2104	0.0179	3.893	14
15	0.0713	4.8244	19.5055	14.0241	67.6578	0.2073	0.0148	4.043	15
16	0.0598	4.8842	20.4024	16.7238	81.6819	0.2047	0.0122	4.177	16
17	0.0501	4.9343	21.2047	19.9431	98.4057	0.2027	0.0102	4.297	17
18	0.0420	4.9764	21.9195	23.7821	118.3488	0.2009	0.0084	4.404	18
19	0.0353	5.0116	22.5542	28.3602	142.1309	0.1995	0.0070	4.500	19
20	0.0296	5.0412	23.1160	33.8195	170.4911	0.1984	0.0059	4.585	20
21	0.0248	5.0660	23.6119	40.3298	204.3107	0.1974	0.0049	4.660	21
22	0.0208	5.0868	24.0485	48.0933	244.6405	0.1966	0.0041	4.727	22
23	0.0174	5.1042	24.4322	57.3513	292.7338	0.1959	0.0034	4.786	23
24	0.0146	5.1188	24.7685	68.3914	350.0850	0.1954	0.0029	4.838	24
25	0.0123	5.1311	25.0627	81.5567	418.4764	0.1949	0.0024	4.884	25
26	0.0103	5.1414	25.3198	97.2564	500.0331	0.1945	0.0020	4.924	26
27	0.0086	5.1500	25.5440	115.9782	597.2895	0.1942	0.0017	4.960	27
28	0.0072	5.1572	25.7392	138.3040	713.2677	0.1939	0.0014	4.990	28
29	0.0061	5.1633	25.9090	164.9276	851.5718	0.1937	0.0012	5.017	29
30	0.0051	5.1684	26.0564	196.6761	1016.4993	0.1935	0.0010	5.041	30
31	0.0043	5.1727	26.1843	234.5363	1213.1754	0.1933	0.0008	5.062	31
32	0.0036	5.1762	26.2952	279.6845	1447.7117	0.1932	0.0007	5.080	32
33	0.0030	5.1792	26.3911	333.5238	1727.3962	0.1931	0.0006	5.095	33
34	0.0025	5.1817	26.4741	397.7271	2060.9200	0.1930	0.0005	5.109	34
35	0.0021	5.1839	26.5458	474.2896	2458.6471	0.1929	0.0004	5.120	35
36	0.0018	5.1856	26.6076	565.5903	2932.9367	0.1928	0.0003	5.131	36
37	0.0015	5.1871	26.6610	674.4664	3498.5270	0.1928	0.0003	5.139	37
38	0.0012	5.1883	26.7070	804.3012	4172.9934	0.1927	0.0002	5.147	38
39	0.0010	5.1894	26.7466	959.1292	4977.2946	0.1927	0.0002	5.154	39
40	0.0009	5.1903	26.7807	1143.7616	5936.4239	0.1927	0.0002	5.159	40
41	0.0007	5.1910	26.8101	1363.9357	7080.1854	0.1926	0.0001	5.164	41
42	0.0006	5.1916	26.8353	1626.4933	8444.1211	0.1926	0.0001	5.169	42
43	0.0005	5.1921	26.8569	1939.5933	10070.6145	0.1926	0.0001	5.172	43
44	0.0004	5.1926	26.8755	2312.9650	12010.2077	0.1926	0.0001	5.175	44
45	0.0004	5.1929	26.8915	2758.2108	14323.1727	0.1926	0.0001	5.178	45
46	0.0003	5.1932	26.9051	3289.1663	17081.3835	0.1926	0.0001	5.180	46
47	0.0003	5.1935	26.9169	3922.3308	20370.5498	0.1925	0.0000	5.182	47
48	0.0002	5.1937	26.9269	4677.3795	24292.8806	0.1925	0.0000	5.184	48
49	0.0002	5.1939	26.9355	5577.7751	28970.2602	0.1925	0.0000	5.186	49
50	0.0002	5.1940	26.9429	6651.4968	34548.0353	0.1925	0.0000	5.187	50
51	0.0001	5.1942	26.9492	7931.9099	41199.5320	0.1925	0.0000	5.188	51
52	0.0001	5.1943	26.9546	9458.8026	49131.4420	0.1925	0.0000	5.189	52
53	0.0001	5.1943	26.9592	11279.6221	58590.2445	0.1925	0.0000	5.190	53
54	0.0001	5.1944	26.9631	13450.9493	69869.8666	0.1925	0.0000	5.190	54
55	0.0001	5.1945	26.9665	16040.2571	83320.8159	0.1925	0.0000	5.191	55
60	0.0000	5.1947	26.9772	38681.4961	200937.6419	0.1925	0.0000	5.193	60
65	0.0000	5.1947	26.9821	93281.4313	484573.6692	0.1925	0.0000	5.194	65
70	0.0000	5.1948	26.9843	224950.5917	1168569.3075	0.1925	0.0000	5.194	70
75	0.0000	5.1948	26.9852	542474.1880	2818042.5350	0.1925	0.0000	5.194	75
80	0.0000	5.1948	26.9857	1308190.5783	6795790.0170	0.1925	0.0000	5.194	80
85	0.0000	5.1948	26.9859	3154735.5191	************	0.1925	0.0000	5.194	85
90	0.0000	5.1948	26.9859	7607726.5508	************	0.1925	0.0000	5.194	90
95	0.0000	5.1948	26.9860	************	************	0.1925	0.0000	5.194	95
100	0.0000	5.1948	26.9860	************	************	0.1925	0.0000	5.194	100

EXPANDED INTEREST TABLES

I = 19.50 %

n	(P/F)	(P/A)	(P/G)	(F/P)	(F/A)	(A/P)	(A/F)	(A/G)	n
1	0.8368	0.8368	0.0000	1.1950	1.0000	1.1950	1.0000	0.000	1
2	0.7003	1.5371	0.7003	1.4280	2.1950	0.6506	0.4556	0.455	2
3	0.5860	2.1231	1.8723	1.7065	3.6230	0.4710	0.2760	0.881	3
4	0.4904	2.6135	3.3434	2.0393	5.3295	0.3826	0.1876	1.279	4
5	0.4104	3.0238	4.9848	2.4369	7.3688	0.3307	0.1357	1.648	5
6	0.3434	3.3672	6.7018	2.9121	9.8057	0.2970	0.1020	1.990	6
7	0.2874	3.6546	8.4259	3.4800	12.7178	0.2736	0.0786	2.305	7
8	0.2405	3.8950	10.1092	4.1586	16.1978	0.2567	0.0617	2.595	8
9	0.2012	4.0963	11.7190	4.9695	20.3563	0.2441	0.0491	2.860	9
10	0.1684	4.2647	13.2346	5.9385	25.3258	0.2345	0.0395	3.103	10
11	0.1409	4.4056	14.6437	7.0965	31.2643	0.2270	0.0320	3.323	11
12	0.1179	4.5235	15.9408	8.4804	38.3609	0.2211	0.0261	3.524	12
13	0.0987	4.6222	17.1249	10.1340	46.8412	0.2163	0.0213	3.705	13
14	0.0826	4.7047	18.1984	12.1102	56.9753	0.2126	0.0176	3.868	14
15	0.0691	4.7738	19.1658	14.4717	69.0855	0.2095	0.0145	4.014	15
16	0.0578	4.8317	20.0332	17.2936	83.5571	0.2070	0.0120	4.146	16
17	0.0484	4.8801	20.8074	20.6659	100.8508	0.2049	0.0099	4.263	17
18	0.0405	4.9205	21.4958	24.6958	121.5167	0.2032	0.0082	4.368	18
19	0.0339	4.9544	22.1057	29.5114	146.2124	0.2018	0.0068	4.461	19
20	0.0284	4.9828	22.6445	35.2662	175.7239	0.2007	0.0057	4.544	20
21	0.0237	5.0065	23.1191	42.1431	210.9900	0.1997	0.0047	4.617	21
22	0.0199	5.0264	23.5360	50.3610	253.1331	0.1990	0.0040	4.682	22
23	0.0166	5.0430	23.9016	60.1813	303.4940	0.1983	0.0033	4.739	23
24	0.0139	5.0569	24.2214	71.9167	363.6754	0.1977	0.0027	4.789	24
25	0.0116	5.0685	24.5007	85.9405	435.5921	0.1973	0.0023	4.833	25
26	0.0097	5.0783	24.7441	102.6988	521.5325	0.1969	0.0019	4.872	26
27	0.0081	5.0864	24.9560	122.7251	624.2314	0.1966	0.0016	4.906	27
28	0.0068	5.0932	25.1401	146.6565	746.9565	0.1963	0.0013	4.936	28
29	0.0057	5.0989	25.2998	175.2545	893.6130	0.1961	0.0011	4.961	29
30	0.0048	5.1037	25.4383	209.4292	1068.8675	0.1959	0.0009	4.984	30
31	0.0040	5.1077	25.5582	250.2679	1278.2967	0.1958	0.0008	5.003	31
32	0.0033	5.1111	25.6618	299.0701	1528.5645	0.1957	0.0007	5.020	32
33	0.0028	5.1139	25.7514	357.3887	1827.6346	0.1955	0.0005	5.035	33
34	0.0023	5.1162	25.8287	427.0796	2185.0233	0.1955	0.0005	5.048	34
35	0.0020	5.1182	25.8953	510.3601	2612.1029	0.1954	0.0004	5.059	35
36	0.0016	5.1198	25.9527	609.8803	3122.4630	0.1953	0.0003	5.069	36
37	0.0014	5.1212	26.0021	728.8069	3732.3432	0.1953	0.0003	5.077	37
38	0.0011	5.1223	26.0445	870.9243	4461.1502	0.1952	0.0002	5.084	38
39	0.0010	5.1233	26.0811	1040.7545	5332.0745	0.1952	0.0002	5.090	39
40	0.0008	5.1241	26.1124	1243.7017	6372.8290	0.1952	0.0002	5.096	40
41	0.0007	5.1248	26.1393	1486.2235	7616.5306	0.1951	0.0001	5.100	41
42	0.0006	5.1253	26.1624	1776.0371	9102.7541	0.1951	0.0001	5.104	42
43	0.0005	5.1258	26.1822	2122.3643	10878.7912	0.1951	0.0001	5.107	43
44	0.0004	5.1262	26.1992	2536.2253	13001.1554	0.1951	0.0001	5.110	44
45	0.0003	5.1265	26.2137	3030.7892	15537.3808	0.1951	0.0001	5.113	45
46	0.0003	5.1268	26.2261	3621.7932	18568.1700	0.1951	0.0001	5.115	46
47	0.0002	5.1270	26.2367	4328.0428	22189.9632	0.1950	0.0000	5.117	47
48	0.0002	5.1272	26.2458	5172.0112	26518.0060	0.1950	0.0000	5.118	48
49	0.0002	5.1274	26.2536	6180.5533	31690.0171	0.1950	0.0000	5.120	49
50	0.0001	5.1275	26.2602	7385.7612	37870.5705	0.1950	0.0000	5.121	50
51	0.0001	5.1276	26.2659	8825.9847	45256.3317	0.1950	0.0000	5.122	51
52	0.0001	5.1277	26.2707	10547.0517	54082.3164	0.1950	0.0000	5.123	52
53	0.0001	5.1278	26.2748	12603.7268	64629.3681	0.1950	0.0000	5.124	53
54	0.0001	5.1279	26.2784	15061.4535	77233.0949	0.1950	0.0000	5.124	54
55	0.0001	5.1279	26.2814	17998.4369	92294.5484	0.1950	0.0000	5.125	55
60	0.0000	5.1281	26.2909	43860.5746	224920.8955	0.1950	0.0000	5.126	60
65	0.0000	5.1282	26.2951	106884.2818	548119.3940	0.1950	0.0000	5.127	65
70	0.0000	5.1282	26.2970	260467.3970	1335725.1128	0.1950	0.0000	5.127	70
75	0.0000	5.1282	26.2978	634735.6575	3255049.5255	0.1950	0.0000	5.128	75
80	0.0000	5.1282	26.2982	1546793.8004	7932270.7712	0.1950	0.0000	5.128	80
85	0.0000	5.1282	26.2984	3769397.5952	************	0.1950	0.0000	5.128	85
90	0.0000	5.1282	26.2984	9185683.4618	************	0.1950	0.0000	5.128	90
95	0.0000	5.1282	26.2985	************	************	0.1950	0.0000	5.128	95
100	0.0000	5.1282	26.2985	************	************	0.1950	0.0000	5.128	100

$$I = 19.75\ \%$$

n	(P/F)	(P/A)	(P/G)	(F/P)	(F/A)	(A/P)	(A/F)	(A/G)	n
1	0.8351	0.8351	0.0000	1.1975	1.0000	1.1975	1.0000	0.000	1
2	0.6973	1.5324	0.6973	1.4340	2.1975	0.6526	0.4551	0.455	2
3	0.5823	2.1148	1.8620	1.7172	3.6315	0.4729	0.2754	0.880	3
4	0.4863	2.6010	3.3209	2.0564	5.3487	0.3845	0.1870	1.276	4
5	0.4061	3.0071	4.9453	2.4625	7.4051	0.3325	0.1350	1.644	5
6	0.3391	3.3463	6.6408	2.9489	9.8676	0.2988	0.1013	1.984	6
7	0.2832	3.6294	8.3399	3.5313	12.8165	0.2755	0.0780	2.297	7
8	0.2365	3.8659	9.9953	4.2287	16.3477	0.2587	0.0612	2.585	8
9	0.1975	4.0634	11.5751	5.0638	20.5764	0.2461	0.0486	2.848	9
10	0.1649	4.2283	13.0593	6.0639	25.6402	0.2365	0.0390	3.088	10
11	0.1377	4.3660	14.4364	7.2616	31.7042	0.2290	0.0315	3.306	11
12	0.1150	4.4810	15.7014	8.6957	38.9657	0.2232	0.0257	3.504	12
13	0.0960	4.5771	16.8538	10.4131	47.6615	0.2185	0.0210	3.682	13
14	0.0802	4.6572	17.8963	12.4697	58.0746	0.2147	0.0172	3.842	14
15	0.0670	4.7242	18.8339	14.9325	70.5444	0.2117	0.0142	3.986	15
16	0.0559	4.7801	19.6727	17.8817	85.4769	0.2092	0.0117	4.115	16
17	0.0467	4.8268	20.4199	21.4133	103.3585	0.2072	0.0097	4.230	17
18	0.0390	4.8658	21.0829	25.6424	124.7719	0.2055	0.0080	4.332	18
19	0.0326	4.8984	21.6691	30.7068	150.4143	0.2041	0.0066	4.423	19
20	0.0272	4.9256	22.1858	36.7714	181.1211	0.2030	0.0055	4.504	20
21	0.0227	4.9483	22.6400	44.0338	217.8926	0.2021	0.0046	4.575	21
22	0.0190	4.9673	23.0382	52.7305	261.9263	0.2013	0.0038	4.638	22
23	0.0158	4.9831	23.3866	63.1447	314.6568	0.2007	0.0032	4.693	23
24	0.0132	4.9963	23.6908	75.6158	377.8015	0.2001	0.0026	4.741	24
25	0.0110	5.0074	23.9559	90.5499	453.4173	0.1997	0.0022	4.784	25
26	0.0092	5.0166	24.1864	108.4335	543.9672	0.1993	0.0018	4.821	26
27	0.0077	5.0243	24.3867	129.8491	652.4007	0.1990	0.0015	4.853	27
28	0.0064	5.0307	24.5603	155.4944	782.2499	0.1988	0.0013	4.882	28
29	0.0054	5.0361	24.7107	186.2045	937.7442	0.1986	0.0011	4.906	29
30	0.0045	5.0406	24.8407	222.9799	1123.9487	0.1984	0.0009	4.928	30
31	0.0037	5.0443	24.9531	267.0184	1346.9286	0.1982	0.0007	4.946	31
32	0.0031	5.0475	25.0500	319.7545	1613.9470	0.1981	0.0006	4.962	32
33	0.0026	5.0501	25.1336	382.9061	1933.7015	0.1980	0.0005	4.976	33
34	0.0022	5.0522	25.2056	458.5300	2316.6076	0.1979	0.0004	4.989	34
35	0.0018	5.0541	25.2675	549.0897	2775.1376	0.1979	0.0004	4.999	35
36	0.0015	5.0556	25.3207	657.5349	3324.2272	0.1978	0.0003	5.008	36
37	0.0013	5.0569	25.3664	787.3980	3981.7621	0.1978	0.0003	5.016	37
38	0.0011	5.0579	25.4057	942.9091	4769.1601	0.1977	0.0002	5.022	38
39	0.0009	5.0588	25.4393	1129.1337	5712.0693	0.1977	0.0002	5.028	39
40	0.0007	5.0595	25.4682	1352.1376	6841.2029	0.1976	0.0001	5.033	40
41	0.0006	5.0602	25.4929	1619.1848	8193.3405	0.1976	0.0001	5.038	41
42	0.0005	5.0607	25.5140	1938.9737	9812.5253	0.1976	0.0001	5.041	42
43	0.0004	5.0611	25.5321	2321.9211	11751.4990	0.1976	0.0001	5.044	43
44	0.0004	5.0615	25.5476	2780.5005	14073.4201	0.1976	0.0001	5.047	44
45	0.0003	5.0618	25.5608	3329.6493	16853.9205	0.1976	0.0001	5.049	45
46	0.0003	5.0620	25.5721	3987.2550	20183.5698	0.1975	0.0000	5.051	46
47	0.0002	5.0622	25.5817	4774.7379	24170.8249	0.1975	0.0000	5.053	47
48	0.0002	5.0624	25.5899	5717.7487	28945.5628	0.1975	0.0000	5.054	48
49	0.0001	5.0626	25.5969	6847.0040	34663.3114	0.1975	0.0000	5.056	49
50	0.0001	5.0627	25.6029	8199.2873	41510.3155	0.1975	0.0000	5.057	50
51	0.0001	5.0628	25.6080	9818.6465	49709.6028	0.1975	0.0000	5.058	51
52	0.0001	5.0629	25.6123	11757.8292	59528.2493	0.1975	0.0000	5.058	52
53	0.0001	5.0629	25.6160	14080.0005	71286.0785	0.1975	0.0000	5.059	53
54	0.0001	5.0630	25.6192	16860.8006	85366.0791	0.1975	0.0000	5.060	54
55	0.0000	5.0630	25.6219	20190.8087	102226.8797	0.1975	0.0000	5.060	55
60	0.0000	5.0632	25.6303	49720.0235	251741.8911	0.1975	0.0000	5.062	60
65	0.0000	5.0632	25.6340	122435.9444	619923.7693	0.1975	0.0000	5.062	65
70	0.0000	5.0633	25.6357	301499.4652	1526574.5071	0.1975	0.0000	5.063	70
75	0.0000	5.0633	25.6364	742444.7772	3759208.9984	0.1975	0.0000	5.063	75
80	0.0000	5.0633	25.6367	1828276.0365	9257088.7923	0.1975	0.0000	5.063	80
85	0.0000	5.0633	25.6368	4502143.9551	***********	0.1975	0.0000	5.063	85
90	0.0000	5.0633	25.6369	***********	***********	0.1975	0.0000	5.063	90
95	0.0000	5.0633	25.6369	***********	***********	0.1975	0.0000	5.063	95
100	0.0000	5.0633	25.6369	***********	***********	0.1975	0.0000	5.063	100

EXPANDED INTEREST TABLES

$I = 20.00\ \%$

n	(P/F)	(P/A)	(P/G)	(F/P)	(F/A)	(A/P)	(A/F)	(A/G)	n
1	0.8333	0.8333	0.0000	1.2000	1.0000	1.2000	1.0000	0.000	1
2	0.6944	1.5278	0.6944	1.4400	2.2000	0.6545	0.4545	0.454	2
3	0.5787	2.1065	1.8519	1.7280	3.6400	0.4747	0.2747	0.879	3
4	0.4823	2.5887	3.2986	2.0736	5.3680	0.3863	0.1863	1.274	4
5	0.4019	2.9906	4.9061	2.4883	7.4416	0.3344	0.1344	1.640	5
6	0.3349	3.3255	6.5806	2.9860	9.9299	0.3007	0.1007	1.978	6
7	0.2791	3.6046	8.2551	3.5832	12.9159	0.2774	0.0774	2.290	7
8	0.2326	3.8372	9.8831	4.2998	16.4991	0.2606	0.0606	2.575	8
9	0.1938	4.0310	11.4335	5.1598	20.7989	0.2481	0.0481	2.836	9
10	0.1615	4.1925	12.8871	6.1917	25.9587	0.2385	0.0385	3.073	10
11	0.1346	4.3271	14.2330	7.4301	32.1504	0.2311	0.0311	3.289	11
12	0.1122	4.4392	15.4667	8.9161	39.5805	0.2253	0.0253	3.484	12
13	0.0935	4.5327	16.5883	10.6993	48.4966	0.2206	0.0206	3.659	13
14	0.0779	4.6106	17.6008	12.8392	59.1959	0.2169	0.0169	3.817	14
15	0.0649	4.6755	18.5095	15.4070	72.0351	0.2139	0.0139	3.958	15
16	0.0541	4.7296	19.3208	18.4884	87.4421	0.2114	0.0114	4.085	16
17	0.0451	4.7746	20.0419	22.1861	105.9306	0.2094	0.0094	4.197	17
18	0.0376	4.8122	20.6805	26.6233	128.1167	0.2078	0.0078	4.297	18
19	0.0313	4.8435	21.2439	31.9480	154.7400	0.2065	0.0065	4.386	19
20	0.0261	4.8696	21.7395	38.3376	186.6880	0.2054	0.0054	4.464	20
21	0.0217	4.8913	22.1742	46.0051	225.0256	0.2044	0.0044	4.533	21
22	0.0181	4.9094	22.5546	55.2061	271.0307	0.2037	0.0037	4.594	22
23	0.0151	4.9245	22.8867	66.2474	326.2369	0.2031	0.0031	4.647	23
24	0.0126	4.9371	23.1760	79.4968	392.4842	0.2025	0.0025	4.694	24
25	0.0105	4.9476	23.4276	95.3962	471.9811	0.2021	0.0021	4.735	25
26	0.0087	4.9563	23.6460	114.4755	567.3773	0.2018	0.0018	4.770	26
27	0.0073	4.9636	23.8353	137.3706	681.8528	0.2015	0.0015	4.802	27
28	0.0061	4.9697	23.9991	164.8447	819.2233	0.2012	0.0012	4.829	28
29	0.0051	4.9747	24.1406	197.8136	984.0680	0.2010	0.0010	4.852	29
30	0.0042	4.9789	24.2628	237.3763	1181.8816	0.2008	0.0008	4.873	30
31	0.0035	4.9824	24.3681	284.8516	1419.2579	0.2007	0.0007	4.890	31
32	0.0029	4.9854	24.4588	341.8219	1704.1095	0.2006	0.0006	4.906	32
33	0.0024	4.9878	24.5368	410.1863	2045.9314	0.2005	0.0005	4.919	33
34	0.0020	4.9898	24.6038	492.2235	2456.1176	0.2004	0.0004	4.930	34
35	0.0017	4.9915	24.6614	590.6682	2948.3411	0.2003	0.0003	4.940	35
36	0.0014	4.9929	24.7108	708.8019	3539.0094	0.2003	0.0003	4.949	36
37	0.0012	4.9941	24.7531	850.5622	4247.8112	0.2002	0.0002	4.956	37
38	0.0010	4.9951	24.7894	1020.6747	5098.3735	0.2002	0.0002	4.962	38
39	0.0008	4.9959	24.8204	1224.8096	6119.0482	0.2002	0.0002	4.968	39
40	0.0007	4.9966	24.8469	1469.7716	7343.8578	0.2001	0.0001	4.972	40
41	0.0006	4.9972	24.8696	1763.7259	8813.6294	0.2001	0.0001	4.976	41
42	0.0005	4.9976	24.8890	2116.4711	10577.3553	0.2001	0.0001	4.980	42
43	0.0004	4.9980	24.9055	2539.7653	12693.8263	0.2001	0.0001	4.983	43
44	0.0003	4.9984	24.9196	3047.7183	15233.5916	0.2001	0.0001	4.985	44
45	0.0003	4.9986	24.9316	3657.2620	18281.3099	0.2001	0.0001	4.987	45
46	0.0002	4.9989	24.9419	4388.7144	21938.5719	0.2000	0.0000	4.989	46
47	0.0002	4.9991	24.9506	5266.4573	26327.2863	0.2000	0.0000	4.991	47
48	0.0002	4.9992	24.9581	6319.7487	31593.7436	0.2000	0.0000	4.992	48
49	0.0001	4.9993	24.9644	7583.6985	37913.4923	0.2000	0.0000	4.993	49
50	0.0001	4.9995	24.9698	9100.4382	45497.1908	0.2000	0.0000	4.994	50
51	0.0001	4.9995	24.9744	10920.5258	54597.6289	0.2000	0.0000	4.995	51
52	0.0001	4.9996	24.9783	13104.6309	65518.1547	0.2000	0.0000	4.996	52
53	0.0001	4.9997	24.9816	15725.5571	78622.7856	0.2000	0.0000	4.996	53
54	0.0001	4.9997	24.9844	18870.6685	94348.3427	0.2000	0.0000	4.997	54
55	0.0000	4.9998	24.9868	22644.8023	113219.0113	0.2000	0.0000	4.997	55
60	0.0000	4.9999	24.9942	56347.5144	281732.5718	0.2000	0.0000	4.998	60
65	0.0000	5.0000	24.9975	140210.6469	701048.2346	0.2000	0.0000	4.999	65
70	0.0000	5.0000	24.9989	348888.9569	1744439.7847	0.2000	0.0000	4.999	70
75	0.0000	5.0000	24.9995	868147.3693	4340731.8466	0.2000	0.0000	4.999	75
80	0.0000	5.0000	24.9998	2160228.4620	************	0.2000	0.0000	5.000	80
85	0.0000	5.0000	24.9999	5375339.6866	************	0.2000	0.0000	5.000	85
90	0.0000	5.0000	25.0000	************	************	0.2000	0.0000	5.000	90
95	0.0000	5.0000	25.0000	************	************	0.2000	0.0000	5.000	95
100	0.0000	5.0000	25.0000	************	************	0.2000	0.0000	5.000	100

$I = 20.25 \%$

n	(P/F)	(P/A)	(P/G)	(F/P)	(F/A)	(A/P)	(A/F)	(A/G)	n
1	0.8316	0.8316	0.0000	1.2025	1.0000	1.2025	1.0000	0.000	1
2	0.6916	1.5232	0.6916	1.4460	2.2025	0.6565	0.4540	0.454	2
3	0.5751	2.0983	1.8418	1.7388	3.6485	0.4766	0.2741	0.877	3
4	0.4783	2.5765	3.2765	2.0909	5.3873	0.3881	0.1856	1.271	4
5	0.3977	2.9742	4.8674	2.5143	7.4783	0.3362	0.1337	1.636	5
6	0.3307	3.3050	6.5211	3.0235	9.9926	0.3026	0.1001	1.973	6
7	0.2750	3.5800	8.1714	3.6358	13.0161	0.2793	0.0768	2.282	7
8	0.2287	3.8088	9.7725	4.3720	16.6519	0.2626	0.0601	2.565	8
9	0.1902	3.9990	11.2942	5.2573	21.0239	0.2501	0.0476	2.824	9
10	0.1582	4.1571	12.7178	6.3219	26.2812	0.2405	0.0380	3.059	10
11	0.1315	4.2887	14.0332	7.6021	32.6032	0.2332	0.0307	3.272	11
12	0.1094	4.3981	15.2365	9.1416	40.2053	0.2274	0.0249	3.464	12
13	0.0910	4.4890	16.3281	10.9927	49.3469	0.2228	0.0203	3.637	13
14	0.0756	4.5647	17.3116	13.2188	60.3396	0.2191	0.0166	3.792	14
15	0.0629	4.6276	18.1923	15.8956	73.5584	0.2161	0.0136	3.931	15
16	0.0523	4.6799	18.9771	19.1144	89.4540	0.2137	0.0112	4.055	16
17	0.0435	4.7234	19.6732	22.9851	108.5684	0.2117	0.0092	4.165	17
18	0.0362	4.7596	20.2882	27.6396	131.5535	0.2101	0.0076	4.262	18
19	0.0301	4.7897	20.8298	33.2366	159.1931	0.2088	0.0063	4.348	19
20	0.0250	4.8147	21.3052	39.9670	192.4297	0.2077	0.0052	4.425	20
21	0.0208	4.8355	21.7213	48.0603	232.3967	0.2068	0.0043	4.492	21
22	0.0173	4.8528	22.0847	57.7926	280.4570	0.2061	0.0036	4.550	22
23	0.0144	4.8672	22.4013	69.4955	338.2496	0.2055	0.0030	4.602	23
24	0.0120	4.8792	22.6765	83.5684	407.7451	0.2050	0.0025	4.647	24
25	0.0100	4.8891	22.9153	100.4910	491.3135	0.2045	0.0020	4.687	25
26	0.0083	4.8974	23.1222	120.8404	591.8045	0.2042	0.0017	4.721	26
27	0.0069	4.9043	23.3011	145.3106	712.6449	0.2039	0.0014	4.751	27
28	0.0057	4.9100	23.4556	174.7360	857.9555	0.2037	0.0012	4.777	28
29	0.0048	4.9148	23.5889	210.1200	1032.6915	0.2035	0.0010	4.799	29
30	0.0040	4.9187	23.7037	252.6693	1242.8116	0.2033	0.0008	4.819	30
31	0.0033	4.9220	23.8024	303.8349	1495.4809	0.2032	0.0007	4.835	31
32	0.0027	4.9248	23.8873	365.3614	1799.3158	0.2031	0.0006	4.850	32
33	0.0023	4.9270	23.9601	439.3471	2164.6772	0.2030	0.0005	4.863	33
34	0.0019	4.9289	24.0226	528.3149	2604.0244	0.2029	0.0004	4.873	34
35	0.0016	4.9305	24.0761	635.2987	3132.3393	0.2028	0.0003	4.883	35
36	0.0013	4.9318	24.1219	763.9467	3767.6380	0.2028	0.0003	4.891	36
37	0.0011	4.9329	24.1611	918.6459	4531.5848	0.2027	0.0002	4.898	37
38	0.0009	4.9338	24.1946	1104.6717	5450.2307	0.2027	0.0002	4.903	38
39	0.0008	4.9346	24.2232	1328.3677	6554.9024	0.2027	0.0002	4.908	39
40	0.0006	4.9352	24.2476	1597.3622	7883.2701	0.2026	0.0001	4.913	40
41	0.0005	4.9357	24.2684	1920.8280	9480.6323	0.2026	0.0001	4.916	41
42	0.0004	4.9361	24.2862	2309.7957	11401.4603	0.2026	0.0001	4.920	42
43	0.0004	4.9365	24.3013	2777.5294	13711.2561	0.2026	0.0001	4.922	43
44	0.0003	4.9368	24.3142	3339.9790	16488.7854	0.2026	0.0001	4.925	44
45	0.0002	4.9370	24.3251	4016.3248	19828.7645	0.2026	0.0001	4.927	45
46	0.0002	4.9372	24.3344	4829.6306	23845.0893	0.2025	0.0000	4.928	46
47	0.0002	4.9374	24.3424	5807.6308	28674.7198	0.2025	0.0000	4.930	47
48	0.0001	4.9376	24.3491	6983.6760	34482.3506	0.2025	0.0000	4.931	48
49	0.0001	4.9377	24.3548	8397.8704	41466.0266	0.2025	0.0000	4.932	49
50	0.0001	4.9378	24.3597	10098.4391	49863.8970	0.2025	0.0000	4.933	50
51	0.0001	4.9379	24.3638	12143.3731	59962.3361	0.2025	0.0000	4.934	51
52	0.0001	4.9379	24.3673	14602.4061	72105.7092	0.2025	0.0000	4.934	52
53	0.0001	4.9380	24.3702	17559.3933	86708.1153	0.2025	0.0000	4.935	53
54	0.0000	4.9380	24.3727	21115.1705	104267.5086	0.2025	0.0000	4.935	54
55	0.0000	4.9381	24.3749	25390.9925	125382.6791	0.2025	0.0000	4.936	55
60	0.0000	4.9382	24.3815	63841.7970	315263.1949	0.2025	0.0000	4.937	60
65	0.0000	4.9382	24.3844	160520.5089	792688.9330	0.2025	0.0000	4.937	65
70	0.0000	4.9383	24.3856	403604.4567	1993103.4900	0.2025	0.0000	4.938	70
75	0.0000	4.9383	24.3861	1014802.1495	5011363.7011	0.2025	0.0000	4.938	75
80	0.0000	4.9383	24.3864	2551565.9835	************	0.2025	0.0000	4.938	80
85	0.0000	4.9383	24.3865	6415525.4022	************	0.2025	0.0000	4.938	85
90	0.0000	4.9383	24.3865	************	************	0.2025	0.0000	4.938	90
95	0.0000	4.9383	24.3865	************	************	0.2025	0.0000	4.938	95
100	0.0000	4.9383	24.3865	************	************	0.2025	0.0000	4.938	100

$I = 20.50\ \%$

n	(P/F)	(P/A)	(P/G)	(F/P)	(F/A)	(A/P)	(A/F)	(A/G)	n
1	0.8299	0.8299	0.0000	1.2050	1.0000	1.2050	1.0000	0.000	1
2	0.6887	1.5186	0.6887	1.4520	2.2050	0.6585	0.4535	0.453	2
3	0.5715	2.0901	1.8318	1.7497	3.6570	0.4784	0.2734	0.876	3
4	0.4743	2.5644	3.2546	2.1084	5.4067	0.3900	0.1850	1.269	4
5	0.3936	2.9580	4.8291	2.5406	7.5151	0.3381	0.1331	1.632	5
6	0.3266	3.2847	6.4623	3.0614	10.0557	0.3044	0.0994	1.967	6
7	0.2711	3.5557	8.0888	3.6890	13.1171	0.2812	0.0762	2.274	7
8	0.2250	3.7807	9.6635	4.4453	16.8061	0.2645	0.0595	2.556	8
9	0.1867	3.9674	11.1570	5.3565	21.2514	0.2521	0.0471	2.812	9
10	0.1549	4.1223	12.5513	6.4546	26.6079	0.2426	0.0376	3.044	10
11	0.1286	4.2509	13.8370	7.7778	33.0625	0.2352	0.0302	3.255	11
12	0.1067	4.3576	15.0107	9.3723	40.8403	0.2295	0.0245	3.444	12
13	0.0885	4.4461	16.0733	11.2936	50.2126	0.2249	0.0199	3.615	13
14	0.0735	4.5196	17.0285	13.6088	61.5062	0.2213	0.0163	3.767	14
15	0.0610	4.5806	17.8823	16.3986	75.1149	0.2183	0.0133	3.903	15
16	0.0506	4.6312	18.6414	19.7603	91.5135	0.2159	0.0109	4.025	16
17	0.0420	4.6732	19.3133	23.8111	111.2737	0.2140	0.0090	4.132	17
18	0.0349	4.7080	19.9058	28.6924	135.0849	0.2124	0.0074	4.228	18
19	0.0289	4.7370	20.4264	34.5743	163.7773	0.2111	0.0061	4.312	19
20	0.0240	4.7610	20.8825	41.6621	198.3516	0.2100	0.0050	4.386	20
21	0.0199	4.7809	21.2809	50.2028	240.0137	0.2092	0.0042	4.451	21
22	0.0165	4.7974	21.6280	60.4944	290.2165	0.2084	0.0034	4.508	22
23	0.0137	4.8111	21.9298	72.8957	350.7109	0.2079	0.0029	4.558	23
24	0.0114	4.8225	22.1917	87.8394	423.6066	0.2074	0.0024	4.601	24
25	0.0094	4.8320	22.4184	105.8464	511.4460	0.2070	0.0020	4.639	25
26	0.0078	4.8398	22.6144	127.5449	617.2924	0.2066	0.0016	4.672	26
27	0.0065	4.8463	22.7836	153.6916	744.8373	0.2063	0.0013	4.701	27
28	0.0054	4.8517	22.9294	185.1984	898.5290	0.2061	0.0011	4.726	28
29	0.0045	4.8562	23.0548	223.1641	1083.7274	0.2059	0.0009	4.747	29
30	0.0037	4.8599	23.1627	268.9128	1306.8915	0.2058	0.0008	4.766	30
31	0.0031	4.8630	23.2553	324.0399	1575.8043	0.2056	0.0006	4.782	31
32	0.0026	4.8656	23.3346	390.4680	1899.8441	0.2055	0.0005	4.795	32
33	0.0021	4.8677	23.4027	470.5140	2290.3122	0.2054	0.0004	4.807	33
34	0.0018	4.8694	23.4609	566.9694	2760.8262	0.2054	0.0004	4.818	34
35	0.0015	4.8709	23.5106	683.1981	3327.7955	0.2053	0.0003	4.826	35
36	0.0012	4.8721	23.5531	823.2537	4010.9936	0.2052	0.0002	4.834	36
37	0.0010	4.8731	23.5894	992.0207	4834.2473	0.2052	0.0002	4.840	37
38	0.0008	4.8740	23.6204	1195.3849	5826.2680	0.2052	0.0002	4.846	38
39	0.0007	4.8747	23.6468	1440.4389	7021.6530	0.2051	0.0001	4.851	39
40	0.0006	4.8752	23.6692	1735.7288	8462.0918	0.2051	0.0001	4.855	40
41	0.0005	4.8757	23.6884	2091.5532	10197.8207	0.2051	0.0001	4.858	41
42	0.0004	4.8761	23.7046	2520.3217	12289.3739	0.2051	0.0001	4.861	42
43	0.0003	4.8764	23.7185	3036.9876	14809.6956	0.2051	0.0001	4.863	43
44	0.0003	4.8767	23.7302	3659.5700	17846.6831	0.2051	0.0001	4.866	44
45	0.0002	4.8769	23.7402	4409.7819	21506.2532	0.2050	0.0000	4.867	45
46	0.0002	4.8771	23.7487	5313.7872	25916.0351	0.2050	0.0000	4.869	46
47	0.0002	4.8773	23.7558	6403.1136	31229.8223	0.2050	0.0000	4.870	47
48	0.0001	4.8774	23.7619	7715.7519	37632.9359	0.2050	0.0000	4.871	48
49	0.0001	4.8775	23.7671	9297.4810	45348.6877	0.2050	0.0000	4.872	49
50	0.0001	4.8776	23.7715	11203.4646	54646.1687	0.2050	0.0000	4.873	50
51	0.0001	4.8777	23.7752	13500.1748	65849.6333	0.2050	0.0000	4.874	51
52	0.0001	4.8777	23.7783	16267.7107	79349.8081	0.2050	0.0000	4.874	52
53	0.0001	4.8778	23.7810	19602.5913	95617.5188	0.2050	0.0000	4.875	53
54	0.0000	4.8778	23.7832	23621.1226	115220.1101	0.2050	0.0000	4.875	54
55	0.0000	4.8779	23.7851	28463.4527	138841.2327	0.2050	0.0000	4.876	55
60	0.0000	4.8780	23.7910	72314.0716	352746.6905	0.2050	0.0000	4.877	60
65	0.0000	4.8780	23.7935	183720.6821	896193.5713	0.2050	0.0000	4.877	65
70	0.0000	4.8780	23.7946	466759.6266	2276871.3494	0.2050	0.0000	4.877	70
75	0.0000	4.8780	23.7950	1185846.6152	5784612.7573	0.2050	0.0000	4.878	75
80	0.0000	4.8780	23.7952	3012754.5629	************	0.2050	0.0000	4.878	80
85	0.0000	4.8780	23.7953	7654185.5747	************	0.2050	0.0000	4.878	85
90	0.0000	4.8780	23.7953	************	************	0.2050	0.0000	4.878	90
95	0.0000	4.8780	23.7954	************	************	0.2050	0.0000	4.878	95
100	0.0000	4.8780	23.7954	************	************	0.2050	0.0000	4.878	100

$I = 20.75\ \%$

n	(P/F)	(P/A)	(P/G)	(F/P)	(F/A)	(A/P)	(A/F)	(A/G)	n
1	0.8282	0.8282	0.0000	1.2075	1.0000	1.2075	1.0000	0.000	1
2	0.6858	1.5140	0.6858	1.4581	2.2075	0.6605	0.4530	0.453	2
3	0.5680	2.0820	1.8218	1.7606	3.6656	0.4803	0.2728	0.875	3
4	0.4704	2.5524	3.2330	2.1259	5.4262	0.3918	0.1843	1.266	4
5	0.3896	2.9419	4.7912	2.5671	7.5521	0.3399	0.1324	1.628	5
6	0.3226	3.2645	6.4042	3.0997	10.1191	0.3063	0.0988	1.961	6
7	0.2672	3.5317	8.0072	3.7429	13.2189	0.2831	0.0756	2.267	7
8	0.2213	3.7530	9.5561	4.5196	16.9618	0.2665	0.0590	2.546	8
9	0.1832	3.9362	11.0220	5.4574	21.4814	0.2541	0.0466	2.800	9
10	0.1517	4.0880	12.3877	6.5898	26.9387	0.2446	0.0371	3.030	10
11	0.1257	4.2136	13.6445	7.9572	33.5285	0.2373	0.0298	3.238	11
12	0.1041	4.3177	14.7893	9.6083	41.4857	0.2316	0.0241	3.425	12
13	0.0862	4.4039	15.8236	11.6020	51.0940	0.2271	0.0196	3.593	13
14	0.0714	4.4753	16.7515	14.0094	62.6960	0.2234	0.0159	3.743	14
15	0.0591	4.5344	17.5791	16.9164	76.7054	0.2205	0.0130	3.876	15
16	0.0490	4.5833	18.3135	20.4265	93.6217	0.2182	0.0107	3.995	16
17	0.0405	4.6239	18.9622	24.6650	114.0483	0.2163	0.0088	4.100	17
18	0.0336	4.6575	19.5330	29.7830	138.7133	0.2147	0.0072	4.193	18
19	0.0278	4.6853	20.0335	35.9630	168.4963	0.2134	0.0059	4.275	19
20	0.0230	4.7083	20.4710	43.4253	204.4593	0.2124	0.0049	4.347	20
21	0.0191	4.7274	20.8524	52.4360	247.8846	0.2115	0.0040	4.411	21
22	0.0158	4.7432	21.1841	63.3165	300.3206	0.2108	0.0033	4.466	22
23	0.0131	4.7562	21.4719	76.4547	363.6371	0.2102	0.0027	4.514	23
24	0.0108	4.7671	21.7210	92.3191	440.0918	0.2098	0.0023	4.556	24
25	0.0090	4.7760	21.9363	111.4753	532.4109	0.2094	0.0019	4.593	25
26	0.0074	4.7835	22.1220	134.6064	643.8861	0.2091	0.0016	4.624	26
27	0.0062	4.7896	22.2820	162.5372	778.4925	0.2088	0.0013	4.652	27
28	0.0051	4.7947	22.4196	196.2637	941.0297	0.2086	0.0011	4.675	28
29	0.0042	4.7989	22.5377	236.9884	1137.2934	0.2084	0.0009	4.696	29
30	0.0035	4.8024	22.6390	286.1635	1374.2817	0.2082	0.0007	4.714	30
31	0.0029	4.8053	22.7259	345.5424	1660.4452	0.2081	0.0006	4.729	31
32	0.0024	4.8077	22.8002	417.2424	2005.9876	0.2080	0.0005	4.742	32
33	0.0020	4.8097	22.8637	503.8202	2423.2300	0.2079	0.0004	4.753	33
34	0.0016	4.8114	22.9179	608.3629	2927.0502	0.2078	0.0003	4.763	34
35	0.0014	4.8127	22.9642	734.5982	3535.4132	0.2078	0.0003	4.771	35
36	0.0011	4.8138	23.0037	887.0274	4270.0114	0.2077	0.0002	4.778	36
37	0.0009	4.8148	23.0373	1071.0855	5157.0388	0.2077	0.0002	4.784	37
38	0.0008	4.8156	23.0659	1293.3358	6228.1243	0.2077	0.0002	4.789	38
39	0.0006	4.8162	23.0902	1561.7030	7521.4601	0.2076	0.0001	4.794	39
40	0.0005	4.8167	23.1109	1885.7563	9083.1631	0.2076	0.0001	4.798	40
41	0.0004	4.8172	23.1285	2277.0508	10968.9194	0.2076	0.0001	4.801	41
42	0.0004	4.8175	23.1434	2749.5388	13245.9702	0.2076	0.0001	4.804	42
43	0.0003	4.8178	23.1560	3320.0681	15995.5090	0.2076	0.0001	4.806	43
44	0.0002	4.8181	23.1667	4008.9823	19315.5772	0.2076	0.0001	4.808	44
45	0.0002	4.8183	23.1758	4840.8461	23324.5594	0.2075	0.0000	4.810	45
46	0.0002	4.8185	23.1835	5845.3216	28165.4055	0.2075	0.0000	4.811	46
47	0.0001	4.8186	23.1901	7058.2259	34010.7271	0.2075	0.0000	4.812	47
48	0.0001	4.8187	23.1956	8522.8078	41068.9530	0.2075	0.0000	4.813	48
49	0.0001	4.8188	23.2002	10291.2904	49591.7608	0.2075	0.0000	4.814	49
50	0.0001	4.8189	23.2042	12426.7331	59883.0510	0.2075	0.0000	4.815	50
51	0.0001	4.8190	23.2075	15005.2802	72309.7843	0.2075	0.0000	4.815	51
52	0.0001	4.8190	23.2103	18118.8759	87315.0645	0.2075	0.0000	4.816	52
53	0.0000	4.8191	23.2127	21878.5426	105433.9404	0.2075	0.0000	4.816	53
54	0.0000	4.8191	23.2147	26418.3402	127312.4830	0.2075	0.0000	4.817	54
55	0.0000	4.8191	23.2164	31900.1458	153730.8232	0.2075	0.0000	4.817	55
60	0.0000	4.8192	23.2216	81889.5275	394643.5062	0.2075	0.0000	4.818	60
65	0.0000	4.8193	23.2238	210215.1745	1013080.3588	0.2075	0.0000	4.819	65
70	0.0000	4.8193	23.2248	539634.5651	2600643.6871	0.2075	0.0000	4.819	70
75	0.0000	4.8193	23.2252	1385273.2781	6676010.9788	0.2075	0.0000	4.819	75
80	0.0000	4.8193	23.2253	3556076.9809	***********	0.2075	0.0000	4.819	80
85	0.0000	4.8193	23.2254	9128656.1969	***********	0.2075	0.0000	4.819	85
90	0.0000	4.8193	23.2254	***********	***********	0.2075	0.0000	4.819	90
95	0.0000	4.8193	23.2254	***********	***********	0.2075	0.0000	4.819	95
100	0.0000	4.8193	23.2254	***********	***********	0.2075	0.0000	4.819	100

EXPANDED INTEREST TABLES

$I = 21.00 \%$

n	(P/F)	(P/A)	(P/G)	(F/P)	(F/A)	(A/P)	(A/F)	(A/G)	n
1	0.8264	0.8264	0.0000	1.2100	1.0000	1.2100	1.0000	0.000	1
2	0.6830	1.5095	0.6830	1.4641	2.2100	0.6625	0.4525	0.452	2
3	0.5645	2.0739	1.8120	1.7716	3.6741	0.4822	0.2722	0.873	3
4	0.4665	2.5404	3.2115	2.1436	5.4457	0.3936	0.1836	1.264	4
5	0.3855	2.9260	4.7537	2.5937	7.5892	0.3418	0.1318	1.624	5
6	0.3186	3.2446	6.3468	3.1384	10.1830	0.3082	0.0982	1.956	6
7	0.2633	3.5079	7.9268	3.7975	13.3214	0.2851	0.0751	2.259	7
8	0.2176	3.7256	9.4502	4.5950	17.1189	0.2684	0.0584	2.536	8
9	0.1799	3.9054	10.8891	5.5599	21.7139	0.2561	0.0461	2.788	9
10	0.1486	4.0541	12.2269	6.7275	27.2738	0.2467	0.0367	3.015	10
11	0.1228	4.1769	13.4553	8.1403	34.0013	0.2394	0.0294	3.221	11
12	0.1015	4.2784	14.5721	9.8497	42.1416	0.2337	0.0237	3.405	12
13	0.0839	4.3624	15.5790	11.9182	51.9913	0.2292	0.0192	3.571	13
14	0.0693	4.4317	16.4804	14.4210	63.9095	0.2256	0.0156	3.718	14
15	0.0573	4.4890	17.2828	17.4494	78.3305	0.2228	0.0128	3.850	15
16	0.0474	4.5364	17.9932	21.1138	95.7799	0.2204	0.0104	3.966	16
17	0.0391	4.5755	18.6195	25.5477	116.8937	0.2186	0.0086	4.069	17
18	0.0323	4.6079	19.1694	30.9127	142.4413	0.2170	0.0070	4.160	18
19	0.0267	4.6346	19.6506	37.4043	173.3540	0.2158	0.0058	4.240	19
20	0.0221	4.6567	20.0704	45.2593	210.7584	0.2147	0.0047	4.310	20
21	0.0183	4.6750	20.4356	54.7637	256.0176	0.2139	0.0039	4.371	21
22	0.0151	4.6900	20.7526	66.2641	310.7813	0.2132	0.0032	4.424	22
23	0.0125	4.7025	21.0269	80.1795	377.0454	0.2127	0.0027	4.471	23
24	0.0103	4.7128	21.2640	97.0172	457.2249	0.2122	0.0022	4.511	24
25	0.0085	4.7213	21.4685	117.3909	554.2422	0.2118	0.0018	4.547	25
26	0.0070	4.7284	21.6445	142.0429	671.6330	0.2115	0.0015	4.577	26
27	0.0058	4.7342	21.7957	171.8719	813.6759	0.2112	0.0012	4.603	27
28	0.0048	4.7390	21.9256	207.9651	985.5479	0.2110	0.0010	4.626	28
29	0.0040	4.7430	22.0368	251.6377	1193.5129	0.2108	0.0008	4.646	29
30	0.0033	4.7463	22.1321	304.4816	1445.1507	0.2107	0.0007	4.663	30
31	0.0027	4.7490	22.2135	368.4228	1749.6323	0.2106	0.0006	4.677	31
32	0.0022	4.7512	22.2830	445.7916	2118.0551	0.2105	0.0005	4.690	32
33	0.0019	4.7531	22.3424	539.4078	2563.8467	0.2104	0.0004	4.700	33
34	0.0015	4.7546	22.3929	652.6834	3103.2545	0.2103	0.0003	4.709	34
35	0.0013	4.7559	22.4360	789.7470	3755.9379	0.2103	0.0003	4.717	35
36	0.0010	4.7569	22.4726	955.5938	4545.6848	0.2102	0.0002	4.724	36
37	0.0009	4.7578	22.5037	1156.2685	5501.2787	0.2102	0.0002	4.729	37
38	0.0007	4.7585	22.5302	1399.0849	6657.5472	0.2102	0.0002	4.734	38
39	0.0006	4.7591	22.5526	1692.8927	8056.6321	0.2101	0.0001	4.738	39
40	0.0005	4.7596	22.5717	2048.4002	9749.5248	0.2101	0.0001	4.742	40
41	0.0004	4.7600	22.5878	2478.5643	11797.9250	0.2101	0.0001	4.745	41
42	0.0003	4.7603	22.6015	2999.0628	14276.4893	0.2101	0.0001	4.747	42
43	0.0003	4.7606	22.6131	3628.8659	17275.5521	0.2101	0.0001	4.750	43
44	0.0002	4.7608	22.6229	4390.9278	20904.4180	0.2100	0.0000	4.751	44
45	0.0002	4.7610	22.6311	5313.0226	25295.3458	0.2100	0.0000	4.753	45
46	0.0002	4.7612	22.6381	6428.7574	30608.3684	0.2100	0.0000	4.754	46
47	0.0001	4.7613	22.6441	7778.7964	37037.1257	0.2100	0.0000	4.755	47
48	0.0001	4.7614	22.6490	9412.3437	44815.9221	0.2100	0.0000	4.756	48
49	0.0001	4.7615	22.6533	11388.9358	54228.2658	0.2100	0.0000	4.757	49
50	0.0001	4.7616	22.6568	13780.6123	65617.2016	0.2100	0.0000	4.758	50
51	0.0001	4.7616	22.6598	16674.5409	79397.8140	0.2100	0.0000	4.758	51
52	0.0000	4.7617	22.6623	20176.1945	96072.3549	0.2100	0.0000	4.759	52
53	0.0000	4.7617	22.6645	24413.1954	116248.5494	0.2100	0.0000	4.759	53
54	0.0000	4.7617	22.6663	29539.9664	140661.7448	0.2100	0.0000	4.760	54
55	0.0000	4.7618	22.6678	35743.3594	170201.7112	0.2100	0.0000	4.760	55
60	0.0000	4.7619	22.6724	92709.0688	441466.9944	0.2100	0.0000	4.761	60
65	0.0000	4.7619	22.6744	240463.4482	1145059.2773	0.2100	0.0000	4.761	65
70	0.0000	4.7619	22.6752	623700.2558	2969996.4561	0.2100	0.0000	4.761	70
75	0.0000	4.7619	22.6755	1617717.8358	7703413.5037	0.2100	0.0000	4.761	75
80	0.0000	4.7619	22.6756	4195943.4391	************	0.2100	0.0000	4.761	80
85	0.0000	4.7619	22.6757	************	************	0.2100	0.0000	4.761	85
90	0.0000	4.7619	22.6757	************	************	0.2100	0.0000	4.761	90
95	0.0000	4.7619	22.6757	************	************	0.2100	0.0000	4.761	95
100	0.0000	4.7619	22.6757	************	************	0.2100	0.0000	4.761	100

$I = 21.25\%$

n	(P/F)	(P/A)	(P/G)	(F/P)	(F/A)	(A/P)	(A/F)	(A/G)	n
1	0.8247	0.8247	0.0000	1.2125	1.0000	1.2125	1.0000	0.000	1
2	0.6802	1.5049	0.6802	1.4702	2.2125	0.6645	0.4520	0.452	2
3	0.5610	2.0659	1.8022	1.7826	3.6827	0.4840	0.2715	0.872	3
4	0.4627	2.5286	3.1902	2.1614	5.4652	0.3955	0.1830	1.261	4
5	0.3816	2.9102	4.7165	2.6206	7.6266	0.3436	0.1311	1.620	5
6	0.3147	3.2249	6.2901	3.1775	10.2472	0.3101	0.0976	1.950	6
7	0.2596	3.4845	7.8474	3.8528	13.4248	0.2870	0.0745	2.252	7
8	0.2141	3.6985	9.3459	4.6715	17.2775	0.2704	0.0579	2.526	8
9	0.1765	3.8751	10.7582	5.6642	21.9490	0.2581	0.0456	2.776	9
10	0.1456	4.0207	12.0687	6.8678	27.6132	0.2487	0.0362	3.001	10
11	0.1201	4.1408	13.2696	8.3272	34.4810	0.2415	0.0290	3.204	11
12	0.0990	4.2398	14.3591	10.0967	42.8082	0.2359	0.0234	3.386	12
13	0.0817	4.3215	15.3393	12.2423	52.9049	0.2314	0.0189	3.549	13
14	0.0674	4.3889	16.2151	14.8438	65.1472	0.2278	0.0153	3.694	14
15	0.0556	4.4444	16.9929	17.9981	79.9910	0.2250	0.0125	3.823	15
16	0.0458	4.4902	17.6803	21.8227	97.9891	0.2227	0.0102	3.937	16
17	0.0378	4.5280	18.2850	26.4600	119.8117	0.2208	0.0083	4.038	17
18	0.0312	4.5592	18.8148	32.0827	146.2717	0.2193	0.0068	4.126	18
19	0.0257	4.5849	19.2776	38.9003	178.3545	0.2181	0.0056	4.204	19
20	0.0212	4.6061	19.6804	47.1666	217.2548	0.2171	0.0046	4.272	20
21	0.0175	4.6236	20.0301	57.1896	264.4214	0.2163	0.0038	4.332	21
22	0.0144	4.6380	20.3329	69.3423	321.6110	0.2156	0.0031	4.384	22
23	0.0119	4.6499	20.5946	84.0776	390.9533	0.2151	0.0026	4.429	23
24	0.0098	4.6597	20.8202	101.9441	475.0309	0.2146	0.0021	4.468	24
25	0.0081	4.6678	21.0144	123.6072	576.9749	0.2142	0.0017	4.502	25
26	0.0067	4.6745	21.1812	149.8737	700.5821	0.2139	0.0014	4.531	26
27	0.0055	4.6800	21.3243	181.7219	850.4558	0.2137	0.0012	4.556	27
28	0.0045	4.6845	21.4468	220.3378	1032.1777	0.2135	0.0010	4.578	28
29	0.0037	4.6883	21.5516	267.1595	1252.5154	0.2133	0.0008	4.596	29
30	0.0031	4.6914	21.6411	323.9309	1519.6750	0.2132	0.0007	4.613	30
31	0.0025	4.6939	21.7175	392.7663	1843.6059	0.2130	0.0005	4.626	31
32	0.0021	4.6960	21.7826	476.2291	2236.3721	0.2129	0.0004	4.638	32
33	0.0017	4.6977	21.8380	577.4278	2712.6012	0.2129	0.0004	4.648	33
34	0.0014	4.6992	21.8852	700.1312	3290.0290	0.2128	0.0003	4.657	34
35	0.0012	4.7003	21.9252	848.9090	3990.1602	0.2128	0.0003	4.664	35
36	0.0010	4.7013	21.9592	1029.3022	4839.0692	0.2127	0.0002	4.670	36
37	0.0008	4.7021	21.9881	1248.0289	5868.3714	0.2127	0.0002	4.676	37
38	0.0007	4.7028	22.0125	1513.2351	7116.4003	0.2126	0.0001	4.680	38
39	0.0005	4.7033	22.0332	1834.7975	8629.6354	0.2126	0.0001	4.684	39
40	0.0004	4.7038	22.0508	2224.6920	10464.4329	0.2126	0.0001	4.687	40
41	0.0004	4.7041	22.0656	2697.4390	12689.1249	0.2126	0.0001	4.690	41
42	0.0003	4.7044	22.0781	3270.6448	15386.5639	0.2126	0.0001	4.693	42
43	0.0003	4.7047	22.0887	3965.6569	18657.2087	0.2126	0.0001	4.695	43
44	0.0002	4.7049	22.0977	4808.3589	22622.8656	0.2125	0.0000	4.696	44
45	0.0002	4.7051	22.1052	5830.1352	27431.2245	0.2125	0.0000	4.698	45
46	0.0001	4.7052	22.1116	7069.0390	33261.3598	0.2125	0.0000	4.699	46
47	0.0001	4.7053	22.1169	8571.2097	40330.3987	0.2125	0.0000	4.700	47
48	0.0001	4.7054	22.1215	10392.5918	48901.6084	0.2125	0.0000	4.701	48
49	0.0001	4.7055	22.1253	12601.0176	59294.2002	0.2125	0.0000	4.702	49
50	0.0001	4.7056	22.1285	15278.7338	71895.2178	0.2125	0.0000	4.702	50
51	0.0001	4.7056	22.1312	18525.4647	87173.9516	0.2125	0.0000	4.703	51
52	0.0000	4.7057	22.1334	22462.1260	105699.4163	0.2125	0.0000	4.703	52
53	0.0000	4.7057	22.1354	27235.3277	128161.5422	0.2125	0.0000	4.703	53
54	0.0000	4.7057	22.1370	33022.8349	155396.8700	0.2125	0.0000	4.704	54
55	0.0000	4.7058	22.1383	40040.1873	188419.7048	0.2125	0.0000	4.704	55
60	0.0000	4.7058	22.1424	104931.2476	493789.4004	0.2125	0.0000	4.705	60
65	0.0000	4.7059	22.1441	274987.8926	1294055.9654	0.2125	0.0000	4.705	65
70	0.0000	4.7059	22.1448	720646.5456	3391273.1558	0.2125	0.0000	4.705	70
75	0.0000	4.7059	22.1451	1888561.1243	8887341.7615	0.2125	0.0000	4.705	75
80	0.0000	4.7059	22.1452	4949254.4466	************	0.2125	0.0000	4.705	80
85	0.0000	4.7059	22.1453	************	************	0.2125	0.0000	4.705	85
90	0.0000	4.7059	22.1453	************	************	0.2125	0.0000	4.705	90
95	0.0000	4.7059	22.1453	************	************	0.2125	0.0000	4.705	95
100	0.0000	4.7059	22.1453	************	************	0.2125	0.0000	4.705	100

EXPANDED INTEREST TABLES

$I = 21.50 \%$

n	(P/F)	(P/A)	(P/G)	(F/P)	(F/A)	(A/P)	(A/F)	(A/G)	n
1	0.8230	0.8230	0.0000	1.2150	1.0000	1.2150	1.0000	0.000	1
2	0.6774	1.5004	0.6774	1.4762	2.2150	0.6665	0.4515	0.451	2
3	0.5575	2.0580	1.7925	1.7936	3.6912	0.4859	0.2709	0.871	3
4	0.4589	2.5169	3.1691	2.1792	5.4848	0.3973	0.1823	1.259	4
5	0.3777	2.8945	4.6798	2.6478	7.6641	0.3455	0.1305	1.616	5
6	0.3108	3.2054	6.2340	3.2170	10.3119	0.3120	0.0970	1.944	6
7	0.2558	3.4612	7.7690	3.9087	13.5289	0.2889	0.0739	2.244	7
8	0.2106	3.6718	9.2430	4.7491	17.4376	0.2723	0.0573	2.517	8
9	0.1733	3.8451	10.6295	5.7701	22.1867	0.2601	0.0451	2.764	9
10	0.1426	3.9877	11.9132	7.0107	27.9568	0.2508	0.0358	2.987	10
11	0.1174	4.1051	13.0872	8.5180	34.9676	0.2436	0.0286	3.188	11
12	0.0966	4.2017	14.1501	10.3494	43.4856	0.2380	0.0230	3.367	12
13	0.0795	4.2813	15.1044	12.5745	53.8350	0.2336	0.0186	3.528	13
14	0.0655	4.3467	15.9553	15.2780	66.4095	0.2301	0.0151	3.670	14
15	0.0539	4.4006	16.7095	18.5628	81.6876	0.2272	0.0122	3.797	15
16	0.0443	4.4449	17.3745	22.5538	100.2504	0.2250	0.0100	3.908	16
17	0.0365	4.4814	17.9584	27.4029	122.8042	0.2231	0.0081	4.007	17
18	0.0300	4.5115	18.4690	33.2945	150.2072	0.2217	0.0067	4.093	18
19	0.0247	4.5362	18.9140	40.4529	183.5017	0.2204	0.0054	4.169	19
20	0.0203	4.5565	19.3005	49.1502	223.9546	0.2195	0.0045	4.235	20
21	0.0167	4.5733	19.6354	59.7175	273.1048	0.2187	0.0037	4.293	21
22	0.0138	4.5871	19.9249	72.5568	332.8223	0.2180	0.0030	4.343	22
23	0.0113	4.5984	20.1744	88.1565	405.3791	0.2175	0.0025	4.387	23
24	0.0093	4.6077	20.3892	107.1102	493.5356	0.2170	0.0020	4.425	24
25	0.0077	4.6154	20.5736	130.1388	600.6458	0.2167	0.0017	4.457	25
26	0.0063	4.6217	20.7317	158.1187	730.7846	0.2164	0.0014	4.485	26
27	0.0052	4.6270	20.8670	192.1142	888.9033	0.2161	0.0011	4.509	27
28	0.0043	4.6312	20.9827	233.4188	1081.0175	0.2159	0.0009	4.530	28
29	0.0035	4.6348	21.0814	283.6038	1314.4363	0.2158	0.0008	4.548	29
30	0.0029	4.6377	21.1656	344.5786	1598.0401	0.2156	0.0006	4.563	30
31	0.0024	4.6401	21.2372	418.6630	1942.6188	0.2155	0.0005	4.576	31
32	0.0020	4.6420	21.2982	508.6756	2361.2818	0.2154	0.0004	4.588	32
33	0.0016	4.6436	21.3500	618.0408	2869.9574	0.2153	0.0003	4.597	33
34	0.0013	4.6450	21.3939	750.9196	3487.9982	0.2153	0.0003	4.605	34
35	0.0011	4.6461	21.4312	912.3673	4238.9178	0.2152	0.0002	4.612	35
36	0.0009	4.6470	21.4628	1108.5263	5151.2852	0.2152	0.0002	4.618	36
37	0.0007	4.6477	21.4895	1346.8595	6259.8115	0.2152	0.0002	4.623	37
38	0.0006	4.6483	21.5121	1636.4343	7606.6709	0.2151	0.0001	4.627	38
39	0.0005	4.6488	21.5312	1988.2676	9243.1052	0.2151	0.0001	4.631	39
40	0.0004	4.6492	21.5473	2415.7452	11231.3728	0.2151	0.0001	4.634	40
41	0.0003	4.6496	21.5610	2935.1304	13647.1180	0.2151	0.0001	4.637	41
42	0.0003	4.6499	21.5725	3566.1834	16582.2483	0.2151	0.0001	4.639	42
43	0.0002	4.6501	21.5822	4332.9128	20148.4317	0.2150	0.0000	4.641	43
44	0.0002	4.6503	21.5903	5264.4891	24481.3446	0.2150	0.0000	4.642	44
45	0.0002	4.6504	21.5972	6396.3542	29745.8336	0.2150	0.0000	4.644	45
46	0.0001	4.6506	21.6030	7771.5704	36142.1879	0.2150	0.0000	4.645	46
47	0.0001	4.6507	21.6079	9442.4580	43913.7583	0.2150	0.0000	4.646	47
48	0.0001	4.6508	21.6120	11472.5865	53356.2163	0.2150	0.0000	4.647	48
49	0.0001	4.6508	21.6154	13939.1926	64828.8028	0.2150	0.0000	4.647	49
50	0.0001	4.6509	21.6183	16936.1190	78767.9954	0.2150	0.0000	4.648	50
51	0.0000	4.6509	21.6207	20577.3846	95704.1144	0.2150	0.0000	4.648	51
52	0.0000	4.6510	21.6228	25001.5223	116281.4990	0.2150	0.0000	4.649	52
53	0.0000	4.6510	21.6245	30376.8496	141283.0213	0.2150	0.0000	4.649	53
54	0.0000	4.6510	21.6259	36907.8722	171659.8708	0.2150	0.0000	4.649	54
55	0.0000	4.6511	21.6271	44843.0648	208567.7431	0.2150	0.0000	4.649	55
60	0.0000	4.6511	21.6308	118734.4312	552248.5172	0.2150	0.0000	4.650	60
65	0.0000	4.6511	21.6323	314382.2847	1462238.5334	0.2150	0.0000	4.651	65
70	0.0000	4.6512	21.6329	832414.1526	3871689.0817	0.2150	0.0000	4.651	70
75	0.0000	4.6512	21.6331	2204046.9681	************	0.2150	0.0000	4.651	75
80	0.0000	4.6512	21.6332	5835824.6587	************	0.2150	0.0000	4.651	80
85	0.0000	4.6512	21.6333	************	************	0.2150	0.0000	4.651	85
90	0.0000	4.6512	21.6333	************	************	0.2150	0.0000	4.651	90
95	0.0000	4.6512	21.6333	************	************	0.2150	0.0000	4.651	95
100	0.0000	4.6512	21.6333	************	************	0.2150	0.0000	4.651	100

$I = 21.75\%$

n	(P/F)	(P/A)	(P/G)	(F/P)	(F/A)	(A/P)	(A/F)	(A/G)	n
1	0.8214	0.8214	0.0000	1.2175	1.0000	1.2175	1.0000	0.000	1
2	0.6746	1.4960	0.6746	1.4823	2.2175	0.6685	0.4510	0.451	2
3	0.5541	2.0501	1.7828	1.8047	3.6998	0.4878	0.2703	0.869	3
4	0.4551	2.5052	3.1482	2.1972	5.5045	0.3992	0.1817	1.256	4
5	0.3738	2.8790	4.6434	2.6751	7.7017	0.3473	0.1298	1.612	5
6	0.3070	3.1861	6.1786	3.2570	10.3769	0.3139	0.0964	1.939	6
7	0.2522	3.4382	7.6917	3.9654	13.6338	0.2908	0.0733	2.237	7
8	0.2071	3.6454	9.1416	4.8278	17.5992	0.2743	0.0568	2.507	8
9	0.1701	3.8155	10.5027	5.8779	22.4270	0.2621	0.0446	2.752	9
10	0.1397	3.9552	11.7603	7.1563	28.3049	0.2528	0.0353	2.973	10
11	0.1148	4.0700	12.9080	8.7128	35.4612	0.2457	0.0282	3.171	11
12	0.0943	4.1643	13.9450	10.6079	44.1741	0.2401	0.0226	3.348	12
13	0.0774	4.2417	14.8742	12.9151	54.7819	0.2358	0.0183	3.506	13
14	0.0636	4.3053	15.7009	15.7241	67.6970	0.2323	0.0148	3.646	14
15	0.0522	4.3575	16.4322	19.1441	83.4211	0.2295	0.0120	3.771	15
16	0.0429	4.4004	17.0758	23.3079	102.5651	0.2272	0.0097	3.880	16
17	0.0352	4.4357	17.6396	28.3774	125.8731	0.2254	0.0079	3.976	17
18	0.0289	4.4646	18.1316	34.5495	154.2505	0.2240	0.0065	4.061	18
19	0.0238	4.4884	18.5596	42.0640	188.7999	0.2228	0.0053	4.135	19
20	0.0195	4.5079	18.9306	51.2129	230.8639	0.2218	0.0043	4.199	20
21	0.0160	4.5240	19.2513	62.3517	282.0768	0.2210	0.0035	4.255	21
22	0.0132	4.5371	19.5280	75.9132	344.4285	0.2204	0.0029	4.304	22
23	0.0108	4.5480	19.7660	92.4243	420.3417	0.2199	0.0024	4.346	23
24	0.0089	4.5568	19.9704	112.5266	512.7661	0.2195	0.0020	4.382	24
25	0.0073	4.5641	20.1456	137.0012	625.2927	0.2191	0.0016	4.413	25
26	0.0060	4.5701	20.2955	166.7989	762.2939	0.2188	0.0013	4.440	26
27	0.0049	4.5751	20.4235	203.0777	929.0928	0.2186	0.0011	4.464	27
28	0.0040	4.5791	20.5327	247.2471	1132.1704	0.2184	0.0009	4.484	28
29	0.0033	4.5824	20.6257	301.0233	1379.4175	0.2182	0.0007	4.501	29
30	0.0027	4.5852	20.7048	366.4959	1680.4408	0.2181	0.0006	4.515	30
31	0.0022	4.5874	20.7721	446.2087	2046.9367	0.2180	0.0005	4.528	31
32	0.0018	4.5892	20.8291	543.2591	2493.1454	0.2179	0.0004	4.538	32
33	0.0015	4.5907	20.8775	661.4180	3036.4046	0.2178	0.0003	4.547	33
34	0.0012	4.5920	20.9185	805.2764	3697.8226	0.2178	0.0003	4.555	34
35	0.0010	4.5930	20.9532	980.4240	4503.0990	0.2177	0.0002	4.562	35
36	0.0008	4.5938	20.9825	1193.6663	5483.5230	0.2177	0.0002	4.567	36
37	0.0007	4.5945	21.0073	1453.2887	6677.1893	0.2176	0.0001	4.572	37
38	0.0006	4.5951	21.0282	1769.3789	8130.4779	0.2176	0.0001	4.576	38
39	0.0005	4.5956	21.0458	2154.2189	9899.8569	0.2176	0.0001	4.579	39
40	0.0004	4.5959	21.0607	2622.7615	12054.0757	0.2176	0.0001	4.582	40
41	0.0003	4.5963	21.0732	3193.2121	14676.8372	0.2176	0.0001	4.584	41
42	0.0003	4.5965	21.0837	3887.7357	17870.0493	0.2176	0.0001	4.586	42
43	0.0002	4.5967	21.0926	4733.3182	21757.7850	0.2175	0.0000	4.588	43
44	0.0002	4.5969	21.1001	5762.8150	26491.1033	0.2175	0.0000	4.590	44
45	0.0001	4.5970	21.1064	7016.2272	32253.9182	0.2175	0.0000	4.591	45
46	0.0001	4.5972	21.1116	8542.2566	39270.1454	0.2175	0.0000	4.592	46
47	0.0001	4.5973	21.1160	10400.1975	47812.4021	0.2175	0.0000	4.593	47
48	0.0001	4.5973	21.1198	12662.2404	58212.5995	0.2175	0.0000	4.593	48
49	0.0001	4.5974	21.1229	15416.2777	70874.8399	0.2175	0.0000	4.594	49
50	0.0001	4.5975	21.1255	18769.3181	86291.1176	0.2175	0.0000	4.595	50
51	0.0000	4.5975	21.1277	22851.6448	105060.4357	0.2175	0.0000	4.595	51
52	0.0000	4.5975	21.1295	27821.8775	127912.0805	0.2175	0.0000	4.595	52
53	0.0000	4.5976	21.1310	33873.1359	155733.9580	0.2175	0.0000	4.596	53
54	0.0000	4.5976	21.1323	41240.5429	189607.0938	0.2175	0.0000	4.596	54
55	0.0000	4.5976	21.1334	50210.3610	230847.6367	0.2175	0.0000	4.596	55
60	0.0000	4.5977	21.1366	134319.2299	617555.0800	0.2175	0.0000	4.597	60
65	0.0000	4.5977	21.1380	359321.3665	1652047.6621	0.2175	0.0000	4.597	65
70	0.0000	4.5977	21.1385	961231.2735	4419449.5334	0.2175	0.0000	4.597	70
75	0.0000	4.5977	21.1387	2571418.3662	************	0.2175	0.0000	4.597	75
80	0.0000	4.5977	21.1388	6878877.7438	************	0.2175	0.0000	4.597	80
85	0.0000	4.5977	21.1388	************	************	0.2175	0.0000	4.597	85
90	0.0000	4.5977	21.1388	************	************	0.2175	0.0000	4.597	90
95	0.0000	4.5977	21.1389	************	************	0.2175	0.0000	4.597	95
100	0.0000	4.5977	21.1389	************	************	0.2175	0.0000	4.597	100

EXPANDED INTEREST TABLES

$I = 22.00 \%$

n	(P/F)	(P/A)	(P/G)	(F/P)	(F/A)	(A/P)	(A/F)	(A/G)	n
1	0.8197	0.8197	0.0000	1.2200	1.0000	1.2200	1.0000	0.000	1
2	0.6719	1.4915	0.6719	1.4884	2.2200	0.6705	0.4505	0.450	2
3	0.5507	2.0422	1.7733	1.8158	3.7084	0.4897	0.2697	0.868	3
4	0.4514	2.4936	3.1275	2.2153	5.5242	0.4010	0.1810	1.254	4
5	0.3700	2.8636	4.6075	2.7027	7.7396	0.3492	0.1292	1.609	5
6	0.3033	3.1669	6.1239	3.2973	10.4423	0.3158	0.0958	1.933	6
7	0.2486	3.4155	7.6154	4.0227	13.7396	0.2928	0.0728	2.229	7
8	0.2038	3.6193	9.0417	4.9077	17.7623	0.2763	0.0563	2.498	8
9	0.1670	3.7863	10.3779	5.9874	22.6700	0.2641	0.0441	2.740	9
10	0.1369	3.9232	11.6100	7.3046	28.6574	0.2549	0.0349	2.959	10
11	0.1122	4.0354	12.7321	8.9117	35.9620	0.2478	0.0278	3.155	11
12	0.0920	4.1274	13.7438	10.8722	44.8737	0.2423	0.0223	3.329	12
13	0.0754	4.2028	14.6485	13.2641	55.7459	0.2379	0.0179	3.485	13
14	0.0618	4.2646	15.4519	16.1822	69.0100	0.2345	0.0145	3.623	14
15	0.0507	4.3152	16.1610	19.7423	85.1922	0.2317	0.0117	3.745	15
16	0.0415	4.3567	16.7838	24.0856	104.9345	0.2295	0.0095	3.852	16
17	0.0340	4.3908	17.3283	29.3844	129.0201	0.2278	0.0078	3.946	17
18	0.0279	4.4187	17.8025	35.8490	158.4045	0.2263	0.0063	4.028	18
19	0.0229	4.4415	18.2141	43.7358	194.2535	0.2251	0.0051	4.100	19
20	0.0187	4.4603	18.5702	53.3576	237.9893	0.2242	0.0042	4.163	20
21	0.0154	4.4756	18.8774	65.0963	291.3469	0.2234	0.0034	4.217	21
22	0.0126	4.4882	19.1418	79.4175	356.4432	0.2228	0.0028	4.264	22
23	0.0103	4.4985	19.3689	96.8894	435.8607	0.2223	0.0023	4.305	23
24	0.0085	4.5070	19.5635	118.2050	532.7501	0.2219	0.0019	4.340	24
25	0.0069	4.5139	19.7299	144.2101	650.9551	0.2215	0.0015	4.370	25
26	0.0057	4.5196	19.8720	175.9364	795.1653	0.2213	0.0013	4.396	26
27	0.0047	4.5243	19.9931	214.6424	971.1016	0.2210	0.0010	4.419	27
28	0.0038	4.5281	20.0962	261.8637	1185.7440	0.2208	0.0008	4.438	28
29	0.0031	4.5312	20.1839	319.4737	1447.6077	0.2207	0.0007	4.454	29
30	0.0026	4.5338	20.2583	389.7579	1767.0813	0.2206	0.0006	4.468	30
31	0.0021	4.5359	20.3214	475.5046	2156.8392	0.2205	0.0005	4.480	31
32	0.0017	4.5376	20.3748	580.1156	2632.3439	0.2204	0.0004	4.490	32
33	0.0014	4.5390	20.4200	707.7411	3212.4595	0.2203	0.0003	4.498	33
34	0.0012	4.5402	20.4582	863.4441	3920.2006	0.2203	0.0003	4.506	34
35	0.0009	4.5411	20.4905	1053.4018	4783.6447	0.2202	0.0002	4.512	35
36	0.0008	4.5419	20.5178	1285.1502	5837.0466	0.2202	0.0002	4.517	36
37	0.0006	4.5426	20.5407	1567.8833	7122.1968	0.2201	0.0001	4.521	37
38	0.0005	4.5431	20.5601	1912.8176	8690.0801	0.2201	0.0001	4.525	38
39	0.0004	4.5435	20.5763	2333.6375	10602.8978	0.2201	0.0001	4.528	39
40	0.0004	4.5439	20.5900	2847.0378	12936.5353	0.2201	0.0001	4.531	40
41	0.0003	4.5441	20.6016	3473.3861	15783.5730	0.2201	0.0001	4.533	41
42	0.0002	4.5444	20.6112	4237.5310	19256.9591	0.2201	0.0001	4.535	42
43	0.0002	4.5446	20.6194	5169.7878	23494.4901	0.2200	0.0000	4.537	43
44	0.0002	4.5447	20.6262	6307.1411	28664.2779	0.2200	0.0000	4.538	44
45	0.0001	4.5449	20.6319	7694.7122	34971.4191	0.2200	0.0000	4.539	45
46	0.0001	4.5450	20.6367	9387.5489	42666.1312	0.2200	0.0000	4.540	46
47	0.0001	4.5451	20.6407	11452.8096	52053.6801	0.2200	0.0000	4.541	47
48	0.0001	4.5451	20.6441	13972.4277	63506.4897	0.2200	0.0000	4.542	48
49	0.0001	4.5452	20.6469	17046.3618	77478.9175	0.2200	0.0000	4.542	49
50	0.0000	4.5452	20.6492	20796.5615	94525.2793	0.2200	0.0000	4.543	50
51	0.0000	4.5453	20.6512	25371.8050	115321.8408	0.2200	0.0000	4.543	51
52	0.0000	4.5453	20.6529	30953.6021	140693.6458	0.2200	0.0000	4.543	52
53	0.0000	4.5453	20.6542	37763.3945	171647.2478	0.2200	0.0000	4.544	53
54	0.0000	4.5454	20.6554	46071.3413	209410.6423	0.2200	0.0000	4.544	54
55	0.0000	4.5454	20.6563	56207.0364	255481.9837	0.2200	0.0000	4.544	55
60	0.0000	4.5454	20.6592	151911.2161	690500.9824	0.2200	0.0000	4.545	60
65	0.0000	4.5454	20.6604	410571.6839	1866230.3813	0.2200	0.0000	4.545	65
70	0.0000	4.5455	20.6609	1109655.4416	5043883.8256	0.2200	0.0000	4.545	70
75	0.0000	4.5455	20.6610	2999074.8205	************	0.2200	0.0000	4.545	75
80	0.0000	4.5455	20.6611	8105623.9993	************	0.2200	0.0000	4.545	80
85	0.0000	4.5455	20.6611	************	************	0.2200	0.0000	4.545	85
90	0.0000	4.5455	20.6611	************	************	0.2200	0.0000	4.545	90
95	0.0000	4.5455	20.6612	************	************	0.2200	0.0000	4.545	95
100	0.0000	4.5455	20.6612	************	************	0.2200	0.0000	4.545	100

$I = 22.25\%$

n	(P/F)	(P/A)	(P/G)	(F/P)	(F/A)	(A/P)	(A/F)	(A/G)	n
1	0.8180	0.8180	0.0000	1.2225	1.0000	1.2225	1.0000	0.000	1
2	0.6691	1.4871	0.6691	1.4945	2.2225	0.6724	0.4499	0.449	2
3	0.5473	2.0344	1.7638	1.8270	3.7170	0.4915	0.2690	0.867	3
4	0.4477	2.4822	3.1069	2.2335	5.5440	0.4029	0.1804	1.251	4
5	0.3662	2.8484	4.5719	2.7305	7.7776	0.3511	0.1286	1.605	5
6	0.2996	3.1480	6.0697	3.3381	10.5081	0.3177	0.0952	1.928	6
7	0.2451	3.3930	7.5401	4.0808	13.8462	0.2947	0.0722	2.222	7
8	0.2005	3.5935	8.9432	4.9887	17.9269	0.2783	0.0558	2.488	8
9	0.1640	3.7574	10.2550	6.0987	22.9157	0.2661	0.0436	2.729	9
10	0.1341	3.8916	11.4621	7.4557	29.0144	0.2570	0.0345	2.945	10
11	0.1097	4.0013	12.5592	9.1146	36.4701	0.2499	0.0274	3.138	11
12	0.0897	4.0910	13.5464	11.1426	45.5847	0.2444	0.0219	3.311	12
13	0.0734	4.1644	14.4274	13.6218	56.7273	0.2401	0.0176	3.464	13
14	0.0601	4.2245	15.2080	16.6527	70.3491	0.2367	0.0142	3.600	14
15	0.0491	4.2736	15.8957	20.3579	87.0018	0.2340	0.0115	3.719	15
16	0.0402	4.3138	16.4984	24.8875	107.3597	0.2318	0.0093	3.824	16
17	0.0329	4.3467	17.0243	30.4250	132.2472	0.2301	0.0076	3.916	17
18	0.0269	4.3735	17.4814	37.1946	162.6723	0.2286	0.0061	3.997	18
19	0.0220	4.3955	17.8772	45.4704	199.8668	0.2275	0.0050	4.067	19
20	0.0180	4.4135	18.2190	55.5875	245.3372	0.2266	0.0041	4.128	20
21	0.0147	4.4282	18.5134	67.9558	300.9247	0.2258	0.0033	4.180	21
22	0.0120	4.4403	18.7661	83.0759	368.8805	0.2252	0.0027	4.226	22
23	0.0098	4.4501	18.9828	101.5603	451.9564	0.2247	0.0022	4.265	23
24	0.0081	4.4582	19.1680	124.1575	553.5167	0.2243	0.0018	4.299	24
25	0.0066	4.4648	19.3261	151.7825	677.6741	0.2240	0.0015	4.328	25
26	0.0054	4.4702	19.4609	185.5541	829.4566	0.2237	0.0012	4.353	26
27	0.0044	4.4746	19.5755	226.8399	1015.0107	0.2235	0.0010	4.374	27
28	0.0036	4.4782	19.6728	277.3118	1241.8506	0.2233	0.0008	4.393	28
29	0.0029	4.4811	19.7554	339.0136	1519.1624	0.2232	0.0007	4.408	29
30	0.0024	4.4835	19.8254	414.4442	1858.1760	0.2230	0.0005	4.421	30
31	0.0020	4.4855	19.8846	506.6580	2272.6202	0.2229	0.0004	4.433	31
32	0.0016	4.4871	19.9347	619.3894	2779.2782	0.2229	0.0004	4.442	32
33	0.0013	4.4884	19.9769	757.2035	3398.6676	0.2228	0.0003	4.450	33
34	0.0011	4.4895	20.0126	925.6813	4155.8712	0.2227	0.0002	4.457	34
35	0.0009	4.4904	20.0426	1131.6454	5081.5525	0.2227	0.0002	4.463	35
36	0.0007	4.4911	20.0679	1383.4365	6213.1979	0.2227	0.0002	4.468	36
37	0.0006	4.4917	20.0892	1691.2512	7596.6344	0.2226	0.0001	4.472	37
38	0.0005	4.4922	20.1071	2067.5545	9287.8856	0.2226	0.0001	4.476	38
39	0.0004	4.4926	20.1221	2527.5854	11355.4402	0.2226	0.0001	4.478	39
40	0.0003	4.4929	20.1348	3089.9732	13883.0256	0.2226	0.0001	4.481	40
41	0.0003	4.4932	20.1453	3777.4922	16972.9988	0.2226	0.0001	4.483	41
42	0.0002	4.4934	20.1542	4617.9843	20750.4910	0.2225	0.0000	4.485	42
43	0.0002	4.4936	20.1617	5645.4857	25368.4753	0.2225	0.0000	4.486	43
44	0.0001	4.4937	20.1679	6901.6063	31013.9610	0.2225	0.0000	4.488	44
45	0.0001	4.4938	20.1731	8437.2137	37915.5673	0.2225	0.0000	4.489	45
46	0.0001	4.4939	20.1775	10314.4938	46352.7811	0.2225	0.0000	4.489	46
47	0.0001	4.4940	20.1811	12609.4687	56667.2749	0.2225	0.0000	4.490	47
48	0.0001	4.4941	20.1842	15415.0754	69276.7435	0.2225	0.0000	4.491	48
49	0.0001	4.4941	20.1867	18844.9297	84691.8189	0.2225	0.0000	4.491	49
50	0.0000	4.4942	20.1888	23037.9266	103536.7487	0.2225	0.0000	4.492	50
51	0.0000	4.4942	20.1906	28163.8652	126574.6752	0.2225	0.0000	4.492	51
52	0.0000	4.4943	20.1921	34430.3253	154738.5405	0.2225	0.0000	4.492	52
53	0.0000	4.4943	20.1933	42091.0726	189168.8657	0.2225	0.0000	4.493	53
54	0.0000	4.4943	20.1944	51456.3363	231259.9383	0.2225	0.0000	4.493	54
55	0.0000	4.4943	20.1952	62905.3711	282716.2746	0.2225	0.0000	4.493	55
60	0.0000	4.4944	20.1978	171763.9693	771968.4015	0.2225	0.0000	4.494	60
65	0.0000	4.4944	20.188	469003.8488	2107877.9723	0.2225	0.0000	4.494	65
70	0.0000	4.4944	20.1992	1280621.3729	5755597.1816	0.2225	0.0000	4.494	70
75	0.0000	4.4944	20.1994	3496754.0348	************	0.2225	0.0000	4.494	75
80	0.0000	4.4944	20.1994	9547934.3378	************	0.2225	0.0000	4.494	80
85	0.0000	4.4944	20.1995	************	************	0.2225	0.0000	4.494	85
90	0.0000	4.4944	20.1995	************	************	0.2225	0.0000	4.494	90
95	0.0000	4.4944	20.1995	************	************	0.2225	0.0000	4.494	95
100	0.0000	4.4944	20.1995	************	************	0.2225	0.0000	4.494	100

EXPANDED INTEREST TABLES

$I = 22.50\%$

n	(P/F)	(P/A)	(P/G)	(F/P)	(F/A)	(A/P)	(A/F)	(A/G)	n
1	0.8163	0.8163	0.0000	1.2250	1.0000	1.2250	1.0000	0.000	1
2	0.6664	1.4827	0.6664	1.5006	2.2250	0.6744	0.4494	0.449	2
3	0.5440	2.0267	1.7544	1.8383	3.7256	0.4934	0.2684	0.865	3
4	0.4441	2.4708	3.0866	2.2519	5.5639	0.4047	0.1797	1.249	4
5	0.3625	2.8333	4.5366	2.7585	7.8158	0.3529	0.1279	1.601	5
6	0.2959	3.1292	6.0163	3.3792	10.5743	0.3196	0.0946	1.922	6
7	0.2416	3.3708	7.4657	4.1395	13.9535	0.2967	0.0717	2.214	7
8	0.1972	3.5680	8.8461	5.0709	18.0931	0.2803	0.0553	2.479	8
9	0.1610	3.7290	10.1340	6.2119	23.1640	0.2682	0.0432	2.717	9
10	0.1314	3.8604	11.3167	7.6096	29.3759	0.2590	0.0340	2.931	10
11	0.1073	3.9677	12.3894	9.3217	36.9855	0.2520	0.0270	3.122	11
12	0.0876	4.0552	13.3527	11.4191	46.3072	0.2466	0.0216	3.292	12
13	0.0715	4.1267	14.2106	13.9884	57.7264	0.2423	0.0173	3.443	13
14	0.0584	4.1851	14.9692	17.1358	71.7148	0.2389	0.0139	3.576	14
15	0.0476	4.2327	15.6362	20.9914	88.8507	0.2363	0.0113	3.694	15
16	0.0389	4.2716	16.2195	25.7145	109.8420	0.2341	0.0091	3.797	16
17	0.0317	4.3034	16.7274	31.5002	135.5565	0.2324	0.0074	3.887	17
18	0.0259	4.3293	17.1680	38.5878	167.0567	0.2310	0.0060	3.965	18
19	0.0212	4.3504	17.5488	47.2700	205.6445	0.2299	0.0049	4.033	19
20	0.0173	4.3677	17.8769	57.9058	252.9145	0.2290	0.0040	4.093	20
21	0.0141	4.3818	18.1589	70.9346	310.8203	0.2282	0.0032	4.144	21
22	0.0115	4.3933	18.4005	86.8948	381.7548	0.2276	0.0026	4.188	22
23	0.0094	4.4027	18.6072	106.4462	468.6496	0.2271	0.0021	4.226	23
24	0.0077	4.4104	18.7836	130.3966	575.0958	0.2267	0.0017	4.259	24
25	0.0063	4.4166	18.9338	159.7358	705.4924	0.2264	0.0014	4.287	25
26	0.0051	4.4217	19.0616	195.6763	865.2282	0.2262	0.0012	4.310	26
27	0.0042	4.4259	19.1701	239.7035	1060.9045	0.2259	0.0009	4.331	27
28	0.0034	4.4293	19.2620	293.6368	1300.6080	0.2258	0.0008	4.348	28
29	0.0028	4.4321	19.3399	359.7051	1594.2448	0.2256	0.0006	4.363	29
30	0.0023	4.4344	19.4057	440.6387	1953.9499	0.2255	0.0005	4.376	30
31	0.0019	4.4362	19.4612	539.7824	2394.5886	0.2254	0.0004	4.386	31
32	0.0015	4.4377	19.5081	661.2335	2934.3710	0.2253	0.0003	4.396	32
33	0.0012	4.4390	19.5476	810.0110	3595.6045	0.2253	0.0003	4.403	33
34	0.0010	4.4400	19.5809	992.2635	4405.6156	0.2252	0.0002	4.410	34
35	0.0008	4.4408	19.6089	1215.5228	5397.8790	0.2252	0.0002	4.415	35
36	0.0007	4.4415	19.6324	1489.0154	6613.4018	0.2252	0.0002	4.420	36
37	0.0005	4.4420	19.6521	1824.0439	8102.4172	0.2251	0.0001	4.424	37
38	0.0004	4.4425	19.6687	2234.4538	9926.4611	0.2251	0.0001	4.427	38
39	0.0004	4.4428	19.6825	2737.2058	12160.9149	0.2251	0.0001	4.430	39
40	0.0003	4.4431	19.6942	3353.0772	14898.1207	0.2251	0.0001	4.432	40
41	0.0002	4.4434	19.7039	4107.5195	18251.1979	0.2251	0.0001	4.434	41
42	0.0002	4.4436	19.7121	5031.7114	22358.7174	0.2250	0.0000	4.436	42
43	0.0002	4.4437	19.7189	6163.8465	27390.4288	0.2250	0.0000	4.437	43
44	0.0001	4.4439	19.7246	7550.7120	33554.2753	0.2250	0.0000	4.438	44
45	0.0001	4.4440	19.7293	9249.6221	41104.9873	0.2250	0.0000	4.439	45
46	0.0001	4.4441	19.7333	11330.7871	50354.6094	0.2250	0.0000	4.440	46
47	0.0001	4.4441	19.7366	13880.2142	61685.3965	0.2250	0.0000	4.441	47
48	0.0001	4.4442	19.7394	17003.2624	75565.6108	0.2250	0.0000	4.441	48
49	0.0000	4.4442	19.7417	20828.9965	92568.8732	0.2250	0.0000	4.442	49
50	0.0000	4.4443	19.7436	25515.5207	113397.8697	0.2250	0.0000	4.442	50
51	0.0000	4.4443	19.7452	31256.5128	138913.3903	0.2250	0.0000	4.442	51
52	0.0000	4.4443	19.7465	38289.2282	170169.9032	0.2250	0.0000	4.443	52
53	0.0000	4.4443	19.7476	46904.3046	208459.1314	0.2250	0.0000	4.443	53
54	0.0000	4.4444	19.7486	57457.7731	255363.4359	0.2250	0.0000	4.443	54
55	0.0000	4.4444	19.7493	70385.7720	312821.2090	0.2250	0.0000	4.443	55
60	0.0000	4.4444	19.7516	194162.4851	862939.9340	0.2250	0.0000	4.444	60
65	0.0000	4.4444	19.7525	535606.4096	2380468.4869	0.2250	0.0000	4.444	65
70	0.0000	4.4444	19.7529	1477495.6436	6566642.8605	0.2250	0.0000	4.444	70
75	0.0000	4.4444	19.7530	4075741.6975	************	0.2250	0.0000	4.444	75
80	0.0000	4.4444	19.7531	************	************	0.2250	0.0000	4.444	80
85	0.0000	4.4444	19.7531	************	************	0.2250	0.0000	4.444	85
90	0.0000	4.4444	19.7531	************	************	0.2250	0.0000	4.444	90
95	0.0000	4.4444	19.7531	************	************	0.2250	0.0000	4.444	95
100	0.0000	4.4444	19.7531	************	************	0.2250	0.0000	4.444	100

$I = 22.75\%$

n	(P/F)	(P/A)	(P/G)	(F/P)	(F/A)	(A/P)	(A/F)	(A/G)	n
1	0.8147	0.8147	0.0000	1.2275	1.0000	1.2275	1.0000	0.000	1
2	0.6637	1.4783	0.6637	1.5068	2.2275	0.6764	0.4489	0.448	2
3	0.5407	2.0190	1.7450	1.8495	3.7343	0.4953	0.2678	0.864	3
4	0.4405	2.4595	3.0664	2.2703	5.5838	0.4066	0.1791	1.246	4
5	0.3588	2.8183	4.5018	2.7868	7.8541	0.3548	0.1273	1.597	5
6	0.2923	3.1106	5.9634	3.4208	10.6409	0.3215	0.0940	1.917	6
7	0.2381	3.3488	7.3923	4.1990	14.0617	0.2986	0.0711	2.207	7
8	0.1940	3.5428	8.7504	5.1543	18.2608	0.2823	0.0548	2.469	8
9	0.1581	3.7009	10.0148	6.3269	23.4151	0.2702	0.0427	2.706	9
10	0.1288	3.8296	11.1737	7.7663	29.7420	0.2611	0.0336	2.917	10
11	0.1049	3.9345	12.2226	9.5332	37.5084	0.2542	0.0267	3.106	11
12	0.0855	4.0200	13.1627	11.7019	47.0415	0.2488	0.0213	3.274	12
13	0.0696	4.0896	13.9981	14.3641	58.7435	0.2445	0.0170	3.422	13
14	0.0567	4.1463	14.7354	17.6320	73.1076	0.2412	0.0137	3.553	14
15	0.0462	4.1925	15.3822	21.6433	90.7396	0.2385	0.0110	3.669	15
16	0.0376	4.2302	15.9468	26.5671	112.3828	0.2364	0.0089	3.769	16
17	0.0307	4.2608	16.4375	32.6111	138.9499	0.2347	0.0072	3.857	17
18	0.0250	4.2858	16.8621	40.0301	171.5610	0.2333	0.0058	3.934	18
19	0.0204	4.3061	17.2285	49.1370	211.5911	0.2322	0.0047	4.000	19
20	0.0166	4.3227	17.5435	60.3157	260.7281	0.2313	0.0038	4.058	20
21	0.0135	4.3362	17.8136	74.0375	321.0438	0.2306	0.0031	4.108	21
22	0.0110	4.3472	18.0447	90.8810	395.0812	0.2300	0.0025	4.150	22
23	0.0090	4.3562	18.2419	111.5564	485.9622	0.2296	0.0021	4.187	23
24	0.0073	4.3635	18.4098	136.9355	597.5186	0.2292	0.0017	4.219	24
25	0.0059	4.3695	18.5526	168.0883	734.4541	0.2289	0.0014	4.246	25
26	0.0048	4.3743	18.6738	206.3284	902.5424	0.2286	0.0011	4.269	26
27	0.0039	4.3782	18.7765	253.2681	1108.8708	0.2284	0.0009	4.288	27
28	0.0032	4.3815	18.8633	310.8866	1362.1390	0.2282	0.0007	4.305	28
29	0.0026	4.3841	18.9367	381.6133	1673.0256	0.2281	0.0006	4.319	29
30	0.0021	4.3862	18.9986	468.4303	2054.6389	0.2280	0.0005	4.331	30
31	0.0017	4.3880	19.0508	574.9983	2523.0692	0.2279	0.0004	4.341	31
32	0.0014	4.3894	19.0947	705.8104	3098.0675	0.2278	0.0003	4.350	32
33	0.0012	4.3905	19.1316	866.3822	3803.8778	0.2278	0.0003	4.357	33
34	0.0009	4.3915	19.1626	1063.4842	4670.2601	0.2277	0.0002	4.363	34
35	0.0008	4.3922	19.1887	1305.4268	5733.7442	0.2277	0.0002	4.368	35
36	0.0006	4.3929	19.2105	1602.4114	7039.1710	0.2276	0.0001	4.373	36
37	0.0005	4.3934	19.2288	1966.9600	8641.5824	0.2276	0.0001	4.376	37
38	0.0004	4.3938	19.2442	2414.4434	10608.5424	0.2276	0.0001	4.379	38
39	0.0003	4.3941	19.2570	2963.7293	13022.9859	0.2276	0.0001	4.382	39
40	0.0003	4.3944	19.2677	3637.9777	15986.7151	0.2276	0.0001	4.384	40
41	0.0002	4.3946	19.2767	4465.6176	19624.6928	0.2276	0.0001	4.386	41
42	0.0002	4.3948	19.2841	5481.5456	24090.3104	0.2275	0.0000	4.387	42
43	0.0001	4.3950	19.2904	6728.5973	29571.8561	0.2275	0.0000	4.389	43
44	0.0001	4.3951	19.2956	8259.3531	36300.4533	0.2275	0.0000	4.390	44
45	0.0001	4.3952	19.2999	10138.3560	44559.8065	0.2275	0.0000	4.391	45
46	0.0001	4.3953	19.3035	12444.8320	54698.1624	0.2275	0.0000	4.391	46
47	0.0001	4.3953	19.3065	15276.0312	67142.9944	0.2275	0.0000	4.392	47
48	0.0001	4.3954	19.3091	18751.3283	82419.0256	0.2275	0.0000	4.393	48
49	0.0000	4.3954	19.3111	23017.2555	101170.3539	0.2275	0.0000	4.393	49
50	0.0000	4.3954	19.3129	28253.6812	124187.6095	0.2275	0.0000	4.393	50
51	0.0000	4.3955	19.3143	34681.3936	152441.2906	0.2275	0.0000	4.394	51
52	0.0000	4.3955	19.3155	42571.4107	187122.6842	0.2275	0.0000	4.394	52
53	0.0000	4.3955	19.3165	52256.4066	229694.0949	0.2275	0.0000	4.394	53
54	0.0000	4.3955	19.3173	64144.7391	281950.5015	0.2275	0.0000	4.394	54
55	0.0000	4.3955	19.3180	78737.6672	346095.2406	0.2275	0.0000	4.394	55
60	0.0000	4.3956	19.3200	219426.9910	964509.8506	0.2275	0.0000	4.395	60
65	0.0000	4.3956	19.3208	611501.5352	2687914.4404	0.2275	0.0000	4.395	65
70	0.0000	4.3956	19.3211	1704139.1572	7490717.1745	0.2275	0.0000	4.395	70
75	0.0000	4.3956	19.3213	4749113.6162	************	0.2275	0.0000	4.395	75
80	0.0000	4.3956	19.3213	************	************	0.2275	0.0000	4.395	80
85	0.0000	4.3956	19.3213	************	************	0.2275	0.0000	4.395	85
90	0.0000	4.3956	19.3213	************	************	0.2275	0.0000	4.395	90
95	0.0000	4.3956	19.3213	************	************	0.2275	0.0000	4.395	95
100	0.0000	4.3956	19.3213	************	************	0.2275	0.0000	4.395	100

EXPANDED INTEREST TABLES

$I = 23.00 \%$

n	(P/F)	(P/A)	(P/G)	(F/P)	(F/A)	(A/P)	(A/F)	(A/G)	n
1	0.8130	0.8130	0.0000	1.2300	1.0000	1.2300	1.0000	0.000	1
2	0.6610	1.4740	0.6610	1.5129	2.2300	0.6784	0.4484	0.448	2
3	0.5374	2.0114	1.7358	1.8609	3.7429	0.4972	0.2672	0.863	3
4	0.4369	2.4483	3.0464	2.2889	5.6038	0.4085	0.1785	1.244	4
5	0.3552	2.8035	4.4672	2.8153	7.8926	0.3567	0.1267	1.593	5
6	0.2888	3.0923	5.9112	3.4628	10.7079	0.3234	0.0934	1.911	6
7	0.2348	3.3270	7.3198	4.2593	14.1708	0.3006	0.0706	2.200	7
8	0.1909	3.5179	8.6560	5.2389	18.4300	0.2843	0.0543	2.460	8
9	0.1552	3.6731	9.8975	6.4439	23.6690	0.2722	0.0422	2.694	9
10	0.1262	3.7993	11.0330	7.9259	30.1128	0.2632	0.0332	2.904	10
11	0.1026	3.9018	12.0588	9.7489	38.0388	0.2563	0.0263	3.090	11
12	0.0834	3.9852	12.9761	11.9912	47.7877	0.2509	0.0209	3.256	12
13	0.0678	4.0530	13.7897	14.7491	59.7788	0.2467	0.0167	3.402	13
14	0.0551	4.1082	14.5063	18.1414	74.5280	0.2434	0.0134	3.531	14
15	0.0448	4.1530	15.1337	22.3140	92.6694	0.2408	0.0108	3.644	15
16	0.0364	4.1894	15.6802	27.4462	114.9834	0.2387	0.0087	3.742	16
17	0.0296	4.2190	16.1542	33.7588	142.4295	0.2370	0.0070	3.828	17
18	0.0241	4.2431	16.5636	41.5233	176.1883	0.2357	0.0057	3.903	18
19	0.0196	4.2627	16.9160	51.0737	217.7116	0.2346	0.0046	3.968	19
20	0.0159	4.2786	17.2185	62.8206	268.7853	0.2337	0.0037	4.024	20
21	0.0129	4.2916	17.4773	77.2694	331.6059	0.2330	0.0030	4.072	21
22	0.0105	4.3021	17.6983	95.0413	408.8753	0.2324	0.0024	4.113	22
23	0.0086	4.3106	17.8865	116.9008	503.9166	0.2320	0.0020	4.149	23
24	0.0070	4.3176	18.0464	143.7880	620.8174	0.2316	0.0016	4.179	24
25	0.0057	4.3232	18.1821	176.8593	764.6054	0.2313	0.0013	4.205	25
26	0.0046	4.3278	18.2970	217.5369	941.4647	0.2311	0.0011	4.227	26
27	0.0037	4.3316	18.3942	267.5704	1159.0016	0.2309	0.0009	4.246	27
28	0.0030	4.3346	18.4763	329.1115	1426.5719	0.2307	0.0007	4.262	28
29	0.0025	4.3371	18.5454	404.8072	1755.6835	0.2306	0.0006	4.276	29
30	0.0020	4.3391	18.6037	497.9129	2160.4907	0.2305	0.0005	4.287	30
31	0.0016	4.3407	18.6526	612.4328	2658.4036	0.2304	0.0004	4.297	31
32	0.0013	4.3421	18.6938	753.2924	3270.8364	0.2303	0.0003	4.305	32
33	0.0011	4.3431	18.7283	926.5496	4024.1287	0.2302	0.0002	4.312	33
34	0.0009	4.3440	18.7573	1139.6560	4950.6783	0.2302	0.0002	4.318	34
35	0.0007	4.3447	18.7815	1401.7769	6090.3344	0.2302	0.0002	4.322	35
36	0.0006	4.3453	18.8018	1724.1856	7492.1113	0.2301	0.0001	4.326	36
37	0.0005	4.3458	18.8188	2120.7483	9216.2969	0.2301	0.0001	4.330	37
38	0.0004	4.3462	18.8330	2608.5204	11337.0451	0.2301	0.0001	4.333	38
39	0.0003	4.3465	18.8449	3208.4801	13945.5655	0.2301	0.0001	4.335	39
40	0.0003	4.3467	18.8547	3946.4305	17154.0456	0.2301	0.0001	4.337	40
41	0.0002	4.3469	18.8630	4854.1095	21100.4761	0.2300	0.0000	4.339	41
42	0.0002	4.3471	18.8698	5970.5547	25954.5856	0.2300	0.0000	4.340	42
43	0.0001	4.3472	18.8756	7343.7823	31925.1403	0.2300	0.0000	4.342	43
44	0.0001	4.3473	18.8803	9032.8522	39268.9225	0.2300	0.0000	4.343	44
45	0.0001	4.3474	18.8843	11110.4082	48301.7747	0.2300	0.0000	4.343	45
46	0.0001	4.3475	18.8876	13665.8021	59412.1829	0.2300	0.0000	4.344	46
47	0.0001	4.3476	18.8903	16808.9365	73077.9850	0.2300	0.0000	4.345	47
48	0.0000	4.3476	18.8926	20674.9919	89886.9215	0.2300	0.0000	4.345	48
49	0.0000	4.3477	18.8945	25430.2401	110561.9135	0.2300	0.0000	4.345	49
50	0.0000	4.3477	18.8960	31279.1953	135992.1536	0.2300	0.0000	4.346	50
51	0.0000	4.3477	18.8973	38473.4102	167271.3489	0.2300	0.0000	4.346	51
52	0.0000	4.3477	18.8984	47322.2946	205744.7591	0.2300	0.0000	4.346	52
53	0.0000	4.3478	18.8993	58206.4224	253067.0537	0.2300	0.0000	4.346	53
54	0.0000	4.3478	18.9000	71593.8995	311273.4761	0.2300	0.0000	4.347	54
55	0.0000	4.3478	18.9007	88060.4964	382867.3756	0.2300	0.0000	4.347	55
60	0.0000	4.3478	18.9025	247917.2160	1077896.5914	0.2300	0.0000	4.347	60
65	0.0000	4.3478	18.9032	697962.7475	3034616.2935	0.2300	0.0000	4.347	65
70	0.0000	4.3478	18.9034	1964978.4905	8543380.3934	0.2300	0.0000	4.347	70
75	0.0000	4.3478	18.9035	5532015.1138	************	0.2300	0.0000	4.347	75
80	0.0000	4.3478	18.9036	************	************	0.2300	0.0000	4.347	80
85	0.0000	4.3478	18.9036	************	************	0.2300	0.0000	4.347	85
90	0.0000	4.3478	18.9036	************	************	0.2300	0.0000	4.347	90
95	0.0000	4.3478	18.9036	************	************	0.2300	0.0000	4.347	95
100	0.0000	4.3478	18.9036	************	************	0.2300	0.0000	4.347	100

$I = 23.25\%$

n	(P/F)	(P/A)	(P/G)	(F/P)	(F/A)	(A/P)	(A/F)	(A/G)	n
1	0.8114	0.8114	0.0000	1.2325	1.0000	1.2325	1.0000	0.000	1
2	0.6583	1.4697	0.6583	1.5191	2.2325	0.6804	0.4479	0.447	2
3	0.5341	2.0038	1.7265	1.8722	3.7516	0.4991	0.2666	0.861	3
4	0.4334	2.4371	3.0266	2.3075	5.6238	0.4103	0.1778	1.241	4
5	0.3516	2.7888	4.4331	2.8440	7.9313	0.3586	0.1261	1.589	5
6	0.2853	3.0740	5.8595	3.5053	10.7754	0.3253	0.0928	1.906	6
7	0.2315	3.3055	7.2483	4.3202	14.2806	0.3025	0.0700	2.192	7
8	0.1878	3.4933	8.5629	5.3247	18.6009	0.2863	0.0538	2.451	8
9	0.1524	3.6457	9.7820	6.5627	23.9256	0.2743	0.0418	2.683	9
10	0.1236	3.7693	10.8946	8.0885	30.4883	0.2653	0.0328	2.890	10
11	0.1003	3.8696	11.8977	9.9691	38.5768	0.2584	0.0259	3.074	11
12	0.0814	3.9510	12.7930	12.2869	48.5459	0.2531	0.0206	3.237	12
13	0.0660	4.0171	13.5854	15.1436	60.8328	0.2489	0.0164	3.381	13
14	0.0536	4.0706	14.2819	18.6645	75.9765	0.2457	0.0132	3.508	14
15	0.0435	4.1141	14.8905	23.0040	94.6410	0.2431	0.0106	3.619	15
16	0.0353	4.1494	15.4196	28.3525	117.6450	0.2410	0.0085	3.716	16
17	0.0286	4.1780	15.8774	34.9444	145.9975	0.2393	0.0068	3.800	17
18	0.0232	4.2012	16.2722	43.0690	180.9419	0.2380	0.0055	3.873	18
19	0.0188	4.2200	16.6113	53.0825	224.0109	0.2370	0.0045	3.936	19
20	0.0153	4.2353	16.9017	65.4242	277.0934	0.2361	0.0036	3.990	20
21	0.0124	4.2477	17.1497	80.6354	342.5176	0.2354	0.0029	4.037	21
22	0.0101	4.2578	17.3610	99.3831	423.1530	0.2349	0.0024	4.077	22
23	0.0082	4.2660	17.5406	122.4896	522.5361	0.2344	0.0019	4.111	23
24	0.0066	4.2726	17.6930	150.9685	645.0257	0.2341	0.0016	4.141	24
25	0.0054	4.2780	17.8219	186.0686	795.9942	0.2338	0.0013	4.166	25
26	0.0044	4.2823	17.9310	229.3296	982.0628	0.2335	0.0010	4.187	26
27	0.0035	4.2859	18.0229	282.6487	1211.3924	0.2333	0.0008	4.205	27
28	0.0029	4.2887	18.1004	348.3646	1494.0412	0.2332	0.0007	4.220	28
29	0.0023	4.2911	18.1657	429.3593	1842.4057	0.2330	0.0005	4.233	29
30	0.0019	4.2929	18.2205	529.1854	2271.7651	0.2329	0.0004	4.244	30
31	0.0015	4.2945	18.2665	652.2210	2800.9505	0.2329	0.0004	4.253	31
32	0.0012	4.2957	18.3050	803.8624	3453.1714	0.2328	0.0003	4.261	32
33	0.0010	4.2967	18.3373	990.7604	4257.0338	0.2327	0.0002	4.267	33
34	0.0008	4.2976	18.3643	1221.1121	5247.7942	0.2327	0.0002	4.273	34
35	0.0007	4.2982	18.3869	1505.0207	6468.9063	0.2327	0.0002	4.277	35
36	0.0005	4.2988	18.4058	1854.9380	7973.9270	0.2326	0.0001	4.281	36
37	0.0004	4.2992	18.4215	2286.2111	9828.8651	0.2326	0.0001	4.284	37
38	0.0004	4.2995	18.4347	2817.7552	12115.0762	0.2326	0.0001	4.287	38
39	0.0003	4.2998	18.4456	3472.8833	14932.8314	0.2326	0.0001	4.289	39
40	0.0002	4.3001	18.4547	4280.3287	18405.7147	0.2326	0.0001	4.291	40
41	0.0002	4.3003	18.4623	5275.5051	22686.0434	0.2325	0.0000	4.293	41
42	0.0002	4.3004	18.4686	6502.0600	27961.5485	0.2325	0.0000	4.294	42
43	0.0001	4.3005	18.4739	8013.7890	34463.6085	0.2325	0.0000	4.295	43
44	0.0001	4.3006	18.4782	9876.9949	42477.3974	0.2325	0.0000	4.296	44
45	0.0001	4.3007	18.4818	12173.3962	52354.3923	0.2325	0.0000	4.297	45
46	0.0001	4.3008	18.4848	15003.7108	64527.7886	0.2325	0.0000	4.298	46
47	0.0001	4.3008	18.4873	18492.0736	79531.4994	0.2325	0.0000	4.298	47
48	0.0000	4.3009	18.4894	22791.4807	98023.5730	0.2325	0.0000	4.299	48
49	0.0000	4.3009	18.4911	28090.5000	120815.0538	0.2325	0.0000	4.299	49
50	0.0000	4.3010	18.4925	34621.5412	148905.5538	0.2325	0.0000	4.299	50
51	0.0000	4.3010	18.4937	42671.0496	183527.0950	0.2325	0.0000	4.299	51
52	0.0000	4.3010	18.4946	52592.0686	226198.1446	0.2325	0.0000	4.300	52
53	0.0000	4.3010	18.4954	64819.7246	278790.2132	0.2325	0.0000	4.300	53
54	0.0000	4.3010	18.4961	79890.3105	343609.9378	0.2325	0.0000	4.300	54
55	0.0000	4.3010	18.4967	98464.8077	423500.2483	0.2325	0.0000	4.300	55
60	0.0000	4.3011	18.4983	280037.1680	1204456.6364	0.2325	0.0000	4.300	60
65	0.0000	4.3011	18.4989	796434.9624	3425522.4189	0.2325	0.0000	4.301	65
70	0.0000	4.3011	18.4991	2265087.3594	9742306.9222	0.2325	0.0000	4.301	70
75	0.0000	4.3011	18.4992	6441983.3232	************	0.2325	0.0000	4.301	75
80	0.0000	4.3011	18.4992	************	************	0.2325	0.0000	4.301	80
85	0.0000	4.3011	18.4992	************	************	0.2325	0.0000	4.301	85
90	0.0000	4.3011	18.4992	************	************	0.2325	0.0000	4.301	90
95	0.0000	4.3011	18.4992	************	************	0.2325	0.0000	4.301	95
100	0.0000	4.3011	18.4992	************	************	0.2325	0.0000	4.301	100

$$I = 23.50 \text{ \%}$$

n	(P/F)	(P/A)	(P/G)	(F/P)	(F/A)	(A/P)	(A/F)	(A/G)	n
1	0.8097	0.8097	0.0000	1.2350	1.0000	1.2350	1.0000	0.000	1
2	0.6556	1.4654	0.6556	1.5252	2.2350	0.6824	0.4474	0.447	2
3	0.5309	1.9962	1.7174	1.8837	3.7602	0.5009	0.2659	0.860	3
4	0.4299	2.4261	3.0070	2.3263	5.6439	0.4122	0.1772	1.239	4
5	0.3481	2.7742	4.3993	2.8730	7.9702	0.3605	0.1255	1.585	5
6	0.2818	3.0560	5.8085	3.5481	10.8432	0.3272	0.0922	1.900	6
7	0.2282	3.2842	7.1777	4.3820	14.3913	0.3045	0.0695	2.185	7
8	0.1848	3.4690	8.4712	5.4117	18.7733	0.2883	0.0533	2.442	8
9	0.1496	3.6186	9.6682	6.6835	24.1850	0.2763	0.0413	2.671	9
10	0.1212	3.7398	10.7586	8.2541	30.8685	0.2674	0.0324	2.876	10
11	0.0981	3.8379	11.7395	10.1938	39.1226	0.2606	0.0256	3.058	11
12	0.0794	3.9173	12.6133	12.5894	49.3164	0.2553	0.0203	3.219	12
13	0.0643	3.9816	13.3851	15.5479	61.9058	0.2512	0.0162	3.361	13
14	0.0521	4.0337	14.0621	19.2016	77.4536	0.2479	0.0129	3.486	14
15	0.0422	4.0759	14.6525	23.7140	96.6552	0.2453	0.0103	3.594	15
16	0.0341	4.1100	15.1647	29.2868	120.3692	0.2433	0.0083	3.689	16
17	0.0276	4.1377	15.6070	36.1691	149.6559	0.2417	0.0067	3.771	17
18	0.0224	4.1601	15.9876	44.6689	185.8251	0.2404	0.0054	3.843	18
19	0.0181	4.1782	16.3139	55.1661	230.4940	0.2393	0.0043	3.904	19
20	0.0147	4.1929	16.5928	68.1301	285.6601	0.2385	0.0035	3.957	20
21	0.0119	4.2047	16.8305	84.1407	353.7902	0.2378	0.0028	4.002	21
22	0.0096	4.2144	17.0326	103.9138	437.9309	0.2373	0.0023	4.041	22
23	0.0078	4.2222	17.2040	128.3335	541.8447	0.2368	0.0018	4.074	23
24	0.0063	4.2285	17.3491	158.4919	670.1782	0.2365	0.0015	4.102	24
25	0.0051	4.2336	17.4717	195.7375	828.6700	0.2362	0.0012	4.126	25
26	0.0041	4.2377	17.5752	241.7358	1024.4075	0.2360	0.0010	4.147	26
27	0.0033	4.2411	17.6622	298.5437	1266.1432	0.2358	0.0008	4.164	27
28	0.0027	4.2438	17.7355	368.7014	1564.6869	0.2356	0.0006	4.179	28
29	0.0022	4.2460	17.7970	455.3463	1933.3883	0.2355	0.0005	4.191	29
30	0.0018	4.2478	17.8485	562.3526	2388.7346	0.2354	0.0004	4.201	30
31	0.0014	4.2492	17.8917	694.5055	2951.0872	0.2353	0.0003	4.210	31
32	0.0012	4.2504	17.9279	857.7143	3645.5927	0.2353	0.0003	4.218	32
33	0.0009	4.2513	17.9581	1059.2771	4503.3070	0.2352	0.0002	4.224	33
34	0.0008	4.2521	17.9833	1308.2073	5562.5841	0.2352	0.0002	4.229	34
35	0.0006	4.2527	18.0043	1615.6360	6870.7914	0.2351	0.0001	4.233	35
36	0.0005	4.2532	18.0219	1995.3104	8486.4274	0.2351	0.0001	4.237	36
37	0.0004	4.2536	18.0365	2464.2084	10481.7378	0.2351	0.0001	4.240	37
38	0.0003	4.2539	18.0487	3043.2974	12945.9462	0.2351	0.0001	4.242	38
39	0.0003	4.2542	18.0588	3758.4722	15989.2435	0.2351	0.0001	4.244	39
40	0.0002	4.2544	18.0672	4641.7132	19747.7158	0.2351	0.0001	4.246	40
41	0.0002	4.2546	18.0741	5732.5158	24389.4290	0.2350	0.0000	4.248	41
42	0.0001	4.2547	18.0799	7079.6570	30121.9448	0.2350	0.0000	4.249	42
43	0.0001	4.2548	18.0847	8743.3764	37201.6018	0.2350	0.0000	4.250	43
44	0.0001	4.2549	18.0887	10798.0699	45944.9783	0.2350	0.0000	4.251	44
45	0.0001	4.2550	18.0920	13335.6163	56743.0482	0.2350	0.0000	4.251	45
46	0.0001	4.2551	18.0948	16469.4862	70078.6645	0.2350	0.0000	4.252	46
47	0.0000	4.2551	18.0970	20339.8154	86548.1506	0.2350	0.0000	4.253	47
48	0.0000	4.2551	18.0989	25119.6720	106887.9660	0.2350	0.0000	4.253	48
49	0.0000	4.2552	18.1004	31022.7949	132007.6380	0.2350	0.0000	4.253	49
50	0.0000	4.2552	18.1017	38313.1518	163030.4330	0.2350	0.0000	4.254	50
51	0.0000	4.2552	18.1028	47316.7424	201343.5847	0.2350	0.0000	4.254	51
52	0.0000	4.2552	18.1036	58436.1769	248660.3272	0.2350	0.0000	4.254	52
53	0.0000	4.2553	18.1044	72168.6784	307096.5040	0.2350	0.0000	4.254	53
54	0.0000	4.2553	18.1050	89128.3179	379265.1825	0.2350	0.0000	4.254	54
55	0.0000	4.2553	18.1055	110073.4726	468393.5004	0.2350	0.0000	4.254	55
60	0.0000	4.2553	18.1069	316240.4765	1345699.9001	0.2350	0.0000	4.255	60
65	0.0000	4.2553	18.1074	908557.1359	3866196.3229	0.2350	0.0000	4.255	65
70	0.0000	4.2553	18.1076	2610279.6146	************	0.2350	0.0000	4.255	70
75	0.0000	4.2553	18.1077	7499318.8621	************	0.2350	0.0000	4.255	75
80	0.0000	4.2553	18.1077	************	************	0.2350	0.0000	4.255	80
85	0.0000	4.2553	18.1077	************	************	0.2350	0.0000	4.255	85
90	0.0000	4.2553	18.1077	************	************	0.2350	0.0000	4.255	90
95	0.0000	4.2553	18.1077	************	************	0.2350	0.0000	4.255	95
100	0.0000	4.2553	18.1077	************	************	0.2350	0.0000	4.255	100

$I = 23.75\ \%$

n	(P/F)	(P/A)	(P/G)	(F/P)	(F/A)	(A/P)	(A/F)	(A/G)	n
1	0.8081	0.8081	0.0000	1.2375	1.0000	1.2375	1.0000	0.000	1
2	0.6530	1.4611	0.6530	1.5314	2.2375	0.6844	0.4469	0.446	2
3	0.5277	1.9887	1.7083	1.8951	3.7689	0.5028	0.2653	0.859	3
4	0.4264	2.4151	2.9875	2.3452	5.6640	0.4141	0.1766	1.237	4
5	0.3446	2.7597	4.3658	2.9022	8.0092	0.3624	0.1249	1.582	5
6	0.2784	3.0382	5.7580	3.5915	10.9114	0.3291	0.0916	1.895	6
7	0.2250	3.2632	7.1080	4.4444	14.5029	0.3065	0.0690	2.178	7
8	0.1818	3.4450	8.3807	5.5000	18.9473	0.2903	0.0528	2.432	8
9	0.1469	3.5919	9.5561	6.8062	24.4473	0.2784	0.0409	2.660	9
10	0.1187	3.7106	10.6247	8.4227	31.2535	0.2695	0.0320	2.863	10
11	0.0959	3.8066	11.5841	10.4231	39.6762	0.2627	0.0252	3.043	11
12	0.0775	3.8841	12.4369	12.8986	50.0994	0.2575	0.0200	3.202	12
13	0.0626	3.9467	13.1887	15.9620	62.9980	0.2534	0.0159	3.341	13
14	0.0506	3.9974	13.8468	19.7530	78.9600	0.2502	0.0127	3.464	14
15	0.0409	4.0383	14.4195	24.4443	98.7130	0.2476	0.0101	3.570	15
16	0.0331	4.0713	14.9154	30.2499	123.1573	0.2456	0.0081	3.663	16
17	0.0267	4.0980	15.3428	37.4342	153.4071	0.2440	0.0065	3.743	17
18	0.0216	4.1196	15.7098	46.3248	190.8413	0.2427	0.0052	3.813	18
19	0.0174	4.1371	16.0238	57.3270	237.1662	0.2417	0.0042	3.873	19
20	0.0141	4.1512	16.2916	70.9421	294.4931	0.2409	0.0034	3.924	20
21	0.0114	4.1626	16.5194	87.7909	365.4352	0.2402	0.0027	3.968	21
22	0.0092	4.1718	16.7127	108.6412	453.2261	0.2397	0.0022	4.006	22
23	0.0074	4.1792	16.8763	134.4435	561.8673	0.2393	0.0018	4.038	23
24	0.0060	4.1852	17.0146	166.3738	696.3108	0.2389	0.0014	4.065	24
25	0.0049	4.1901	17.1312	205.8876	862.6846	0.2387	0.0012	4.088	25
26	0.0039	4.1940	17.2293	254.7859	1068.5722	0.2384	0.0009	4.108	26
27	0.0032	4.1972	17.3117	315.2976	1323.3581	0.2383	0.0008	4.124	27
28	0.0026	4.1997	17.3809	390.1807	1638.6557	0.2381	0.0006	4.138	28
29	0.0021	4.2018	17.4389	482.8486	2028.8364	0.2380	0.0005	4.150	29
30	0.0017	4.2035	17.4875	597.5252	2511.6851	0.2379	0.0004	4.160	30
31	0.0014	4.2048	17.5280	739.4374	3109.2103	0.2378	0.0003	4.168	31
32	0.0011	4.2059	17.5619	915.0538	3848.6477	0.2378	0.0003	4.175	32
33	0.0009	4.2068	17.5902	1132.3791	4763.7015	0.2377	0.0002	4.181	33
34	0.0007	4.2075	17.6137	1401.3192	5896.0807	0.2377	0.0002	4.186	34
35	0.0006	4.2081	17.6333	1734.1325	7297.3998	0.2376	0.0001	4.190	35
36	0.0005	4.2086	17.6496	2145.9889	9031.5323	0.2376	0.0001	4.193	36
37	0.0004	4.2089	17.6632	2655.6613	11177.5212	0.2376	0.0001	4.196	37
38	0.0003	4.2092	17.6745	3286.3808	13833.1825	0.2376	0.0001	4.199	38
39	0.0002	4.2095	17.6838	4066.8963	17119.5633	0.2376	0.0001	4.200	39
40	0.0002	4.2097	17.6915	5032.7841	21186.4596	0.2375	0.0000	4.202	40
41	0.0002	4.2099	17.6980	6228.0704	26219.2437	0.2375	0.0000	4.203	41
42	0.0001	4.2100	17.7033	7707.2371	32447.3141	0.2375	0.0000	4.205	42
43	0.0001	4.2101	17.7077	9537.7059	40154.5512	0.2375	0.0000	4.206	43
44	0.0001	4.2102	17.7113	11802.9111	49692.2571	0.2375	0.0000	4.206	44
45	0.0001	4.2102	17.7143	14606.1024	61495.1682	0.2375	0.0000	4.207	45
46	0.0001	4.2103	17.7168	18075.0518	76101.2706	0.2375	0.0000	4.208	46
47	0.0000	4.2103	17.7189	22367.8766	94176.3224	0.2375	0.0000	4.208	47
48	0.0000	4.2104	17.7206	27680.2472	116544.1989	0.2375	0.0000	4.208	48
49	0.0000	4.2104	17.7220	34254.3060	144224.4462	0.2375	0.0000	4.209	49
50	0.0000	4.2104	17.7231	42389.7036	178478.7522	0.2375	0.0000	4.209	50
51	0.0000	4.2104	17.7241	52457.2583	220868.4558	0.2375	0.0000	4.209	51
52	0.0000	4.2105	17.7249	64915.8571	273325.7141	0.2375	0.0000	4.209	52
53	0.0000	4.2105	17.7255	80333.3731	338241.5711	0.2375	0.0000	4.209	53
54	0.0000	4.2105	17.7261	99412.5493	418574.9443	0.2375	0.0000	4.210	54
55	0.0000	4.2105	17.7265	123023.0297	517987.4936	0.2375	0.0000	4.210	55
60	0.0000	4.2105	17.7278	357036.3683	1503306.8140	0.2375	0.0000	4.210	60
65	0.0000	4.2105	17.7283	1036187.8471	4362891.9877	0.2375	0.0000	4.210	65
70	0.0000	4.2105	17.7284	3007215.3699	***********	0.2375	0.0000	4.210	70
75	0.0000	4.2105	17.7285	8727514.3270	***********	0.2375	0.0000	4.210	75
80	0.0000	4.2105	17.7285	***********	***********	0.2375	0.0000	4.210	80
85	0.0000	4.2105	17.7285	***********	***********	0.2375	0.0000	4.210	85
90	0.0000	4.2105	17.7285	***********	***********	0.2375	0.0000	4.210	90
95	0.0000	4.2105	17.7285	***********	***********	0.2375	0.0000	4.210	95
100	0.0000	4.2105	17.7285	***********	***********	0.2375	0.0000	4.210	100

EXPANDED INTEREST TABLES

$I = 24.00 \%$

n	(P/F)	(P/A)	(P/G)	(F/P)	(F/A)	(A/P)	(A/F)	(A/G)	n
1	0.8065	0.8065	0.0000	1.2400	1.0000	1.2400	1.0000	0.000	1
2	0.6504	1.4568	0.6504	1.5376	2.2400	0.6864	0.4464	0.446	2
3	0.5245	1.9813	1.6993	1.9066	3.7776	0.5047	0.2647	0.857	3
4	0.4230	2.4043	2.9683	2.3642	5.6842	0.4159	0.1759	1.234	4
5	0.3411	2.7454	4.3327	2.9316	8.0484	0.3642	0.1242	1.578	5
6	0.2751	3.0205	5.7081	3.6352	10.9801	0.3311	0.0911	1.889	6
7	0.2218	3.2423	7.0392	4.5077	14.6153	0.3084	0.0684	2.171	7
8	0.1789	3.4212	8.2915	5.5895	19.1229	0.2923	0.0523	2.423	8
9	0.1443	3.5655	9.4458	6.9310	24.7125	0.2805	0.0405	2.649	9
10	0.1164	3.6819	10.4930	8.5944	31.6434	0.2716	0.0316	2.849	10
11	0.0938	3.7757	11.4313	10.6571	40.2379	0.2649	0.0249	3.027	11
12	0.0757	3.8514	12.2637	13.2148	50.8950	0.2596	0.0196	3.184	12
13	0.0610	3.9124	12.9960	16.3863	64.1097	0.2556	0.0156	3.321	13
14	0.0492	3.9616	13.6358	20.3191	80.4961	0.2524	0.0124	3.442	14
15	0.0397	4.0013	14.1915	25.1956	100.8151	0.2499	0.0099	3.546	15
16	0.0320	4.0333	14.6716	31.2426	126.0108	0.2479	0.0079	3.637	16
17	0.0258	4.0591	15.0846	38.7408	157.2534	0.2464	0.0064	3.716	17
18	0.0208	4.0799	15.4385	48.0386	195.9942	0.2451	0.0051	3.784	18
19	0.0168	4.0967	15.7406	59.5679	244.0328	0.2441	0.0041	3.842	19
20	0.0135	4.1103	15.9979	73.8641	303.6006	0.2433	0.0033	3.892	20
21	0.0109	4.1212	16.2162	91.5915	377.4648	0.2426	0.0026	3.934	21
22	0.0088	4.1300	16.4011	113.5735	469.0563	0.2421	0.0021	3.971	22
23	0.0071	4.1371	16.5574	140.8312	582.6298	0.2417	0.0017	4.002	23
24	0.0057	4.1428	16.6891	174.6306	723.4610	0.2414	0.0014	4.028	24
25	0.0046	4.1474	16.7999	216.5420	898.0916	0.2411	0.0011	4.050	25
26	0.0037	4.1511	16.8930	268.5121	1114.6336	0.2409	0.0009	4.069	26
27	0.0030	4.1542	16.9711	332.9550	1383.1457	0.2407	0.0007	4.085	27
28	0.0024	4.1566	17.0365	412.8642	1716.1007	0.2406	0.0006	4.098	28
29	0.0020	4.1585	17.0912	511.9516	2128.9648	0.2405	0.0005	4.109	29
30	0.0016	4.1601	17.1369	634.8199	2640.9164	0.2404	0.0004	4.119	30
31	0.0013	4.1614	17.1750	787.1767	3275.7363	0.2403	0.0003	4.127	31
32	0.0010	4.1624	17.2067	976.0991	4062.9130	0.2402	0.0002	4.133	32
33	0.0008	4.1632	17.2332	1210.3629	5039.0122	0.2402	0.0002	4.139	33
34	0.0007	4.1639	17.2552	1500.8500	6249.3751	0.2402	0.0002	4.144	34
35	0.0005	4.1644	17.2734	1861.0540	7750.2251	0.2401	0.0001	4.147	35
36	0.0004	4.1649	17.2886	2307.7070	9611.2791	0.2401	0.0001	4.151	36
37	0.0003	4.1652	17.3012	2861.5567	11918.9861	0.2401	0.0001	4.153	37
38	0.0003	4.1655	17.3116	3548.3303	14780.5428	0.2401	0.0001	4.156	38
39	0.0002	4.1657	17.3202	4399.9295	18328.8731	0.2401	0.0001	4.157	39
40	0.0002	4.1659	17.3274	5455.9126	22728.8026	0.2400	0.0000	4.159	40
41	0.0001	4.1661	17.3333	6765.3317	28184.7152	0.2400	0.0000	4.160	41
42	0.0001	4.1662	17.3382	8389.0113	34950.0469	0.2400	0.0000	4.161	42
43	0.0001	4.1663	17.3422	10402.3740	43339.0581	0.2400	0.0000	4.162	43
44	0.0001	4.1663	17.3456	12898.9437	53741.4321	0.2400	0.0000	4.163	44
45	0.0001	4.1664	17.3483	15994.6902	66640.3758	0.2400	0.0000	4.163	45
46	0.0001	4.1665	17.3506	19833.4158	82635.0660	0.2400	0.0000	4.164	46
47	0.0000	4.1665	17.3524	24593.4356	102468.4818	0.2400	0.0000	4.164	47
48	0.0000	4.1665	17.3540	30495.8602	127061.9174	0.2400	0.0000	4.165	48
49	0.0000	4.1666	17.3553	37814.8666	157557.7776	0.2400	0.0000	4.165	49
50	0.0000	4.1666	17.3563	46890.4346	195372.6442	0.2400	0.0000	4.165	50
51	0.0000	4.1666	17.3572	58144.1389	242263.0788	0.2400	0.0000	4.165	51
52	0.0000	4.1666	17.3579	72098.7323	300407.2178	0.2400	0.0000	4.165	52
53	0.0000	4.1666	17.3584	89402.4280	372505.9500	0.2400	0.0000	4.166	53
54	0.0000	4.1666	17.3589	110859.0107	461908.3780	0.2400	0.0000	4.166	54
55	0.0000	4.1666	17.3593	137465.1733	572767.3888	0.2400	0.0000	4.166	55
60	0.0000	4.1667	17.3604	402996.3473	1679147.2802	0.2400	0.0000	4.166	60
65	0.0000	4.1667	17.3609	1181434.1917	4922638.2987	0.2400	0.0000	4.166	65
70	0.0000	4.1667	17.3610	3463522.0859	***********	0.2400	0.0000	4.166	70
75	0.0000	4.1667	17.3611	***********	***********	0.2400	0.0000	4.166	75
80	0.0000	4.1667	17.3611	***********	***********	0.2400	0.0000	4.166	80
85	0.0000	4.1667	17.3611	***********	***********	0.2400	0.0000	4.166	85
90	0.0000	4.1667	17.3611	***********	***********	0.2400	0.0000	4.166	90
95	0.0000	4.1667	17.3611	***********	***********	0.2400	0.0000	4.166	95
100	0.0000	4.1667	17.3611	***********	***********	0.2400	0.0000	4.166	100

$$I = 24.25 \%$$

n	(P/F)	(P/A)	(P/G)	(F/P)	(F/A)	(A/P)	(A/F)	(A/G)	n
1	0.8048	0.8048	0.0000	1.2425	1.0000	1.2425	1.0000	0.000	1
2	0.6477	1.4526	0.6477	1.5438	2.2425	0.6884	0.4459	0.445	2
3	0.5213	1.9739	1.6904	1.9182	3.7863	0.5066	0.2641	0.856	3
4	0.4196	2.3935	2.9491	2.3833	5.7045	0.4178	0.1753	1.232	4
5	0.3377	2.7312	4.2999	2.9613	8.0878	0.3661	0.1236	1.574	5
6	0.2718	3.0030	5.6588	3.6794	11.0491	0.3330	0.0905	1.884	6
7	0.2187	3.2217	6.9712	4.5717	14.7285	0.3104	0.0679	2.163	7
8	0.1760	3.3977	8.2036	5.6803	19.3002	0.2943	0.0518	2.414	8
9	0.1417	3.5394	9.3371	7.0578	24.9805	0.2825	0.0400	2.638	9
10	0.1140	3.6535	10.3634	8.7693	32.0383	0.2737	0.0312	2.836	10
11	0.0918	3.7452	11.2812	10.8958	40.8076	0.2670	0.0245	3.012	11
12	0.0739	3.8191	12.0937	13.5381	51.7034	0.2618	0.0193	3.166	12
13	0.0594	3.8786	12.8071	16.8211	65.2415	0.2578	0.0153	3.302	13
14	0.0478	3.9264	13.4291	20.9002	82.0625	0.2547	0.0122	3.420	14
15	0.0385	3.9649	13.9682	25.9684	102.9627	0.2522	0.0097	3.523	15
16	0.0310	3.9959	14.4331	32.2658	128.9311	0.2503	0.0078	3.612	16
17	0.0249	4.0209	14.8322	40.0902	161.1969	0.2487	0.0062	3.688	17
18	0.0201	4.0409	15.1735	49.8121	201.2872	0.2475	0.0050	3.755	18
19	0.0162	4.0571	15.4643	61.8916	251.0993	0.2465	0.0040	3.811	19
20	0.0130	4.0701	15.7114	76.9003	312.9909	0.2457	0.0032	3.860	20
21	0.0105	4.0806	15.9207	95.5486	389.8911	0.2451	0.0026	3.901	21
22	0.0084	4.0890	16.0976	118.7191	485.4398	0.2446	0.0021	3.936	22
23	0.0068	4.0958	16.2467	147.5085	604.1589	0.2442	0.0017	3.966	23
24	0.0055	4.1012	16.3722	183.2794	751.6674	0.2438	0.0013	3.992	24
25	0.0044	4.1056	16.4776	227.7246	934.9468	0.2436	0.0011	4.013	25
26	0.0035	4.1091	16.5660	282.9478	1162.6714	0.2434	0.0009	4.031	26
27	0.0028	4.1120	16.6399	351.5627	1445.6192	0.2432	0.0007	4.046	27
28	0.0023	4.1143	16.7017	436.8166	1797.1818	0.2431	0.0006	4.059	28
29	0.0018	4.1161	16.7533	542.7446	2233.9984	0.2429	0.0004	4.070	29
30	0.0015	4.1176	16.7963	674.3602	2776.7430	0.2429	0.0004	4.079	30
31	0.0012	4.1188	16.8321	837.8925	3451.1032	0.2428	0.0003	4.086	31
32	0.0010	4.1198	16.8619	1041.0815	4288.9958	0.2427	0.0002	4.092	32
33	0.0008	4.1205	16.8866	1293.5437	5330.0772	0.2427	0.0002	4.098	33
34	0.0006	4.1211	16.9072	1607.2281	6623.6210	0.2427	0.0002	4.102	34
35	0.0005	4.1216	16.9242	1996.9809	8230.8490	0.2426	0.0001	4.106	35
36	0.0004	4.1220	16.9383	2481.2488	10227.8299	0.2426	0.0001	4.109	36
37	0.0003	4.1224	16.9500	3082.9516	12709.0787	0.2426	0.0001	4.111	37
38	0.0003	4.1226	16.9596	3830.5673	15792.0303	0.2426	0.0001	4.113	38
39	0.0002	4.1228	16.9676	4759.4799	19622.5976	0.2426	0.0001	4.115	39
40	0.0002	4.1230	16.9742	5913.6538	24382.0775	0.2425	0.0000	4.116	40
41	0.0001	4.1232	16.9797	7347.7148	30295.7313	0.2425	0.0000	4.118	41
42	0.0001	4.1233	16.9842	9129.5357	37643.4462	0.2425	0.0000	4.119	42
43	0.0001	4.1233	16.9879	11343.4481	46772.9819	0.2425	0.0000	4.119	43
44	0.0001	4.1234	16.9909	14094.2343	58116.4300	0.2425	0.0000	4.120	44
45	0.0001	4.1235	16.9934	17512.0861	72210.6642	0.2425	0.0000	4.121	45
46	0.0000	4.1235	16.9955	21758.7670	89722.7503	0.2425	0.0000	4.121	46
47	0.0000	4.1236	16.9972	27035.2679	111481.5173	0.2425	0.0000	4.122	47
48	0.0000	4.1236	16.9986	33591.3204	138516.7852	0.2425	0.0000	4.122	48
49	0.0000	4.1236	16.9997	41737.2156	172108.1056	0.2425	0.0000	4.122	49
50	0.0000	4.1236	17.0007	51858.4904	213845.3212	0.2425	0.0000	4.122	50
51	0.0000	4.1236	17.0015	64434.1743	265703.8116	0.2425	0.0000	4.122	51
52	0.0000	4.1237	17.0021	80059.4616	330137.9859	0.2425	0.0000	4.123	52
53	0.0000	4.1237	17.0026	99473.8810	410197.4475	0.2425	0.0000	4.123	53
54	0.0000	4.1237	17.0031	123596.2972	509671.3285	0.2425	0.0000	4.123	54
55	0.0000	4.1237	17.0034	153568.3992	633267.6257	0.2425	0.0000	4.123	55
60	0.0000	4.1237	17.0044	454761.6613	1875301.6960	0.2425	0.0000	4.123	60
65	0.0000	4.1237	17.0048	1346684.4064	5553333.6347	0.2425	0.0000	4.123	65
70	0.0000	4.1237	17.0049	3987932.6797	************	0.2425	0.0000	4.123	70
75	0.0000	4.1237	17.0050	************	************	0.2425	0.0000	4.123	75
80	0.0000	4.1237	17.0050	************	************	0.2425	0.0000	4.123	80
85	0.0000	4.1237	17.0050	************	************	0.2425	0.0000	4.123	85
90	0.0000	4.1237	17.0050	************	************	0.2425	0.0000	4.123	90
95	0.0000	4.1237	17.0050	************	************	0.2425	0.0000	4.123	95
100	0.0000	4.1237	17.0050	************	************	0.2425	0.0000	4.123	100

EXPANDED INTEREST TABLES

$I = 24.50\%$

n	(P/F)	(P/A)	(P/G)	(F/P)	(F/A)	(A/P)	(A/F)	(A/G)	n
1	0.8032	0.8032	0.0000	1.2450	1.0000	1.2450	1.0000	0.000	1
2	0.6452	1.4484	0.6452	1.5500	2.2450	0.6904	0.4454	0.445	2
3	0.5182	1.9666	1.6815	1.9298	3.7950	0.5085	0.2635	0.855	3
4	0.4162	2.3828	2.9302	2.4026	5.7248	0.4197	0.1747	1.229	4
5	0.3343	2.7171	4.2674	2.9912	8.1274	0.3680	0.1230	1.570	5
6	0.2685	2.9856	5.6101	3.7241	11.1186	0.3349	0.0899	1.879	6
7	0.2157	3.2013	6.9042	4.6364	14.8426	0.3124	0.0674	2.156	7
8	0.1732	3.3745	8.1168	5.7724	19.4791	0.2963	0.0513	2.405	8
9	0.1391	3.5137	9.2300	7.1866	25.2515	0.2846	0.0396	2.626	9
10	0.1118	3.6254	10.2359	8.9473	32.4381	0.2758	0.0308	2.823	10
11	0.0898	3.7152	11.1336	11.1394	41.3854	0.2692	0.0242	2.996	11
12	0.0721	3.7873	11.9268	13.8686	52.5248	0.2640	0.0190	3.149	12
13	0.0579	3.8452	12.6218	17.2664	66.3934	0.2601	0.0151	3.282	13
14	0.0465	3.8918	13.2265	21.4967	83.6598	0.2570	0.0120	3.398	14
15	0.0374	3.9291	13.7496	26.7633	105.1565	0.2545	0.0095	3.499	15
16	0.0300	3.9591	14.1998	33.3204	131.9198	0.2526	0.0076	3.586	16
17	0.0241	3.9832	14.5855	41.4838	165.2402	0.2511	0.0061	3.661	17
18	0.0194	4.0026	14.9146	51.6474	206.7240	0.2498	0.0048	3.726	18
19	0.0156	4.0182	15.1946	64.3010	258.3714	0.2489	0.0039	3.781	19
20	0.0125	4.0306	15.4319	80.0547	322.6724	0.2481	0.0031	3.828	20
21	0.0100	4.0407	15.6326	99.6681	402.7271	0.2475	0.0025	3.868	21
22	0.0081	4.0487	15.8018	124.0868	502.3953	0.2470	0.0020	3.902	22
23	0.0065	4.0552	15.9442	154.4881	626.4821	0.2466	0.0016	3.931	23
24	0.0052	4.0604	16.0638	192.3377	780.9702	0.2463	0.0013	3.956	24
25	0.0042	4.0646	16.1640	239.4604	973.3079	0.2460	0.0010	3.976	25
26	0.0034	4.0679	16.2479	298.1283	1212.7684	0.2458	0.0008	3.994	26
27	0.0027	4.0706	16.3179	371.1697	1510.8966	0.2457	0.0007	4.008	27
28	0.0022	4.0728	16.3764	462.1062	1882.0663	0.2455	0.0005	4.020	28
29	0.0017	4.0745	16.4250	575.3223	2344.1726	0.2454	0.0004	4.031	29
30	0.0014	4.0759	16.4655	716.2762	2919.4948	0.2453	0.0003	4.039	30
31	0.0011	4.0771	16.4992	891.7639	3635.7711	0.2453	0.0003	4.046	31
32	0.0009	4.0780	16.5271	1110.2461	4527.5350	0.2452	0.0002	4.052	32
33	0.0007	4.0787	16.5502	1382.2564	5637.7811	0.2452	0.0002	4.057	33
34	0.0006	4.0793	16.5694	1720.9092	7020.0374	0.2451	0.0001	4.061	34
35	0.0005	4.0797	16.5853	2142.5319	8740.9466	0.2451	0.0001	4.065	35
36	0.0004	4.0801	16.5984	2667.4522	10883.4785	0.2451	0.0001	4.068	36
37	0.0003	4.0804	16.6092	3320.9780	13550.9307	0.2451	0.0001	4.070	37
38	0.0002	4.0806	16.6182	4134.6177	16871.9088	0.2451	0.0001	4.072	38
39	0.0002	4.0808	16.6256	5147.5990	21006.5264	0.2450	0.0000	4.074	39
40	0.0002	4.0810	16.6317	6408.7607	26154.1254	0.2450	0.0000	4.075	40
41	0.0001	4.0811	16.6367	7978.9071	32562.8861	0.2450	0.0000	4.076	41
42	0.0001	4.0812	16.6408	9933.7393	40541.7932	0.2450	0.0000	4.077	42
43	0.0001	4.0813	16.6442	12367.5055	50475.5326	0.2450	0.0000	4.078	43
44	0.0001	4.0814	16.6470	15397.5443	62843.0381	0.2450	0.0000	4.078	44
45	0.0001	4.0814	16.6493	19169.9427	78240.5824	0.2450	0.0000	4.079	45
46	0.0000	4.0815	16.6512	23866.5786	97410.5251	0.2450	0.0000	4.079	46
47	0.0000	4.0815	16.6527	29713.8904	121277.1037	0.2450	0.0000	4.080	47
48	0.0000	4.0815	16.6540	36993.7936	150990.9941	0.2450	0.0000	4.080	48
49	0.0000	4.0815	16.6550	46057.2730	187984.7877	0.2450	0.0000	4.080	49
50	0.0000	4.0816	16.6559	57341.3049	234042.0607	0.2450	0.0000	4.080	50
51	0.0000	4.0816	16.6566	71389.9246	291383.3655	0.2450	0.0000	4.080	51
52	0.0000	4.0816	16.6571	88880.4561	362773.2901	0.2450	0.0000	4.081	52
53	0.0000	4.0816	16.6576	110656.1678	451653.7462	0.2450	0.0000	4.081	53
54	0.0000	4.0816	16.6580	137766.9289	562309.9140	0.2450	0.0000	4.081	54
55	0.0000	4.0816	16.6583	171519.8265	700076.8429	0.2450	0.0000	4.081	55
60	0.0000	4.0816	16.6592	513051.6467	2094084.2724	0.2450	0.0000	4.081	60
65	0.0000	4.0816	16.6595	1534644.6972	6263851.8253	0.2450	0.0000	4.081	65
70	0.0000	4.0816	16.6597	4590443.0121	***********	0.2450	0.0000	4.081	70
75	0.0000	4.0816	16.6597	***********	***********	0.2450	0.0000	4.081	75
80	0.0000	4.0816	16.6597	***********	***********	0.2450	0.0000	4.081	80
85	0.0000	4.0816	16.6597	***********	***********	0.2450	0.0000	4.081	85
90	0.0000	4.0816	16.6597	***********	***********	0.2450	0.0000	4.081	90
95	0.0000	4.0816	16.6597	***********	***********	0.2450	0.0000	4.081	95
100	0.0000	4.0816	16.6597	***********	***********	0.2450	0.0000	4.081	100

$I = 24.75\%$

n	(P/F)	(P/A)	(P/G)	(F/P)	(F/A)	(A/P)	(A/F)	(A/G)	n
1	0.8016	0.8016	0.0000	1.2475	1.0000	1.2475	1.0000	0.000	1
2	0.6426	1.4442	0.6426	1.5563	2.2475	0.6924	0.4449	0.444	2
3	0.5151	1.9593	1.6727	1.9414	3.8038	0.5104	0.2629	0.853	3
4	0.4129	2.3721	2.9114	2.4219	5.7452	0.4216	0.1741	1.227	4
5	0.3310	2.7031	4.2353	3.0214	8.1671	0.3699	0.1224	1.566	5
6	0.2653	2.9684	5.5619	3.7691	11.1885	0.3369	0.0894	1.873	6
7	0.2127	3.1811	6.8379	4.7020	14.9576	0.3144	0.0669	2.149	7
8	0.1705	3.3516	8.0313	5.8658	19.6596	0.2984	0.0509	2.396	8
9	0.1367	3.4883	9.1246	7.3175	25.5254	0.2867	0.0392	2.615	9
10	0.1095	3.5978	10.1105	9.1286	32.8429	0.2779	0.0304	2.810	10
11	0.0878	3.6856	10.9886	11.3880	41.9716	0.2713	0.0238	2.981	11
12	0.0704	3.7560	11.7629	14.2065	53.3595	0.2662	0.0187	3.131	12
13	0.0564	3.8124	12.4400	17.7226	67.5660	0.2623	0.0148	3.263	13
14	0.0452	3.8577	13.0280	22.1089	85.2886	0.2592	0.0117	3.377	14
15	0.0363	3.8939	13.5356	27.5809	107.3975	0.2568	0.0093	3.476	15
16	0.0291	3.9230	13.9715	34.4072	134.9784	0.2549	0.0074	3.561	16
17	0.0233	3.9463	14.3443	42.9229	169.3856	0.2534	0.0059	3.634	17
18	0.0187	3.9649	14.6618	53.5464	212.3085	0.2522	0.0047	3.697	18
19	0.0150	3.9799	14.9312	66.7991	265.8549	0.2513	0.0038	3.751	19
20	0.0120	3.9919	15.1592	83.3319	332.6540	0.2505	0.0030	3.797	20
21	0.0096	4.0015	15.3516	103.9565	415.9858	0.2499	0.0024	3.836	21
22	0.0077	4.0092	15.5136	129.6857	519.9423	0.2494	0.0019	3.869	22
23	0.0062	4.0154	15.6496	161.7829	649.6281	0.2490	0.0015	3.897	23
24	0.0050	4.0204	15.7635	201.8242	811.4110	0.2487	0.0012	3.920	24
25	0.0040	4.0244	15.8588	251.7757	1013.2353	0.2485	0.0010	3.940	25
26	0.0032	4.0275	15.9384	314.0902	1265.0110	0.2483	0.0008	3.957	26
27	0.0026	4.0301	16.0048	391.8275	1579.1012	0.2481	0.0006	3.971	27
28	0.0020	4.0321	16.0600	488.8049	1970.9287	0.2480	0.0005	3.983	28
29	0.0016	4.0338	16.1059	609.7841	2459.7336	0.2479	0.0004	3.992	29
30	0.0013	4.0351	16.1441	760.7056	3069.5177	0.2478	0.0003	4.000	30
31	0.0011	4.0361	16.1757	948.9803	3830.2233	0.2478	0.0003	4.007	31
32	0.0008	4.0370	16.2019	1183.8529	4779.2036	0.2477	0.0002	4.013	32
33	0.0007	4.0377	16.2235	1476.8565	5963.0565	0.2477	0.0002	4.018	33
34	0.0005	4.0382	16.2414	1842.3785	7439.9129	0.2476	0.0001	4.021	34
35	0.0004	4.0386	16.2562	2298.3671	9282.2914	0.2476	0.0001	4.025	35
36	0.0003	4.0390	16.2684	2867.2130	11580.6585	0.2476	0.0001	4.027	36
37	0.0003	4.0393	16.2785	3576.8482	14447.8715	0.2476	0.0001	4.030	37
38	0.0002	4.0395	16.2868	4462.1181	18024.7197	0.2476	0.0001	4.031	38
39	0.0002	4.0397	16.2936	5566.4924	22486.8378	0.2475	0.0000	4.033	39
40	0.0001	4.0398	16.2992	6944.1992	28053.3302	0.2475	0.0000	4.034	40
41	0.0001	4.0399	16.3039	8662.8885	34997.5294	0.2475	0.0000	4.035	41
42	0.0001	4.0400	16.3077	10806.9534	43660.4179	0.2475	0.0000	4.036	42
43	0.0001	4.0401	16.3108	13481.6744	54467.3714	0.2475	0.0000	4.037	43
44	0.0001	4.0402	16.3133	16818.3888	67949.0458	0.2475	0.0000	4.037	44
45	0.0000	4.0402	16.3154	20980.9401	84767.4346	0.2475	0.0000	4.038	45
46	0.0000	4.0402	16.3171	26173.7227	105748.3747	0.2475	0.0000	4.038	46
47	0.0000	4.0403	16.3185	32651.7191	131922.0974	0.2475	0.0000	4.039	47
48	0.0000	4.0403	16.3197	40733.0196	164573.8166	0.2475	0.0000	4.039	48
49	0.0000	4.0403	16.3206	50814.4420	205306.8362	0.2475	0.0000	4.039	49
50	0.0000	4.0403	16.3214	63391.0163	256121.2781	0.2475	0.0000	4.039	50
51	0.0000	4.0404	16.3221	79080.2929	319512.2944	0.2475	0.0000	4.039	51
52	0.0000	4.0404	16.3226	98652.6654	398592.5873	0.2475	0.0000	4.039	52
53	0.0000	4.0404	16.3230	123069.2000	497245.2527	0.2475	0.0000	4.040	53
54	0.0000	4.0404	16.3233	153528.8271	620314.4527	0.2475	0.0000	4.040	54
55	0.0000	4.0404	16.3236	191527.2117	773843.2798	0.2475	0.0000	4.040	55
60	0.0000	4.0404	16.3244	578673.0512	2338068.8936	0.2475	0.0000	4.040	60
65	0.0000	4.0404	16.3247	1748380.8024	7064160.8179	0.2475	0.0000	4.040	65
70	0.0000	4.0404	16.3248	5282491.4243	************	0.2475	0.0000	4.040	70
75	0.0000	4.0404	16.3248	************	************	0.2475	0.0000	4.040	75
80	0.0000	4.0404	16.3249	************	************	0.2475	0.0000	4.040	80
85	0.0000	4.0404	16.3249	************	************	0.2475	0.0000	4.040	85
90	0.0000	4.0404	16.3249	************	************	0.2475	0.0000	4.040	90
95	0.0000	4.0404	16.3249	************	************	0.2475	0.0000	4.040	95
100	0.0000	4.0404	16.3249	************	************	0.2475	0.0000	4.040	100

EXPANDED INTEREST TABLES

I = 25.00 %

n	(P/F)	(P/A)	(P/G)	(F/P)	(F/A)	(A/P)	(A/F)	(A/G)	n
1	0.8000	0.8000	0.0000	1.2500	1.0000	1.2500	1.0000	0.000	1
2	0.6400	1.4400	0.6400	1.5625	2.2500	0.6944	0.4444	0.444	2
3	0.5120	1.9520	1.6640	1.9531	3.8125	0.5123	0.2623	0.852	3
4	0.4096	2.3616	2.8928	2.4414	5.7656	0.4234	0.1734	1.224	4
5	0.3277	2.6893	4.2035	3.0518	8.2070	0.3718	0.1218	1.563	5
6	0.2621	2.9514	5.5142	3.8147	11.2588	0.3388	0.0888	1.868	6
7	0.2097	3.1611	6.7725	4.7684	15.0735	0.3163	0.0663	2.142	7
8	0.1678	3.3289	7.9469	5.9605	19.8419	0.3004	0.0504	2.387	8
9	0.1342	3.4631	9.0207	7.4506	25.8023	0.2888	0.0388	2.604	9
10	0.1074	3.5705	9.9870	9.3132	33.2529	0.2801	0.0301	2.797	10
11	0.0859	3.6564	10.8460	11.6415	42.5661	0.2735	0.0235	2.966	11
12	0.0687	3.7251	11.6020	14.5519	54.2077	0.2684	0.0184	3.114	12
13	0.0550	3.7801	12.2617	18.1899	68.7596	0.2645	0.0145	3.243	13
14	0.0440	3.8241	12.8334	22.7374	86.9495	0.2615	0.0115	3.355	14
15	0.0352	3.8593	13.3260	28.4217	109.6868	0.2591	0.0091	3.453	15
16	0.0281	3.8874	13.7482	35.5271	138.1085	0.2572	0.0072	3.536	16
17	0.0225	3.9099	14.1085	44.4089	173.6357	0.2558	0.0058	3.608	17
18	0.0180	3.9279	14.4147	55.5112	218.0446	0.2546	0.0046	3.669	18
19	0.0144	3.9424	14.6741	69.3889	273.5558	0.2537	0.0037	3.722	19
20	0.0115	3.9539	14.8932	86.7362	342.9447	0.2529	0.0029	3.766	20
21	0.0092	3.9631	15.0777	108.4202	429.6809	0.2523	0.0023	3.804	21
22	0.0074	3.9705	15.2326	135.5253	538.1011	0.2519	0.0019	3.836	22
23	0.0059	3.9764	15.3625	169.4066	673.6264	0.2515	0.0015	3.863	23
24	0.0047	3.9811	15.4711	211.7582	843.0329	0.2512	0.0012	3.886	24
25	0.0038	3.9849	15.5618	264.6978	1054.7912	0.2509	0.0009	3.905	25
26	0.0030	3.9879	15.6373	330.8722	1319.4890	0.2508	0.0008	3.921	26
27	0.0024	3.9903	15.7002	413.5903	1650.3612	0.2506	0.0006	3.934	27
28	0.0019	3.9923	15.7524	516.9879	2063.9515	0.2505	0.0005	3.945	28
29	0.0015	3.9938	15.7957	646.2349	2580.9394	0.2504	0.0004	3.955	29
30	0.0012	3.9950	15.8316	807.7936	3227.1743	0.2503	0.0003	3.962	30
31	0.0010	3.9960	15.8614	1009.7420	4034.9678	0.2502	0.0002	3.969	31
32	0.0008	3.9968	15.8859	1262.1774	5044.7098	0.2502	0.0002	3.974	32
33	0.0006	3.9975	15.9062	1577.7218	6306.8872	0.2502	0.0002	3.979	33
34	0.0005	3.9980	15.9229	1972.1523	7884.6091	0.2501	0.0001	3.982	34
35	0.0004	3.9984	15.9367	2465.1903	9856.7613	0.2501	0.0001	3.985	35
36	0.0003	3.9987	15.9481	3081.4879	12321.9516	0.2501	0.0001	3.988	36
37	0.0003	3.9990	15.9574	3851.8599	15403.4396	0.2501	0.0001	3.990	37
38	0.0002	3.9992	15.9651	4814.8249	19255.2994	0.2501	0.0001	3.992	38
39	0.0002	3.9993	15.9714	6018.5311	24070.1243	0.2500	0.0000	3.993	39
40	0.0001	3.9995	15.9766	7523.1638	30088.6554	0.2500	0.0000	3.994	40
41	0.0001	3.9996	15.9809	9403.9548	37611.8192	0.2500	0.0000	3.995	41
42	0.0001	3.9997	15.9843	11754.9435	47015.7740	0.2500	0.0000	3.996	42
43	0.0001	3.9997	15.9872	14693.6794	58770.7175	0.2500	0.0000	3.997	43
44	0.0001	3.9998	15.9895	18367.0992	73464.3969	0.2500	0.0000	3.997	44
45	0.0000	3.9998	15.9915	22958.8740	91831.4962	0.2500	0.0000	3.998	45
46	0.0000	3.9999	15.9930	28698.5925	114790.3702	0.2500	0.0000	3.998	46
47	0.0000	3.9999	15.9943	35873.2407	143488.9627	0.2500	0.0000	3.998	47
48	0.0000	3.9999	15.9954	44841.5509	179362.2034	0.2500	0.0000	3.998	48
49	0.0000	3.9999	15.9962	56051.9386	224203.7543	0.2500	0.0000	3.999	49
50	0.0000	3.9999	15.9969	70064.9232	280255.6929	0.2500	0.0000	3.999	50
51	0.0000	4.0000	15.9975	87581.1540	350320.6161	0.2500	0.0000	3.999	51
52	0.0000	4.0000	15.9980	109476.4425	437901.7701	0.2500	0.0000	3.999	52
53	0.0000	4.0000	15.9983	136845.5532	547378.2126	0.2500	0.0000	3.999	53
54	0.0000	4.0000	15.9986	171056.9414	684223.7658	0.2500	0.0000	3.999	54
55	0.0000	4.0000	15.9989	213821.1768	855280.7072	0.2500	0.0000	3.999	55
60	0.0000	4.0000	15.9996	652530.4468	2610117.7872	0.2500	0.0000	3.999	60
65	0.0000	4.0000	15.9999	1991364.8889	7965455.5557	0.2500	0.0000	4.000	65
70	0.0000	4.0000	16.0000	6077163.3573	************	0.2500	0.0000	4.000	70
75	0.0000	4.0000	16.0000	************	************	0.2500	0.0000	4.000	75
80	0.0000	4.0000	16.0000	************	************	0.2500	0.0000	4.000	80
85	0.0000	4.0000	16.0000	************	************	0.2500	0.0000	4.000	85
90	0.0000	4.0000	16.0000	************	************	0.2500	0.0000	4.000	90
95	0.0000	4.0000	16.0000	************	************	0.2500	0.0000	4.000	95
100	0.0000	4.0000	16.0000	************	************	0.2500	0.0000	4.000	100

$I = 30.00\ \%$

n	(P/F)	(P/A)	(P/G)	(F/P)	(F/A)	(A/P)	(A/F)	(A/G)	n
1	0.7692	0.7692	0.0000	1.3000	1.0000	1.3000	1.0000	0.000	1
2	0.5917	1.3609	0.5917	1.6900	2.3000	0.7348	0.4348	0.434	2
3	0.4552	1.8161	1.5020	2.1970	3.9900	0.5506	0.2506	0.827	3
4	0.3501	2.1662	2.5524	2.8561	6.1870	0.4616	0.1616	1.178	4
5	0.2693	2.4356	3.6297	3.7129	9.0431	0.4106	0.1106	1.490	5
6	0.2072	2.6427	4.6656	4.8268	12.7560	0.3784	0.0784	1.765	6
7	0.1594	2.8021	5.6218	6.2749	17.5828	0.3569	0.0569	2.006	7
8	0.1226	2.9247	6.4800	8.1573	23.8577	0.3419	0.0419	2.215	8
9	0.0943	3.0190	7.2343	10.6045	32.0150	0.3312	0.0312	2.396	9
10	0.0725	3.0915	7.8872	13.7858	42.6195	0.3235	0.0235	2.551	10
11	0.0558	3.1473	8.4452	17.9216	56.4053	0.3177	0.0177	2.683	11
12	0.0429	3.1903	8.9173	23.2981	74.3270	0.3135	0.0135	2.795	12
13	0.0330	3.2233	9.3135	30.2875	97.6250	0.3102	0.0102	2.889	13
14	0.0254	3.2487	9.6437	39.3738	127.9125	0.3078	0.0078	2.968	14
15	0.0195	3.2682	9.9172	51.1859	167.2863	0.3060	0.0060	3.034	15
16	0.0150	3.2832	10.1426	66.5417	218.4722	0.3046	0.0046	3.089	16
17	0.0116	3.2948	10.3276	86.5042	285.0139	0.3035	0.0035	3.134	17
18	0.0089	3.3037	10.4788	112.4554	371.5180	0.3027	0.0027	3.171	18
19	0.0068	3.3105	10.6019	146.1920	483.9734	0.3021	0.0021	3.202	19
20	0.0053	3.3158	10.7019	190.0496	630.1655	0.3016	0.0016	3.227	20
21	0.0040	3.3198	10.7828	247.0645	820.2151	0.3012	0.0012	3.248	21
22	0.0031	3.3230	10.8482	321.1839	1067.2796	0.3009	0.0009	3.264	22
23	0.0024	3.3254	10.9009	417.5391	1388.4635	0.3007	0.0007	3.278	23
24	0.0018	3.3272	10.9433	542.8008	1806.0026	0.3006	0.0006	3.289	24
25	0.0014	3.3286	10.9773	705.6410	2348.8033	0.3004	0.0004	3.297	25
26	0.0011	3.3297	11.0045	917.3333	3054.4443	0.3003	0.0003	3.305	26
27	0.0008	3.3305	11.0263	1192.5333	3971.7776	0.3003	0.0003	3.310	27
28	0.0006	3.3312	11.0437	1550.2933	5164.3109	0.3002	0.0002	3.315	28
29	0.0005	3.3317	11.0576	2015.3813	6714.6042	0.3001	0.0001	3.318	29
30	0.0004	3.3321	11.0687	2619.9956	8729.9855	0.3001	0.0001	3.321	30
31	0.0003	3.3324	11.0775	3405.9943	11349.9811	0.3001	0.0001	3.324	31
32	0.0002	3.3326	11.0845	4427.7926	14755.9755	0.3001	0.0001	3.326	32
33	0.0002	3.3328	11.0901	5756.1304	19183.7681	0.3001	0.0001	3.327	33
34	0.0001	3.3329	11.0945	7482.9696	24939.8985	0.3000	0.0000	3.328	34
35	0.0001	3.3330	11.0980	9727.8604	32422.8681	0.3000	0.0000	3.329	35
36	0.0001	3.3331	11.1007	12646.2186	42150.7285	0.3000	0.0000	3.330	36
37	0.0001	3.3331	11.1029	16440.0841	54796.9471	0.3000	0.0000	3.331	37
38	0.0000	3.3332	11.1047	21372.1094	71237.0312	0.3000	0.0000	3.331	38
39	0.0000	3.3332	11.1060	27783.7422	92609.1405	0.3000	0.0000	3.331	39
40	0.0000	3.3332	11.1071	36118.8648	120392.8827	0.3000	0.0000	3.332	40
41	0.0000	3.3333	11.1080	46954.5243	156511.7475	0.3000	0.0000	3.332	41
42	0.0000	3.3333	11.1086	61040.8815	203466.2718	0.3000	0.0000	3.332	42
43	0.0000	3.3333	11.1092	79353.1460	264507.1533	0.3000	0.0000	3.332	43
44	0.0000	3.3333	11.1096	103159.0898	343860.2993	0.3000	0.0000	3.332	44
45	0.0000	3.3333	11.1099	134106.8167	447019.3890	0.3000	0.0000	3.333	45
46	0.0000	3.3333	11.1102	174338.8617	581126.2058	0.3000	0.0000	3.333	46
47	0.0000	3.3333	11.1104	226640.5202	755465.0675	0.3000	0.0000	3.333	47
48	0.0000	3.3333	11.1105	294632.6763	982105.5877	0.3000	0.0000	3.333	48
49	0.0000	3.3333	11.1107	383022.4792	1276738.2640	0.3000	0.0000	3.333	49
50	0.0000	3.3333	11.1108	497929.2230	1659760.7433	0.3000	0.0000	3.333	50

$I = 35.00\%$

n	(P/F)	(P/A)	(P/G)	(F/P)	(F/A)	(A/P)	(A/F)	(A/G)	n
1	0.7407	0.7407	0.0000	1.3500	1.0000	1.3500	1.0000	0.000	1
2	0.5487	1.2894	0.5487	1.8225	2.3500	0.7755	0.4255	0.425	2
3	0.4064	1.6959	1.3616	2.4604	4.1725	0.5897	0.2397	0.802	3
4	0.3011	1.9969	2.2648	3.3215	6.6329	0.5008	0.1508	1.134	4
5	0.2230	2.2200	3.1568	4.4840	9.9544	0.4505	0.1005	1.422	5
6	0.1652	2.3852	3.9828	6.0534	14.4384	0.4193	0.0693	1.669	6
7	0.1224	2.5075	4.7170	8.1722	20.4919	0.3988	0.0488	1.881	7
8	0.0906	2.5982	5.3515	11.0324	28.6640	0.3849	0.0349	2.059	8
9	0.0671	2.6653	5.8886	14.8937	39.6964	0.3752	0.0252	2.209	9
10	0.0497	2.7150	6.3363	20.1066	54.5902	0.3683	0.0183	2.333	10
11	0.0368	2.7519	6.7047	27.1439	74.6967	0.3634	0.0134	2.436	11
12	0.0273	2.7792	7.0049	36.6442	101.8406	0.3598	0.0098	2.520	12
13	0.0202	2.7994	7.2474	49.4697	138.4848	0.3572	0.0072	2.588	13
14	0.0150	2.8144	7.4421	66.7841	187.9544	0.3553	0.0053	2.644	14
15	0.0111	2.8255	7.5974	90.1585	254.7385	0.3539	0.0039	2.688	15
16	0.0082	2.8337	7.7206	121.7139	344.8970	0.3529	0.0029	2.724	16
17	0.0061	2.8398	7.8180	164.3138	466.6109	0.3521	0.0021	2.753	17
18	0.0045	2.8443	7.8946	221.8236	630.9247	0.3516	0.0016	2.775	18
19	0.0033	2.8476	7.9547	299.4619	852.7483	0.3512	0.0012	2.793	19
20	0.0025	2.8501	8.0017	404.2736	1152.2103	0.3509	0.0009	2.807	20
21	0.0018	2.8519	8.0384	545.7693	1556.4838	0.3506	0.0006	2.818	21
22	0.0014	2.8533	8.0669	736.7886	2102.2532	0.3505	0.0005	2.827	22
23	0.0010	2.8543	8.0890	994.6646	2839.0418	0.3504	0.0004	2.834	23
24	0.0007	2.8550	8.1061	1342.7973	3833.7064	0.3503	0.0003	2.839	24
25	0.0006	2.8556	8.1194	1812.7763	5176.5037	0.3502	0.0002	2.843	25
26	0.0004	2.8560	8.1296	2447.2480	6989.2800	0.3501	0.0001	2.846	26
27	0.0003	2.8563	8.1374	3303.7848	9436.5280	0.3501	0.0001	2.849	27
28	0.0002	2.8565	8.1435	4460.1095	12740.3128	0.3501	0.0001	2.850	28
29	0.0002	2.8567	8.1481	6021.1478	17200.4222	0.3501	0.0001	2.852	29
30	0.0001	2.8568	8.1517	8128.5495	23221.5700	0.3500	0.0000	2.853	30
31	0.0001	2.8569	8.1545	10973.5418	31350.1195	0.3500	0.0000	2.854	31
32	0.0001	2.8569	8.1565	14814.2815	42323.6613	0.3500	0.0000	2.855	32
33	0.0001	2.8570	8.1581	19999.2800	57137.9428	0.3500	0.0000	2.855	33
34	0.0000	2.8570	8.1594	26999.0280	77137.2228	0.3500	0.0000	2.855	34
35	0.0000	2.8571	8.1603	36448.6878	104136.2508	0.3500	0.0000	2.856	35
36	0.0000	2.8571	8.1610	49205.7285	140584.9385	0.3500	0.0000	2.856	36
37	0.0000	2.8571	8.1616	66427.7334	189790.6670	0.3500	0.0000	2.856	37
38	0.0000	2.8571	8.1620	89677.4402	256218.4004	0.3500	0.0000	2.856	38
39	0.0000	2.8571	8.1623	121064.5442	345895.8406	0.3500	0.0000	2.856	39
40	0.0000	2.8571	8.1625	163437.1347	466960.3848	0.3500	0.0000	2.856	40
41	0.0000	2.8571	8.1627	220640.1318	630397.5195	0.3500	0.0000	2.857	41
42	0.0000	2.8571	8.1628	297864.1780	851037.6513	0.3500	0.0000	2.857	42
43	0.0000	2.8571	8.1629	402116.6402	1148901.8293	0.3500	0.0000	2.857	43
44	0.0000	2.8571	8.1630	542857.4643	1551018.4695	0.3500	0.0000	2.857	44
45	0.0000	2.8571	8.1631	732857.5768	2093875.9338	0.3500	0.0000	2.857	45
46	0.0000	2.8571	8.1631	989357.7287	2826733.5107	0.3500	0.0000	2.857	46
47	0.0000	2.8571	8.1632	1335632.9338	3816091.2394	0.3500	0.0000	2.857	47
48	0.0000	2.8571	8.1632	1803104.4606	5151724.1732	0.3500	0.0000	2.857	48
49	0.0000	2.8571	8.1632	2434191.0218	6954828.6338	0.3500	0.0000	2.857	49
50	0.0000	2.8571	8.1632	3286157.8795	9389019.6556	0.3500	0.0000	2.857	50

PROFESSIONAL PUBLICATIONS, INC. ● Belmont, CA

$I = 40.00\%$

n	(P/F)	(P/A)	(P/G)	(F/P)	(F/A)	(A/P)	(A/F)	(A/G)	n
1	0.7143	0.7143	0.0000	1.4000	1.0000	1.4000	1.0000	0.000	1
2	0.5102	1.2245	0.5102	1.9600	2.4000	0.8167	0.4167	0.416	2
3	0.3644	1.5889	1.2391	2.7440	4.3600	0.6294	0.2294	0.779	3
4	0.2603	1.8492	2.0200	3.8416	7.1040	0.5408	0.1408	1.092	4
5	0.1859	2.0352	2.7637	5.3782	10.9456	0.4914	0.0914	1.358	5
6	0.1328	2.1680	3.4278	7.5295	16.3238	0.4613	0.0613	1.581	6
7	0.0949	2.2628	3.9970	10.5414	23.8534	0.4419	0.0419	1.766	7
8	0.0678	2.3306	4.4713	14.7579	34.3947	0.4291	0.0291	1.918	8
9	0.0484	2.3790	4.8585	20.6610	49.1526	0.4203	0.0203	2.042	9
10	0.0346	2.4136	5.1696	28.9255	69.8137	0.4143	0.0143	2.141	10
11	0.0247	2.4383	5.4166	40.4957	98.7391	0.4101	0.0101	2.221	11
12	0.0176	2.4559	5.6106	56.6939	139.2348	0.4072	0.0072	2.284	12
13	0.0126	2.4685	5.7618	79.3715	195.9287	0.4051	0.0051	2.334	13
14	0.0090	2.4775	5.8788	111.1201	275.3002	0.4036	0.0036	2.372	14
15	0.0064	2.4839	5.9688	155.5681	386.4202	0.4026	0.0026	2.403	15
16	0.0046	2.4885	6.0376	217.7953	541.9883	0.4018	0.0018	2.426	16
17	0.0033	2.4918	6.0901	304.9135	759.7837	0.4013	0.0013	2.444	17
18	0.0023	2.4941	6.1299	426.8789	1064.6971	0.4009	0.0009	2.457	18
19	0.0017	2.4958	6.1601	597.6304	1491.5760	0.4007	0.0007	2.468	19
20	0.0012	2.4970	6.1828	836.6826	2089.2064	0.4005	0.0005	2.476	20
21	0.0009	2.4979	6.1998	1171.3556	2925.8889	0.4003	0.0003	2.482	21
22	0.0006	2.4985	6.2127	1639.8978	4097.2445	0.4002	0.0002	2.486	22
23	0.0004	2.4989	6.2222	2295.8569	5737.1423	0.4002	0.0002	2.490	23
24	0.0003	2.4992	6.2294	3214.1997	8032.9993	0.4001	0.0001	2.492	24
25	0.0002	2.4994	6.2347	4499.8796	11247.1990	0.4001	0.0001	2.494	25
26	0.0002	2.4996	6.2387	6299.8314	15747.0785	0.4001	0.0001	2.495	26
27	0.0001	2.4997	6.2416	8819.7640	22046.9099	0.4000	0.0000	2.496	27
28	0.0001	2.4998	6.2438	12347.6696	30866.6739	0.4000	0.0000	2.497	28
29	0.0001	2.4999	6.2454	17286.7374	43214.3435	0.4000	0.0000	2.498	29
30	0.0000	2.4999	6.2466	24201.4324	60501.0809	0.4000	0.0000	2.498	30
31	0.0000	2.4999	6.2475	33882.0053	84702.5132	0.4000	0.0000	2.499	31
32	0.0000	2.4999	6.2482	47434.8074	118584.5185	0.4000	0.0000	2.499	32
33	0.0000	2.5000	6.2487	66408.7304	166019.3260	0.4000	0.0000	2.499	33
34	0.0000	2.5000	6.2490	92972.2225	232428.0563	0.4000	0.0000	2.499	34
35	0.0000	2.5000	6.2493	130161.1116	325400.2789	0.4000	0.0000	2.499	35
36	0.0000	2.5000	6.2495	182225.5562	455561.3904	0.4000	0.0000	2.499	36
37	0.0000	2.5000	6.2496	255115.7786	637786.9466	0.4000	0.0000	2.499	37
38	0.0000	2.5000	6.2497	357162.0901	892902.7252	0.4000	0.0000	2.499	38
39	0.0000	2.5000	6.2498	500026.9261	1250064.8153	0.4000	0.0000	2.499	39
40	0.0000	2.5000	6.2498	700037.6966	1750091.7415	0.4000	0.0000	2.499	40
41	0.0000	2.5000	6.2499	980052.7752	2450129.4381	0.4000	0.0000	2.500	41
42	0.0000	2.5000	6.2499	1372073.8853	3430182.2133	0.4000	0.0000	2.500	42
43	0.0000	2.5000	6.2499	1920903.4394	4802256.0986	0.4000	0.0000	2.500	43
44	0.0000	2.5000	6.2500	2689264.8152	6723159.5381	0.4000	0.0000	2.500	44
45	0.0000	2.5000	6.2500	3764970.7413	9412424.3533	0.4000	0.0000	2.500	45

EXPANDED INTEREST TABLES

$I = 45.00 \%$

n	(P/F)	(P/A)	(P/G)	(F/P)	(F/A)	(A/P)	(A/F)	(A/G)	n
1	0.6897	0.6897	0.0000	1.4500	1.0000	1.4500	1.0000	0.000	1
2	0.4756	1.1653	0.4756	2.1025	2.4500	0.8582	0.4082	0.408	2
3	0.3280	1.4933	1.1317	3.0486	4.5525	0.6697	0.2197	0.757	3
4	0.2262	1.7195	1.8103	4.4205	7.6011	0.5816	0.1316	1.052	4
5	0.1560	1.8755	2.4344	6.4097	12.0216	0.5332	0.0832	1.298	5
6	0.1076	1.9831	2.9723	9.2941	18.4314	0.5043	0.0543	1.498	6
7	0.0742	2.0573	3.4176	13.4765	27.7255	0.4861	0.0361	1.661	7
8	0.0512	2.1085	3.7758	19.5409	41.2019	0.4743	0.0243	1.790	8
9	0.0353	2.1438	4.0581	28.3343	60.7428	0.4665	0.0165	1.893	9
10	0.0243	2.1681	4.2772	41.0847	89.0771	0.4612	0.0112	1.972	10
11	0.0168	2.1849	4.4450	59.5728	130.1618	0.4577	0.0077	2.034	11
12	0.0116	2.1965	4.5724	86.3806	189.7346	0.4553	0.0053	2.081	12
13	0.0080	2.2045	4.6682	125.2518	276.1151	0.4536	0.0036	2.117	13
14	0.0055	2.2100	4.7398	181.6151	401.3670	0.4525	0.0025	2.144	14
15	0.0038	2.2138	4.7929	263.3419	582.9821	0.4517	0.0017	2.165	15
16	0.0026	2.2164	4.8322	381.8458	846.3240	0.4512	0.0012	2.180	16
17	0.0018	2.2182	4.8611	553.6764	1228.1699	0.4508	0.0008	2.191	17
18	0.0012	2.2195	4.8823	802.8308	1781.8463	0.4506	0.0006	2.199	18
19	0.0009	2.2203	4.8978	1164.1047	2584.6771	0.4504	0.0004	2.205	19
20	0.0006	2.2209	4.9090	1687.9518	3748.7818	0.4503	0.0003	2.210	20
21	0.0004	2.2213	4.9172	2447.5301	5436.7336	0.4502	0.0002	2.213	21
22	0.0003	2.2216	4.9231	3548.9187	7884.2638	0.4501	0.0001	2.216	22
23	0.0002	2.2218	4.9274	5145.9321	11433.1824	0.4501	0.0001	2.217	23
24	0.0001	2.2219	4.9305	7461.6015	16579.1145	0.4501	0.0001	2.219	24
25	0.0001	2.2220	4.9327	10819.3222	24040.7161	0.4500	0.0000	2.219	25
26	0.0001	2.2221	4.9343	15688.0172	34860.0383	0.4500	0.0000	2.220	26
27	0.0000	2.2221	4.9354	22747.6250	50548.0556	0.4500	0.0000	2.221	27
28	0.0000	2.2222	4.9362	32984.0563	73295.6806	0.4500	0.0000	2.221	28
29	0.0000	2.2222	4.9368	47826.8816	106279.7368	0.4500	0.0000	2.221	29
30	0.0000	2.2222	4.9372	69348.9783	154106.6184	0.4500	0.0000	2.221	30
31	0.0000	2.2222	4.9375	100556.0185	223455.5967	0.4500	0.0000	2.221	31
32	0.0000	2.2222	4.9378	145806.2269	324011.6152	0.4500	0.0000	2.222	32
33	0.0000	2.2222	4.9379	211419.0289	469817.8421	0.4500	0.0000	2.222	33
34	0.0000	2.2222	4.9380	306557.5920	681236.8710	0.4500	0.0000	2.222	34
35	0.0000	2.2222	4.9381	444508.5083	987794.4630	0.4500	0.0000	2.222	35

I = 50.00 %

n	(P/F)	(P/A)	(P/G)	(F/P)	(F/A)	(A/P)	(A/F)	(A/G)	n
1	0.6667	0.6667	0.0000	1.5000	1.0000	1.5000	1.0000	0.000	1
2	0.4444	1.1111	0.4444	2.2500	2.5000	0.9000	0.4000	0.400	2
3	0.2963	1.4074	1.0370	3.3750	4.7500	0.7105	0.2105	0.736	3
4	0.1975	1.6049	1.6296	5.0625	8.1250	0.6231	0.1231	1.015	4
5	0.1317	1.7366	2.1564	7.5937	13.1875	0.5758	0.0758	1.241	5
6	0.0878	1.8244	2.5953	11.3906	20.7812	0.5481	0.0481	1.422	6
7	0.0585	1.8829	2.9465	17.0859	32.1719	0.5311	0.0311	1.564	7
8	0.0390	1.9220	3.2196	25.6289	49.2578	0.5203	0.0203	1.675	8
9	0.0260	1.9480	3.4277	38.4434	74.8867	0.5134	0.0134	1.759	9
10	0.0173	1.9653	3.5838	57.6650	113.3301	0.5088	0.0088	1.823	10
11	0.0116	1.9769	3.6994	86.4976	170.9951	0.5058	0.0058	1.871	11
12	0.0077	1.9846	3.7842	129.7463	257.4927	0.5039	0.0039	1.906	12
13	0.0051	1.9897	3.8459	194.6195	387.2390	0.5026	0.0026	1.932	13
14	0.0034	1.9931	3.8904	291.9293	581.8585	0.5017	0.0017	1.951	14
15	0.0023	1.9954	3.9224	437.8939	873.7878	0.5011	0.0011	1.965	15
16	0.0015	1.9970	3.9452	656.8408	1311.6817	0.5008	0.0008	1.975	16
17	0.0010	1.9980	3.9614	985.2613	1968.5225	0.5005	0.0005	1.982	17
18	0.0007	1.9986	3.9729	1477.8919	2953.7838	0.5003	0.0003	1.987	18
19	0.0005	1.9991	3.9811	2216.8378	4431.6756	0.5002	0.0002	1.991	19
20	0.0003	1.9994	3.9868	3325.2567	6648.5135	0.5002	0.0002	1.994	20
21	0.0002	1.9996	3.9908	4987.8851	9973.7702	0.5001	0.0001	1.995	21
22	0.0001	1.9997	3.9936	7481.8276	14961.6553	0.5001	0.0001	1.997	22
23	0.0001	1.9998	3.9955	11222.7415	22443.4829	0.5000	0.0000	1.998	23
24	0.0001	1.9999	3.9969	16834.1122	33666.2244	0.5000	0.0000	1.998	24
25	0.0000	1.9999	3.9979	25251.1683	50500.3366	0.5000	0.0000	1.999	25
26	0.0000	1.9999	3.9985	37876.7524	75751.5049	0.5000	0.0000	1.999	26
27	0.0000	2.0000	3.9990	56815.1287	113628.2573	0.5000	0.0000	1.999	27
28	0.0000	2.0000	3.9993	85222.6930	170443.3860	0.5000	0.0000	1.999	28
29	0.0000	2.0000	3.9995	127834.0395	255666.0790	0.5000	0.0000	1.999	29
30	0.0000	2.0000	3.9997	191751.0592	383500.1185	0.5000	0.0000	1.999	30
31	0.0000	2.0000	3.9998	287626.5888	575251.1777	0.5000	0.0000	1.999	31
32	0.0000	2.0000	3.9998	431439.8833	862877.7665	0.5000	0.0000	1.999	32
33	0.0000	2.0000	3.9999	647159.8249	1294317.6498	0.5000	0.0000	1.999	33
34	0.0000	2.0000	3.9999	970739.7374	1941477.4747	0.5000	0.0000	2.000	34
35	0.0000	2.0000	3.9999	1456109.6060	2912217.2121	0.5000	0.0000	2.000	35